THE WAY THINGS WORK

Special Edition for Young People

THE WAY THINGS WORK

An Illustrated Encyclopedia of Technology

Special Edition for Young People

by T. Lodewijk
and others

Simon and Schuster ■ New York

SPECIAL EDITION FOR YOUNG PEOPLE

Published by Simon and Schuster, Children's Book Division
Rockefeller Center, 630 Fifth Avenue
New York, New York 10020

SBN 671-65212-5
Library of Congress Catalog Card Number: 73-13009
Type design by Jack Jaget
The publisher's special thanks to Miss Dorothy L. Gordineer for
her creative adaptations of the art and
attention to minute detail in the page layouts.
Manufactured in the United States of America

2 3 4 5 6 7 8 9 10

FOREWORD

This book is an adaptation of the longer, more technical reference volumes, *The Way Things Work,* which was originally published in Germany under the title *Wie funktioniert das?* (*How Does That Work?*).

This edition, intended for use by readers of junior- and senior-high-school age, is a shorter version. Like the original, it is designed to give the layman an understanding of how things work, from simple mechanical functions like the block and tackle to basic scientific principles such as those involved in supersonic speed or radioactivity, and such complex industrial processes as those which convert energy into work, use light to make pictures or use radio waves to make sounds. Subjects of special interest to young people have been included, while those of a more technical or esoteric nature have been omitted. The text has been simplified to make the information more accessible to less experienced readers, and the illustrations have been enlarged and simplified as well.

The book is divided into ten sections; there are ninety-one individual entries, each one accompanied by a two-color diagram or illustration supplementing the text. The Table of Contents lists the various subjects and the general divisions into which they fall. At the back of the book, there is an alphabetical listing of the subjects as well, for ease of reference.

THE PUBLISHERS

Contents

THE WAY THINGS WORK

Special Edition for Young People

I Pushing, Pulling, Floating, Flying

BLOCK AND TACKLE

A block and tackle allows one to lift heavy loads while applying only a small force. It consists of two or more pulley blocks and a length of rope that passes around the pulleys.

In Fig. 1, a 100-pound boy is suspended in mid-air in a cage. His two friends, who weigh 200 pounds between them, know perfectly well that he can't counterbalance them.

In Fig. 2, something has changed. There is the same top "fixed" pulley, but also a moving pulley. The moving pulley is suspended by two "falls" of rope, each of which carries half the load. This arrangement, in which the moving pulley is hauled by two ropes, allows a load of 200 pounds to be matched by a pull of only 100 pounds.

What the top pulley does in Fig. 2 is to change the direction of the pulling rope, so that the force needed on the right can act as a downward pull. But to see what the *moving* pulley does, imagine the boy on the right going down by 2 feet. The moving pulley will then move upward—but by only 1 foot. The distance moved is split between the two ropes carrying the pulley.

Incidentally, both sides are performing the same amount of *work*. The way to measure work is to multiply the weight by the distance

Fig. 1 FIXED PULLEY

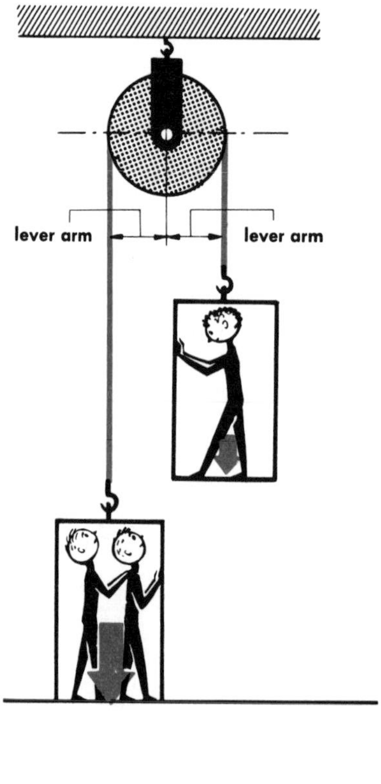

Fig. 2 FIXED PULLEY AND MOVING PULLEY

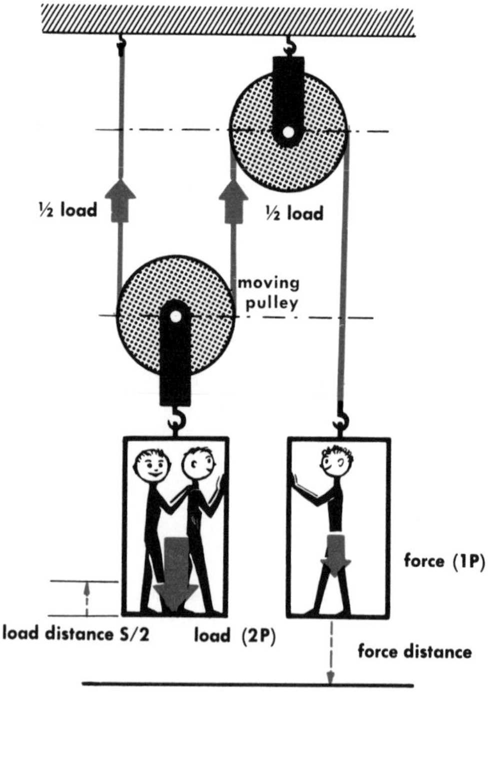

Fig. 3 **MULTIPLE BLOCK AND TACKLE**

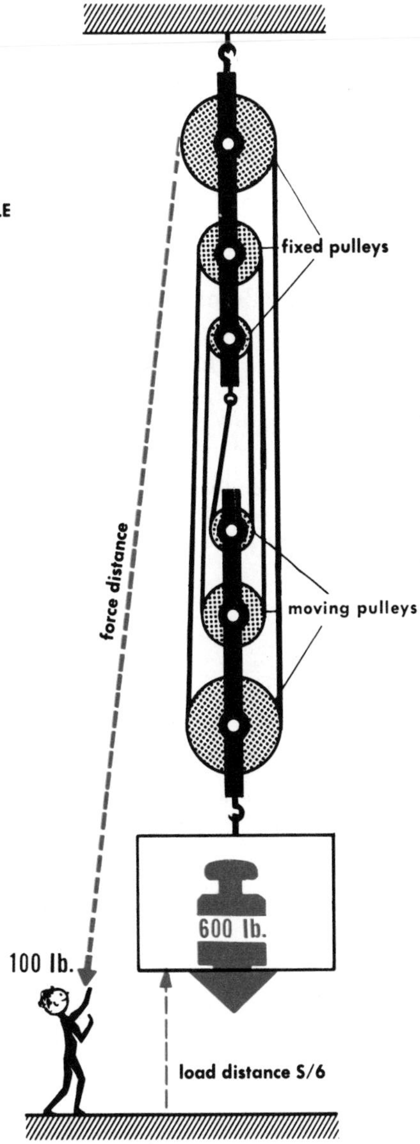

moved. On the left, 200 pounds were moved by a distance of 1 foot; on the right, 100 pounds were moved by a distance of 2 feet. No matter which side goes up or which side goes down, both sides perform the same amount of work. The use of pulleys can make work *easier* because less weight or force has to be applied on the pulling end. But the amount of work performed is not affected.

The kind of help one is given by a block and tackle is called *mechanical advantage*. Since the moving pulley in Fig. 2 is supported by two falls of rope, the mechanical advantage is 2. In Fig. 3, the pulley is supported by six falls of rope; the mechanical advantage is 6. It would allow a 100-pound boy to balance a 600-pound piano!

CRANES

To raise a heavy bucket from a well, it is helpful to have a *windlass*. This is a horizontal axle (turned by a handle) on which a rope can be wound.

To carry heavy loads of raw material from a railroad siding to a factory is much the same problem—but the rope (or cable) has to pass over a pulley held high over the work, and since the railroad

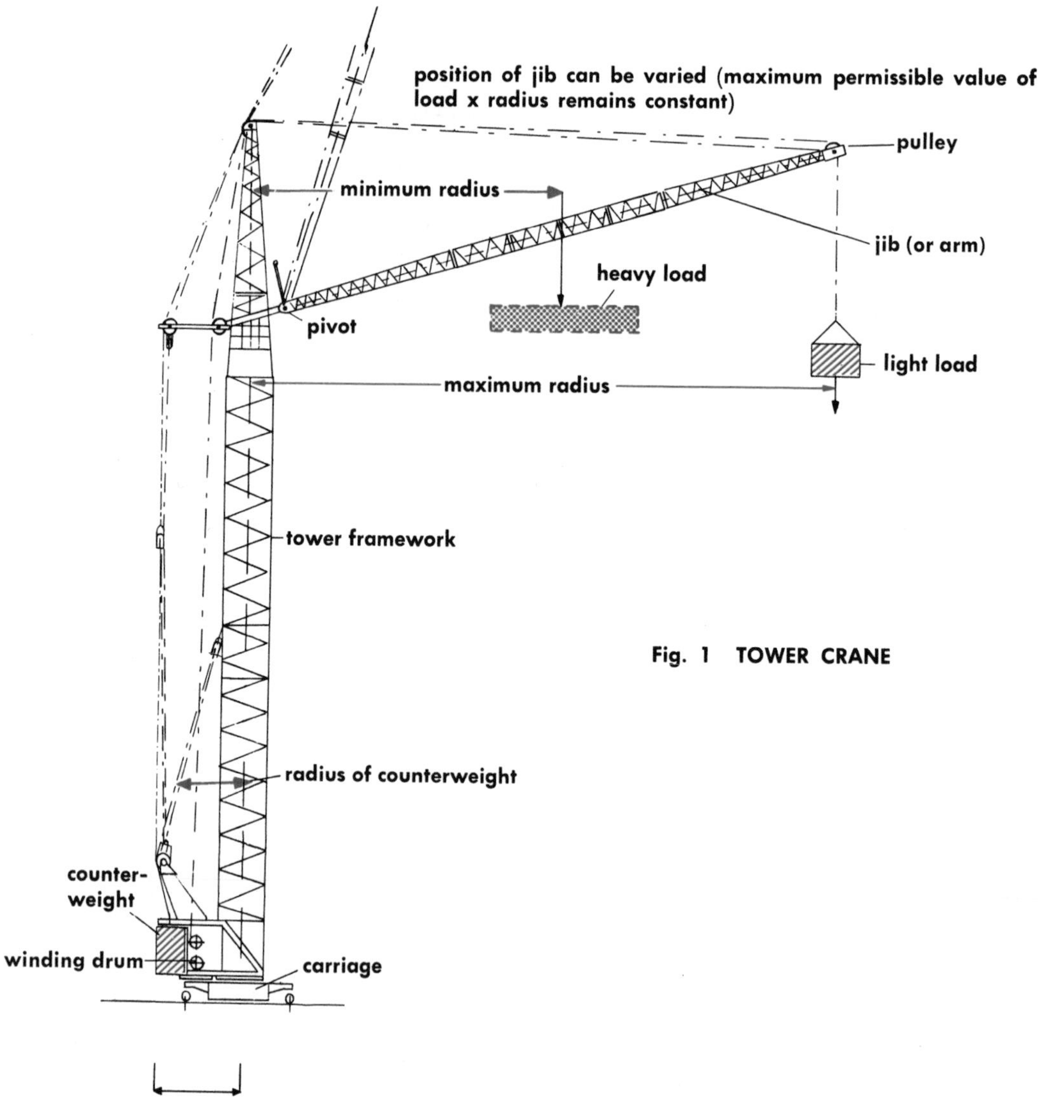

Fig. 1 TOWER CRANE

tracks may be 50 yards from the factory, the pulley must be free to move over a wide area.

The **tower crane** (Fig. 1) has all these features. Its pulley is held high, at the tip of a steel *jib,* or arm. This arm can be raised or lowered on a *pivot,* and the tower is free to turn so that the arm can be swerved around from over the tracks to over the factory yard. In the modern crane the simple windlass is replaced by *winding drums* that are driven by a Diesel-electric engine.

If the load is very heavy, the crane operator has to be careful not to stretch out his jib too far horizontally or the load will pull the crane off balance. (If his maximum load 100 feet out from the tower is 2,000 pounds, his maximum load 200 feet out is only 1,000 pounds.)

Loads that are all in one piece—like a crate—are attached to a hook at the end of the cable. Bulk loads—like gravel—are picked up by a *grab,* or "clam." In Fig. 2, the cable holding the clam is shown in red. The opening and closing of the two "half shells" of the clam are controlled by the *closing rope.*

In large factories and shipyards one sometimes sees a tall structure with *two* towers. This is a **bridge crane.** The load is lifted by a traveling trolley, or "crab," that can move along overhead tracks from one tower to the other. Often the towers themselves can also move (together) by riding along railroad tracks. This arrangement, with the trolley traveling crosswise and the towers lengthwise, enables loads to be lifted over a wide area.

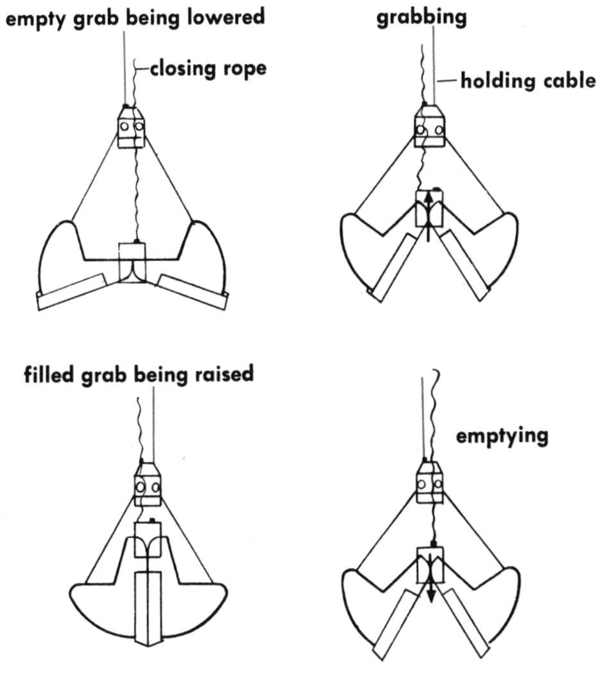

Fig. 2
HOW A GRAB IS OPERATED

BICYCLE, I

PEDALING, FREEWHEELING, BRAKING

The pedals of a bicycle make the rear wheel turn—but the rear wheel, when *it* is turning, does not force the pedals to keep turning. This freedom, which allows the rider to rest his legs, is known as **free-wheeling.**

The design that makes this possible is shown in Fig. 1. The bicycle is seen from the right. The ring marked *hub sleeve* is actually part of the wheel—pedaling does not affect it directly. The bicycle chain transmits force directly only to the *drive rollers*. When the rider begins to pedal, the rollers move clockwise in the space between the *ratchet* and the hub sleeve. As the rollers move, the sloping faces of the ratchet jam them against the hub sleeve (Fig. 1a). The hub sleeve now begins to turn—turning the rear wheel of the bicycle along with it.

Fig. 1 FREEWHEELING HUB

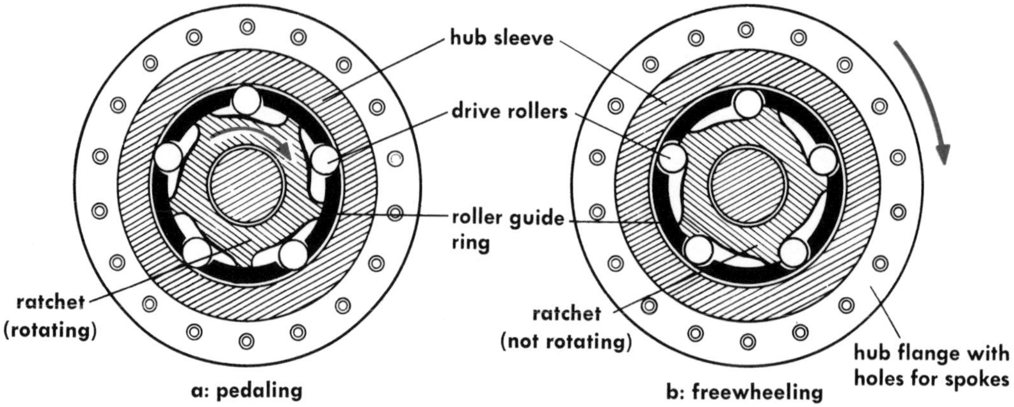

The bicycle is now moving along. If the rider stops pedaling for a while, the rear wheel still turns, carrying the hub sleeve around with it (Fig. 1b). The bicycle is freewheeling. Since the pedaling has stopped, there is no pressure on the drive rollers; they slip back and float free in the empty pockets around the ratchet. The hub sleeve and drive rollers are now disconnected and the pedals can stay motionless in any position the rider likes.

In bicycles that do not carry hand brakes, the freewheeling hub is also adapted to **brake** when the rider backpedals. The mechanism designed to do this consists of a great many parts (the whole assembly is shown in cross section in Fig. 2). The job of pushing against

Fig. 2 BRAKING MECHANISM AS INSTALLED

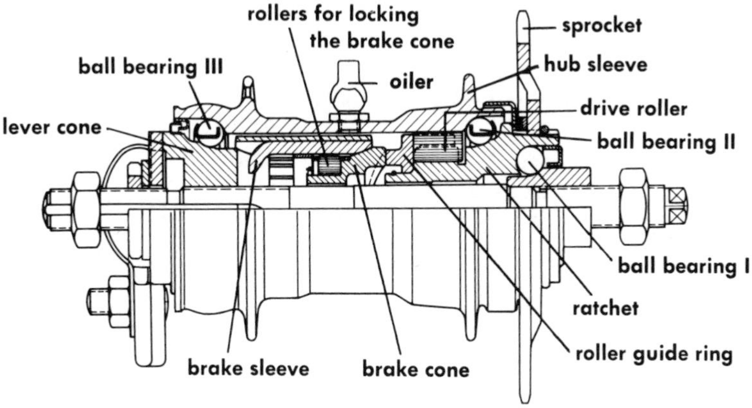

the wheel's turning hub to make it stop is done by a cylinder called the *brake sleeve* (Fig. 3). This brake sleeve is forced to expand by having two conelike parts pushed into it, somewhat as in Fig. 4. But if all the brake parts themselves are turning, they can't stop the hub from turning too. So there is a second group of parts that anchor some of the brake parts to the frame of the bicycle. In combination,

Fig. 3 PARTS IN THE BRAKING MECHANISM

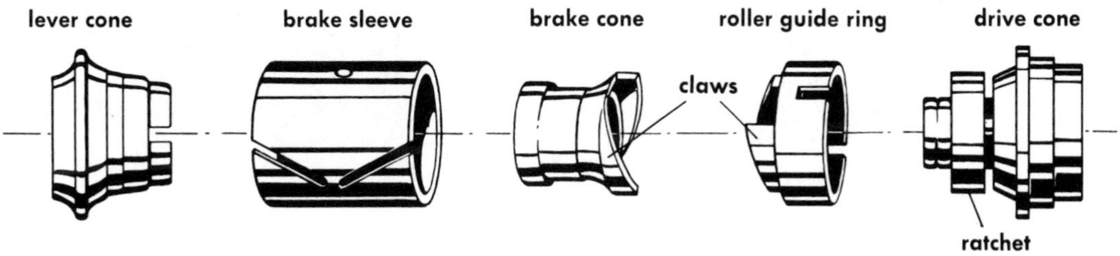

the brake sleeve, expansion parts and holding parts work together like this:

When the rider backpedals, the *brake cone* slides into the brake sleeve and pushes it onto the *lever cone*—so that the brake sleeve expands from both ends. (To prevent the brake cone from turning when it is put to work, the inside of the *roller guide ring* is provided with two *claws* (Fig. 3) that grip the brake cone.) This rigidly held brake cone now slides into the brake sleeve and, at the same time, pushes it onto the lever cone.

Fig. 4 HOW THE BRAKING MECHANISM WORKS

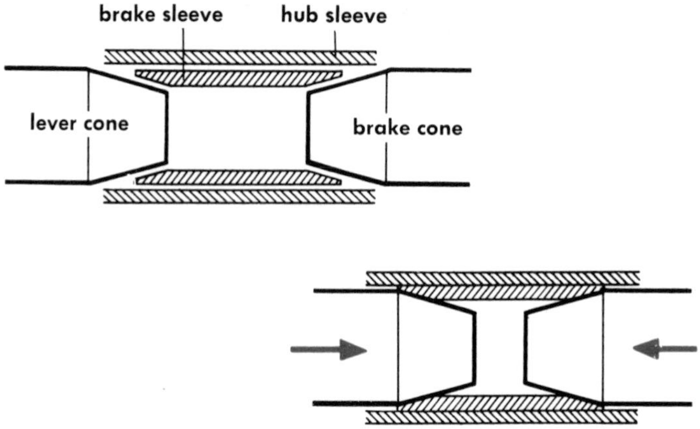

Fig. 5 HOW ROLLERS LOCK BRAKE CONE

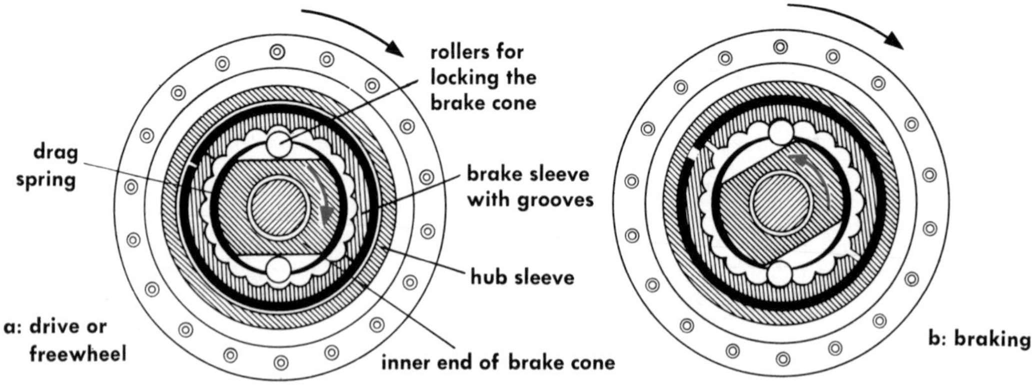

The remaining mechanisms are concerned with keeping the brake cone from turning when the brake sleeve is pressed against it. A lever attaches it to the frame of the bicycle, enabling it to hold steady against the braking force that develops when the rider backpedals. To keep it from rotating, the brake cone is also provided with two flat surfaces (Fig. 5). Between each of these surfaces and the grooved inner surface of the brake sleeve are rollers, held in position by springs. When the rider moves the pedals backward, one end of each flat surface presses each roller into a groove, and the brake cone is locked in. The thrust exerted by the claws on the roller guide ring then forces the brake sleeve over the lever cone. The brake sleeve, now pried apart from both ends, expands against the wheel's hub sleeve and stops it from turning.

BICYCLE, II

VARIABLE-GEAR HUB

Many gearshifts on bicycles in the United States and Canada have the variable gear set in the hub of the rear wheel. It is built around a pair of planetary gear systems like the one in Fig. 1. The central gear, called the *sun wheel,* can move the three planet wheels, which then slowly turn the outer ring, or *annulus.* (Or the annulus can spin the planet wheels, which would then drive the sun wheel.)

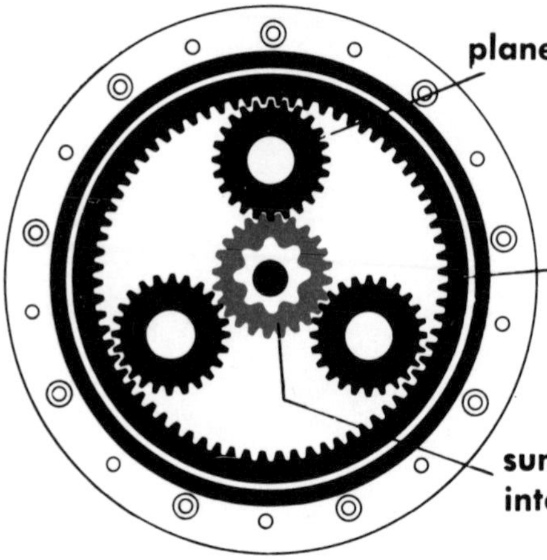

Fig. 1 PLANETARY GEAR SYSTEM OF THREE-SPEED VARIABLE-GEAR HUB

Figure 2 shows the planetary gear system with, for simplicity, a single planet wheel instead of three. (The principle is the same.) The short red line marked *cage,* which joins the spindles of sun wheel and planet wheel, stands for a component that occurs twice in the actual gear system. This cage encloses the sun and planet wheels and allows the planet wheels to be locked so that they cannot spin. If the sun wheel is free to turn, the annulus will then turn at the same speed as the red line.

This last condition, in which the planet wheels are locked, is the one used when the gearshift of a bicycle is in **normal gear.** The internal teeth of the sun wheel are disengaged from the hub spindle so that this wheel is free to rotate. As the same time, its *outer* teeth (which remain engaged with those of the planet wheels) mesh with the internal teeth of the cage that carries the three planet wheels. The planetary gear sets—of which there are two—are locked. The drive is thus directly transmitted from the sprocket (the outer wheel whose teeth catch the bicycle chain) to the rear wheel of the bicycle.

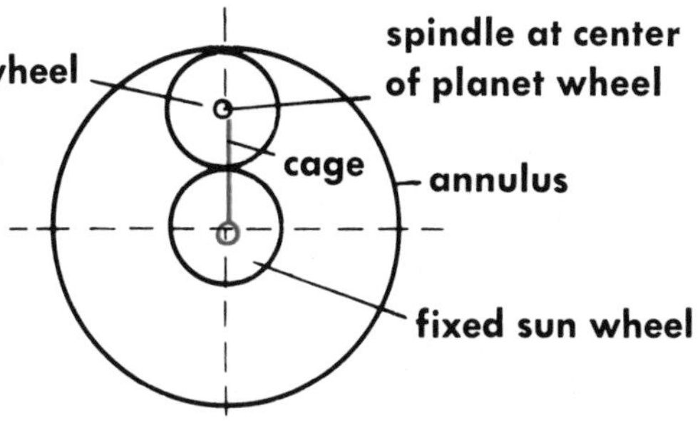

Fig. 2 PLANETARY GEAR SET WITH FIXED SUN WHEEL

To shift into high or low gear, the rider works a lever on the handle bars. This lever pushes or pulls a control wire connected to the gear control chain. Of course, whatever happens has to affect the bicycle's rear wheel, of which there is only one; and there is only one annulus, seen in profile near the top of Fig 3. But there are *two* cages, each containing its own sun-and-planet gear system. What the rider does when he shifts out of "normal gear" is to call one or the other of these two systems into play. (At the same time, the design takes advantage of the fact that the other one is locked.)

If the rider selects **high gear,** for a swift ride on a level road, he brings the planetary system shown on the right side of Fig. 3 into operation. Its sun gear, shown in red in Fig. 1, has *internal* teeth, which lock into the hub spindle. The sprocket that receives the bicycle

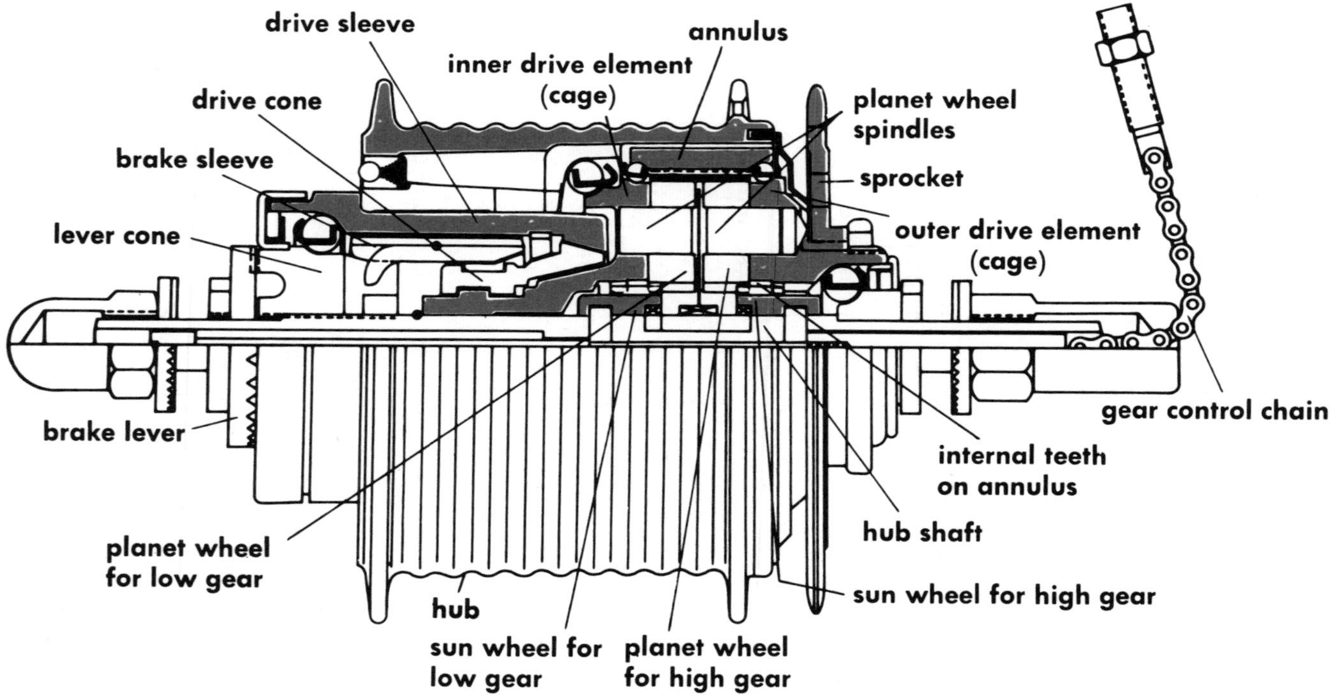

Fig. 3 SECTION THROUGH A THREE-SPEED VARIABLE-GEAR HUB
Setting: "normal" gear

chain is fixed to the planet-wheel cage (in Fig. 3, the *outer* drive element of the right-hand gear set). The power is transmitted from this cage through the annulus to the left-hand gear set. This set, being locked, simply transmits the power to its planet-wheel cage (the *inner* drive element), which transmits it to the drive sleeve. It is the drive sleeve that is fixed to the hub and thus turns the rear wheel of the bicycle.

To climb hills, the rider shifts into **low gear.** The control wire from the handle bars then puts the gear set on the *left* to work and locks the one on the right.

ESCALATOR

To a shopper or a traveler, an escalator is more attractive than an elevator—he doesn't have to wait for his climb. To the management of a building, it is an even greater convenience because it handles about ten times as many people as an elevator does in the course of an hour—and if it breaks down, it can still be used as stairs.

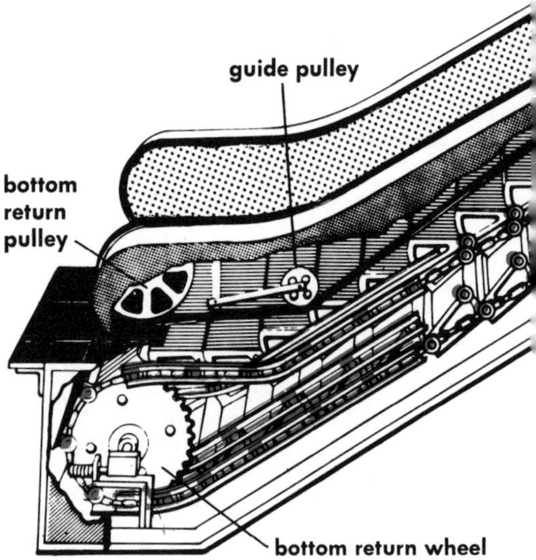

Fig. 1 SECTION THROUGH ESCALATOR

Each step of an escalator is a separate little truck on four wheels (Fig. 2). The top pair runs on one set of rails (the outer set), the bottom pair on another. For most of the climb, the inner and outer rails run right alongside each other. As the top stepping-off point is neared, the inner rails, which hold the lower wheels, begin to level off; the outer rails level off a bit later, in such a way that the upper surfaces—the "treads"—of the top steps develop into an even platform (Fig. 3). A similar separate control of the angles of the two pairs of rails makes for a level stepping-on area at the bottom. These rails, which support the steps and control the way their treads are set, are continued on the underside of the escalator for the steps' return journey.

What *pulls* the steps is a pair of "endless" (that is, looped) chains that run on sprocket wheels at the top and bottom of the escalator.

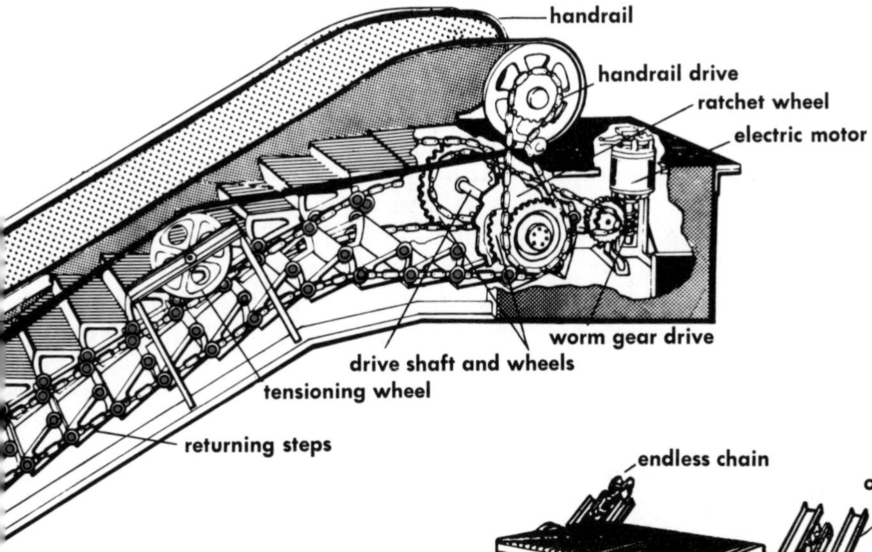

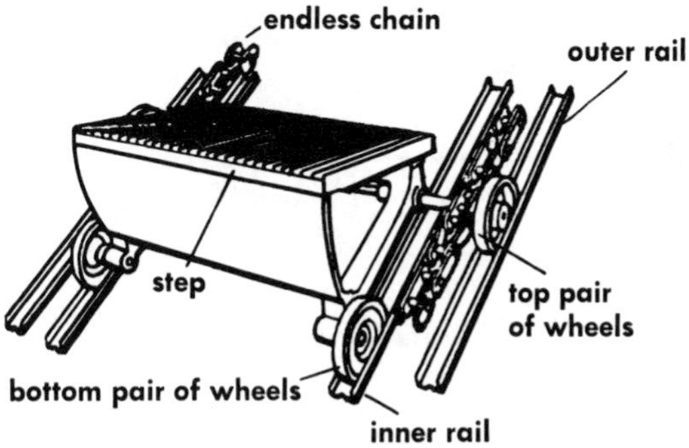

Fig. 2 STEP OF ESCALATOR

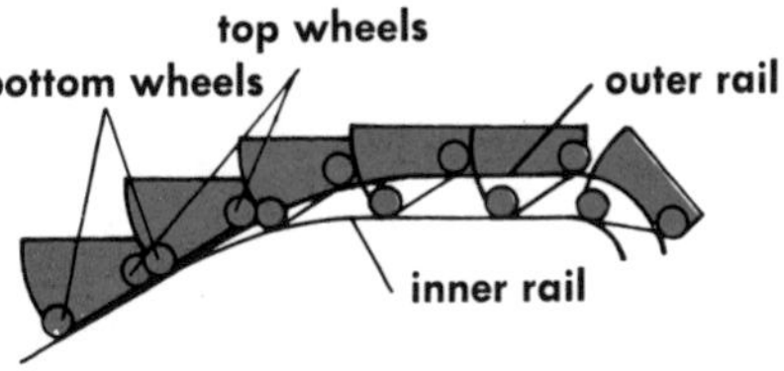

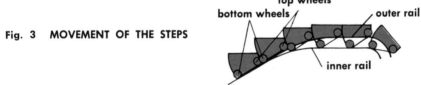

Fig. 3 MOVEMENT OF THE STEPS

(These toothed wheels can be seen in Fig. 1.) The top sprocket wheels are driven by an electric motor, which can be reversed to make the steps move downward.

The handrails—which are made of canvas-backed rubber or of coiled metal—not only help the passengers keep their balance but warn them, by curving, that they must soon step off. These belts are driven by the same motor as the escalator itself. A *tensioning wheel,* which pushes the belts outward on their return trip under the escalator, keeps them taut.

PUMPS

In raising liquids or gases, or in moving them across great distances, one does not have to use up energy in hauling containers. One can use pipes, which stay where they are. But one still has to nudge the fluid itself along: this job is done by pumps.

A **piston pump** appears in Fig. 1. The piston, which is free to move back and forth in a cylinder, is attached to a motor by a connecting rod. When the piston is pulled to the right, liquid is sucked up into the empty space in the cylinder (Fig. 1a). (That, at least, is the way it *seems*. In fact, the liquid simply moves up into the empty space

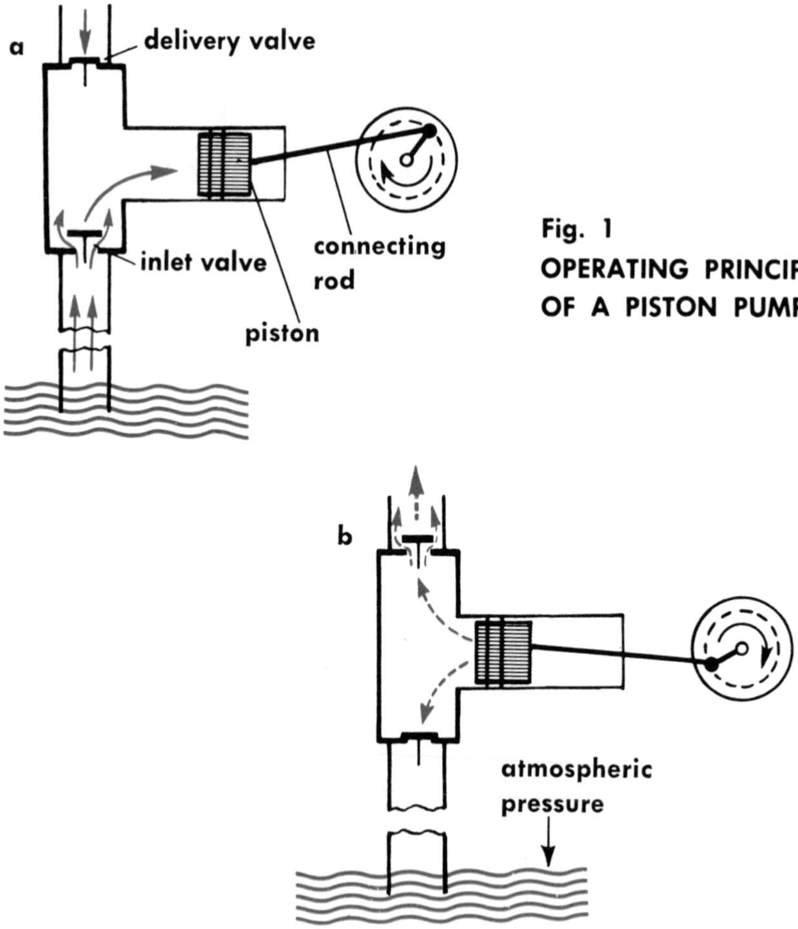

Fig. 1
OPERATING PRINCIPLE OF A PISTON PUMP

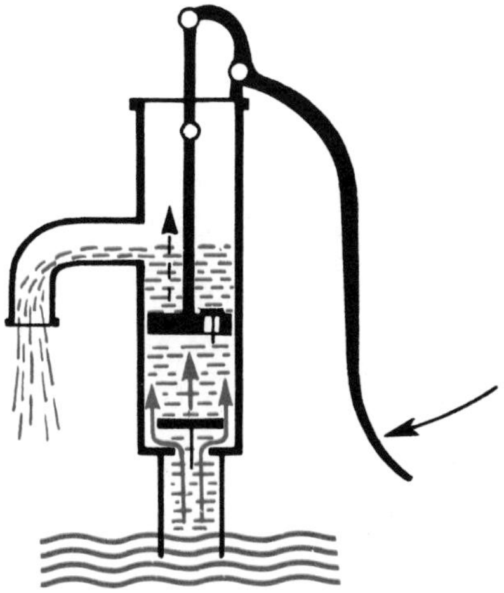

Fig. 2
LIFTING PUMP

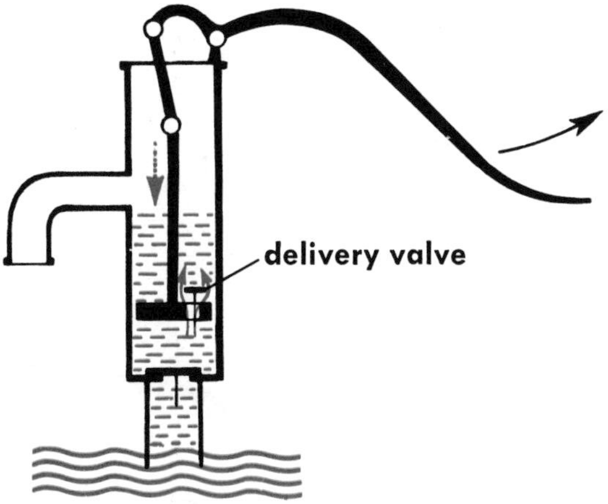

because the weight of the earth's atmosphere, outside the cylinder, is pressing on it.) As the motor keeps turning, the piston is pushed back to the left (Fig. 1b). It now produces pressure on the liquid in the cylinder. This pressure closes the inlet valve but forces open the delivery valve. The piston now pushes the liquid upward, out of the cylinder.

The **lifting pump** (Fig. 2), which has long been used to raise water in villages and on farms, is a form of piston pump. (Its delivery valve is set *in* the piston.) Each new load of water that it brings up is spilled out immediately. Another variety of piston pump is the **diaphragm pump.** (Diaphragm—pronounced *DIE-ah-fram,* only faster!—is here used to mean a tough sheet of plastic that is flexible but lets nothing get through it.) Instead of a piston, this pump uses a flexible diaphragm (Fig. 3), which is moved back and forth by a rod connected to a motor.

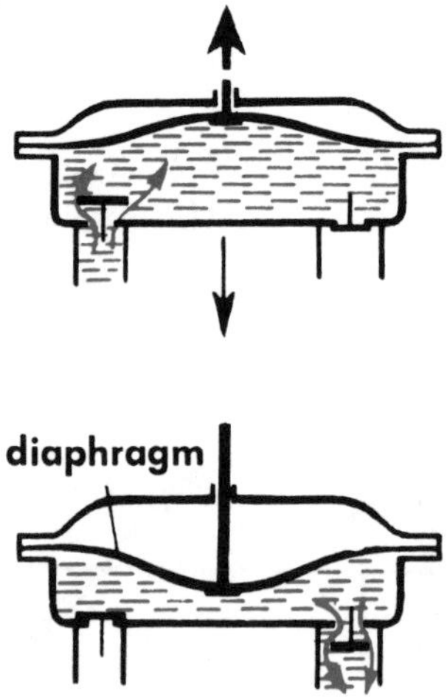

Fig. 3
DIAPHRAGM PUMP

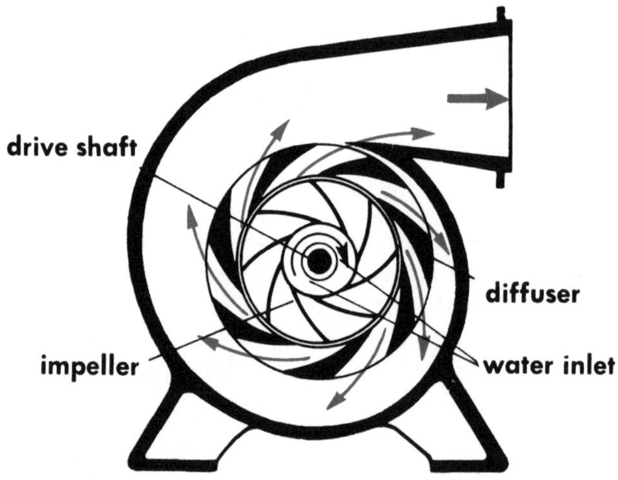

Fig. 4 CENTRIFUGAL PUMP
(*schematic*)

Centrifugal pumps work in a completely different way. They are something like the FRANCIS TURBINE (page 38), but working backward: in a turbine, the water makes the rotor turn, whereas in a centrifugal pump, the rotor moves the water. In the pump, this rotor —which is fitted with curved blades—is called the *impeller*. When water meets this rotating impeller, the impeller's blades push it onward at great speed but at angles that are not immediately useful. The gradually widening snail-shell casing (Fig. 4) allows the high-speed jets to collect themselves into a stream.

PNEUMATIC HAMMER

Opening up a roadbed with a pick used to be a whole day's work. For the pick to pierce the roadbed, it had to come down with speed—the roadworker had each time to raise it high enough for it to *develop* the speed as it came down. This took time. Today this work is done by pneumatic hammer (Fig. 1), in which a chisel-like tool is pushed by a piston that works on compressed air. It hits several times per second.

The air is supplied through a hose after it has been put under pressure by a Diesel-powered compressor. When the operator presses the control lever on the underside of the handle (Fig. 2), compressed air flows through the diaphragm valve into the *outer compartment.* This valve is rounded, so that it rocks, or flutters, to and fro. In Fig. 2, it is shown at the moment it opens the inlet passage into the outer compartment. From there the air flows into the *inner compartment* from below, forcing the piston upward. The air in the space above the piston is now under pressure; it presses on the underside of the

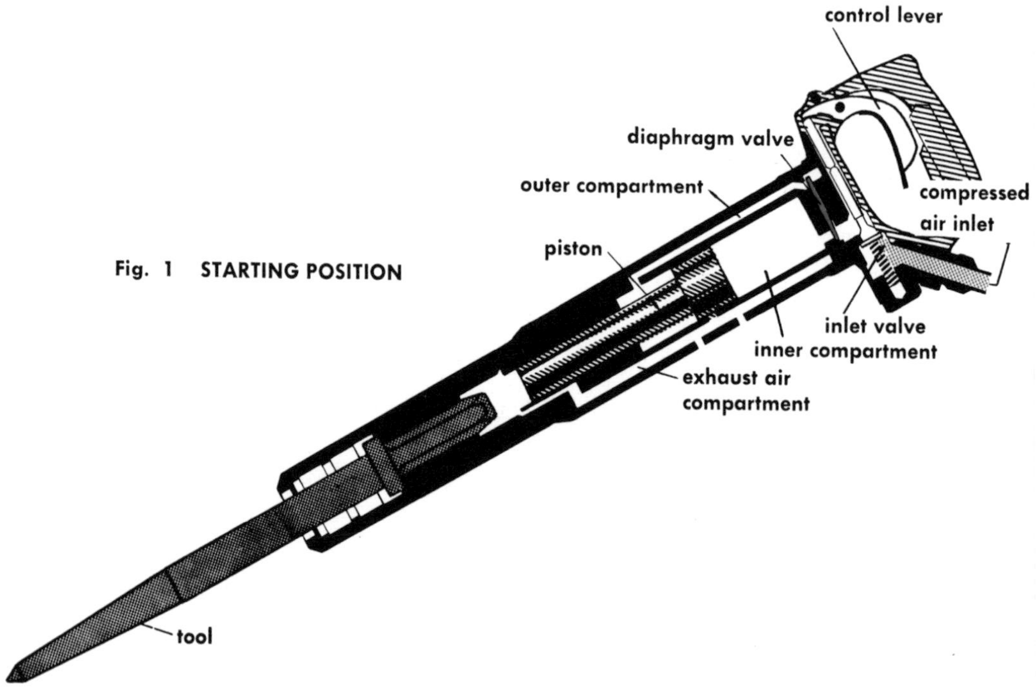

Fig. 1 STARTING POSITION

diaphragm valve, tilting it the other way. This closes the inlet passage to the outer compartmen but opens it to the inner compartment (Fig. 3).

The compressed air now rushes in over the top of the piston and forces it downward, so that it strikes the upper end of the chisel. Exhaust air is discharged (as if from an air rifle) during both the upward and downward strokes of the piston—with a noise that can be heard several blocks away!

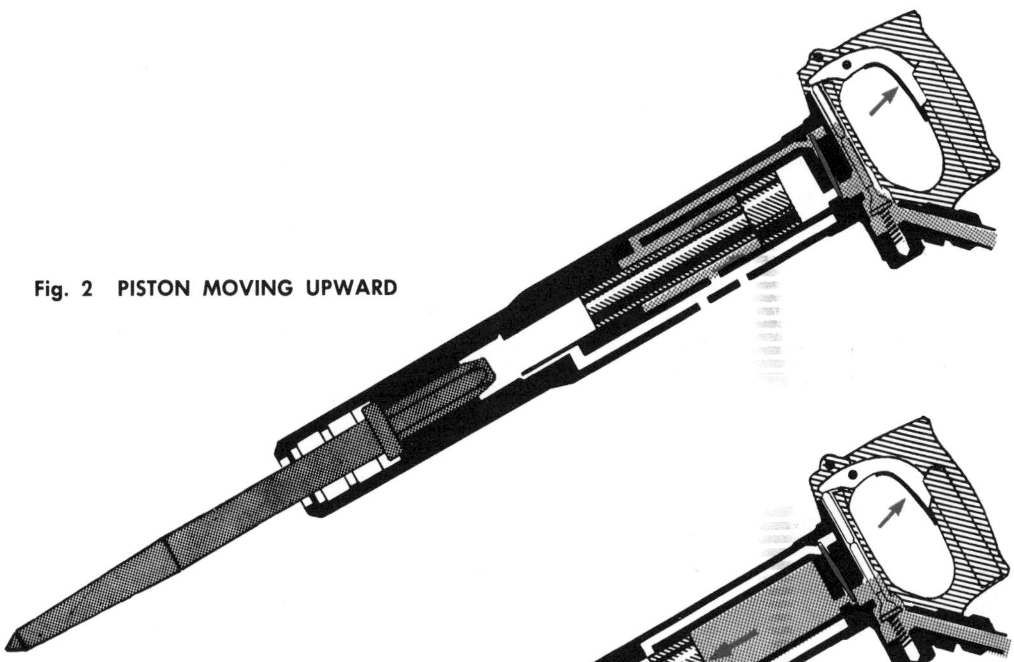

Fig. 2 PISTON MOVING UPWARD

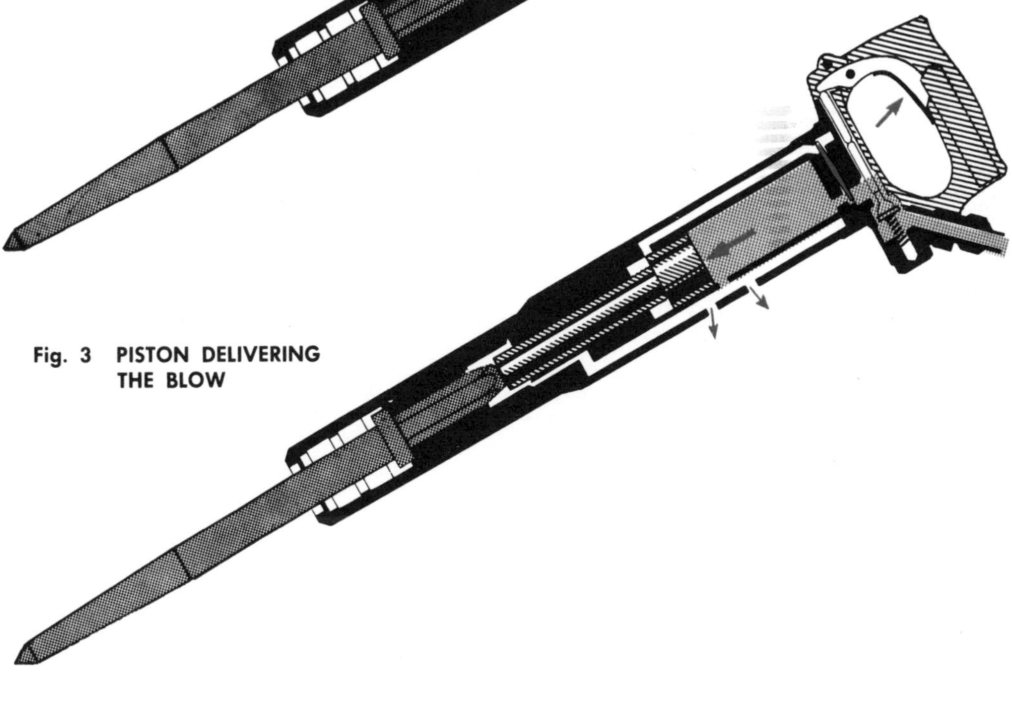

Fig. 3 PISTON DELIVERING THE BLOW

SHIPS' PROPELLERS

Ships are large. Propellers, in proportion, are small. And yet propellers are successful in moving ships, often across large oceans. They do this by pushing against water—the way a swimmer in a swimming pool gives himself a start by pushing against the wall and then keeps going by pushing against the water with his arms.

A propeller doesn't look at all like what it really is. What it really is is a screw—the kind of screw that is used to hold metal parts together and has a straight cylindrical shank. The way to picture this is to think of just one of a propeller's blades and notice the slight angle at which it is set. If one extends the line made by this angle, letting it go around and come back again, and then go around again, and so on, the shape it will carve in the air will be an enlarged version of a little machine screw. This shape, which advances steadily as it goes round and round, is called a *helix*.

Why doesn't a propeller look like a *helix*? Because each of its blades is borrowed from a different part of the helix, then moved back so that it starts as far back as the first blade. But all three blades (or four, if there are four) are set at the same angle, and all move forward by the same amount as they go full circle. This amount, called the *pitch*, is shown in Fig. 1.

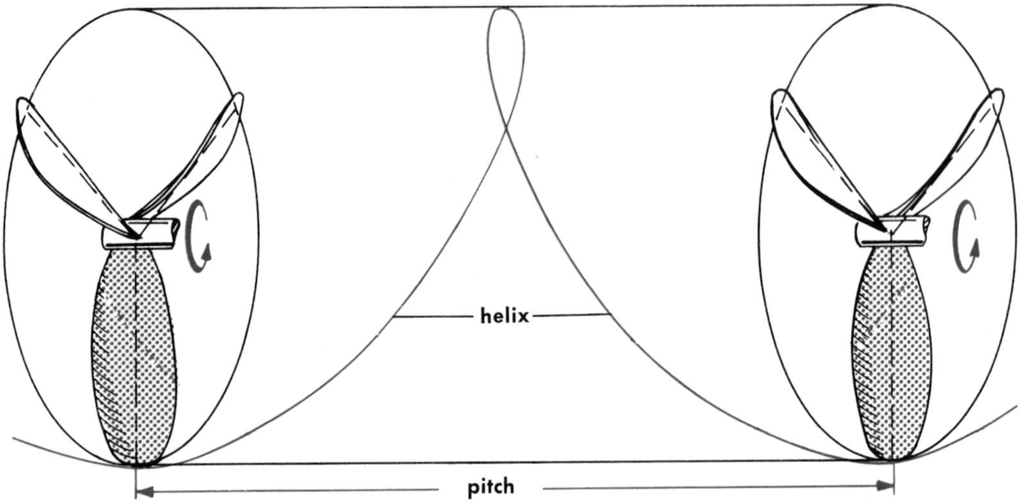

Fig. 1 PRINCIPLE OF SCREW MOTION

We can imagine a propeller pushing its way through some kind of cheese, so that every time it would have spun through one whole turn, it would have carried a ship forward with it by a length equal to the pitch. In the real world of water—as water actually behaves—a ship moves forward a little less far than that (only about two-thirds as far).

There is one thing that makes propeller design difficult. The blades are set at a slight angle, and as they turn, they push against the water behind them. So far so good. But what happens in front of them? The front faces of a propeller should have water filling in, clinging to them as they turn. But when a propeller is turning fast, water doesn't always move in fast enough. Bubbles of water vapor form and wear out the metal of the blades.

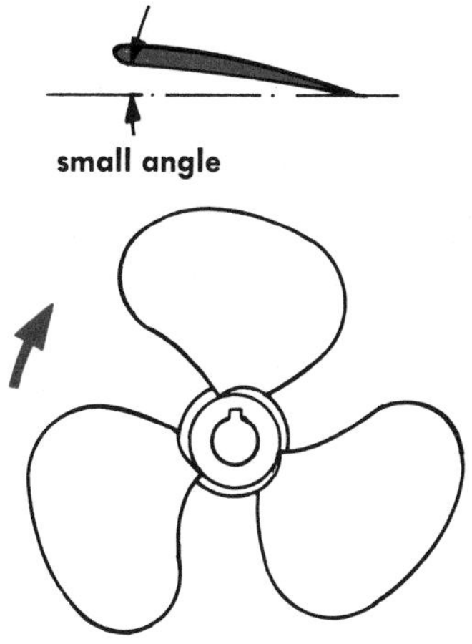

Fig. 2 HIGH-SPEED PROPELLER (*wide, flat blades*)

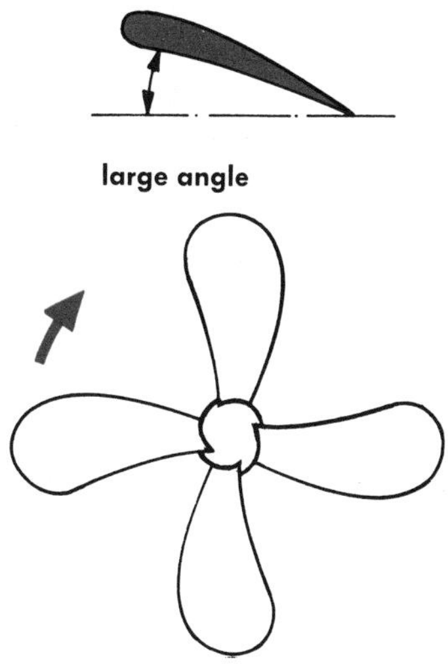

Fig. 3 LOW-SPEED PROPELLER (*narrow blades strongly curved in section*)

To prevent this, the propellers of ocean liners, which move great masses of water with their blades, are allowed to run slowly (Fig. 3). But the propellers of small boats, which are themselves small and move very little water per turn, have to whiz around much faster to let each turn give the water a fast push; the only way to prevent bubbles from forming on the forward faces of their blades is to keep the angle of the blades very slight (Fig. 2).

WATER TURBINES

We are now so accustomed to obtaining power by burning fuel in an engine that the power of flowing water, in rivers and their waterfalls, hardly seems important. But there is only so much coal, and so much petroleum, in the world. Once we have burned the coal, or used up the petroleum, it's gone. A power source like flowing river water, which renews itself every minute, is worth putting to work.

What's more, we don't have to move to Buffalo to use the energy of Niagara Falls. ELECTRIC GENERATORS can convert it into electricity, which can be sent several hundred miles away without great loss. But first, we have to *capture* the energy that is in the flowing water.

The old **water wheel** is the simplest way. If the water passes *under* the wheel, as in Fig. 1, the wheel is an *undershot wheel.* If the water is dammed up and then is allowed to fall on the vanes of the wheel

Fig. 1 UNDERSHOT WATER WHEEL

from above, the design is called an *overshot wheel.* The overshot does a slightly better job of capturing the energy of the moving water, but neither design is very effective. The water gives the flat vanes a glancing blow and flows right on with practically as much energy as it had before.

What is needed is a system that will really *catch* the water, the way a catcher catches a ball. That is what the **Pelton wheel** provides. The water is channeled into a nozzle (something like the nozzle of a fireman's hose) and is shot at deeply scooped-out buckets set on a wheel fixed to a shaft, which is thus driven by the water from the nozzle. (The Pelton wheel shown in Fig. 2 uses *two* nozzles.) The operator adjusts a control needle within the nozzle (Fig. 3) in such a way as to keep the buckets moving about half as fast as the jet.

An engineer installs a Pelton wheel only when he is lucky enough to find water coming down from a great height. What he more often finds, however, is a good flow of water but no great height. He then installs a Francis or a Kaplan turbine.

Fig. 2 TWO-NOZZLE PELTON WHEEL

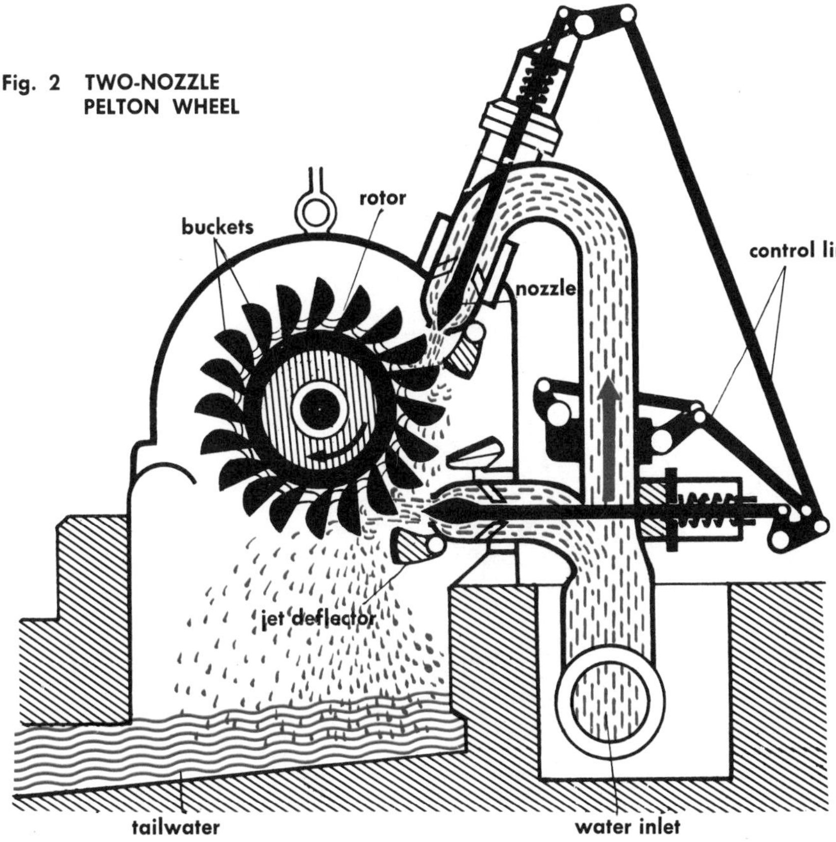

Fig. 3 NOZZLE AND BUCKET OF A PELTON WHEEL

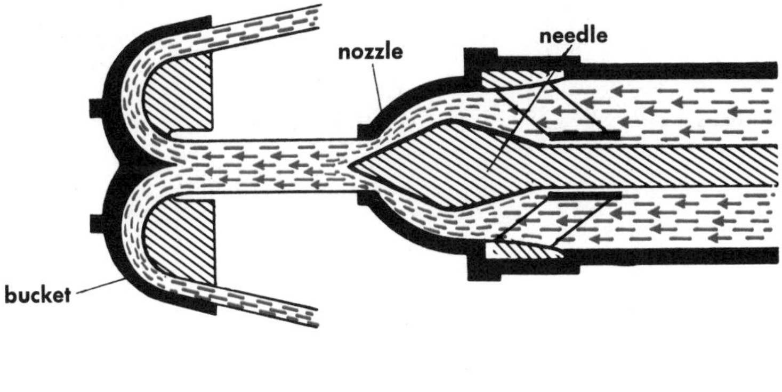

In the **Francis turbine** (Fig. 4), water first enters a channel in the shape of a snail shell, then comes out from between *guide vanes* set in a circle to hit the curved blades of the *runner* from the side. The blades are sent whirling, leaving the water to flow down along the shaft of the runner—at right angles to the way it came in.

The **Kaplan turbine** is the one most often used to run generators at

Fig. 4 FRANCIS TURBINE, SIDE VIEW
(*schematic*)

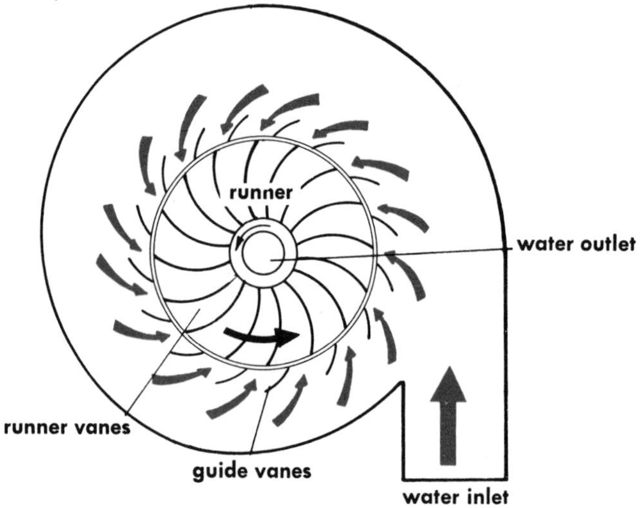

Fig. 5 KAPLAN TURBINE
(*schematic*)

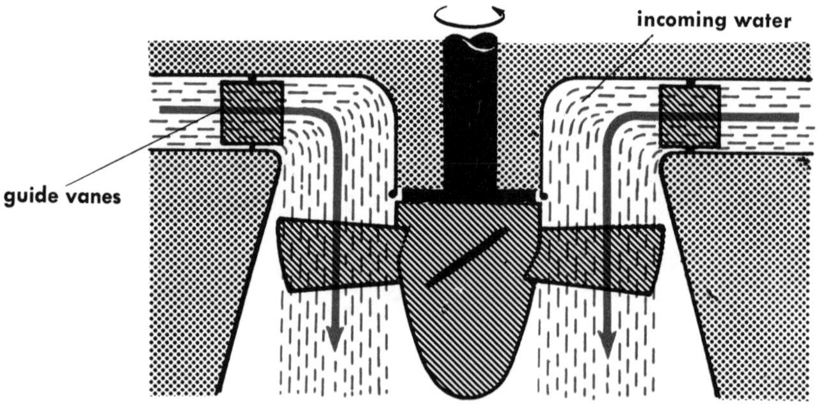

Fig. 6 PROPELLER OF KAPLAN TURBINE

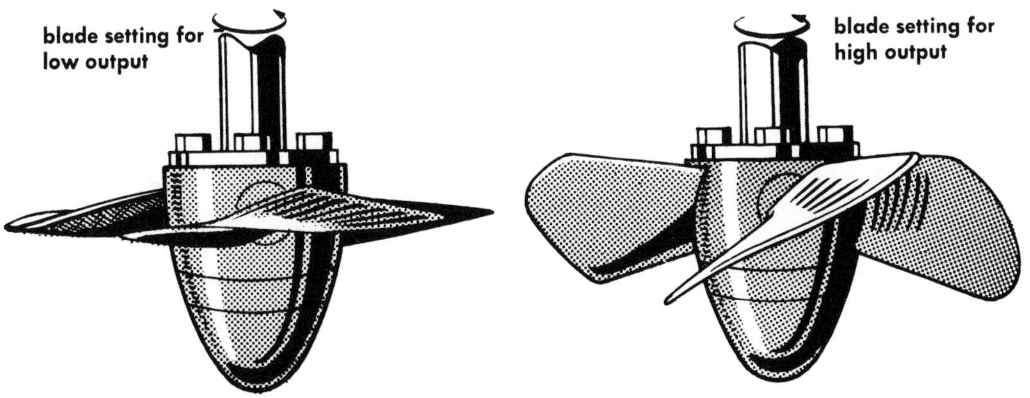

dams. Water enters it from the sides (Fig. 5), from which guide vanes direct it so that it falls along the shaft of what looks very much like the propeller of a ship! Only here, the blades don't move the water—it's the water that drives the blades. When not much power is needed, the guide vanes of the Kaplan turbine can be adjusted to reduce the flow of water, and the angle made by the blades of the propeller (Fig. 6) is then also adjusted to meet the new rate of flow.

Almost all turbines in use today are connected to ELECTRIC GENERATORS to produce electricity.

CENTRIFUGE

A centrifuge is a device that separates certain liquids (or solids) out of another liquid. If one substance is actually *dissolved* in the other (the way a lump of sugar will dissolve in a quart of water), the centrifuge will not separate them. But to separate *mixtures*—as in separating fat out of milk—a centrifuge is the most practical device there is. It is used not only in dairies and factories, but also in hospitals, where it serves to separate blood into cells and plasma.

Most mixtures (sand in water, cream in milk) will separate out if left standing long enough. Each grain of sand is heavier than a small unit of water of the same size, and sinks (Fig. 1). But it often hap-

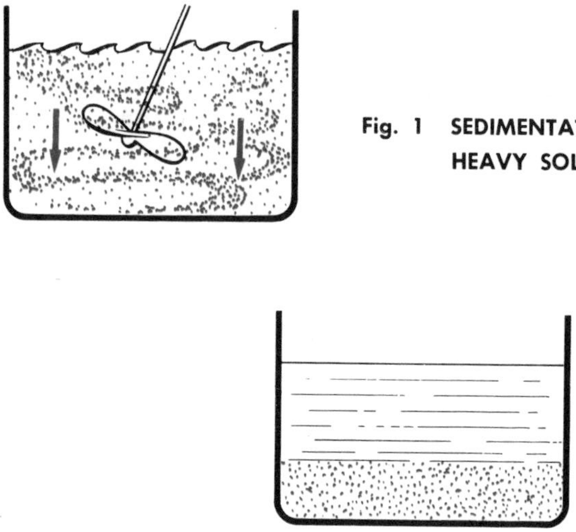

Fig. 1 SEDIMENTATION OF A HEAVY SOLID IN A LIQUID

pens that mixtures are sluggish about separating. For these, hospitals and factories use a centrifuge.

In a centrifuge, the mixture is made to spin. When one is spinning a stone at the end of a string (Fig. 2), it tends to pull outward—to prevent it from flying off, we keep a good grip on the string. If we replaced it with a *heavier* stone, it would take *more* force to pull it in as it spins. In a centrifuge, no one is pulling back with extra force on the heavy particles, so they collect near the outer rim (Fig. 3). The separated parts can then be drained through separate outlet holes. To do this, one would have to stop the drum.

Sometimes, in industry, it is more practical to keep the centrifuge going all the time, feeding it a steady stream of raw material and withdrawing the separated parts without stopping the machine. In one such system (Fig. 4a), the mixture is fed continuously, through a pipe, into the spinning drum; inside the drum are cone-shaped metal plates (like a family of funnels) stacked one above the other. The lighter liquid flows upward along the backs of the plates and is piped out. The heavier liquid is flung outward, toward the inside of

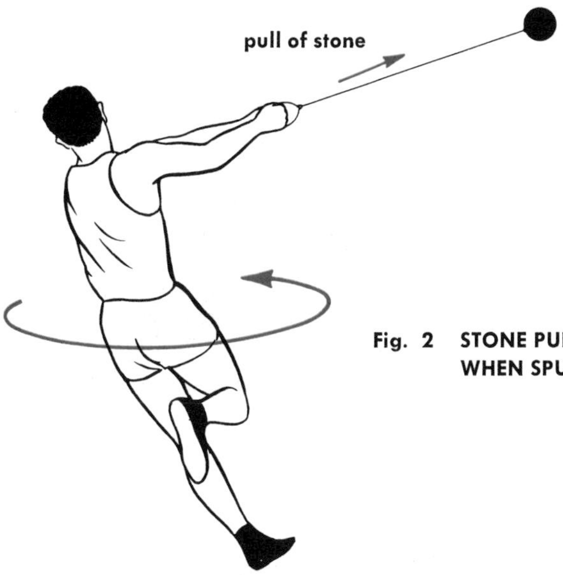

Fig. 2 STONE PULLS ON STRING WHEN SPUN AROUND

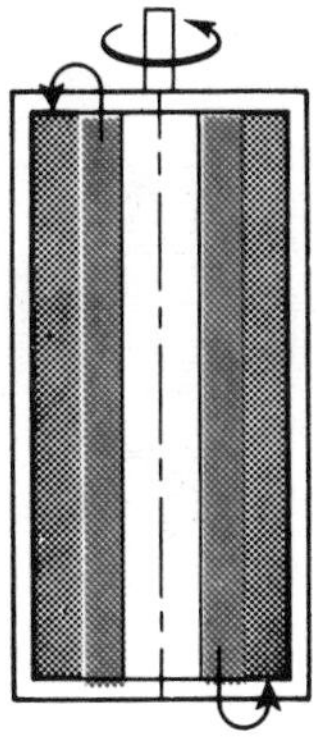

Fig. 3 SEPARATION OF THE PARTS OF A MIXTURE IN A SPINNING DRUM

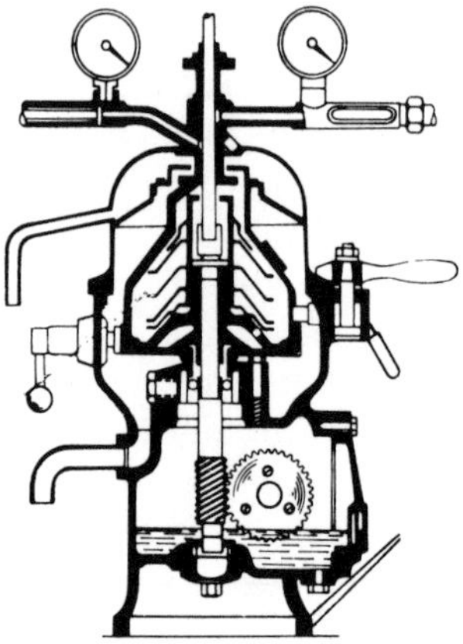

Fig. 4a CENTRIFUGE FOR THE SEPARATION OF TWO LIQUIDS

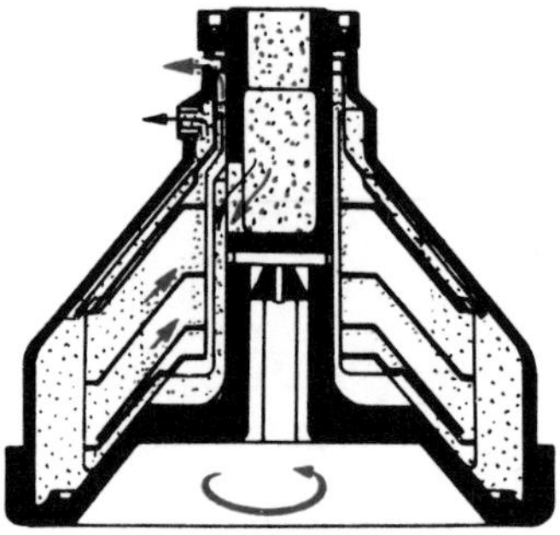

Fig. 4b
CENTRIFUGING DRUM WITH PLATES
(*detail of Fig. 4a*)

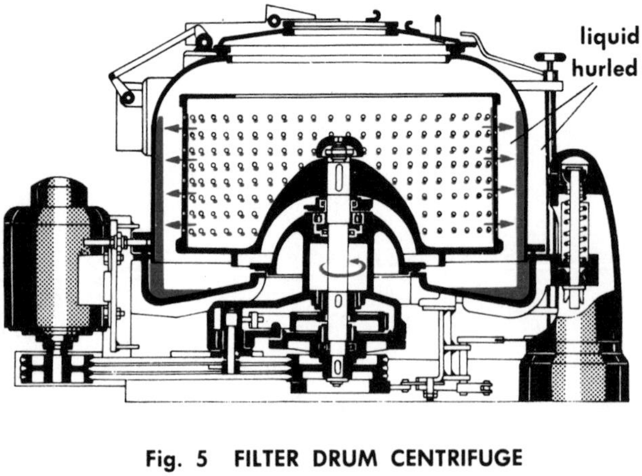

Fig. 5 FILTER DRUM CENTRIFUGE

the outer drum. The drum is cone-shaped—the heavy liquid presses against its narrowing roof (Fig. 4b) and is let out.

There is one kind of centrifuge that acts in a different way. It is used to filter solid particles suspended in a liquid. It requires a filter cloth, and the wall of its inside drum (Fig. 5) is pierced. As the drum spins, the solid particles are stopped by the filter in the inner drum, while the liquid is hurled through the holes and is collected in the outer casing. The liquid is easily drained off (as in the spin-dryers used in laundries); to collect the solid particles, the motor is stopped and the deposit is scraped off. In some designs, internal scrapers remove the solids so that the machine does not have to be stopped.

STAYING AFLOAT

When ships were made of wood, and stayed afloat, it wasn't so surprising. But today most ships are made of metal. How do they stay afloat?

According to Archimedes' principle, an object in water loses the weight of the water it displaces. When the object displaces a quantity of water equal to (or greater than) its own weight, the object floats. An aluminum cube with sides 1 foot long weighs 168 pounds when it is weighed in the air (Fig. 1a). When it is weighed in water (Fig. 1b),

ARCHIMEDES' PRINCIPLE

Fig. 1a

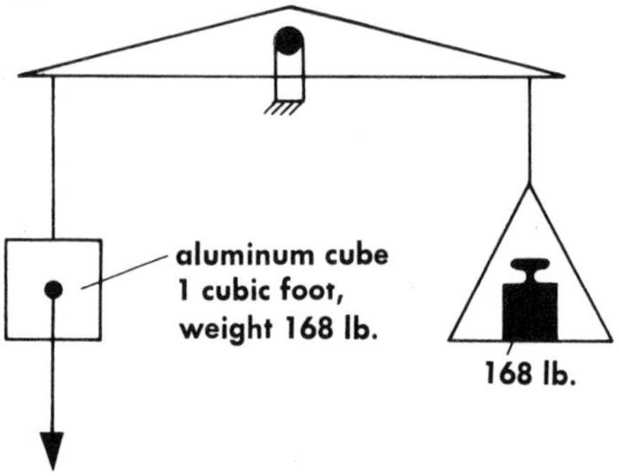

Fig. 1b

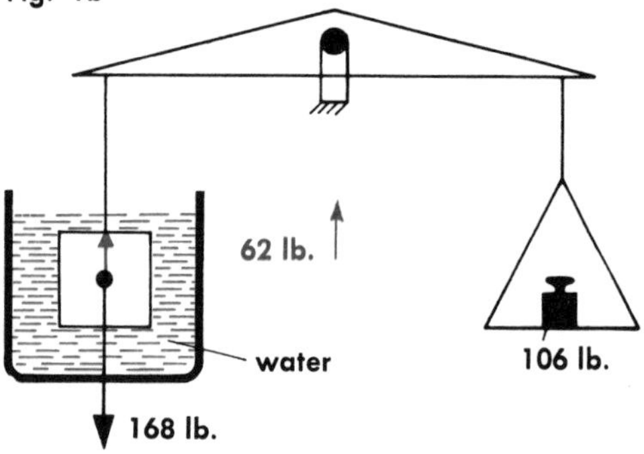

its weight registers only 106 pounds. The 62 pounds it has lost is the weight of a cube of water with sides 1 foot long. But a loss of 62 pounds is still not enough to keep the 168-pound cube from sinking—and if we let go of it, it sinks.

A wooden cube of the same size, weighing 50 pounds, would behave differently (Fig. 2). As we eased it into the water, it would settle in, pushing some of the water out of the way—but it would sink in only deep enough for the weight of this water to amount to 50 pounds. At that point, the cube would be *floating.*

Fig. 2 FLOATING

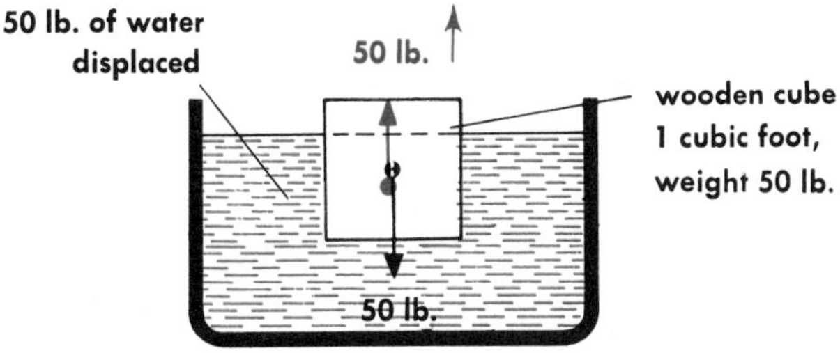

But it *is* possible to make the aluminum cube float. It can be reworked into the shape of a hollowed-out shell or box. Then, as soon as it settled in the water, it would displace an enormous amount of water (enough to make up a weight of 168 pounds)—and would float. That is how a ship can be made of metals, even though these same metals if melted down into one huge cube would sink on the spot.

But as soon as the metal has been reworked into the shape of an open shell, there is danger of its tipping over. If the hull of a hollow ship starts filling up with water, the weight that has been subtracted from the weight of its metal is added right back again—and the ship sinks. So it is not enough for a metal-hulled ship to float: it has to stay upright as well.

As it meets wind and waves, a ship can't possibly stay bolt upright all the time—sometimes it will lean to one side, or heel (Fig. 3a); sometimes it will be *trimmed* by the bow (Fig. 3b) or by the stern. When this happens, what will enable a ship to right itself?

Every object can be considered as having a *center of gravity*—a point so placed that the object will behave as if all its weight were concentrated at this point. In Fig. 4a, the ship's center of gravity is marked G. The counterbalancing upward thrust of the water that has been moved out of the way by the ship's hull can also be thought of as acting from a single point, U. When the ship is riding upright (Fig. 4a), point U is right under point G. But when the ship heels over (Fig. 4b), the upward thrust comes from a new point, U_a. This

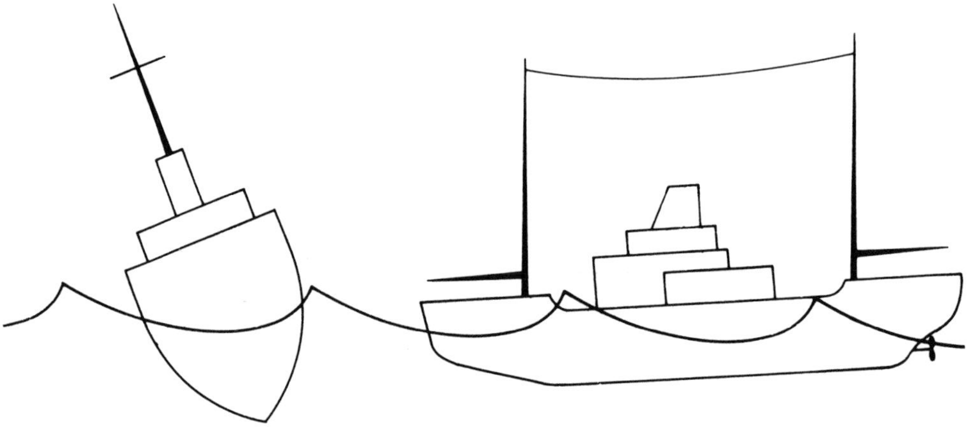

Fig. 3a **HEELING**

Fig. 3b **TRIM**

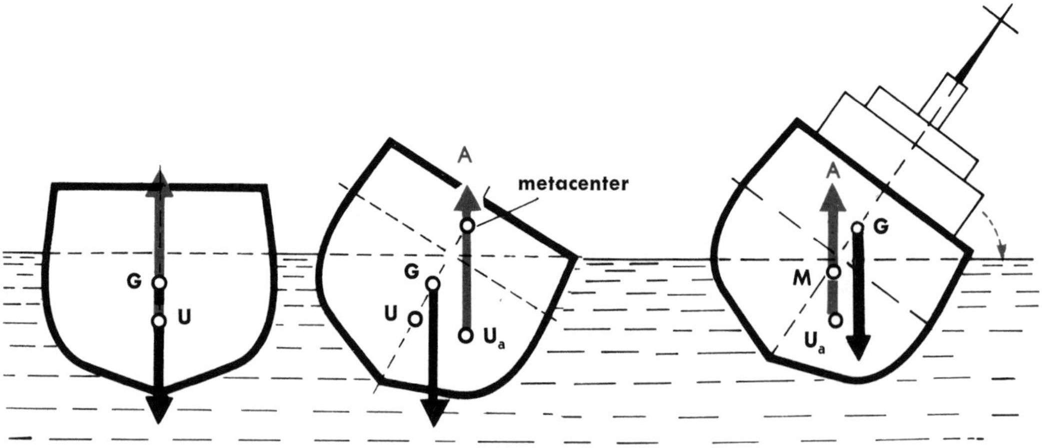

Fig. 4a

Fig. 4b

Fig. 4c

thrust may right the ship, and it may not. The only way of telling is to find out where the *metacenter* is going to be.

The metacenter can be found by drawing a straight line through the ship from the keel up, passing through its center of gravity, and another line vertically through the center of upthrust U_a. It's the point at which these two lines meet that is called the *metacenter*, M. If M is above G, the ship will right itself. If M is below G (Fig. 4c), the ship will heel over more and more and will capsize.

SAILING

A modern sailboat allows one to sail just where one wants to go, whether the wind happens to be going there or not. It does this by an arrangement called the *fore-and-aft rig,* which appears in Fig. 1. The boat's *mainsail* (pronounced MAIN-sel) is hung from the mast but is also attached to the *boom,* which can swing about the mast (as in Fig. 2, in which the boat is seen from above).

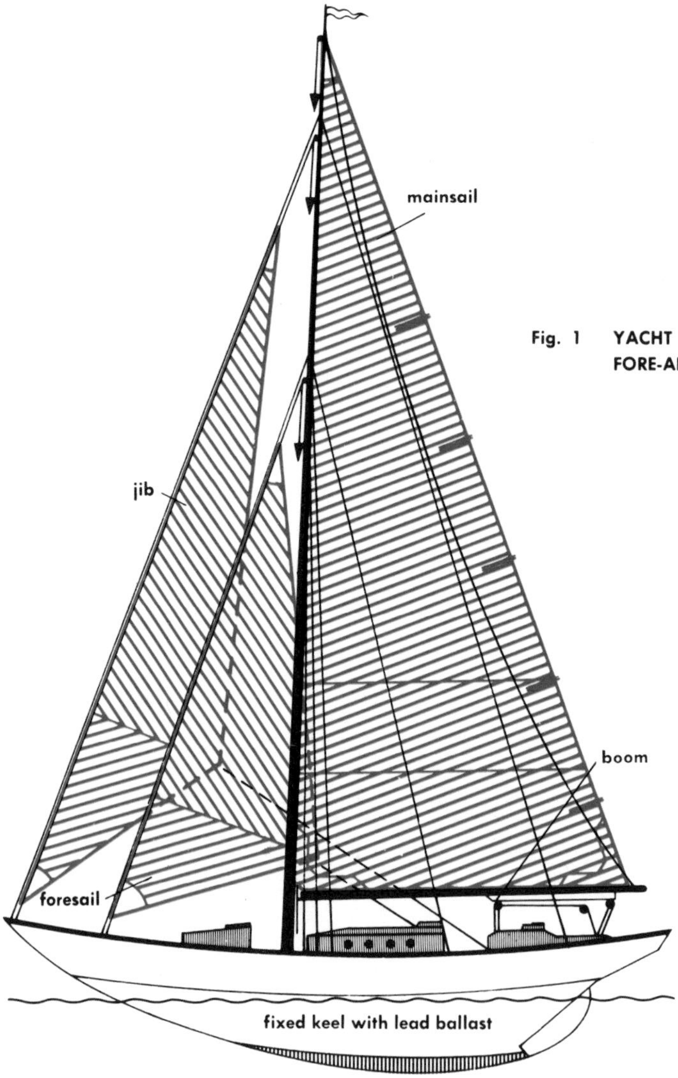

Fig. 1 YACHT WITH FORE-AND-AFT RIG

The boat can "run before the wind" (Fig. 2a), but she can also make use of a wind coming "on her quarter" (Fig. 2b) or "on her beam" (at right angles to the way she is heading, Fig. 2c); this is known as *reaching*. If she is designed for racing, she may even be able to "beat" almost into the wind (Fig. 2d). To sail in the direction the wind is coming from requires *tacking*, a zigzag course that gets one out of actually trying to sail into the wind.

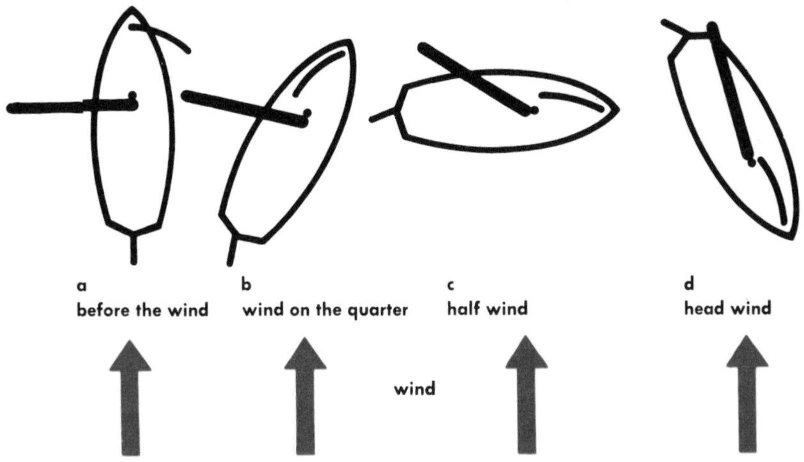

Fig. 2 WIND DIRECTIONS IN RELATION TO BOAT

The ability of a boat with a fore-and-aft rig to use the wind even when it is not coming from behind her grows out of a combination of effects. First, the sail acts simply as a wind-catching area. Then, because of its curvature under the pressure of the wind, the sail causes the air on the side *away* from the wind to take a long path behind the sail; as a result, it moves faster than the wind on the windward side, creating a difference in pressure on the two sides of the sail. As in the airplane wing (page 52), this resulting force can be used to move the whole craft. And because this boat has more than one sail, the "slot" between sails can be adjusted so that the foresail increases the speed of the jet of air back of the mainsail, with the jib doing the same thing for the foresail. This gives further usable force.

A fore-and-aft rig is set at an angle to the wind, but also at another angle to the direction of the boat. How the boat's skipper can use a

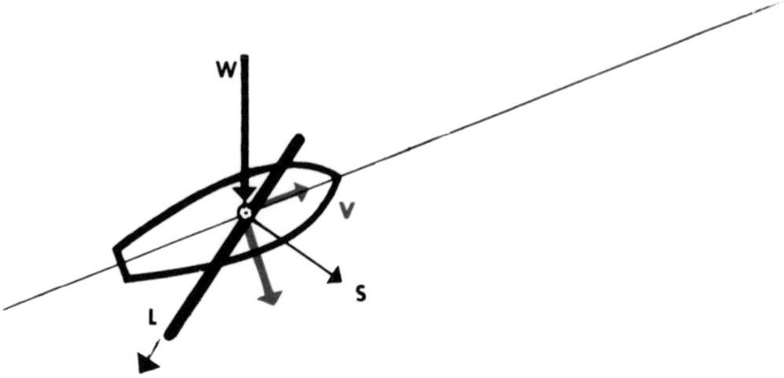

Fig. 3 FORCES ON BOAT

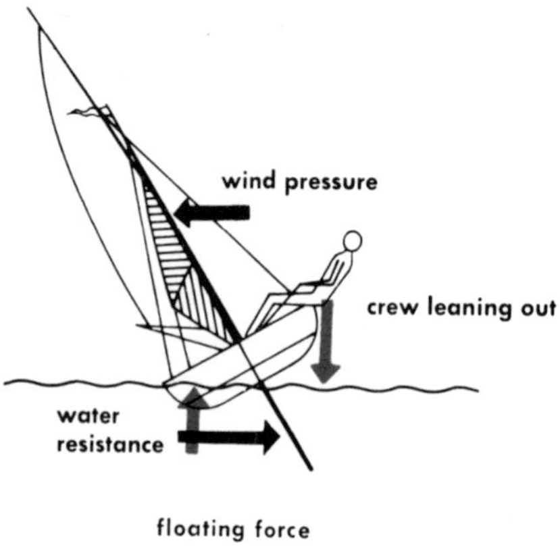

Fig. 4 FORCES ACTING ON BOAT WITH MOVABLE KEEL

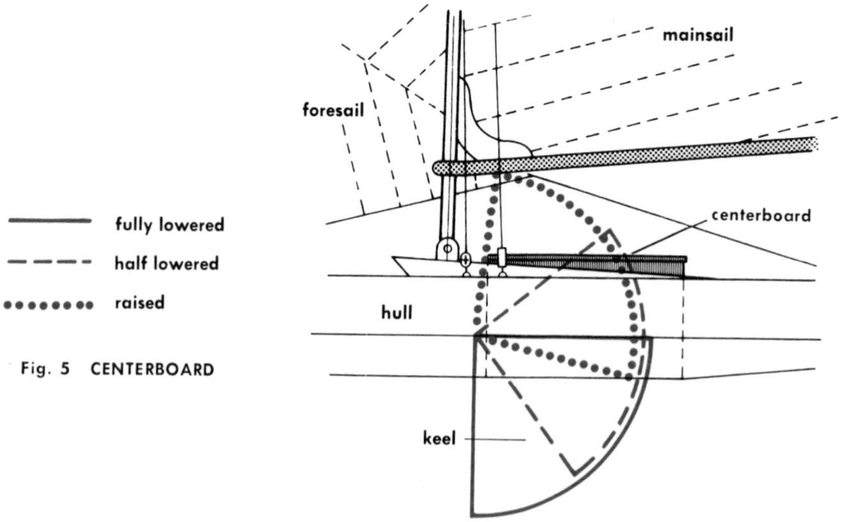

Fig. 5 CENTERBOARD

wind that is not coming from behind depends on how he manages to adjust these two angles to his advantage. For instance, in pulling a sled over the snow, one wants to produce horizontal motion forward; but because of the height of one's hand, one has to pull the sled at an upward angle. Only a *part* of one's pulling force actually moves the sled forward.

In the same way, the black arrow W (Fig. 3) represents the force of the wind. Of this force, only the portion marked S, at right angles to the sail, acts on the boat. Its effect is to push her in the direction of arrow S. If the skipper now uses the boat's keel to fight the part of S that pushes at right angles to the boat, he is left with a forward portion V. Compared with the original wind force W, V looks pretty small—but it *is* directed forward, and enables the boat to advance when the wind is seemingly "against" her.

Most yachts and other large sailing craft have lead-ballasted fixed keels (Fig. 1) that enable them to stand up against the wind. What smaller boats and dinghies have instead is a movable keel, or *centerboard,* that can be tucked back into the hull (Fig. 5); to avoid capsizing, the crew must lean far out every so often to counterbalance the sideways force of the wind (Fig. 4).

WILL IT FLY?

Planes are enormously heavy. They carry tons of aluminum and steel, tons of fuel and sometimes tons of people. When a plane is cruising four miles above the earth, what force is there that counteracts this weight and keeps the plane aloft?

The force is called *lift*. A plane's wings are designed to produce lift as soon as the plane moves forward. When the wing cuts through the air of the atmosphere, the air layers just above it are made to travel a slightly longer route than those beneath it (Fig. 1). The air stream

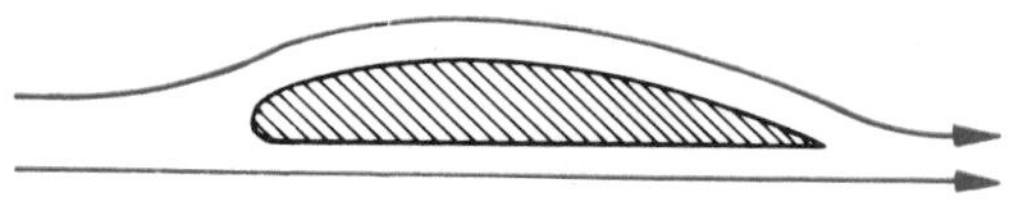

Fig. 1 AIR FLOW AT WING

above the wing moves very fast, producing a lowering of pressure on the wing's upper surface. With less pressure above it than below it, the wing is subject to an upward force—*lift*. If the lift pushing the wings upward is greater than a plane's weight, the plane will rise.

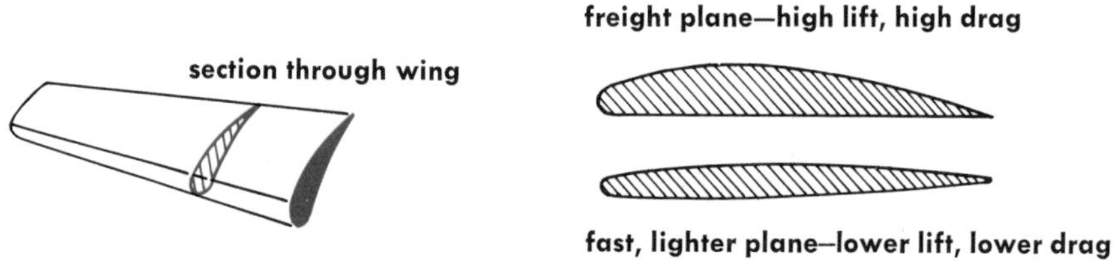

Fig. 2 WINGS SEEN IN PROFILE

Meanwhile, a plane's forward speed makes it encounter air resistance—*drag*. If it is to continue flying, it has to keep up its forward speed. The drag can be kept small by streamlining the wings, as they are seen in profile (Fig. 2), and by keeping them smooth, so that the air layers flowing by remain unruffled. But the engines—through propellers or through JET ENGINES—still have to produce enough *thrust,* or forward force, to overcome the drag. The tug of war between weight and lift, drag and thrust, is shown in Fig. 3.

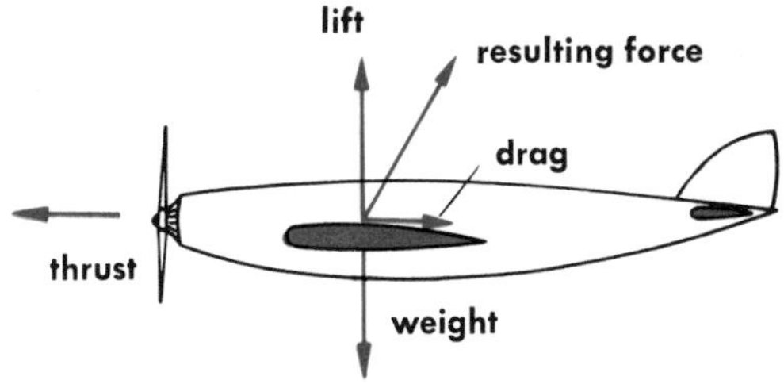

Fig. 3 FORCES ACTING ON AIRCRAFT'S WING

In the course of his flight, a pilot can change the angle at which the wings meet the air. This angle, called the *angle of attack,* appears in Fig. 4, in which the forces acting on the plane are shown as if acting on a single spot, the *center of pressure.* As a pilot increases the angle of attack, this point moves forward. If he increases it too much, he risks losing control of the plane: the air flow along the upper surface of the wing can be pulled too far out (Fig. 5) and the plane can lose its lift and "stall."

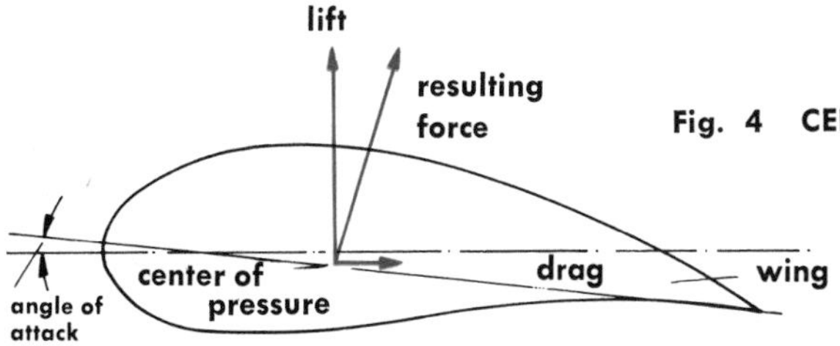

Fig. 4 CENTER OF PRESSURE

Fig. 5 STALLING CONDITION

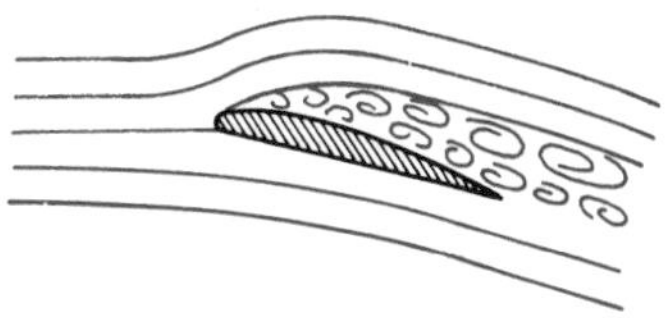

If one were to cut through the blade of a propeller, one would discover that it is shaped just like the wing section shown in Fig. 4. It, too, has to cut its way through the air in such a way as to produce a force "lifting" it toward its curved surface. Only since the propeller's "lift" is directed forward, the plane uses it as a *thrust.*

The angle at which a propeller blade is twisted as it cuts through the air is called its *pitch.* (It corresponds to the angle of attack of a wing.) During flight, a pilot makes adjustments in the pitch of the propeller to give it maximum effectiveness for the speed at which the plane is flying. A control in the cockpit allows him to do this while the propeller is turning.

GLIDERS

Any craft that is heavier than air cannot fly without a device that will produce *lift* (page 52) to counteract its weight. In powered aircraft, the wings are so designed that if engine power moves them forward, they will develop lift. But gliders have no engines—yet they commonly fly three miles above the earth and often stay up for hours. How do they manage it?

A glider pilot keeps his eyes open for signs of rising air currents. If he sees a hawk or a gull soaring in the air without flapping its wings, he will suspect a rising air current and try to take advantage of it. He also learns to expect rising currents on hillsides (Fig. 1) and under "fair weather" cumulus clouds just as they are forming (Fig. 2); sometimes he uses the updrafts that rise along the boundaries between warm and cold air masses at the edge of a thunderstorm.

Fig. 1 RISING CURRENT ON HILLSIDE

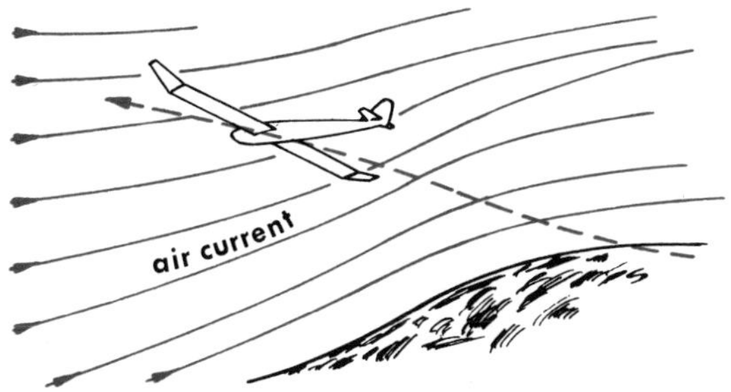

Fig. 2 UPDRAFTS OF WARM AIR

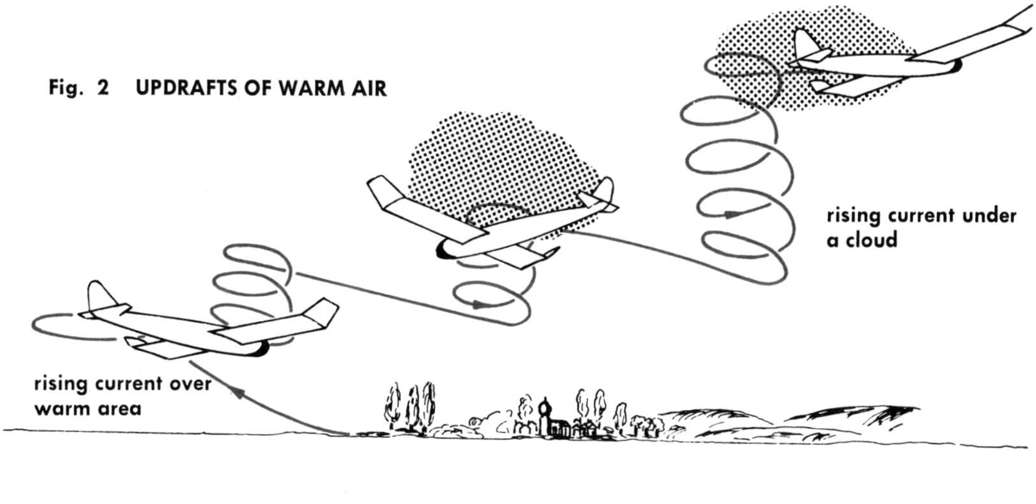

When a glider pilot has reached a great height, it is because he has found these updrafts and "hitched a ride" on them. But whenever he is in perfectly calm air, he can only coast downward. This is gliding in its purest form. But if a pilot can string out his downward glide for hours, with only an occasional updraft to help hitch him up again, it's because gliders are not designed like powered planes.

Fig. 3 HIGH-DRAG CRAFT IN DIVE

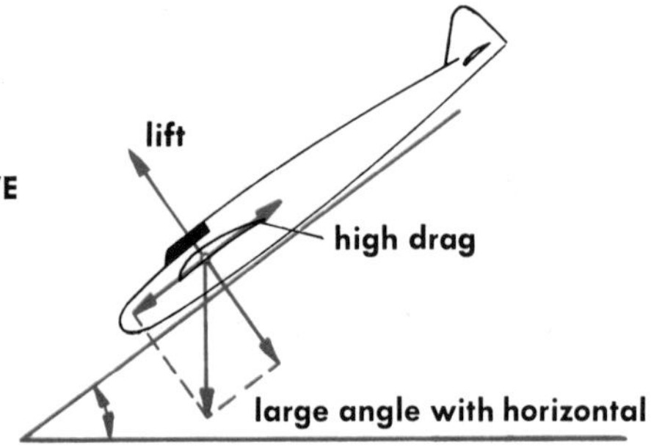

Fig. 4 FORCES ON GLIDER

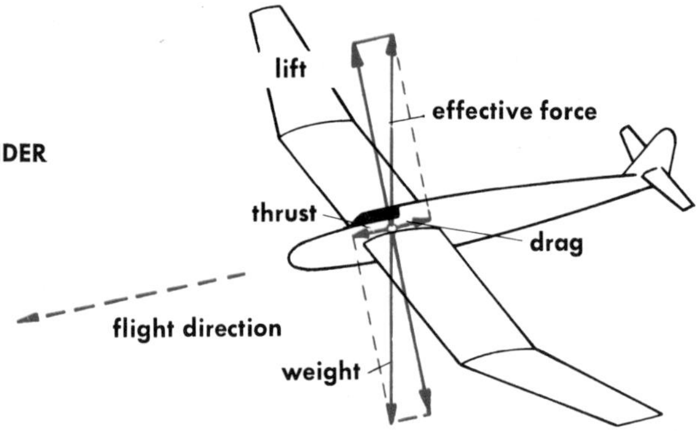

Fig. 5 LOW-DRAG CRAFT IN GLIDE

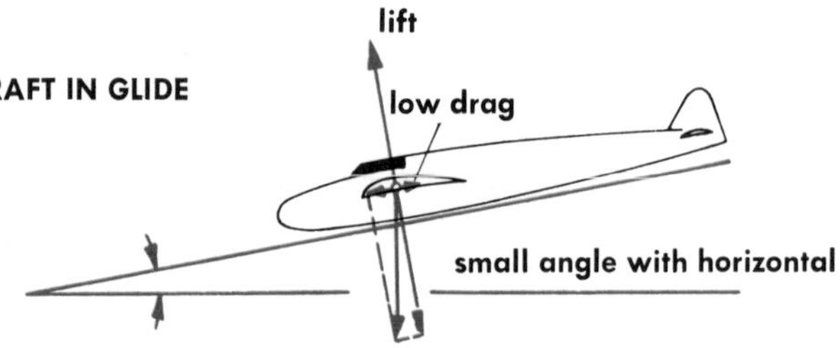

In a powered plane, the lift is not much greater than the drag (Fig. 3). But a glider has to work up all the lift it can get (Fig. 4) and has to force air to flow over its wings to produce it. Since it lacks engines, the only way for it to do this is to glide at a slightly downward angle.

If gliders were designed like powered planes, they would come down at a very steep angle—they would "dive." To prevent them from doing this, engineers design them with something like 30 times as much lift as drag (Fig. 5). In practice, this means that as a glider drops 1 mile downward, it moves 30 miles forward. This gives a pilot a chance to search for another updraft, to regain whatever height he has lost—after which he starts gliding slowly downward again.

One thing gliders are not good at is taking off from the ground by themselves. Two common ways of launching them from the ground are to tow them behind an automobile (at the end of a rope several hundred feet long) or to pull them from far away by means of a high-speed winch. (That is, by using hoisting machinery—but horizontally.) If a powered airplane tows them into the air, they can be launched from a great height and cover hundreds of miles.

II Energy and Where to Find It

STEAM ENGINE

A steam engine converts the energy of heat into mechanical power—the ability to pull, push, raise or turn. It does this by applying the original energy—heat—to water, producing steam under high pressure, then cooling the steam suddenly, so that it shrinks. The expansion and shrinkage of the steam can then be used to move a *piston* back and forth in a *cylinder* (Fig. 1). A *connecting rod* uses the back-and-forth motion of the piston to make a crank (Fig. 3) or a wheel (Fig. 1) turn.

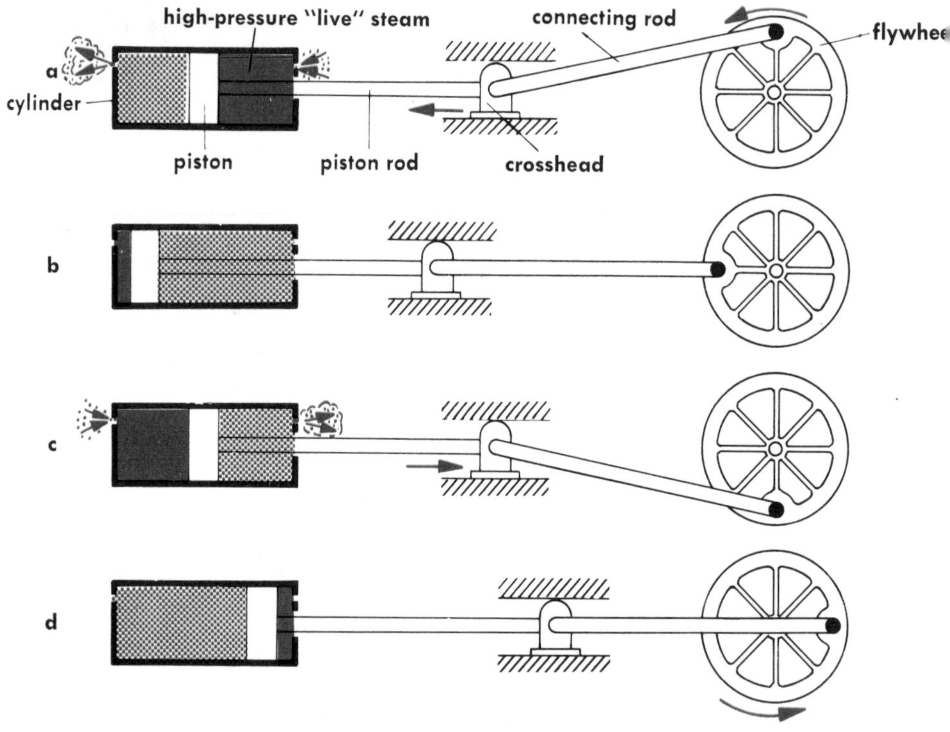

Fig. 1 FOUR MOMENTS IN THE CYCLE OF A DOUBLE-ACTING ENGINE

The water is first heated in a *boiler*, becoming steam under high pressure. The steam is let into the cylinder, where it expands, pushing the piston to the left (Fig. 1a). When the steam has pushed the piston all the way to the left (Fig. 1b), it is allowed to escape, cool off (Fig. 2) and shrink. Meanwhile new "live" steam is allowed in on the left

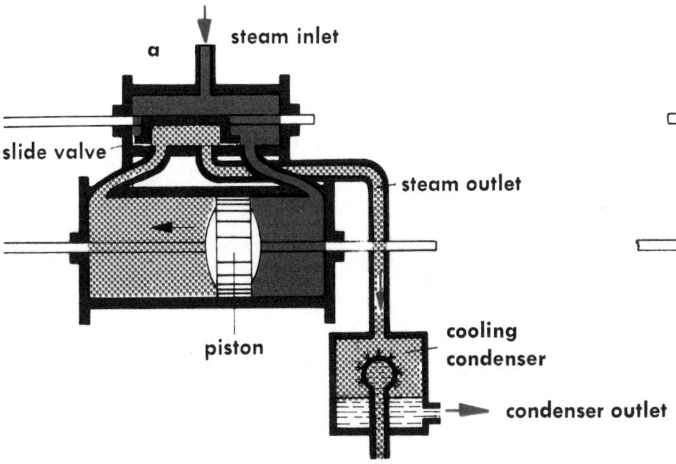

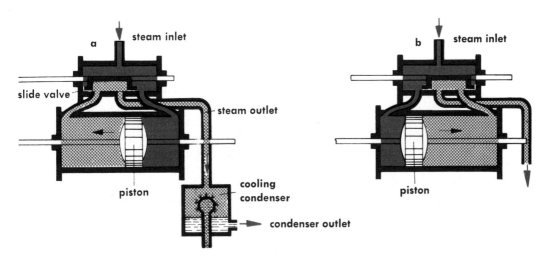

Fig. 2 HOW THE SLIDE VALVE WORKS

—and the piston now moves toward the right (Fig. 1c), until it reaches the end of its stroke (Fig. 1d), when the cycle begins all over again. This kind of steam engine, in which the steam is let in first from one side of the piston, then from the other, is called **double-acting.**

Controlling the comings and goings of the steam is the job of the *slide valve,* which appears in Fig. 2 as a squarish black lid. When the slide valve is on the left (Fig. 2a), it allows live steam in on the right and lets the spent steam escape on the left; when it moves to the right, it lets live steam in on the left and lets the spent steam out on the right.

But the slide valve doesn't merely let steam in and out—it lets it in and out *at the right time.* To make this timing automatic, it is con-

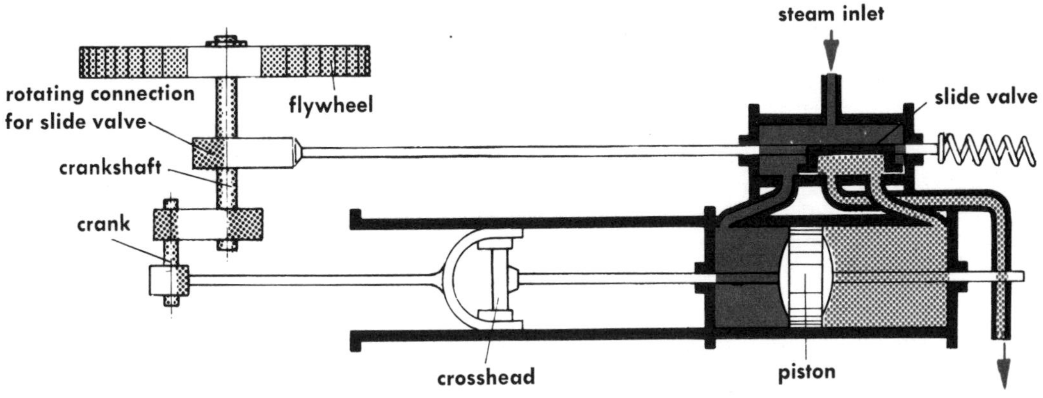

Fig. 3 HOW THE SLIDE VALVE IS CONTROLLED

nected to the *crankshaft,* the shaft that receives the power from the engine.

Steam engines would have been of no use in locomotives, and of very little use in industry, were it not for the system that allows their original back-and-forth motion to be converted to *rotary,* or round-and-round, motion. The piston rod first passes the back-and-forth motion to the *crosshead* (Fig. 1a), which slides back and forth between guides, so that it has no up-and-down motion. The crosshead passes this motion to the *connecting rod* through an "elbow" whose design can be seen from above in Fig. 3. The part with the most interesting motion is the connecting rod: one end of it goes back and forth *at the same time* that the other end goes round and round. (It's not an easy motion to describe—to imitate it with one's forearm, it is best to keep one's fist sliding back and forth on a table.)

The connecting rod does succeed in changing the piston's back-and-forth motion to rotary motion, but since the piston transmits power push by push, the resulting motion is jerky. To smooth out the crankshaft's speed of rotation, a heavy cast-iron *flywheel* is mounted on it.

With all their heating and cooling and friction between parts, steam engines are hardly efficient—they deliver only about 15% of the energy offered by the coal they burn to heat their boilers. But a hundred years ago, neither trains nor industry could have run without them.

STEAM LOCOMOTIVE

A steam locomotive combines a large STEAM ENGINE (with special features) with ways that are all its own of transmitting the power to the wheels. Its source of energy is the heat released as it burns coal in its *firebox*. The resulting hot gases are channeled in "fire tubes" (Fig. 1) that cross the boiler. The steam that develops in the boiler is let into a cylinder, where it pushes a piston. After that, the spent steam is simply released into the air. Unlike other steam engines,

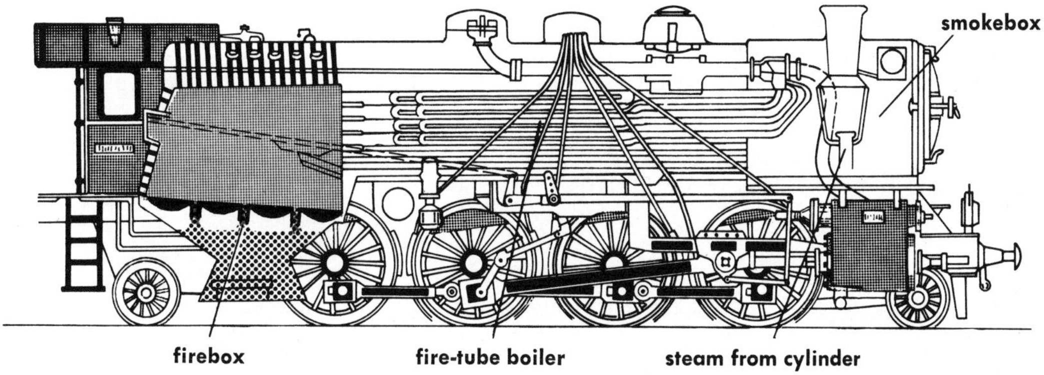

Fig. 1 THE INSIDE OF A STEAM LOCOMOTIVE

locomotives do not have a *condenser* to chill the steam and recirculate it as water. As a result, they need to take on water during each run.

Before being put to work in the cylinder, the steam passes through the *slide-valve chest* (Fig. 2), which allows it to reach the piston from either side. In Fig. 2, the live steam (deep red) is entering the cylinder from behind (that is, from the left as we see it); as it expands, the piston will be pushed forward and used-up steam from the previous stroke (pink stippling) will be pushed out. The forward part of the cylinder will then be ready for live steam from the slide valve. This new steam will push the piston backward.

Almost everything that happens from then on can be seen from the outside. The back-and-forth ("reciprocating") motion of the piston has to be converted into the round-and-round ("rotary") motion of the wheels. This is done by introducing a *crosshead* between them.

The crosshead receives simple back-and-forth motion from the piston through the *piston rod,* but it transmits power to one pair of driving wheels (the third) through a *driving rod,* of which one end moves back and forth while the other, connected to the *driving pin,* moves round and round. (Its motion is best seen on page 60, Fig. 1, where it is labeled *connecting rod.*) Although there are four pairs of driving wheels, only one pair receives power directly—the other driving wheels receive their power through *coupling rods.*

The locomotive in Fig. 2 is traveling backward—as the piston

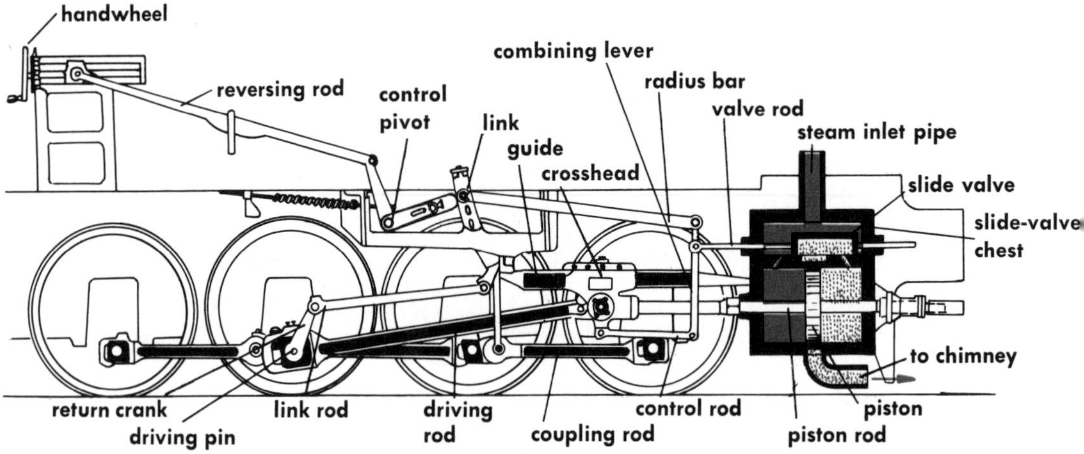

Fig. 2 HOW THE MOTION OF THE CYLINDER IS TRANSMITTED TO THE DRIVING WHEELS

pushes forward, the driving rod pulls the driving pin forward from below, making the wheel turn counterclockwise. For the locomotive to move forward, the slide valve would have to make the piston move backward when the driving pin is low. To make this happen, the back-and-forth motion of the slide valve would have to be reversed. In the locomotive shown here, this is done by changing the motion of the *combining lever,* which controls the slide valve through the *valve rod.*

The combining lever is so called because it combines two motions. One of these, acting at its bottom end, can't be changed—it comes fairly directly from the crosshead; but the other, acting at its top through the *radius bar,* can be switched by taking advantage of the motion of the *link.*

The link is pivoted near its mid-point—when its top rocks forward, its bottom rocks backward. At its bottom end it is connected to the *link rod,* so that when the link rod moves forward, the bottom end of the link moves forward with it—and the top moves backward. To put the locomotive into forward motion, the engineer turns the *hand-wheel* (top left) to pull back the *reversing rod;* this forces the radius bar to act from above its pivot, pulling the slide valve back whenever the link rod moves forward, and vice versa.

On a slippery track, none of this would get a locomotive anywhere. But a locomotive like the one shown weighs more than 400 tons (800,000 pounds), and the wheels get a good grip on the rails. When weather makes the tracks slippery, the engineer can blow a jet of sand in front of the driving wheels while the train is running.

STEAM TURBINES

Steam engines are used primarily to make an axle or shaft *turn*. But they go about their job first by making a piston move back and forth, then by converting this motion into a turning motion. Much of their energy is wasted in the rubbing and clanking of their metal parts against one another.

What a steam *turbine* does is to take the high-pressure steam from the boiler and send it against the blades of a wheel *directly*. The wheel (Fig. 2) is called a *rotor*, just as it is in WATER TURBINES. The turbine design is quite efficient, with the result that electric-power stations use large steam-turbine installations, as did the great steamships of a generation ago.

But the efficiency of a steam turbine depends on solving a difficult problem: the only thing that will make the blades turn is speed, and when the steam leaves the boiler, it has pressure but no speed. The Swedish engineer Gustav de Laval solved the problem a century ago by releasing the steam through *nozzles* in which the steam is briefly channeled into a narrowing throat to build up its speed, then is allowed to increase slightly in volume in the nozzle's flare (Fig. 1). The steam jet can then be directed at the blades of the rotor (Fig. 4).

But De Laval's first steam turbines released the steam's energy to the rotor in a single stage—and the shaft of the rotor turned much too fast. Other systems have been developed since in which the energy

Fig. 1 PASSAGE OF STEAM THROUGH DE LAVAL NOZZLE

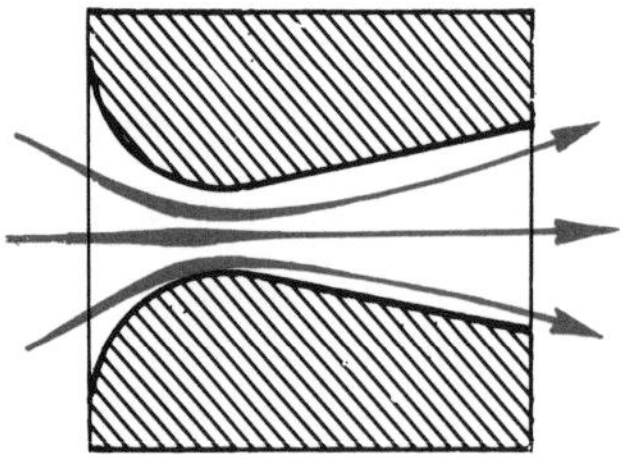

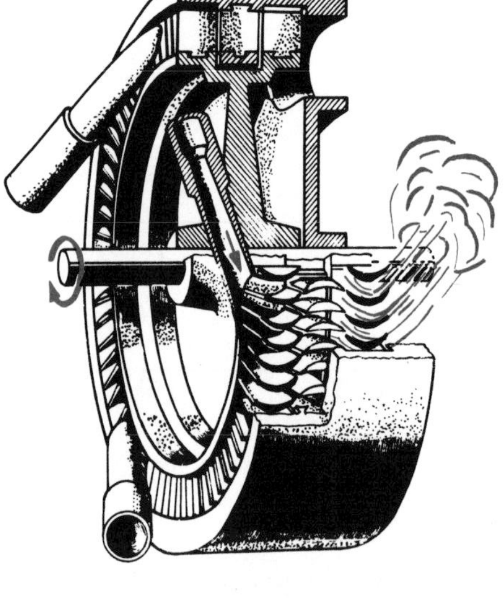

Fig. 2 DRIVE OF WHEEL WITH ROTOR BLADES

is released in installments to a series of wheels, all mounted on the same shaft. (In this design, the whole multiwheel assembly is called the *rotor.*)

One such system appears in Fig. 3, which shows a portion of the Curtis turbine, in which the rows marked 1 and 2 are made of moving blades mounted on a single shaft; they form part of the rotor. Between them is a row of fixed blades mounted on a stationary ring; these blades catch the steam jets coming from blade ring 1 and redirect them for the benefit of blade ring 2.

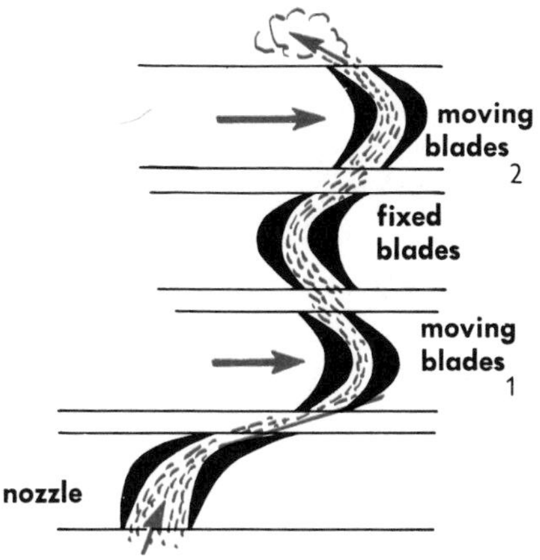

Fig. 3 BLADE WHEELS OF A CURTIS TURBINE

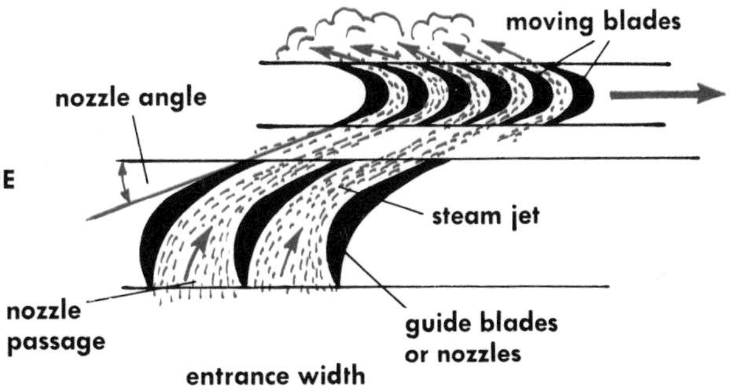

Fig. 4 FLOW OF STEAM JETS IN TURBINE THAT USES PRESSURE STAGING

Engineers have adapted the idea of alternating rows of fixed and rotating blade rings to obtain special advantages. In **pressure staging** (Fig. 4), the rings keep increasing in blade spacing and even in diameter from one fixed ring to the next, allowing for a gradual decrease in steam pressure until all the pressure is used up. In **reaction turbines,** even the blade rings of the rotor are shaped to transform pressure into speed—so that the steam leaves them at a greater speed than it had before, giving them a recoil action, like a ROCKET.

PETROLEUM

Petroleum has been found under the earth's crust in a number of places—Texas, Rumania, Arabia, North Africa, and (in 1968) Alaska. It is slightly different wherever it occurs, showing different proportions of sulfur compounds and gasolinelike compounds. From the layers of rock found around it, geologists have decided that most of it comes from deposits of dead sea plants laid down in shallow water (Fig. 1)—most of them within the last 200 million years.

In former centuries, the tar of natural seepages had sometimes been used to make ships watertight, and from about the time of the Civil War, petroleum had been a source of kerosene for oil lamps. This was before the days of automobiles and airplanes. Today 1 billion tons of it are used every year; there is now much less petroleum left in the earth's crust than there was, say, in 1900. It is not certain how much there is left today—perhaps 50 billion tons.

Petroleum is what chemical engineers call a *raw material.* It is not used as it comes from the **wells** (Fig. 2), but is broken down into a great many "fractions"—among them, gasoline. The system, which is called distillation, works like this:

After the petroleum has been brought to the surface, it is shipped in tankers or pumped through a pipeline to a *refinery.* Here it is heated until it vaporizes, and the vapor is then released at the foot of a tall *fractionating tower,* where its heavy parts condense and sink to the bottom in the form of a black tar, *petroleum asphalt,* used by roofers and road builders. The lighter vapors rise, weaving their way among steel trays in which the heating fuels (for buildings) and Diesel oil (for trucks) condense as liquids. The lighter fractions keep on rising into higher and hotter regions of the tower, where kerosene, then gasoline, condense as liquids in the trays. Some very light gases go right to the top and are also collected.

The most valuable fraction is the *gasoline.* Gasoline is a mixture of a number of liquids, of which the three most useful are made up of molecules that contain only carbon and hydrogen. But the heavier oils can *also* be made into gasoline by "cracking" their large molecules into smaller ones. To do this, they are heated under pressure in the presence of a compound called a *catalyst.* The catalyst itself does not get used up but allows the chemical changes to take place.

The main result of cracking is an extra supply of gasoline beyond what was in the original petroleum. But cracking also yields some very light gases (themselves also carbon-hydrogen compounds) whose molecules are *too small.* But industrial chemists have found ways of building these up into larger groups.

Fig. 1 THE BEGINNINGS OF AN OIL FIELD

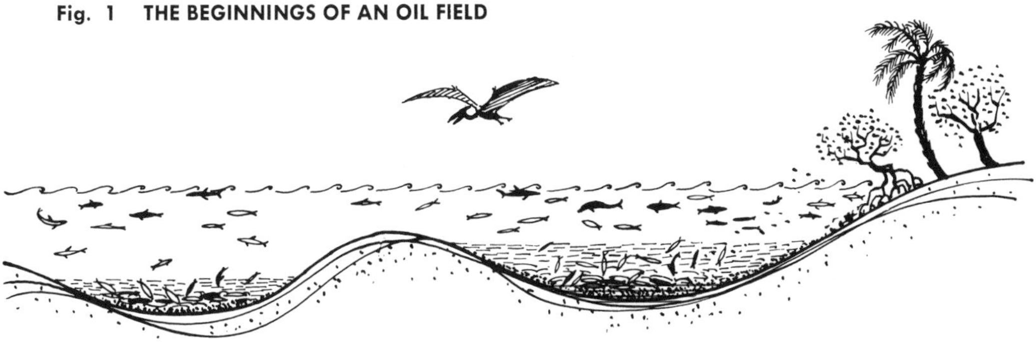

Fig. 2 WAYS IN WHICH PETROLEUM CAN LIE UNDER THE EARTH'S SURFACE

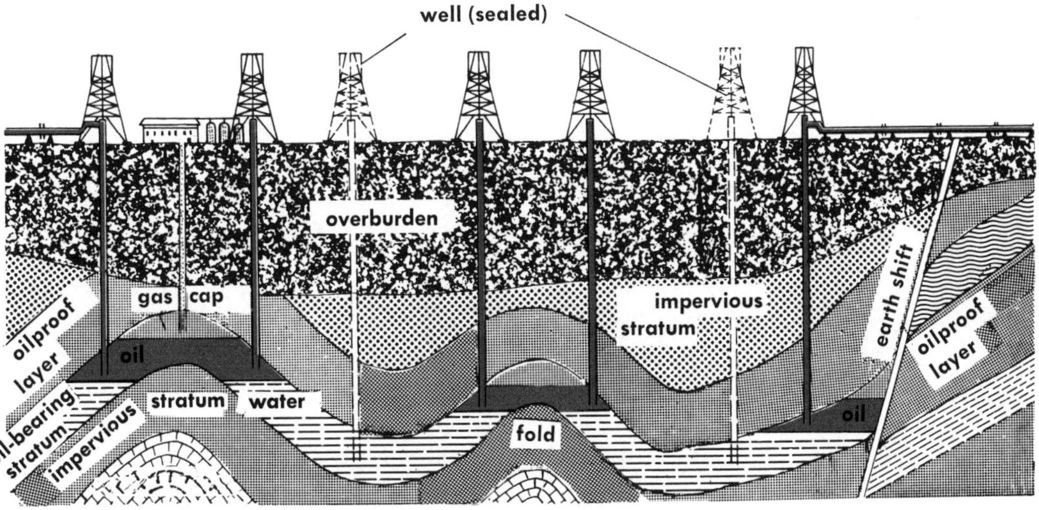

Our demand for gasoline in this country is enormous: in 1967 alone, American passenger cars burned 55 billion gallons of it. Even kerosene has made a comeback, as a fuel for jet airplanes: when a Boeing 747 flies from New York to London, it carries 35,000 gallons of kerosene fuel at take-off. But petroleum is not merely a source of fuels. Through chemical tinkering, its various "fractions" have also yielded drugs, insecticides, synthetic RUBBER, synthetic fibers (for cloth), PLASTICS and DETERGENTS.

NATURAL GAS AND COAL GAS

The natural gas that supplies the kitchen gas range and burns with the familiar blue flame may not seem of great importance, but it is: after coal and petroleum, it is the world's most important source of power. In fact, in the United States it's the *leading* source, accounting for 36% of all energy used.

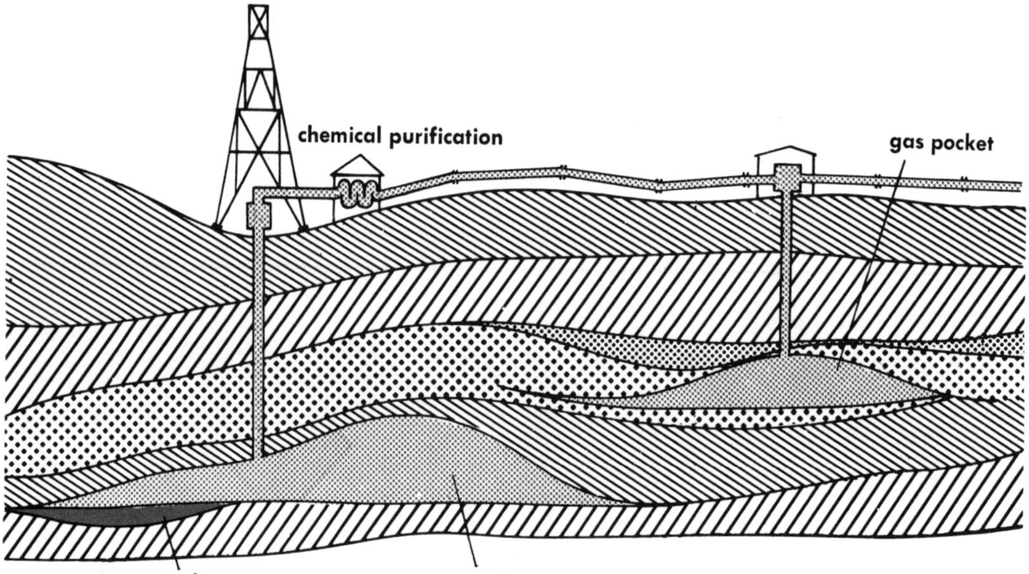

THE RELEASE OF NATURAL GAS FROM THE EARTH'S CRUST

Natural gas is found in the *gas cap* above the petroleum in oil wells (as in Fig. 2, page 69), as well as in underground pockets that have little or no petroleum (opposite). In parts of the world, like Pennsylvania, where there are nearby cities to benefit, oil wells are a rich source of top-quality gas for kitchens and gas furnaces, though around oil wells in the Middle East, millions of cubic feet of it have been wasted every year—it is often burned away day and night, for lack of local use.

The most valuable kinds of natural gas are made up almost entirely of *methane* (or "marsh gas") and one or two other related compounds of carbon and hydrogen that produce a great deal of heat when burned. But natural gas varies from one well to the next, often reaching the surface carrying small amounts of other gases, such as hydrogen sulfide, carbon dioxide and nitrogen.

In Los Angeles, which has a severe air-pollution problem, it has been found worth while to bring in natural gas by pipeline because its use as fuel and kitchen gas does not befoul the air. But most cities not within reach of local natural gas and not served by continent-crossing pipelines usually end up using other gases.

One of these is **coal gas,** which is a mixture of different gases that varies from city to city. For instance, it might contain 50% hydrogen (a dandy rocket fuel, but dangerous), 20% to 30% methane, 7% to 17% carbon monoxide (poisonous to man and beast—it can be removed), 3% carbon dioxide (safe enough, but useless), 8% nitrogen (wholly safe, also useless) and 2% random gases, related to methane, that burn nicely. If the mixture doesn't have a properly "gassy" smell, extra compounds are added by the gas company to allow one to detect leaks quickly.

Coal gas can be made by heating water away from air, as well as by slightly more devious processing, also starting from coal. In some parts of the world it is mixed with **water gas,** which contains an even more dangerous proportion of carbon monoxide. (Water gas is also produced from coal, but by blowing steam through it.) Although coal gas is dangerous, other ways of cooking—coal stoves, electric ranges—also have their dangers. Coal gas continues to be used because, once the pipes have been laid under the streets, it's a cheap and convenient source of heat.

Gas is considered a source of energy because it can be burned to perform work—such as raising the temperature of water. If one has 3 quarts of water sitting on a stove in a kettle at room temperature, it will take about 2 cubic feet of coal gas (at the usual range pressure) to bring the water to a boil. (One half that amount of natural gas would accomplish the same result.)

As the world's energy needs increase, less and less natural gas will be allowed to go to waste. For instance, the countries around the Persian Gulf (such as Saudi Arabia) still have low energy needs; but Japan uses a great deal of fuel gas. What the Japanese are now doing is to ship the natural gas from the Persian Gulf as a *liquid*—they do this by putting it under pressure and keeping its temperature very low in refrigerated tanks.

MATCHES

More than 500 billion matches are made each year in the United States—each one a little power pack of chemical energy (enough to light a fire), stored safely until it is needed. A match, today, is usually a little splint of wood—or a narrow strip of cardboard, as in book matches—with a double ability: it can hold back its chemical power for years, then light up immediately when struck. This is the result of carefully balanced burning and nonburning properties that have been built into it.

The wood is from a log of softwood—pine or aspen—that has first been peeled into long shavings, called *veneers,* about a tenth of an inch thick. These ribbons are cut up into splints—the future matchsticks—which are soaked in a bath of ammonium phosphate. This is a kind of fireproofing that will prevent the wood from glowing after the match has been put out.

The splints are now packed into the small holes of trays fitted to a conveyor belt that carries them upside down for part of their journey, giving their heads a soaking in paraffin that will someday help them catch fire. They are then dipped in tanks containing the souplike concoction that will give them their visible "head."

This composition bastes their head with four ingredients: (1) the fuel—sulfur, in the form of a sulfide, (2) an oxygen releaser like potassium chlorate or potassium dichromate that will help the fuel burn, (3) an abrasive, like powdered glass, that will help the head scrape against the side of the box when it is struck and (4) a binder —dextrin (made from starch) and glue—to cement the whole head together. A color is usually mixed in—it looks cheerful and it helps the user tell one end from the other. The matches circulate on the conveyor belt for about an hour, until they are dry. (At one point during the ride their heads are sprayed with a coating that will prevent them from falling apart in damp weather.) They are then pushed out of the little holes in the trays and packed into boxes.

As a safety measure, most matches are made so they cannot be struck except on the side of the box, where a striking patch has been painted with a variety of phosphorus. Strike-anywhere matches have very little phosphorus in the main "bulb" of the head, but are given a second dipping in which the phosphorus, along with the ground glass, is concentrated in the tip of the head only. Packed in a box, they are reasonably safe—bulbs touch, the tips don't.

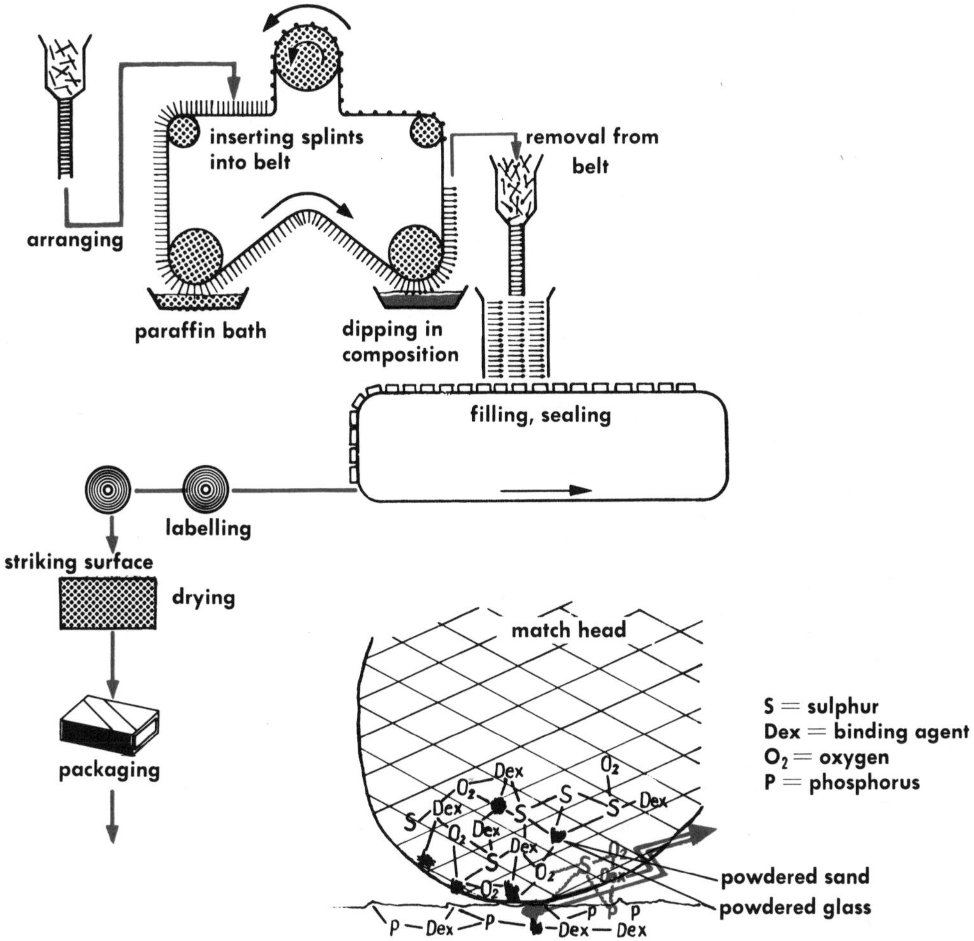

Book matches are made in long "combs" of 60 or 100 matches. After the heads have dried, the combs are usually stacked two or three deep, then sliced to produce combs only ten matches wide. These are always "safety matches"—they cannot be struck except on the phosphorus patch on the flap of the book.

When a match is struck, the friction produces enough heat to get the sulfur to react with oxygen being released by the potassium chlorate. Once this reaction is under way (and fumes of sulfur dioxide begin to fill the air), more heat is released, until the whole match head catches fire.

EXPLOSIVES

Many chemical reactions produce gases that take up more space than the original material. Sometimes they also produce heat, making the gases expand even more. These sudden increases in volume can take place just slowly enough to push the pistons of an automobile engine (see page 88). If they happen faster than that, they can push a bullet out of a rifle. If they are faster than *that,* all they can do is shatter everything around them. But even this can be useful—for instance, in cutting a tunnel through rock.

Gunpowder explodes just slowly enough not to shatter. It is made up of little grains that contain saltpeter, charcoal, and sulfur (Fig. 1). The saltpeter (potassium nitrate—used by meat packers to give canned ham a nice red color) is a good oxygen releaser; in gunpowder its job is to give oxygen to sulfur and to the charcoal. When the gunpowder is fired (simple jarring won't set it off), hot gases that take up 4,000 times as much space as the original gunpowder push the bullet out of the rifle. Because gunpowder explodes just slowly enough to propel a bullet, it is called a *propellant.*

Gunpowder is no longer used in rifles today—partly because it is smoky and dirty, partly because newer propellants, such as **cordite,** move the bullet a bit faster, so that gravity has less time to act on it and drag it off target.

Explosives used in blasting are **high explosives** that detonate with a sudden release of gases. One of these is **blasting gelatin**—made of guncotton (an explosive) that has soaked up nitroglycerin (another explosive). When a single pound of it explodes, it produces a temperature of 8500° Fahrenheit, in which the gases try to expand to about 9 cubic feet. Trapped in a rock formation, they develop a pressure of about 190,000 pounds per square inch.

In coal mines, explosives can save the miners a great deal of work. But some mines contain *firedamp*—gases consisting mostly of methane (page 71). What used to happen is that the flame of the blast would set off an explosion in the firedamp, killing the miners. Since early in this century this has been avoided by adding about 40% common salt to the explosives. The salt absorbs the heat of the explosion before the exploding gases reach the firedamp.

The man who invented blasting gelatin was Alfred Nobel, the Swedish industrial chemist remembered today for the Nobel Prizes, which he founded. It was Nobel also who invented **dynamite,** as well as the principle—*detonation*—by which high explosives are set off. That is, propellants like gunpowder have to be set off by the flame

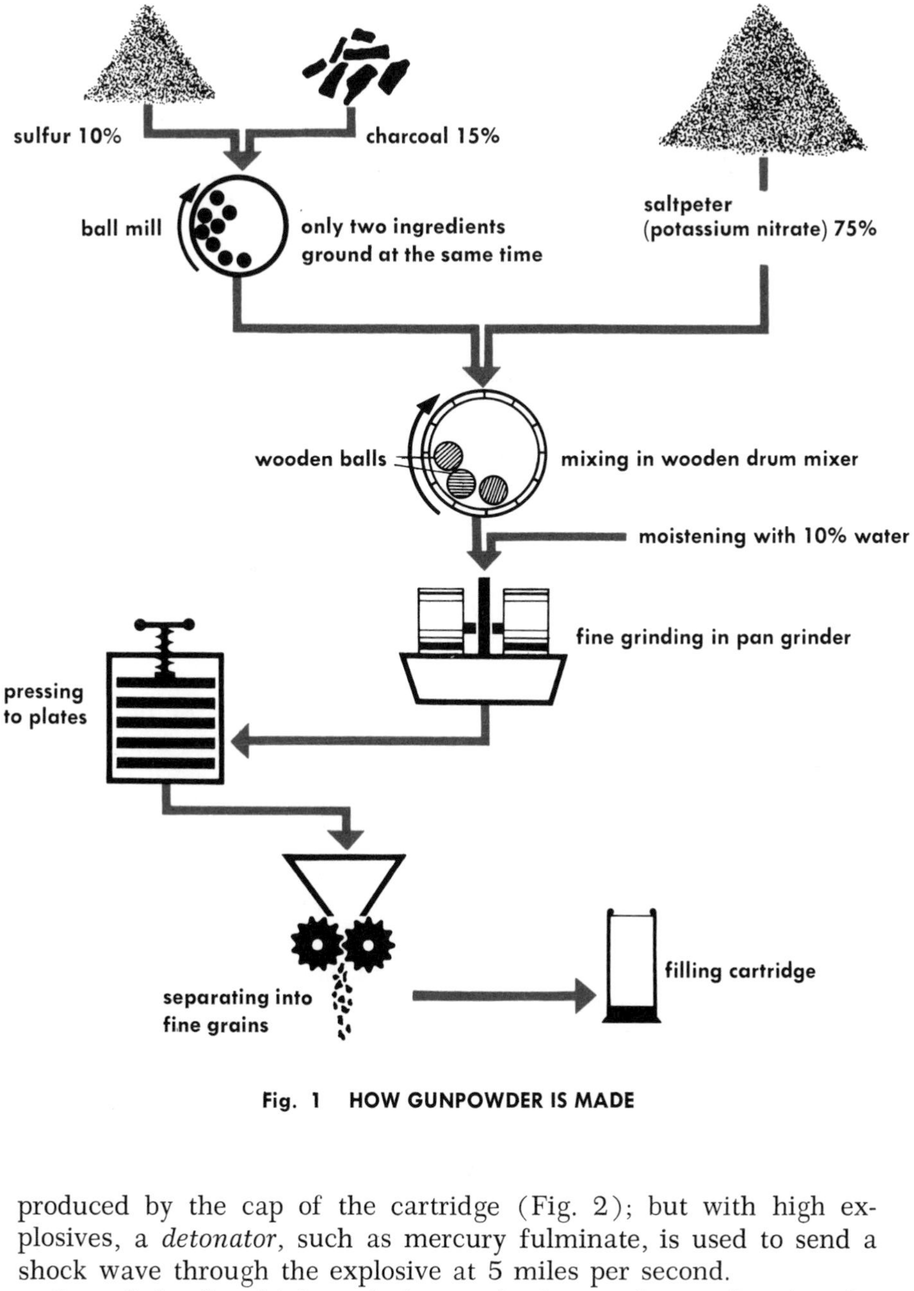

Fig. 1 HOW GUNPOWDER IS MADE

produced by the cap of the cartridge (Fig. 2); but with high explosives, a *detonator*, such as mercury fulminate, is used to send a shock wave through the explosive at 5 miles per second.

One of the first high explosives to be invented was **nitroglycerin,** a heavy colorless liquid that explodes violently when slightly jarred,

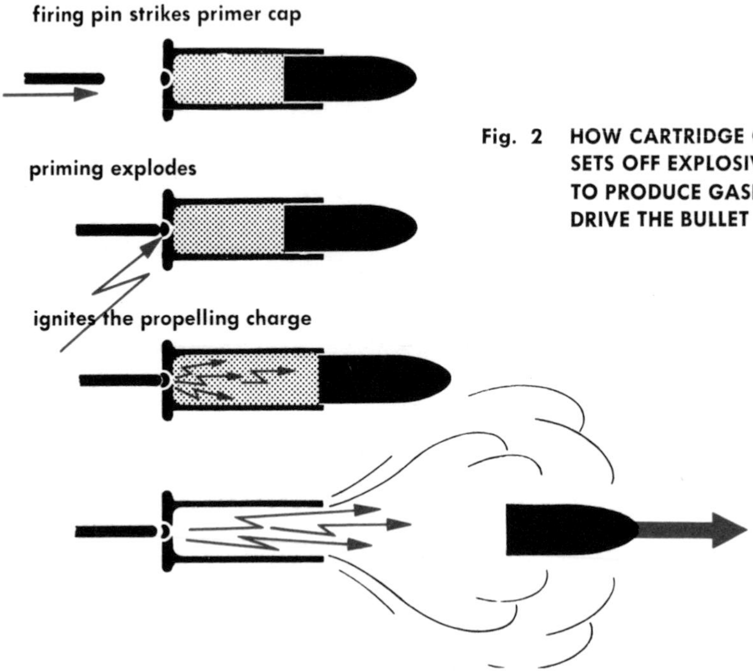

Fig. 2 HOW CARTRIDGE CAP SETS OFF EXPLOSIVE CHARGE TO PRODUCE GASES THAT DRIVE THE BULLET

transforming itself into hot gases that take up 10,000 times its own volume. It is made by treating glycerin with nitric acid (with sulfuric acid at hand to remove the unwanted water). It caused many accidental deaths until Nobel invented dynamite, in which the nitroglycerin is mixed with a fine, absorbent variety of earth. Other absorbents have been used since.

Another well-known high explosive is **TNT**—trinitrotoluene. It is made by letting nitric acid go to work on toluene, a compound obtained from coal tar. When an explosion starts in TNT, it goes 17 times as fast as in gunpowder.

BATTERIES

To get a flashlight to work, we have to pass a current of electrons through the very thin wire in the glass bulb. One way of getting the electrons moving is to connect the bulb's terminals (it has two—collar and bottom) to a strip of copper and a strip of zinc, then dip the two strips in a weak solution of sulfuric acid in water (Fig. 1).

The water is important—it allows the atom groupings in the sulfuric acid to break up into smaller packages that have too many or too few electrons. When the electric circuit is closed (by a switch), a chemical reaction takes place in which the copper releases electrons into the solution and the zinc picks them up. Outside the tank, the electrons keep flowing—from the zinc through the light bulb (which

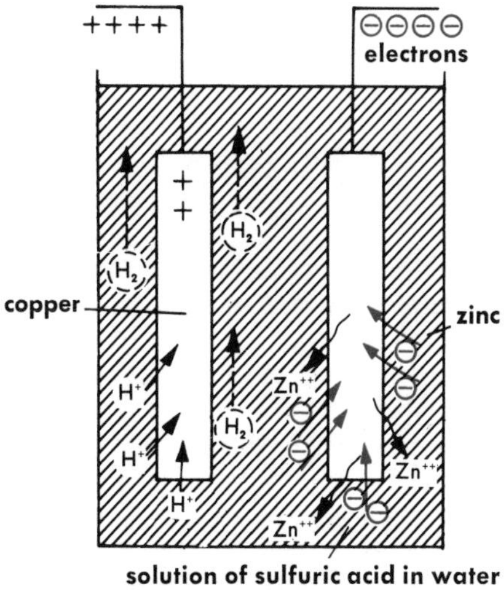

Fig. 1 A CHEMICAL WAY OF OBTAINING ELECTRICAL ENERGY

may or may not light up) and back to the copper. (If the bulb does not light up with a single tank, we connect two or three tanks end to end.)

After the current has been flowing for a while, chemical by-products develop that clog up the plates and make the reaction less and less efficient. How this problem is met will be seen in the two batteries in greatest use today, the **dry cell** and the **automobile battery.**

The dry cell is a sealed zinc can in which the two electric terminals are the can itself and a stick of carbon in the middle of it; the space between them is filled with a paste of ammonium chloride (which is not totally dry but has moisture in it). When the electric circuit is closed, chemical reactions allow the zinc to pick up free electrons and pass them into the outside circuit. But the carbon, meanwhile, becomes surrounded by a cloud of hydrogen bubbles that make it less and less efficient; to prevent this, it is surrounded by a sheath of manganese dioxide (Fig. 2). The hydrogen reacts with the manganese

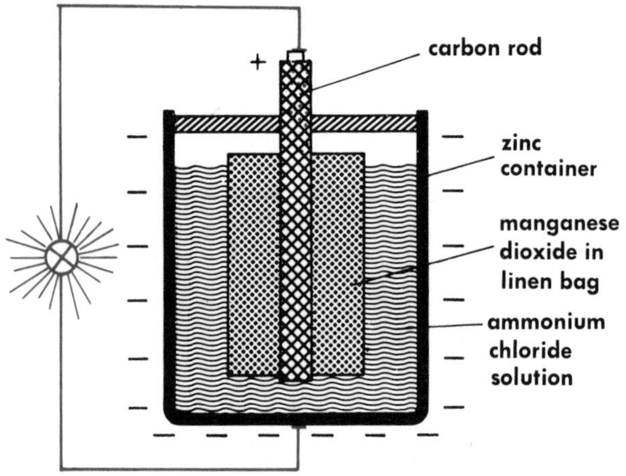

Fig. 2 INSIDE A FLASHLIGHT BATTERY, OR "DRY CELL"

dioxide and produces water, which has no place to go. After a while, it is an excellent idea to throw out the old cell and buy a new one.

Automobile batteries don't have to be thrown out when they run down—they are rechargeable. Basic units of a battery are a plate of brown lead dioxide soaking between two plates of gray lead in a bath of dilute sulfuric acid (Fig. 3). When the battery is connected into an electric circuit (for instance, to light up the speedometer on the dashboard), electrons accumulate at the gray lead terminal, go through the panel lights, and return to the lead dioxide terminal. Both terminals develop a coating of lead sulfate; then they are hardly different anymore and the battery is "dead."

But it can be recharged. Direct (one-way) current from the submarine's ELECTRIC GENERATORS can now send electrons into the former lead terminal; the surface coating is broken up, the old lead reappears, and the battery is ready to give current again.

The individual cells of lead batteries offer about 2 volts; in automobiles they are usually packed in groups (Fig. 4) in such a way that their voltages add up. What happens when a lead battery is charged is that it is *given* electrical energy, which it stores in the form of a high-energy chemical situation. When the battery is used to give ELECTRIC CURRENT, this situation settles down little by little into a state of low chemical energy. The battery is then recharged—given new energy from the outside. Since it has hardly ever produced energy of its own, it is called a *secondary cell.* (The little dry cell used in a portable radio is a *primary cell.*)

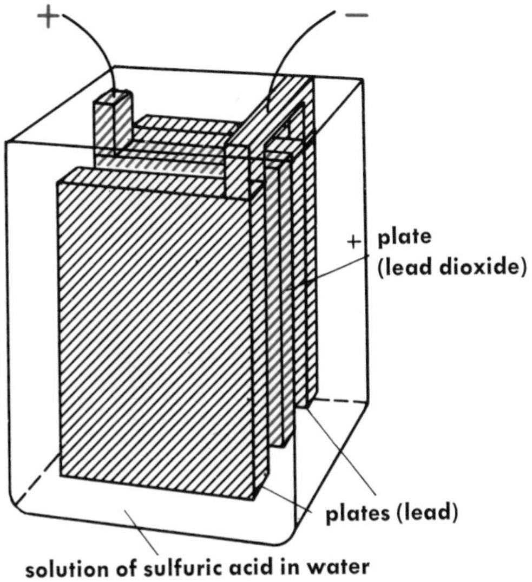

Fig. 3 LEAD "SANDWICH" OF AUTOMOBILE BATTERY

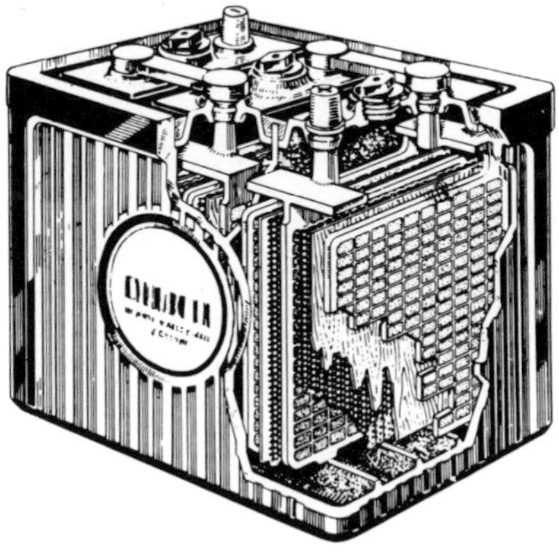

Fig. 4 "WET CELLS" GROUPED IN AUTOMOBILE BATTERY

RADIOACTIVITY

Natural radioactivity is a peculiar kind of energy produced when atoms—the smallest unit of an element having the properties of that particular element—disintegrate. This natural radioactivity is extremely powerful, and it can't be turned off. A little lead tube containing radium, for instance, is always about 3° Fahrenheit warmer than its surroundings—it is as if, day after day, it were quietly burning. But in fact what is going on within it releases about a million times as much energy as one could get by burning the same amount of material.

Within every small quantity of radium, there are always a few atoms that are *disintegrating,* or falling apart. For instance, in any sample of 1 million atoms of radium, 427 will "decay" before the year is out. Since atoms are very small (a single gram would contain 2,660,000,000,000,000,000,000 atoms—and a gram weighs less than a dime), every sample of radium is giving off heat from the breakup of its atoms every moment.

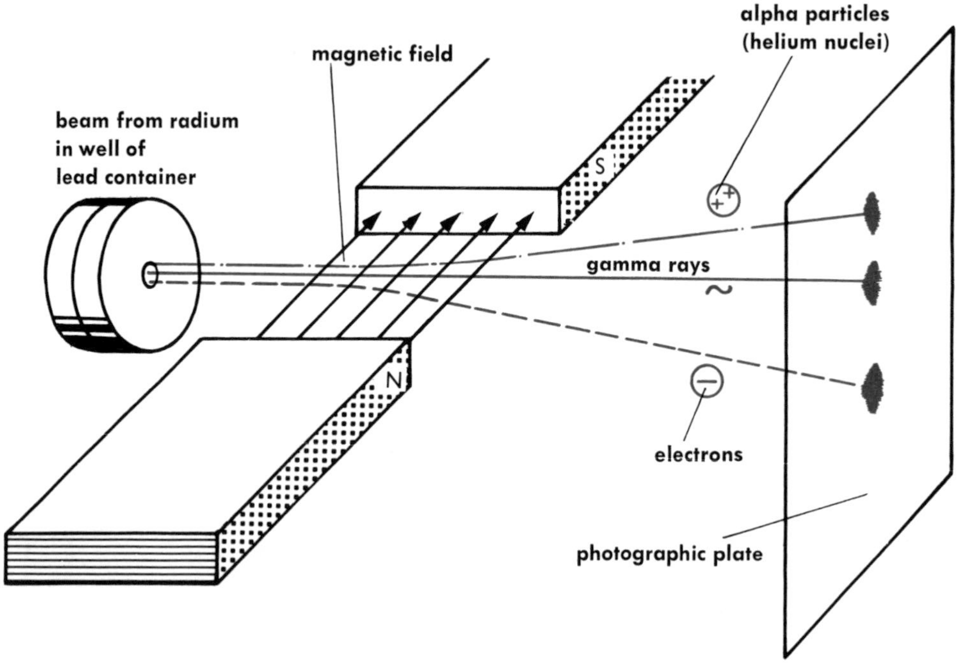

Fig. 1 HOW RAYS FROM RADIUM CAN BE SORTED OUT BY PASSING THEM BETWEEN POLES OF A MAGNET

As they break up, the atoms give off not only heat but three kinds of radiation (Fig. 1). These are little bits of matter called **alpha particles,** which are no different from the core, or *nucleus,* of a helium atom; a shower of fast-moving **electrons;** and **gamma rays,** a variety of X RAY that is so penetrating that it can go right through several inches of lead.

The atoms that give off these particles and gamma rays don't remain the same afterward—when a radium atom shoots out an alpha particle, the particle catches two electrons on the fly and becomes an atom of helium gas; what is left of the original radium atom is then no longer radium but a radioactive gas called *radon.* These

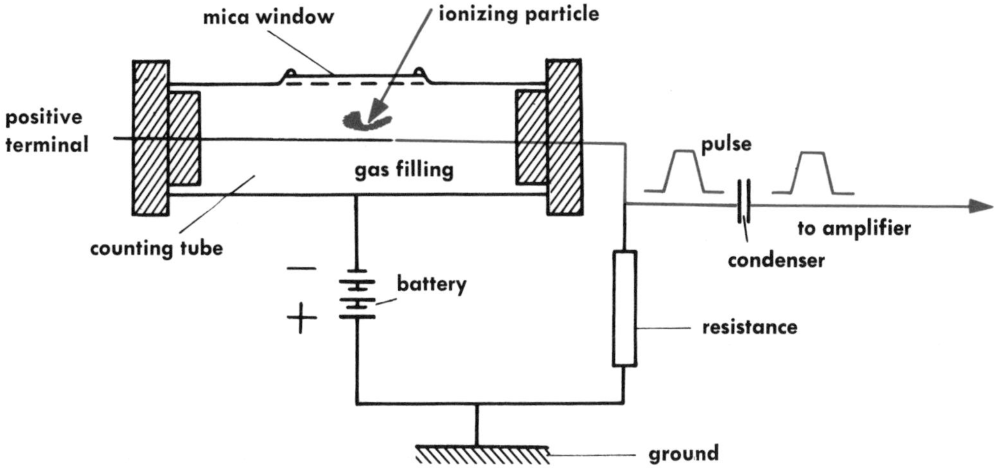

Fig. 2 HOW IONIZING PARTICLE TRIGGERS ELECTRIC DISCHARGE IN GEIGER COUNTER

changes happen deep in the atom's core—its nucleus. The nucleus is very small—it is less than one ten-thousandth as wide as the atom.

Uranium and thorium are among the other elements that are naturally radioactive; when they are part of minerals in a rock, the rock as a whole is slightly radioactive. To check whether it is, one can test it with a **Geiger counter** (Fig. 2).

A Geiger counter takes advantage of the fact that the radiations from radioactive materials *ionize* the atoms they knock into—that is, they disturb their outer rings of electrons, suddenly making them good conductors of electricity. The atoms available in a Geiger counter belong to gases at low pressure that fill the space between two electric terminals. Normally, an ELECTRIC CURRENT is prevented from flowing—the direct-current voltage is set just a little bit too low. But as soon as an ionizing particle crosses the gases in the tube, it produces a shower of electrical discharges that trigger current flow through the whole circuit. These happenings can be fed to an electronic amplifier, as in Fig. 2, so that they register on a meter. Or a LOUDSPEAKER can be connected into the circuit—the discharges then show up as a crackling sound. Prospectors carry Geiger counters with them as they search for uranium rocks.

Radioactivity is like nothing else we know. There is nothing we can do to stop it or to make it go faster. If we have eight thousandths of a gram (8 milligrams) of radium in a lead box, in another 1,590 years there will be only 4 milligrams left; and 1,590 years after that there will be only 2 milligrams. Another way of saying this is that radium has a *half-life* of 1,590 years—*any* sample of radium, of *any* size, will be reduced by half in 1,590 years. The half-life of uranium is 4.7 billion years.

One thing that can be done, however, is to convert innocent, stable chemical elements into **artificially radioactive elements.** This is done by bombarding their atoms with heavy particles of the kind that make up an atomic nucleus. Such artificially radioactive substances occur in the fallout from atomic bombs and in the waste products of nuclear reactors.

Though we cannot stop natural radioactivity, we can control the *chain reactions* that occur when naturally radioactive material is gathered together or when radioactive material is artifically produced. And thus we are enabled to utilize this great source of energy. The machine that makes this possible is called a NUCLEAR REACTOR.

NUCLEAR REACTOR

Within the cores, or *nuclei*, of atoms is the greatest concentration of power known. Unfortunately, there is no *direct* way of harnessing this power to put it to work for us—for instance, in providing a city with electric power. So although the source of power—RADIOACTIVITY—is modern, the way in which it is put to work in a nuclear reactor is old-fashioned: it simply heats water to make steam; the steam drives STEAM TURBINES and the turbines drive ELECTRIC GENERATORS.

The nuclear reactor itself is a large structure in which a variety of uranium, uranium 235, is bombarded with particles called *neutrons,* which come from its atoms or from the atoms of other varieties of uranium that occur with it. The process is very delicate: only a certain proportion of the flying neutrons may hit the nuclei of the uranium 235; and their speed has to be controlled—as well as the temperature, pressure and radioactivity of everything in the building and everything coming out of it.

Every sample of natural uranium is made up of three varieties of uranium, whose atoms are built differently in their core, or nucleus.

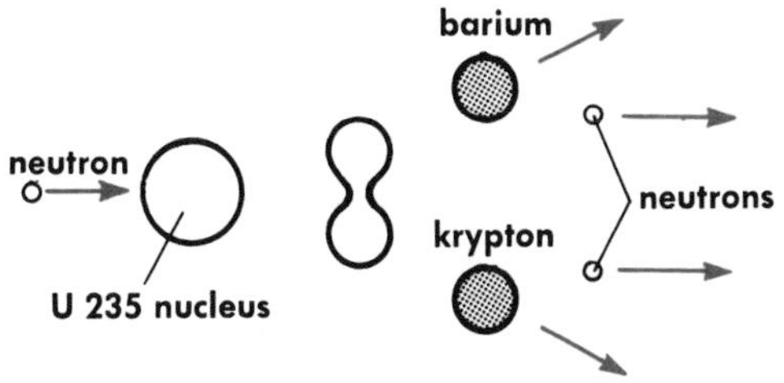

Fig. 1 WHAT HAPPENS WHEN THE NUCLEUS OF AN ATOM OF URANIUM 235 IS SPLIT BY A NEUTRON

In one of these, which has 235 particles in its nucleus and is called uranium 235, the atoms have a peculiar way of breaking up when hit by a slow neutron (Fig. 1). They divide (usually into atoms of barium and krypton) and shoot out *extra* neutrons. If these fresh neutrons are allowed to hit the nuclei of other atoms, they can split them and keep the process going. This is called a **chain reaction.**

In atomic bombs, the chain reaction is used to make an explosion. In nuclear reactors, where the rate at which neutrons are released is carefully controlled, it is used as a source of power.

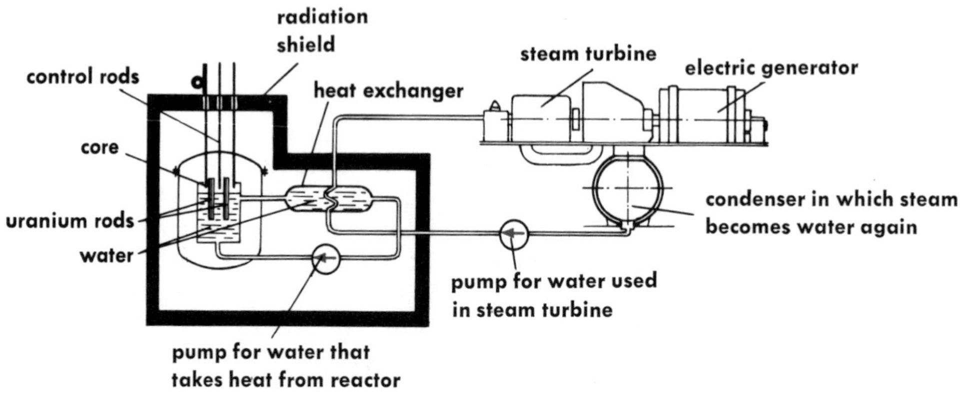

Fig. 2 NUCLEAR REACTOR WITH WATER AS MODERATOR

Nuclear reactors (of which there were 16 in the United States in 1970) can be used for several purposes: to breed plutonium, a radioactive metal that can be used as fuel in other reactors; to produce heat, which can be converted to electric power; or to produce a thick stream of neutrons, for use in making materials radioactive for the study of animals and plants.

The reactor in Fig. 2 uses rods of metallic uranium in its core (*left*) and water as the moderator that slows down its neutrons. (Only slow neutrons will split the nuclei of uranium 235—fast ones go right by.) A neutron released by a uranium rod will bounce off a number of nuclei of oxygen atoms in the water, losing speed before it enters another uranium rod. Some of these slow neutrons split

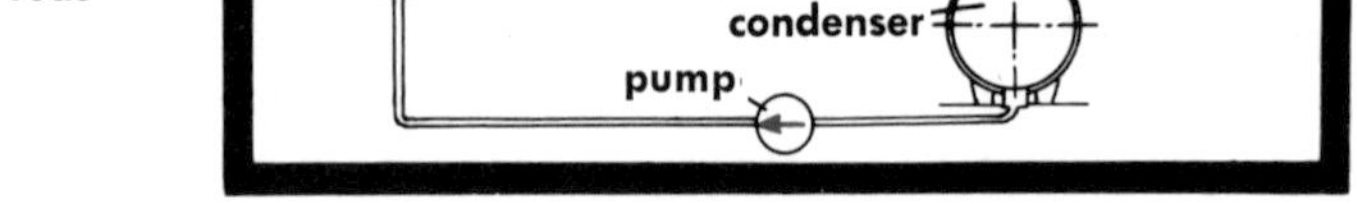

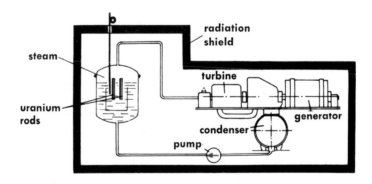

Fig. 3 BOILING-WATER REACTOR

atoms in their path, releasing energy in the form of heat. Water in the circuit on the left picks up the heat but becomes radioactive; it passes on the heat to the second water circuit (*right*) through a *heat exchanger* (page 138). Control rods, made of a material that soaks up the neutrons, can be pushed into the core. In this way, the engineer separates the rods of radioactive material from one another, which slows down or stops the chain reaction in which the energy of radioactivity is gathered together. The radioactive parts of the reactor are enclosed in a *shield*—an iron-lined concrete wall several feet thick.

It is possible to arrange things so that the water used as moderator is also the water that becomes steam for the turbines. This makes a much smaller reactor, called a **boiling-water reactor** (Fig. 3). It cannot use natural uranium as fuel, but requires a more expensive enriched uranium in which the proportion of uranium 235 has been boosted from the usual 1 part in 140 to 7 parts in 140.

III Internal Combustion Engines

FOUR-STROKE GASOLINE ENGINE

More than 200 million cars, trucks, and buses carry people and freight throughout the world, 96 million of them in the United States. American trucks and buses use DIESEL ENGINES, passenger cars use the four-stroke gasoline engine, and motorcycles use the TWO-STROKE GASOLINE ENGINE. All are varieties of the **internal-combustion engine.**

In STEAM ENGINES (page 60), coal is burned to produce heat, the heat turns water into steam, and the pressure of the steam drives the piston. In internal-combustion engines, the heat is produced *right inside* the cylinder by burning droplets of gasoline in air; the resulting hot gases expand directly against the piston.

In the four-stroke gasoline engine, four things happen over and over as the piston moves up and down. Following the numbers in Fig. 1, they are:

1. *Piston* moves down, drawing mixture of vaporized gasoline and air into cylinder through *inlet valve,* which is open;
2. No valves now open; as the piston moves up, it *compresses* the fuel mixture;
3. Gases in cylinder ignited by spark; gases burn, producing large quantities of carbon dioxide and water vapor, pushing piston down; piston transmits *power* to *crankshaft;*
4. Piston moves up, pushing *exhaust* through open *exhaust valve.*

Since only stroke 3 is a power stroke, the motion of an engine running on simply one cylinder would be jerky. So a flywheel is mounted on the crankshaft, storing some of the energy and helping the piston move up and down during the three strokes that are not power strokes. Another thing that makes for smoothness is that the engine has a number of cylinders arranged so that each produces its power stroke at a different time—when the crankshaft has turned to a different angle. In Fig. 2 this is illustrated for an **in-line engine,** in which the cylinders are all in one line. (The ignition occurs at a different time for each cylinder.)

Smoothness is not the only reason for having many cylinders. A gasoline engine cannot have simply one big cylinder—it would get too hot and the fuel mixture would fire too early. By dividing the volume of one large cylinder into six or eight small cylinders, a great deal more cooling surface is obtained. Of course, this also adds to the

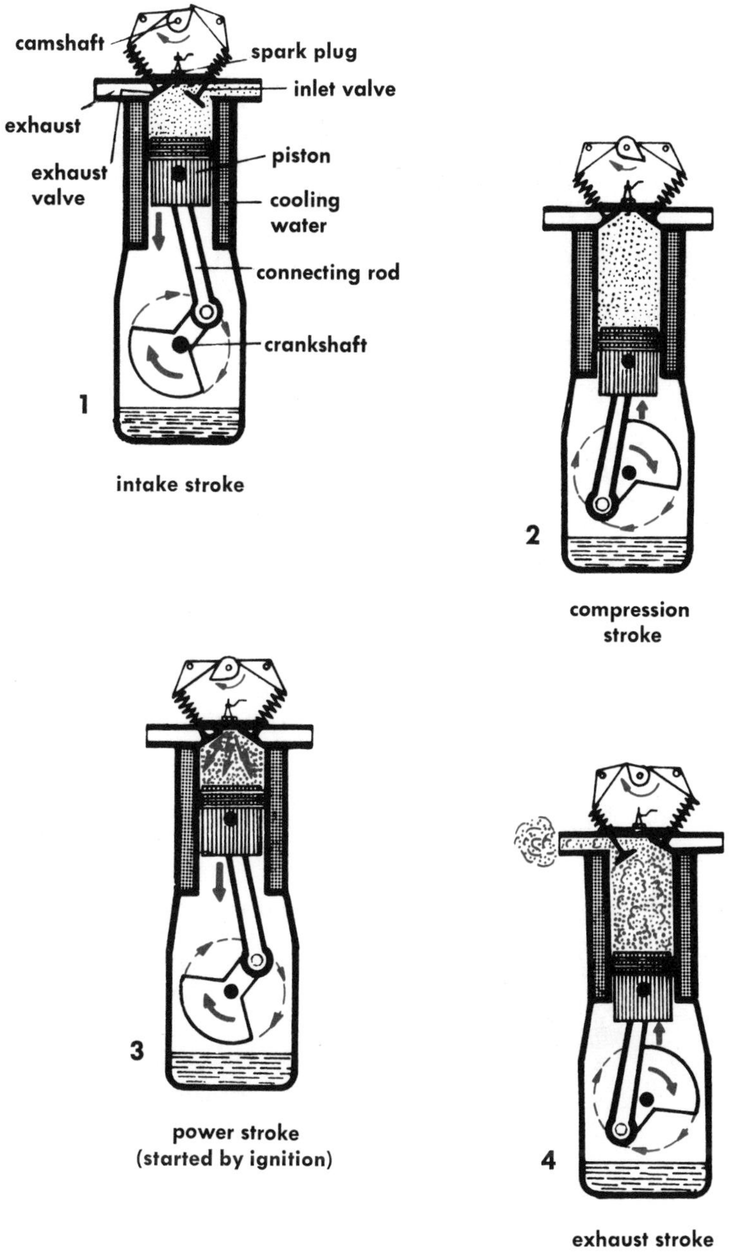

Fig. 1 WHAT HAPPENS IN EACH OF THE FOUR STROKES

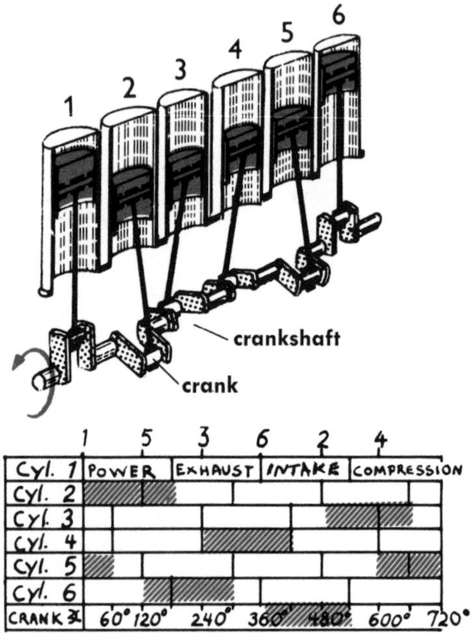

Fig. 2 HOW SIX CYLINDERS TAKE TURNS IN MOVING THE CRANKSHAFT OF AN IN-LINE ENGINE

Fig. 3 THE PISTONS OF A RADIAL ENGINE TRANSMIT THEIR POWER TO A SINGLE ROTATING CRANK

engine's weight. In early airplanes, where every pound counted, it was discovered that much weight could be saved by arranging the cylinders **radially**—like the spokes of a wheel—as in Fig. 3. The rods all connect to a single crank.

By itself, a cylinder is not an engine and an engine is not an automobile. Liquid gasoline, produced from PETROLEUM, will not ignite in the cylinder unless it has first been changed into vapor—or at least very small droplets—in the CARBURETOR. Making the fuel in each cylinder ignite at the right time is the job of the electrical IGNITION system. And the way the engine's power is passed on to the wheels is taken up in the following pages under CLUTCH, GEAR TRANSMISSION, AUTOMATIC TRANSMISSIONS and DIFFERENTIAL, along with BRAKES and the SPEEDOMETER.

TWO-STROKE GASOLINE ENGINE— MOTORCYCLES

Model airplanes, lawnmowers, motorcycles, skimobiles and boats with outboard motors all run on engines noisy enough to be heard a mile away. These are gasoline engines, but with only two strokes to each cycle instead of four. They come in several varieties. The simplest (Fig. 1) has a special way of making use of the *crankcase,* the empty space in which the crankshaft moves. It works like this:

In the **first stroke,** an electric spark ignites a mixture of gasoline

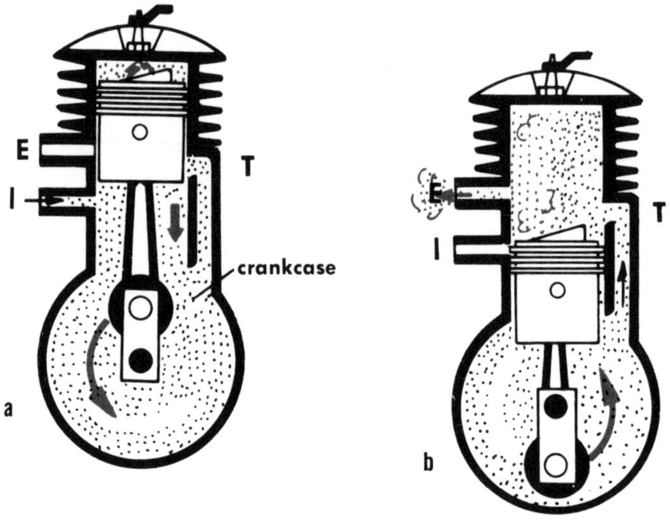

Fig. 1 TWO-STROKE GASOLINE ENGINE IN WHICH FUEL IS TRANSFERRED FROM CRANKCASE

droplets and air. The fuel catches fire, producing gases and water vapor that kick down the piston (Fig. 1a). As the piston moves down, its top clears an opening called the *exhaust port,* E, allowing the gases to escape. The piston keeps on moving down, squeezing the new gasoline-and-air mixture in the crankcase. When the piston is low enough to open the *transfer port,* T, the fuel mixture is released from the crankcase and fills the cylinder above it (Fig. 1b).

In the **second stroke,** the piston moves up, compressing the fuel mixture above it in the cylinder. As it moves up, it clears the *intake* *port*, I, allowing fresh gasoline and air to enter the crankcase. Just before it reaches the top, a spark is set off in the cylinder, and everything begins again.

In two-stroke engines that use the crankcase as a waiting room and pump to bring the fuel mixture up to the cylinder, oil that is used to lubricate the crankshaft tends to be carried into the cylinder, where it helps nobody. A sure sign of its wanderings is a blue color in the exhaust fumes.

To avoid this waste of oil, some two-stroke engines use a fan, as in Fig. 2, to push the fuel mixture into the cylinder. The crankcase stays free of fuel, and the crankshaft can be lubricated with oil that will stay where it's needed.

Two-stroke engines are simple and light, and they provide one power stroke out of every two strokes—instead of one out of every four as in four-stroke engines. As a result, they offer a great deal of power per pound of engine weight. But apart from filling the neighborhood with fumes and noise, they are expensive to run for any length of time—every time spent gases are pushed out, some of the incoming fuel is swept out with them.

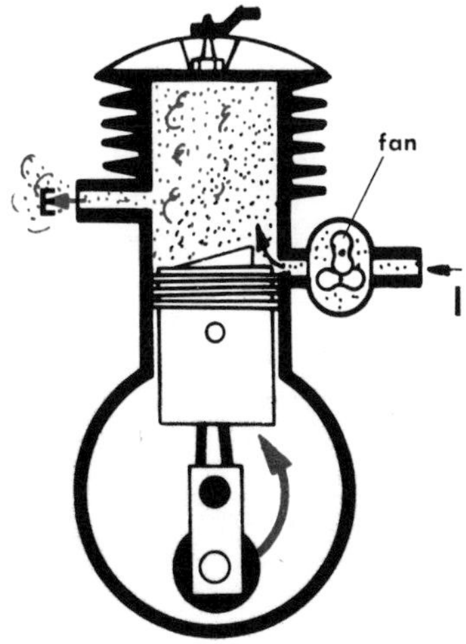

Fig. 2 TWO-STROKE GASOLINE ENGINE IN WHICH FUEL IS PUMPED IN BY A FAN

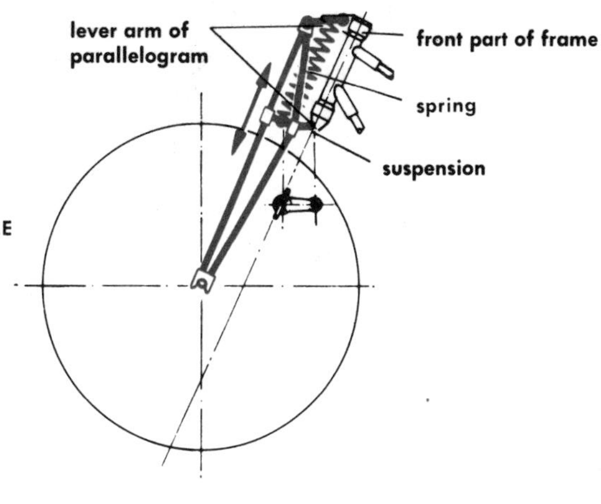

Fig. 3 PARALLELOGRAM SUSPENSION FOR FRONT WHEEL OF MOTORCYCLE

One important use of the two-stroke engine is on *motorcycles*, in which engine power is added to what looks at first sight like a bicycle. But because of their speed, motorcycles would give a very jolty ride unless special shock-absorbing ways of supporting their weight had been invented.

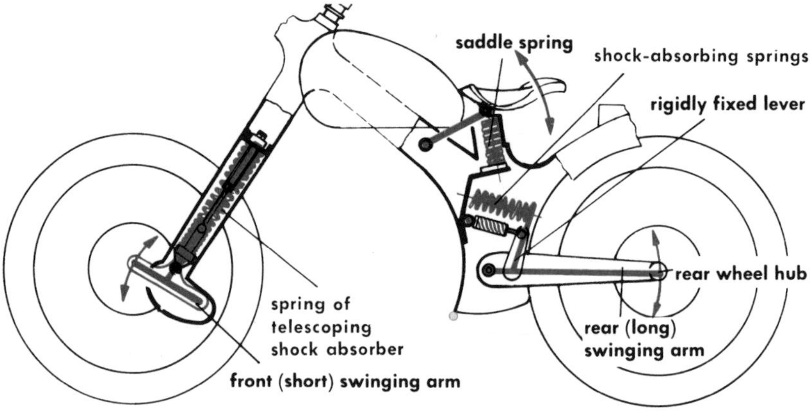

Fig. 4 SHOCK ABSORBERS AND SWINGING ARMS IN SUSPENSION ON BOTH WHEELS

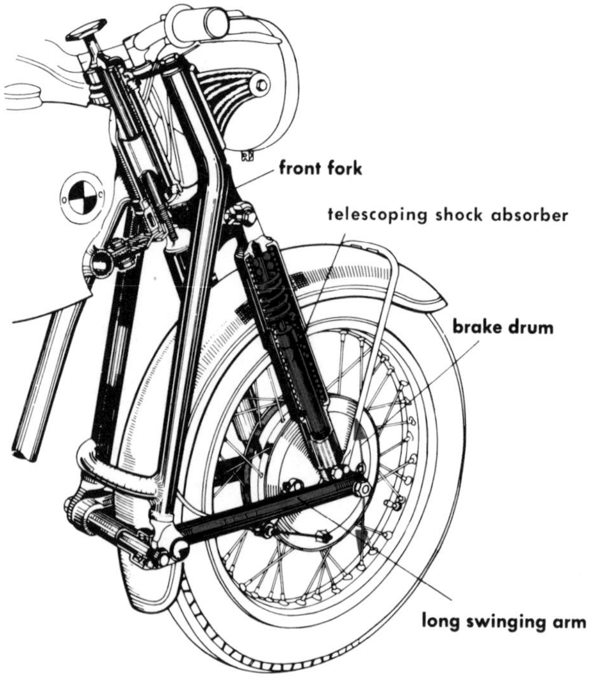

Fig. 5
SHOCK ABSORBER COMBINED WITH LONG SWINGING ARM FOR FRONT-WHEEL SUSPENSION

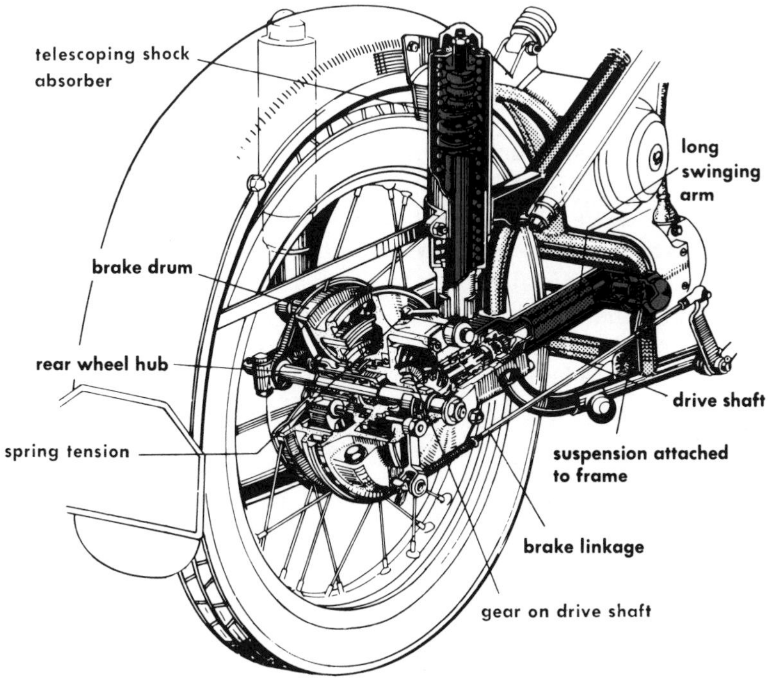

Fig. 6 REAR WHEEL OF MOTORCYCLE SHOWING MECHANISMS THAT PROVIDE DRIVE, BRAKING, AND SUSPENSION

The weight of the rider and engine rests on a frame that joins the axles only indirectly. In the **parallelogram suspension,** Fig. 3, the frame is hung from a spring that absorbs the oscillations of the entire front wheel and of the two-pronged fork that holds the axle. Other suspensions (Figs. 4 and 5) combine *telescoping shock absorbers* (containing springs and oil pots) and *swinging arms.*

Since the rear wheel is the motorcycle's only powered wheel, it carries the *drive shaft* and related mechanisms as well as a *brake drum* and a shock-absorbing suspension (Fig. 6).

ROTARY PISTON ENGINE

The rotary piston engine, also known as the Wankel engine, is another kind of internal combustion engine. It works on the same general principle as the four-stroke gasoline engine but is more efficient. The energy produced in a four-stroke or two-stroke engine drives the piston up and down. This up-and-down motion must then be converted by connecting rods into a round-and-round, or rotary, motion. In a rotary piston engine, the piston moves by rotating in circles. Since the rotary piston engine needs only two moving parts, the energy that would otherwise be lost in converting up-and-down motion into rotary motion is saved. In addition, because the rotary piston engine has only two moving parts (the two rotors), it makes almost no noise. The pounding of pistons moving up and down that we hear in four-stroke and two-stroke engines is eliminated. All we hear when a rotary piston engine is running is a quiet hum. This reduction in noise is an important ecological factor.

The rotary piston engine has a piston shaped like a triangle with convex (curved outward) sides. This piston rotates in a chamber shaped like an oval that has been slightly pinched in the middle (see Fig. 1). When the piston rotates, the seals mounted at its three corners

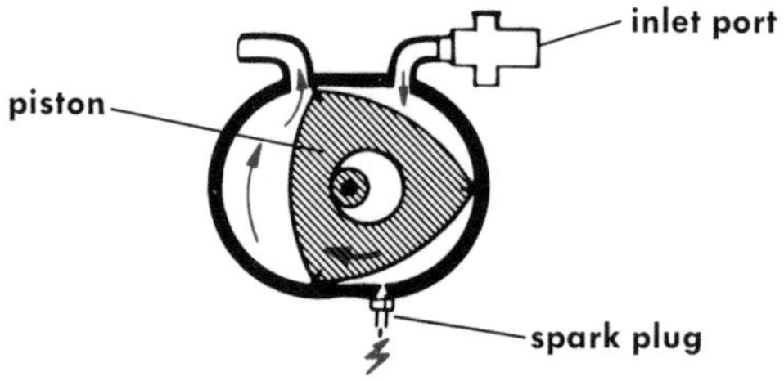

Fig. 1 ROTARY PISTON ENGINE

sweep continuously along the wall of the chamber. The three spaces formed between the piston and the chamber wall get larger and smaller as the piston rotates. These changes in the size of the spaces are used for drawing in the mixture of gasoline and air, for compressing the mixture, for combustion, and for discharging the burned gases, so that the full four-stroke working cycle is performed. The four "strokes" for the space in the chamber between corners A and C of the piston (see Fig. 2) are as follows:

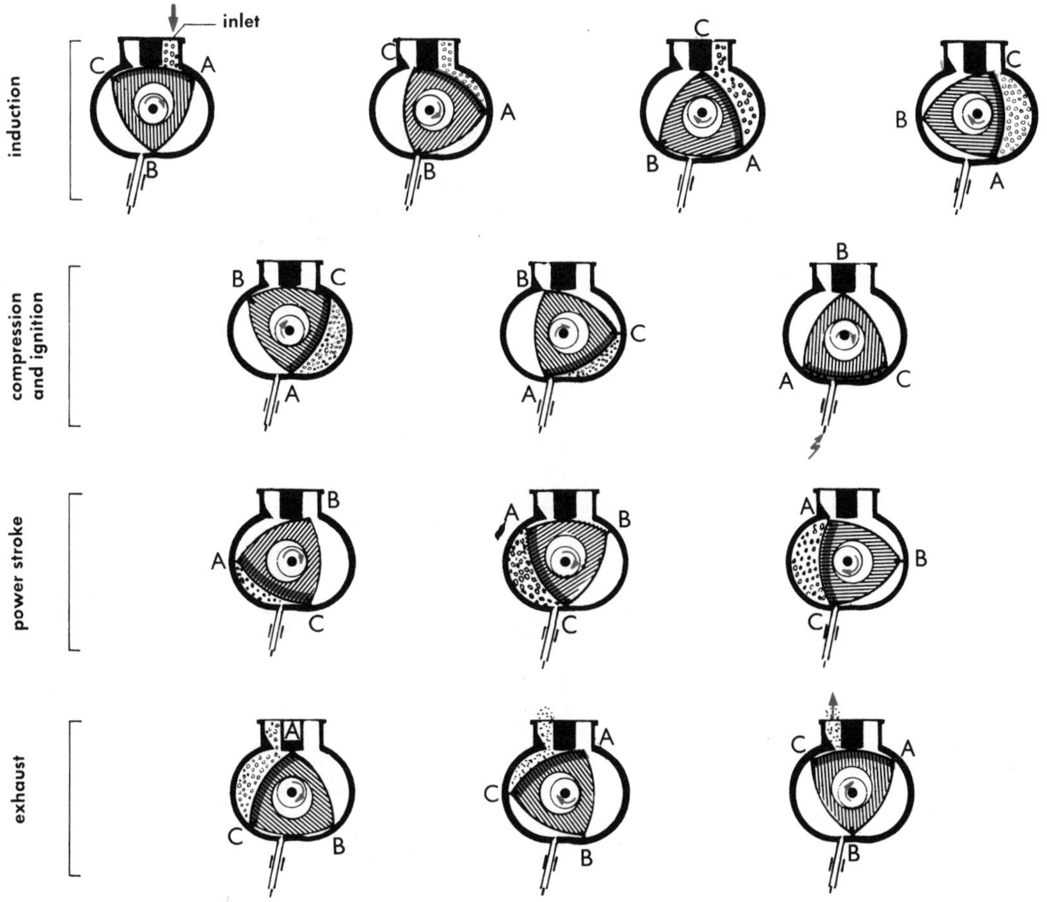

Fig. 2 **SEQUENCE OF OPERATIONS IN THE ROTARY PISTON ENGINE**
(***shown for one combustion chamber***)

1. The rotary piston uncovers the inlet port; the mixture of gasoline and air flows in.
2. As the space gets smaller, the mixture is compressed.
3. The compressed mixture is ignited by the spark plug, burns, and drives the piston around.
4. The exhaust gas is discharged through the outlet port.

The same process occurs in the other two spaces in the combustion chamber. During the course of one full rotation of the piston, there are three ignitions, or three power "strokes."

CARBURETOR

In an INTERNAL-COMBUSTION ENGINE, the fuel is burned right inside the cylinder. It is the carburetor's job to mix the gasoline with the air in which it will burn and to feed the mixture to the cylinder.

There is no difficulty about bringing in the air—whenever one of the pistons goes down (stroke 1 on page 89), the pressure of the atmosphere pushes the air right into the cylinder. The difficulty comes with the gasoline, which is stored in the gas tank as a liquid but

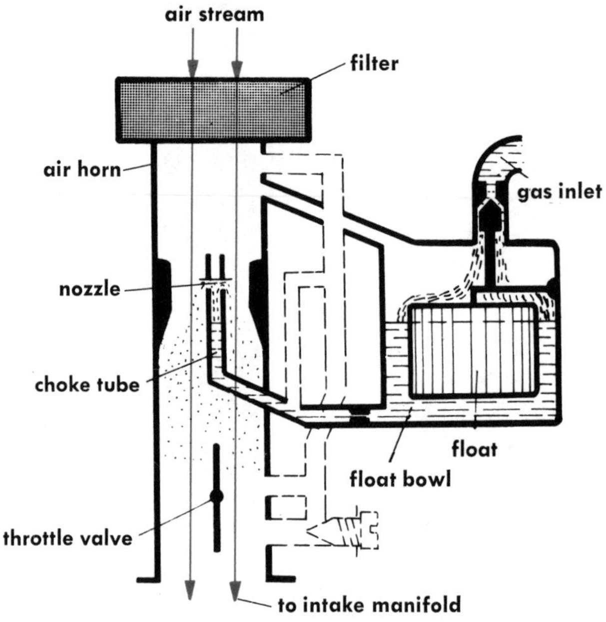

Fig. 1 GASOLINE ENTERING FLOAT BOWL OF CARBURETOR

which must reach the cylinder as a vapor mixed with air. And the amount of gasoline in the mixture must be close to 6% (by weight) or the spark won't set it off.

To keep the flow of incoming gasoline steady, the carburetor includes a *float bowl* in which a round can with a needle on top floats in gasoline. When there is enough gasoline in the bowl, the *float* rises, closing the gas inlet with its needle. No more gasoline flows in. As soon as some of this gasoline has been used, the float sinks, pulling the needle away from the intake (Fig. 1) and letting new gasoline pour in.

At this point the gasoline is still liquid. A *nozzle* brings it into the air stream at the narrow part of the *air horn,* where the air speed increases and the pressure is reduced. The gasoline is drawn to this low-pressure area, leaving the nozzle as a spray of droplets. These droplets evaporate, becoming gasoline vapor. The mixture of air and gasoline vapor is then sucked in by the cylinder through a branching pipeline called the *intake manifold.*

When a car is moving along a road, the driver holds the *throttle valve* open by keeping his foot on the accelerator pedal. A normal gas-and-air mixture passes on to the cylinders. But a few other situations have to be allowed for.

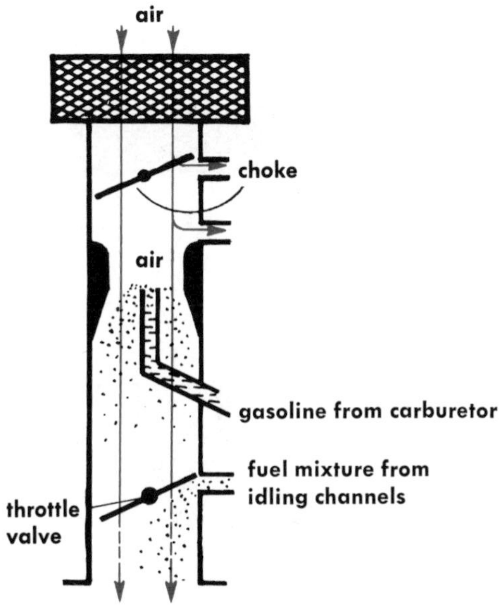

Fig. 2 HOW CHOKE IS USED TO REDUCE AIR INTAKE

In **starting** an engine, one has to allow for the fact that the engine is cold—gasoline droplets settle on the cold walls of the cylinders and the mixture actually burned lacks gasoline. To offset this, a hinged flap called the *choke* is tilted across the air horn (Fig. 2), cutting off part of the air supply and restoring the gasoline-to-air balance. In modern cars its operation is automatic.

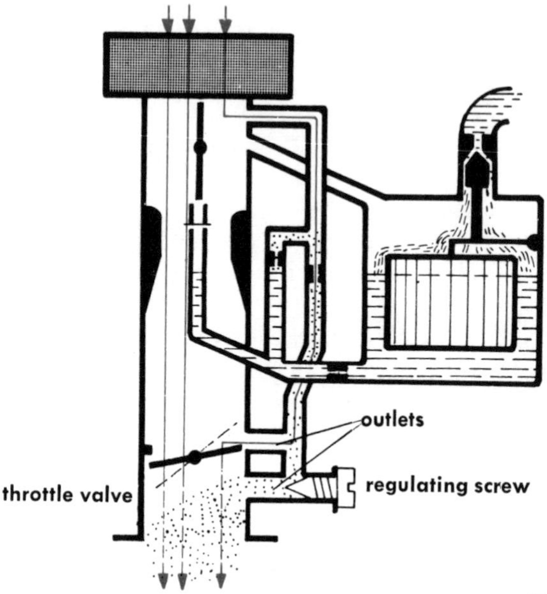

Fig. 3 HOW BYPASS CHANNELS ALLOW AIR AND GASOLINE TO BE DELIVERED WHEN THROTTLE VALVE IS CLOSED WHEN MOTOR IS IDLING

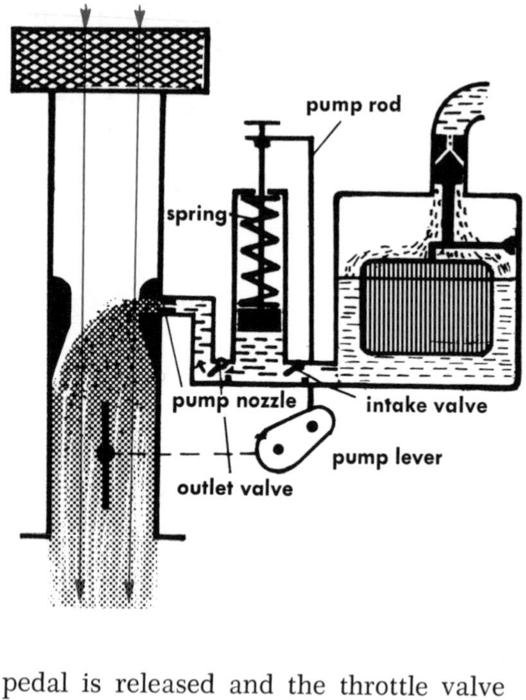

Fig. 4 HOW ACCELERATING PUMP DELIVERS EXTRA GASOLINE

In **idling,** the accelerator pedal is released and the throttle valve swings shut. Since no air is flowing in the air horn, there is no drop in pressure in the horn's narrow part and no fuel is drawn from the nozzle. The only way the engine can be kept going is to sneak in gasoline through a special channel—one that can bring in air from the upper part of the air horn and lead it to a spot just below the throttle valve (Fig. 3), picking up a small amount of gasoline on the way. With the engine going and the throttle closed, a good vacuum develops below the throttle and the weight of the atmosphere pushes the air-and-fuel mixture to the cylinders.

A special problem arises when the driver wants to **accelerate** from low to high speed. He opens the throttle—but the gasoline inflow is slow in picking up. In many modern engines, an accelerating pump helps out: its piston is pushed downward, forcing gasoline through a special passage (Fig. 4).

Apart from these improvements, the great value of the carburetor is that it allows internal-combustion engines to use gasoline. When these engines were first invented (around 1860), they ran on coal gas. As soon as carburetors became reliable, in the 1890's, drivers could turn to gasoline—and the great PETROLEUM industry got under way.

IGNITION

Every car runs on *chemical energy*—the energy released by a chemical reaction in each cylinder during the third stroke (page 88). But cars also use *electrical energy,* which they obtain from their batteries. They use it to control exactly *when* the fuel will ignite. The engine is kept just cool enough to prevent the fuel mixture from igniting by itself. Then, *just* before the piston reaches the top, a spark passes between the two metal tips of the **spark plug** and triggers the chemical reaction that powers the car.

The spark leaps across a small gap—hardly four hundredths of an inch wide—between the tips of the two pins, or *electrodes,* at the

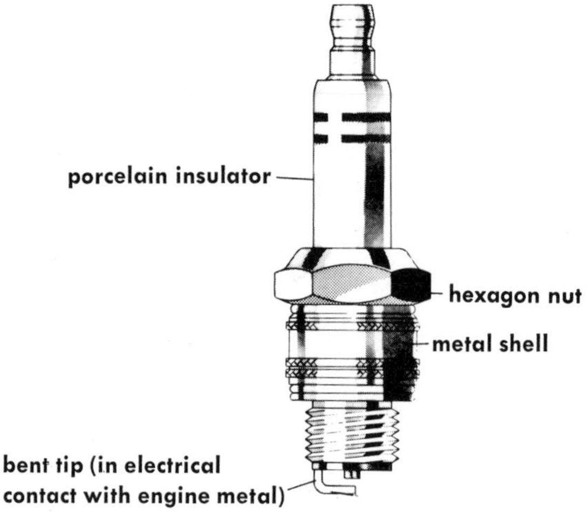

Fig. 1 SPARK PLUG SEEN FROM OUTSIDE

bottom of the spark plug. Seen from the outside (Fig. 1), the plug's bottom half is a *metal shell* that screws into the top of the cylinder and can exchange electricity with the engine walls, which are also made of metal. The top half is a white porcelain collar that acts as an *insulator—preventing* electrical contact. Running straight through the middle is a structure (Fig. 2) that conducts electricity between the center tip and the terminal at the top. (The metal shell has a screw base, like a light bulb, so that the whole plug can be removed to be cleaned or replaced.)

Sending electricity to a single spark plug at the right moment would be tricky enough, but suppose the engine speeds up? This can be handled by having an electric switch, or *contact breaker*, turned on and off by an ignition cam that turns only once during the engine's complete four-stroke cycle. (It is easy to find gears that turn at this rate, since it is also the rate at which the cylinder's intake and exhaust valves open and close.)

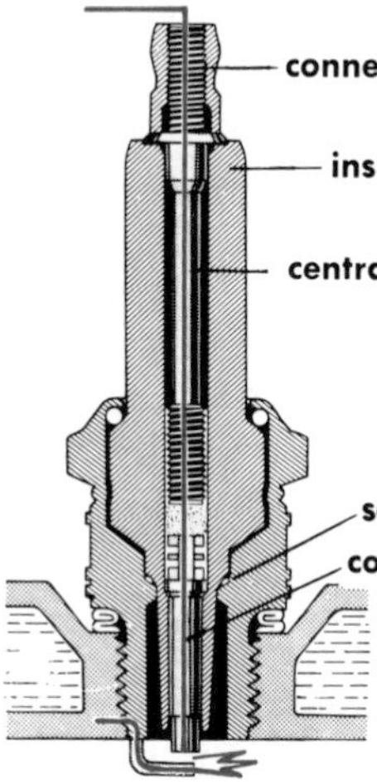

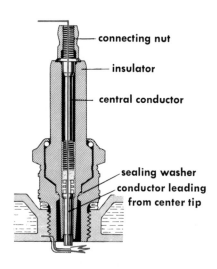

Fig. 2 THE INSIDE OF A SPARK PLUG

But what if the engine has four cylinders? Something has to keep switching the ELECTRIC CURRENT from one spark plug to another, until each cylinder has received its range of high voltage. This is done by the **distributor** (Fig. 3), which has a little *rotor* that sends current to each spark plug in turn as it rotates. It is mounted on the same shaft as the *breaker cam* that controls the *ignition coil*. As soon as a broken circuit in the coil's primary, or outside, winding triggers a surge of electricity, the rotor makes contact with one of the distributor's terminals and the current is sent straight to one of the spark plugs.

None of this explains how 6 or 12 volts in the storage battery can reappear as *thousands* of volts in the spark plug. But this is where the ignition coil comes in. It is built somewhat like a transformer, with two coils of wire, one inside the other. Whenever the contact

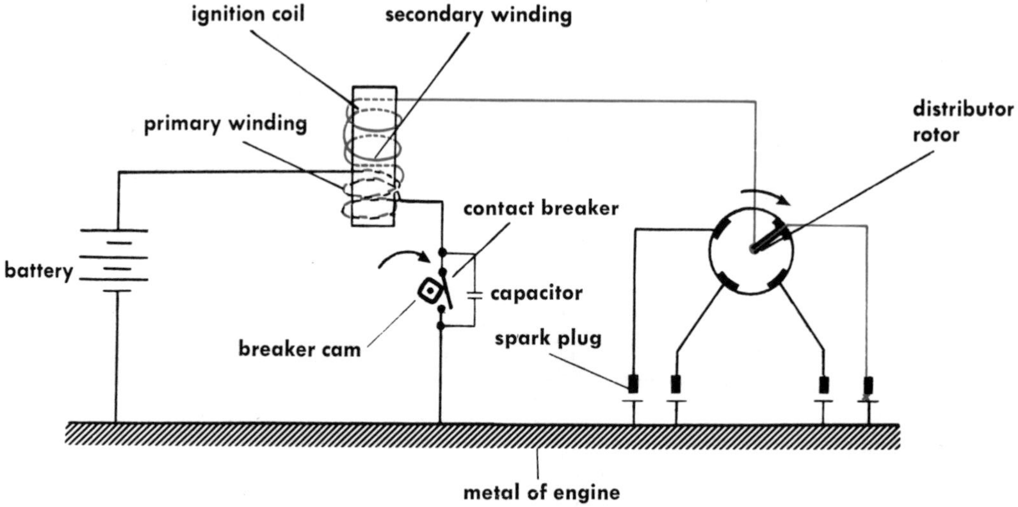

Fig. 3 HOW DISTRIBUTOR CONTROLS ELECTRICAL PATHS BETWEEN METAL OF ENGINE AND IGNITION COIL

breaker interrupts current from the battery, a magnetic field builds up around the outside winding, which has only a few hundred turns of thick wire. When this magnetic field sweeps over the inside winding, which has thousands of turns of very fine wire, it produces a surge of electricity of more than a hundred times the original voltage —enough to cross the gap between the two tips of the spark plug.

If the battery "dies," the entire engine fails. But cars use *storage batteries,* and these can be recharged (see BATTERIES). A separate electrical system takes care of this. It is built around an ELECTRIC GENERATOR, which can produce electricity whenever the engine is running. Depending on the speed of the engine, this power is produced at various high voltages that batteries can't digest, so a regulator is inserted between the generator and the battery; it trims the voltages down to the 6 or 12 volts of the battery system.

CLUTCH

All the pistons of an automobile engine transmit their power to a single axle called the *crankshaft*. As soon as the engine starts working, the crankshaft starts turning—at first at no more than a few hundred revolutions per minute. But the car's *wheels*, at that moment, may be receiving no power at all from the engine.

This comes about because the car's rear wheels are not directly connected to the crankshaft. Between the two are the TRANSMISSION (which allows the driver to "shift gears") and the DIFFERENTIAL (which transmits power to each of the two rear wheels). These units will not transmit power unless they receive it from the crankshaft. And whether they do or not depends on the **clutch** (Fig. 1).

Fig. 1 THE MAIN PARTS INVOLVED IN THE TRANSMISSION OF POWER FROM THE ENGINE TO THE WHEELS

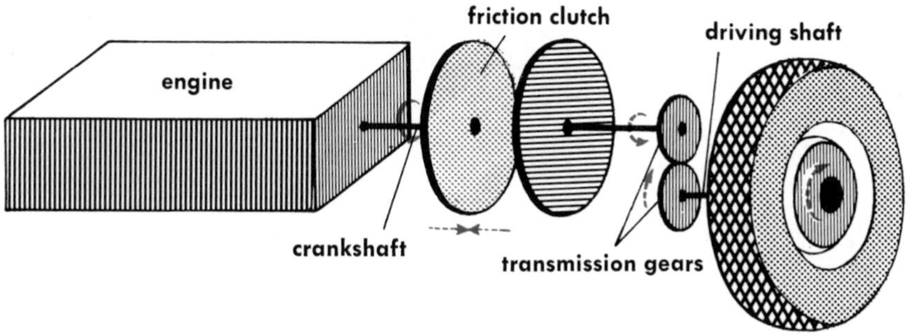

What the clutch connects is the *crankshaft* of the engine and the *clutch shaft* (which leads to the *transmission*). The driver can't suddenly, directly, connect the two to start the car moving. He has to let the clutch shaft *gradually* come up to the speed of the crankshaft. This is done by bringing a disk on the clutch shaft (the *drive plate*) flat up against the rear face of the *flywheel* on the clutch shaft. The two disks won't settle on the same speed right away—there will be a certain amount of "slip" as they rub against each other. This friction will cause them to heat up a bit—they are built with a lining that allows for this.

In the clutch shown in Fig. 2a, all parts colored red turn whenever the crankshaft turns. (These parts are the crankshaft itself and the engine's flywheel—a heavy wheel that keeps the shaft turning evenly

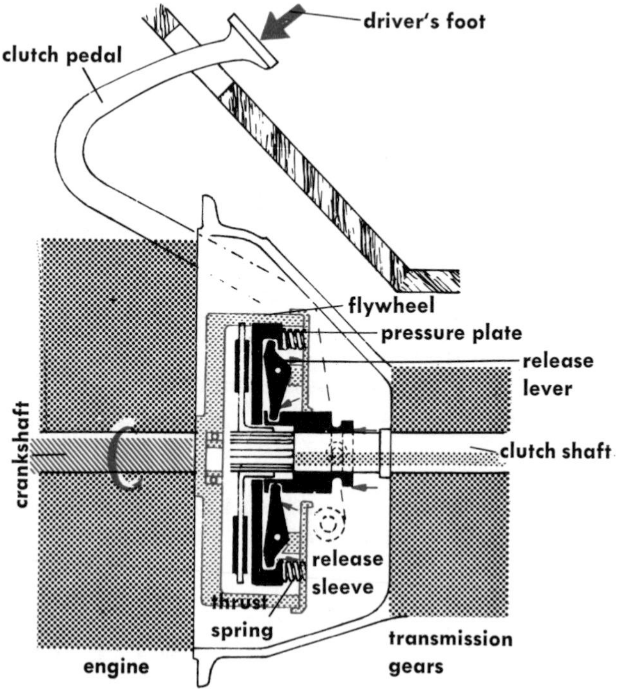

Fig. 2a CLUTCH DISENGAGED—ONLY THE PARTS SHOWN IN RED ARE TURNING

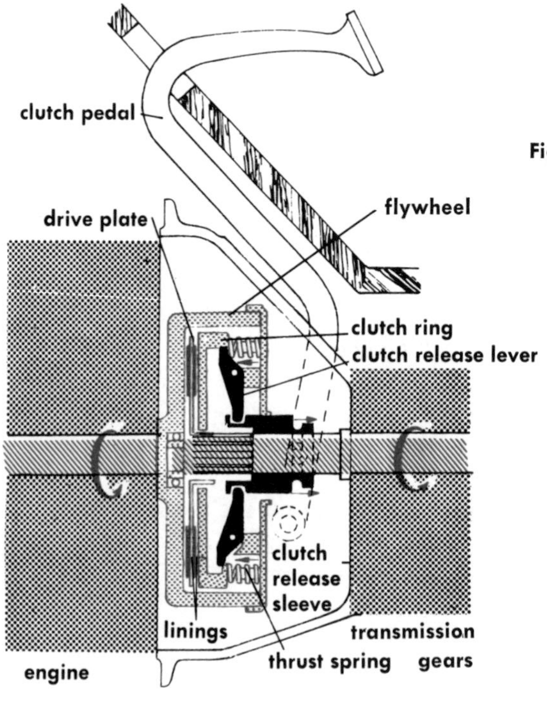

Fig. 2b CLUTCH ENGAGED, TRANSMITTING POWER OF CRANKSHAFT TO CLUTCH SHAFT

between the power stroke of one cylinder and the power stroke of the next.)

The remaining parts in Fig. 2a do not turn because the driver, by putting his foot down on the pedal, has **disengaged** (or "let out") the clutch. The *clutch release sleeve* is moved forward, toward the engine, forcing its *clutch release lever* to shift the *pressure plate* backward against the pressure of the *thrust springs:* there is now no mechanical connection between the crankshaft (red) and the clutch shaft (white).

In Fig. 2b, the driver has taken his foot off the pedal, letting it spring up again. The clutch release sleeve has moved back, away from the engine, allowing the thrust springs to press the pressure plate against the *drive plates* and the drive plates against the flywheel. (Although the pressure plate can slip backward and forward *along* the clutch shaft, it is mounted in such a way that whenever it turns, it makes the clutch shaft turn with it.)

Since the "driven" parts of the clutch have now been pressed forward, the flywheel forces the friction disk to turn along with it, the disk makes the pressure plate turn, and the plate makes the clutch shaft turn. In other words, with the clutch **engaged,** all its parts stick together and transmit the turning power of the engine shaft to the clutch shaft, which passes it on to the transmission.

Apart from connecting the crankshaft of a running engine to a shaft that has been idle, the clutch is also used to disengage shafts from one another in shifting gears. If the gearshift is worked by hand, the driver has to remember to release the clutch with his foot while changing, say, from first, or low, gear into second gear.

In many cars the clutch is **automatic**—it disengages whenever the driver's hand applies pressure to the speed-shift lever under the steering wheel. It is also disengaged when the engine is idling, but "lets in" as soon as the crankshaft turns fast enough to push some spinning weights outward (as in a CENTRIFUGE).

GEAR TRANSMISSION

One simple reason for having gears in a car is that the speed at which the crankshaft turns is greater than the speed (in revolutions per minute) of the rear wheels. But there is another reason, which is more difficult to follow but at least as important.

The automobile engine delivers power through a rotating shaft, the *crankshaft*. Now, when work is done in a straight line (as in the BLOCK AND TACKLE, page 14) it is measured by how much force is used over how much distance, or how much weight is raised how far. With a rotating shaft, what counts is how much *torque* is used over how wide a turning angle. Torque (pronounced TORK) simply refers to a push that goes round and round, like the twist one gives to the lid of a jar.

Gasoline engines are not good at developing *starting torque*. That is why a driver, in starting a car, lets out the CLUTCH to disconnect the engine from the rest of the car. It allows the engine to come up to a usable speed without the drag of an extra load. But it is also why the engine, once started, is connected in first, or "low," gear. The amount of *work* done by the crankshaft is as great as it would be without gearing, but if it is performed by a shaft turning through a smaller angle than the crankshaft, greater *torque* can be developed (work = torque × angle). Once the car has developed speed, this extra starting torque is no longer needed; the driver shifts into second gear—and later into high gear, in which the turning of the crankshaft is passed on without any reduction at all.

To keep the gears lubricated, they are kept in a *gearbox* partly filled with oil. The gearbox receives its power from the *clutch shaft* (Fig. 1), which receives it from the engine's crankshaft whenever the clutch allows it through; it passes the power on through the *transmission main shaft*, which sends it to the DIFFERENTIAL, which distributes it to each rear wheel. The gearbox also includes a *countershaft*, which acts as a go-between for the other two shafts.

In **first gear** (Fig. 1), a small gear on the clutch shaft drives a larger one (with more teeth) on the countershaft, which as a result turns more slowly. A small gear on the countershaft then drives a larger many-toothed gear on the main shaft, which now turns more slowly than the clutch shaft but offers more torque, or "twisting push."

In **second gear** (Fig. 2), the countershaft is slowed down exactly as much as in first gear, but there is less of a step-down in speed from countershaft to main shaft. (Notice that in first and second

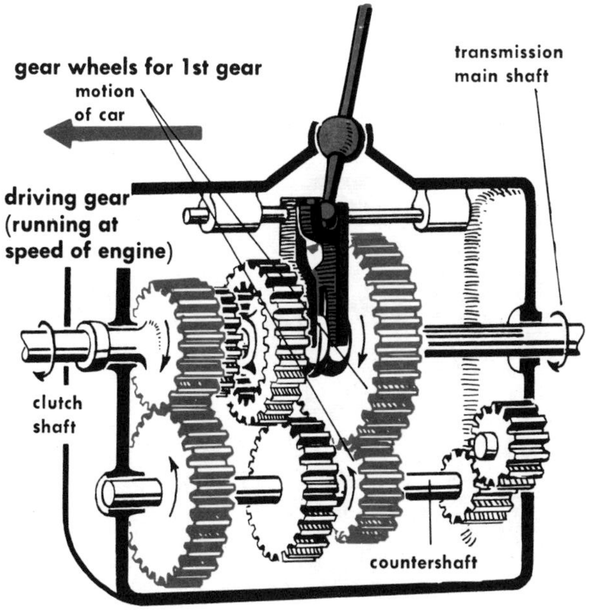

Fig. 1 VIEW INTO GEARBOX, SHOWING CLUTCH SHAFT, COUNTERSHAFT AND TRANSMISSION MAIN SHAFT. GEARS SHOWN IN RED ARE USED IN FIRST GEAR

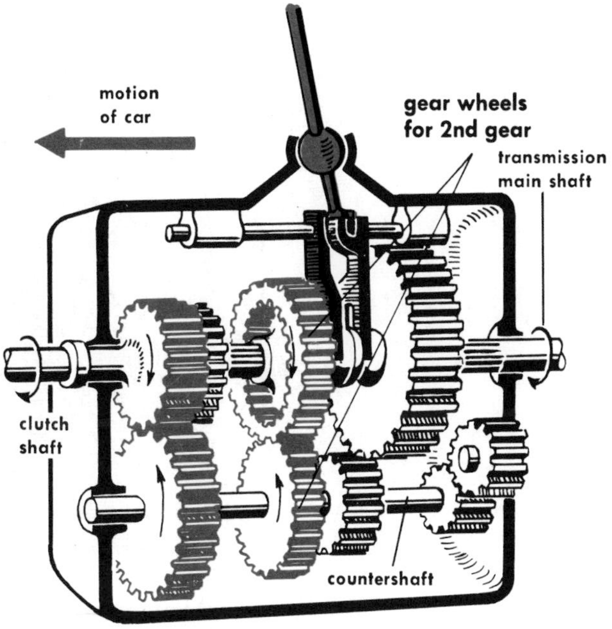

Fig. 2 ARRANGEMENT OF GEARS FOR DRIVING IN SECOND GEAR. POWER IS TRANSMITTED ONLY BY THE GEARS SHOWN IN RED

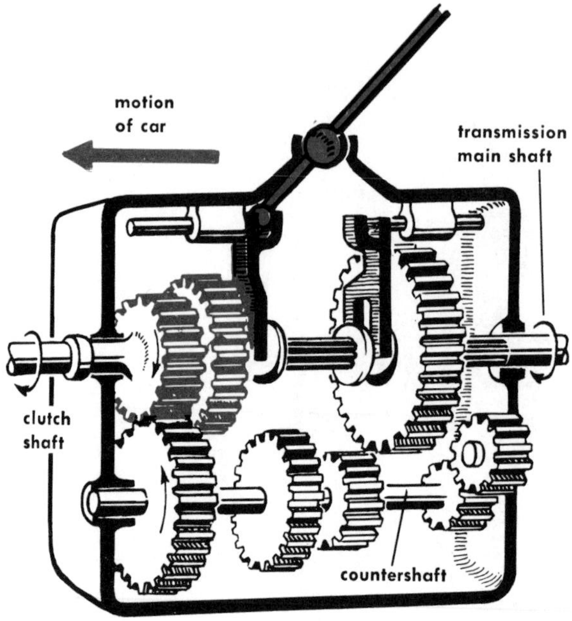

Fig. 3 POSITION OF GEARS IN HIGH GEAR. THE MAIN SHAFT IS LOCKED TO THE CLUTCH SHAFT. COUNTERSHAFT TURNS BUT DOES NOT TRANSMIT POWER

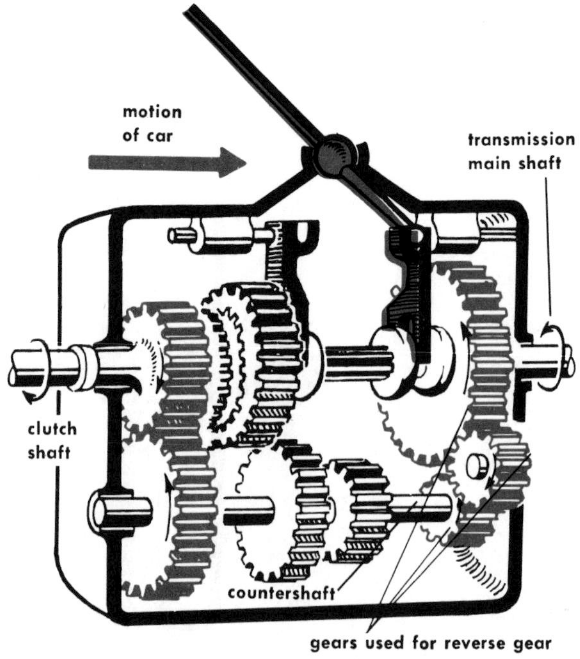

Fig. 4 ARRANGEMENT OF GEARS FOR DRIVING IN REVERSE. EXTRA GEAR, ON SEPARATE SHAFT, IS NEEDED TO REVERSE MOTION OF MAIN SHAFT

gears, the countershaft turns the opposite way from the clutch shaft but the motion is re-reversed when it is passed on to the main shaft. As a result, the output of the gearbox as a whole is in the same direction as the input.)

In **high gear** (Fig. 3), a special little clutch (not visible but between the two red gears) allows the main shaft to lock in to the clutch shaft. Although the countershaft keeps on turning, it is not transmitting power: power is passed on directly, without gear reduction, from clutch shaft to main shaft.

In **reverse** (Fig. 4), the countershaft picks up power as before but passes it on to an idler gear on an extra little shaft, which then passes it on to the main shaft. Because of this extra gear the main shaft now turns in reverse (see arrows).

AUTOMATIC TRANSMISSIONS

The gear shifting that all early cars used to require can also be accomplished automatically by having it depend on the speeds at which the crankshaft and the wheels are turning. Gears by themselves are too clumsy for this, too sudden in their operation. But a *hydraulic* system, in which rotating parts are joined by a liquid instead of by solid chunks of steel, can make it possible.

The heart of a hydraulic system is the **fluid coupling.** To see how it works, imagine two electric fans set up facing each other (Fig. 1). The fan on the left is turned on. As soon as it starts pushing air forward, the blades of the second fan begin to turn—first slowly, then faster, like a pinwheel. The second fan is said to be "coupled" to the first. (In this particular setup the coupling is inefficient—much of the draft escapes into the room before reaching the second fan.)

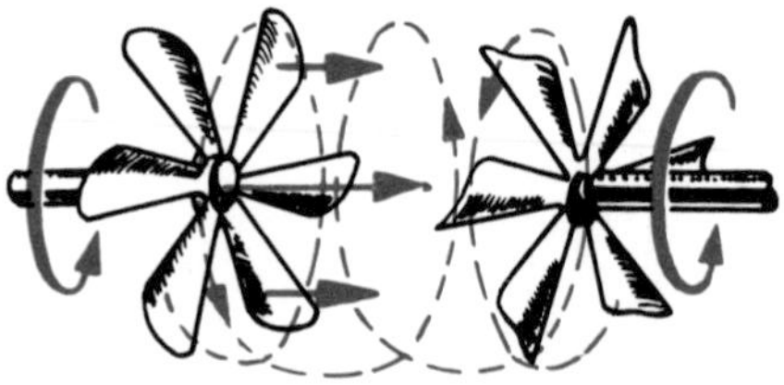

Fig. 1 HOW MOTION OF ONE FAN CAN CONTROL MOTION OF ANOTHER

As installed in a car, a fluid coupling uses oil instead of air and is used in combination with gears placed ahead of it. As the driving fan, called the *impeller*, receives its power from the *crankshaft*, it flings the surrounding oil at the blades of a second fan, called the *turbine;* the oil streams then bounce off the turbine and the surrounding casing and back into the impeller (Fig. 2). After the driver has started the car, the turbine gradually picks up speed until it moves almost as fast as the impeller. In this way, a fluid coupling helps a car to start smoothly.

Since World War II, two kinds of automatic transmission have been common in American cars. In the first kind, the fluid coupling is combined with gears (Fig. 3). The torque, or "twisting push," delivered by the fluid coupling to the gears is not very different from what the coupling itself received from the crankshaft—any increase

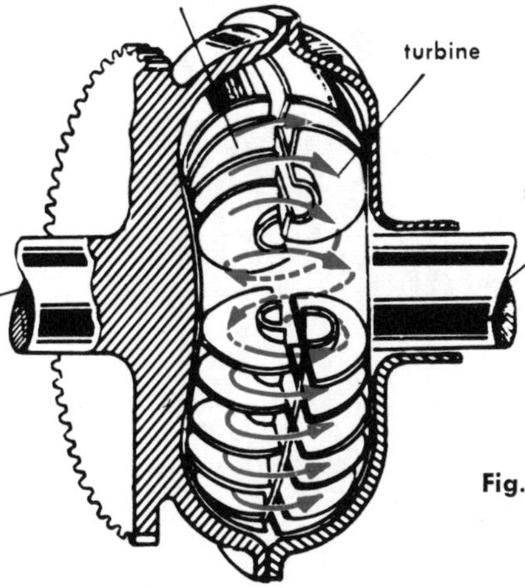

Fig. 2 HOW A FLUID COUPLING WORKS

in torque that is needed for starting (page 108) is left to the two sets of gears. These are of the kind called *planetary gears*, somewhat like the ones shown on page 22 for the VARIABLE-GEAR HUB of bicycles. (These gears do not have a fixed countershaft like the one on page 109—the spindles of the *planet wheels* not only are free to spin but are themselves carried by a frame, or "cage," that can either be locked to its own shaft or be left free to turn, carrying the planet wheels with it.) The whole system taken together allows the driver four forward gear combinations and one position for reverse.

The second kind of automatic transmission also combines gears and fluid coupling, but this time the fluid coupling also acts as a **torque converter.** In addition to the usual impeller and turbine, it uses an extra circle of vanes, called a *reactor*, mounted on a "free wheel." The freewheeling arrangement is much the same as that used on bicycles (as in diagrams on page 18), where the sprockets carrying the bicycle chain merely "freewheel" unless the rider, by pedaling, gives them a rotary speed faster than the speed of the rear axle.

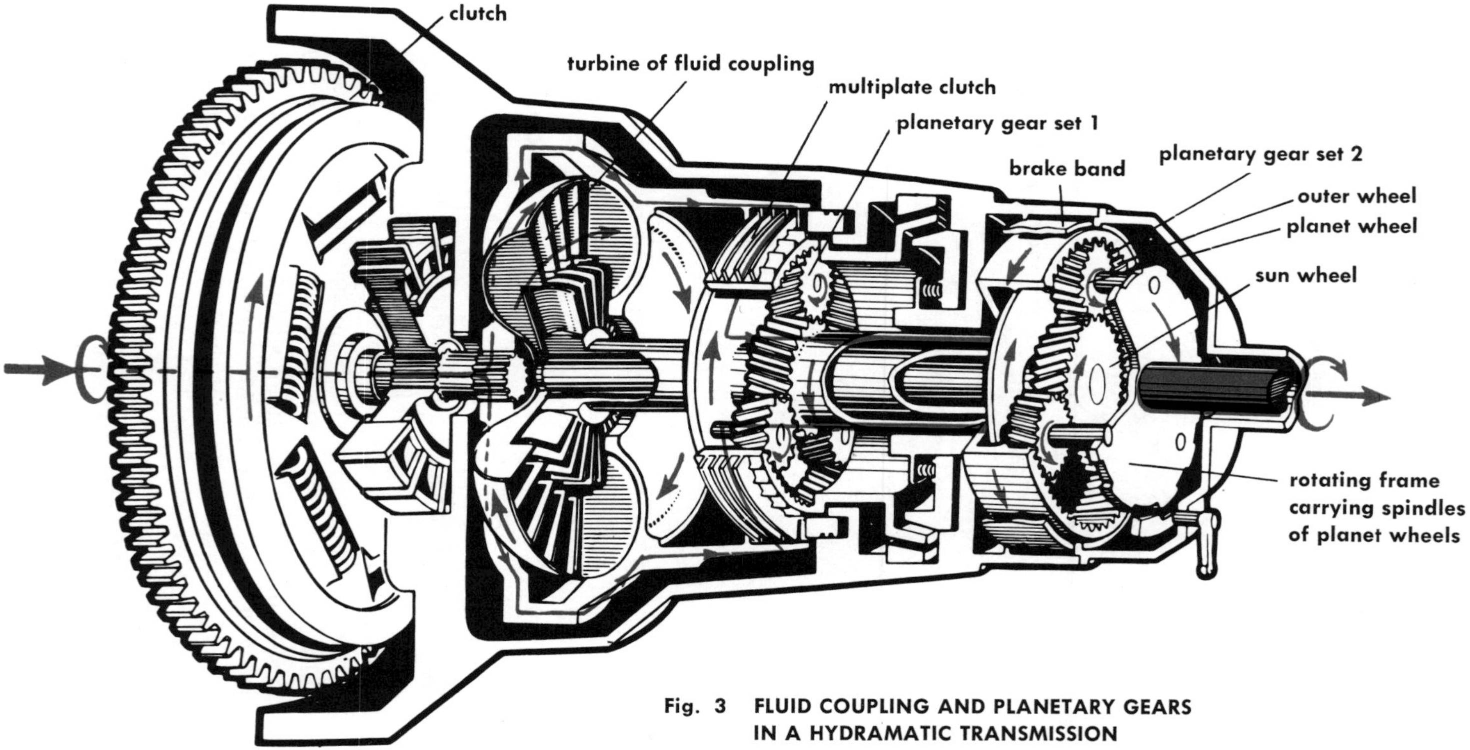

Fig. 3 FLUID COUPLING AND PLANETARY GEARS IN A HYDRAMATIC TRANSMISSION

In the torque converter, the same device is used—the reactor hugs the housing (and stalls, letting its vanes shape the oil stream) only when the torque of the crankshaft is smaller than the output torque of the transmission as a whole. As soon as the car is fully under way and the two torques are equal, the reactor drifts loose from the housing and "freewheels" along with the turbine. At that point the torque converter becomes a simple fluid coupling.

DIFFERENTIAL

When a car makes a right turn, its left wheels have a longer road to travel than its right wheels (Fig. 1). For the front wheels, this makes no difference—each rides on a short, stubby axle of its own and simply turns as fast as it needs to. But both the rear wheels get their power from the same shaft (called the *propeller shaft*); if they were both forced to make the same number of turns while the car was taking a curve, the one going too fast would skid. What is needed is

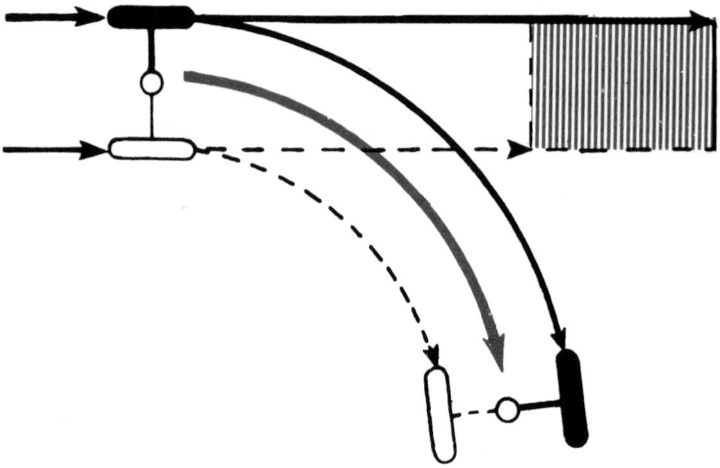

Fig. 1 WHEN CAR TURNS, INSIDE AND OUTSIDE WHEELS COVER DIFFERENT DISTANCES

a set of gears that will keep feeding power to both rear wheels while letting them adjust their speeds between them.

This set of gears exists. It's an ingenious contraption called a **differential.** To see how it works, imagine you are looking down at the car from above, as in Fig. 2. There is no single rear axle; instead, there are two half-axles. At the outer end of each half-axle is a wheel (not shown); at the inner end is a small gear, labeled *bevel gear.* To make the car's rear wheels turn, power from the propeller shaft has to reach these two bevel gears. But to keep them independent from each other, power reaches them in a roundabout way.

First through the *drive pinion,* at the rear end of the propeller shaft, which passes its motion (at right angles, and slowed down) to the large *ring gear.* Notice that the ring gear rides on the left half-axle *but is not connected to it*—what the ring gear passes its motion to is not the axle but a case that contains small gears called the *differential pinions.* This case turns round and round over itself, carrying

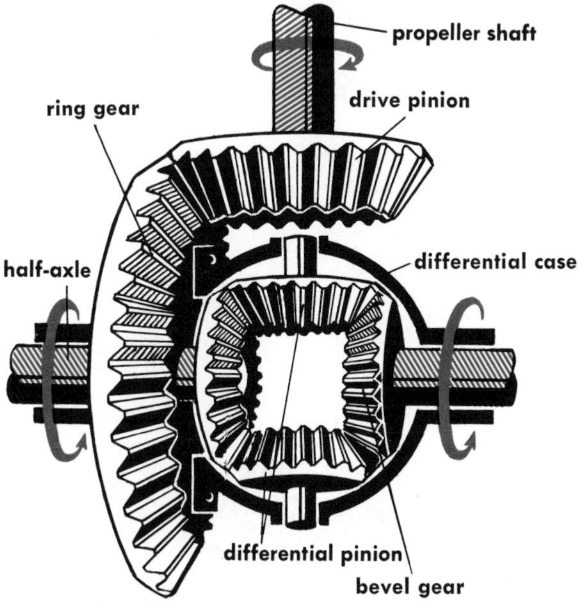

Fig. 2 HOW THE GEARS OF A DIFFERENTIAL LOOK WHEN SEEN FROM ABOVE

the differential pinions with it. It is these pinions that finally transmit the power to the two bevel gears.

When the car is going straight ahead, the ring gear makes the case turn round and round; the case makes the differential pinions go round with it, but the pinions don't spin on their own spindles. They might just as well be rigid pieces of steel, as they turn round and round, forcing the bevel wheels to rotate.

It's when the car is taking a curve that the differential pinions start spinning. To see why, consider what happens to a pinion that is caught between two toothed racks, as in Fig. 3a. As long as the two racks don't move in relation to each other, the pinion won't turn. But as soon as one of them moves backward or forward in relation to the other, the pinion starts rotating.

Fig. 3a THE PINION TURNS ONLY WHEN THE TWO RACKS MOVE AT DIFFERENT SPEEDS

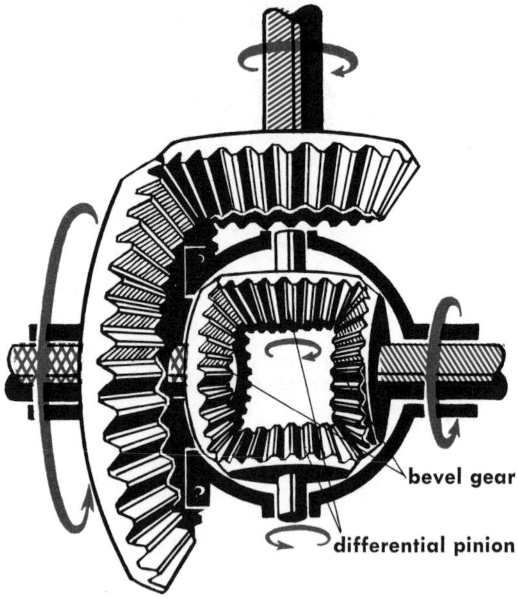

Fig. 3b THE CAR IS MAKING A TURN. THE BEVEL GEARS TURN AT DIFFERENT SPEEDS, FORCING THE DIFFERENTIAL PINIONS TO SPIN

This is exactly what happens in the differential of a car. When the two rear wheels are moving at the same rate (Fig. 2), the differential pinions don't spin on their spindles; they simply go round and round with the whole case. But as soon as the car is taking a curve, the wheel on the inside of the curve holds back a bit, while the wheel on the outside needs to make one or two extra turns. As a result, the two bevel gears turn at different rates from each other. The differential pinions now begin to turn, each on its own spindle, while still going round and round with the case as a whole and bringing power to the wheels.

BRAKES

A brake usually works by producing so much friction between a moving object and some other object we think of as stationary that the moving object stops. And so when a boy on a bicycle "brakes with his foot"—that is, by dragging his foot along the ground—we think of the foot as the brake.

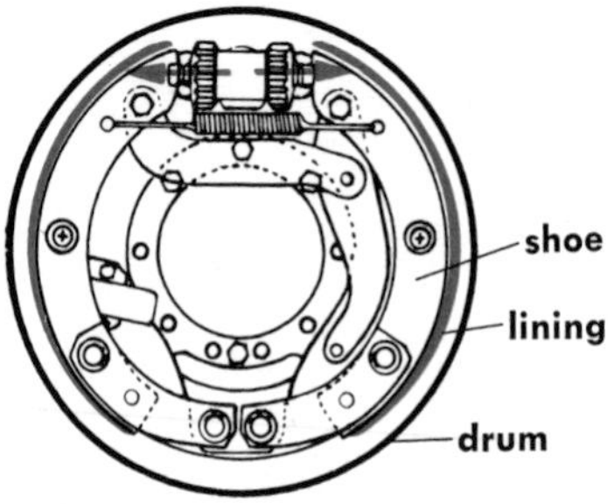

Fig. 1 SHOE BRAKE IN WHICH SHOES PRESS LININGS AGAINST DRUM

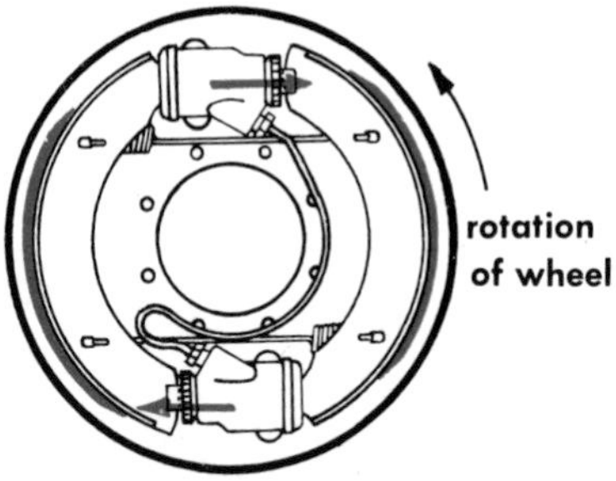

Fig. 2 SHOE BRAKE IN WHICH SEPARATE PIVOTS ENABLE BOTH SHOES TO ACT IN THE SAME DIRECTION

Actually, things are not that simple. Braking involves not only the brake itself but the signal from the rider (or the driver) to the brake. When a boy on a bike uses his foot, we don't notice the signal path, which is built into his body. But in designing a car, engineers have to think up not only a good brake but a good way of getting the braking signal from the driver to the brake.

In brakes of the kind used in cars, two "*shoes*"—that is what they are called—press against the inside of a *drum* that is part of each of the four wheels. In the simple shoe brake of Fig. 1, each shoe is in the form of a banana, both shoes being pivoted from the same base when the brake is applied. (One of these is applied "with," the other "against," the rotation of the wheel.) When the brake is released, springs stretched between the two bananas pull them away from the drum. In the brake design shown in Fig. 2, the shoes are pivoted from opposite sides; this brake is more effective and the friction and wear are more even.

It is also possible to have the friction of the brake apply evenly in a full circle, as in the full-disk brake of Fig. 3. Here a circle of fixed

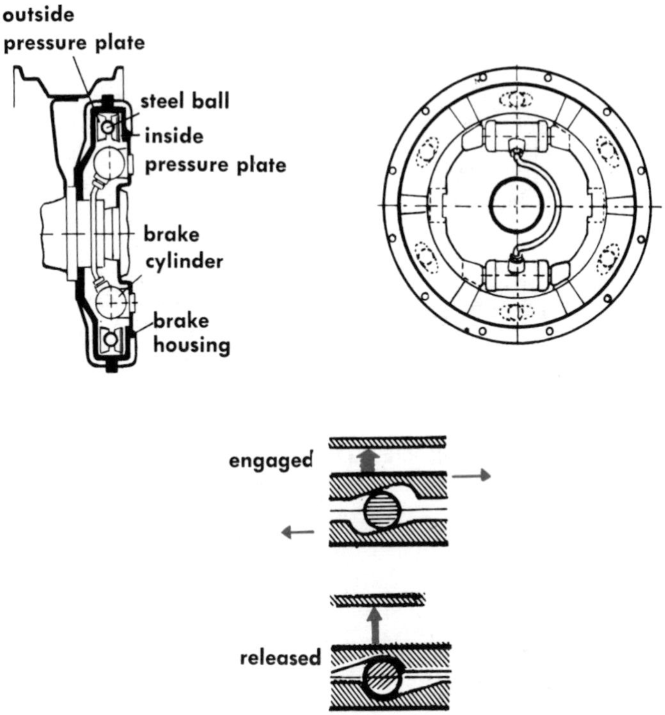

Fig. 3 FULL-DISK BRAKE, SEEN HEAD ON AND FROM THE SIDE. ENLARGED DIAGRAM (BELOW) SHOWS HOW STEEL BALLS FORCE THE TWO PLATES APART

pads (Fig. 3, *middle*) pushes outward within the folded-over rim (Fig. 3, *left*) of a rotating drum, pressing the two *pressure plates* against it. The effectiveness of the braking is increased by the fact that the two pressure plates can rotate with regard to each other (like the lid and bottom of a round candy box)—but by only a few degrees. *Steel balls* are trapped in grooves, set at an angle, between the two plates. When the brake is applied, the two plates shift position (Fig. 3, *right*) in such a way that the steel balls, pressing against the sides of the grooves, pry the plates apart, driving their linings against the two inner faces of the drum.

Whether it uses shoes or pressure plates, each brake still has to be controlled from a distance by the driver. The system used is almost

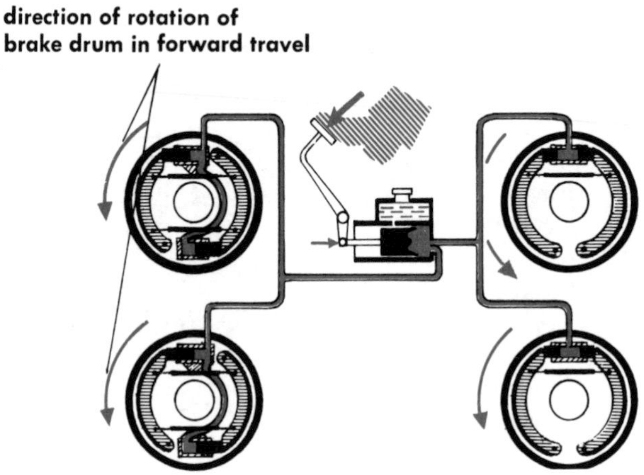

Fig. 4 HOW OIL PRESSURE IS CARRIED FROM MASTER CYLINDER TO BRAKES IN WHEELS

always hydraulic. When the driver's foot presses down on the brake pedal, he forces oil out of a *brake cylinder* and outward into tubes that carry the oil pressure to small cylinders in each of the four wheels; in each cylinder, the oil then pushes a piston that acts on the shoes or disk pads. (When the brake is released, a compressed spring in the brake cylinder pushes the piston out again.) A simple hydraulic circuit, connected to shoe brakes, appears in Fig. 4.

When a driver applies the brakes to bring his car to a stop, the car's energy of motion is converted into heat. For this reason, the brake drums are given a large outer surface and are mounted on the wheels in a way that allows the outside air to flow over them; and the linings are made of a tough heat-resistant material, usually containing asbestos.

SPEEDOMETER

When a driver wants to know *How fast am I going?* chances are that he doesn't mean how fast in relation to this or that car he can see on the road, but how fast in relation to the road itself. Unfortunately, because of the way it works, the speedometer cannot really tell him that—but it can give him a good approximation.

Under its *dial*, each speedometer has a *spring* in the form of a spiral that keeps the pointer at 0 when the car is not moving. (Whether the engine is running or not should make no difference.) The car will move forward when its *propeller shaft* (page 116), taking power to the DIFFERENTIAL and from there to the rear wheels, starts turning.

So the propeller shaft is a good place to connect a speedometer—usually right behind the TRANSMISSION. Once the shaft of the speedometer has been connected, a way has to be found to make the pointer of the dial indicate speed as it moves away from the 0 mark. For this, speedometers use a whirling *magnet*.

Above the whirling magnet is a metal *speed cup* (colored red in Fig. 1), mounted so that it is free to turn. Now, a peculiar thing about a magnet is that when it is whirled, it starts ELECTRIC CURRENTS in a metal that lies alongside it. But as the currents move about in the speed cup, they, in turn, set up concentrations of magnetic force around themselves. The stronger the electric currents, the more the speed cup begins to act like a magnet. The more it acts like a magnet, the more its newly developed magnetic poles tend to follow around the poles of the permanent magnet whirling clockwise under them.

The dial pointer and the speed cup are both fixed to the same shaft, and the spiral spring always acts to pull the two of them back to the position marked 0. But as the car's speed picks up, and the magnetic forces in the speed cup become stronger, the cup's clockwise push overcomes the spring and carries the pointer clockwise away from 0.

After a series of tests, the manufacturer has had tick marks for 40, 50, 60 and so on spaced out on the dial for a particular car model. But the speedometer does not work *directly* to register the passage of a stretch of road—it works from a shaft or axle on the car, which in turn "knows" about the road only through the tires. If the tires are worn thin, blown up to a new pressure or turned in for tires of a different thickness, the speedometer (through no fault of its own) will no longer be registering true road speed.

For a more modern indicator—the vertical pointer moving straight to the right as speeds increase—the shaft of the speed cup can drive a cylinder placed on its side. The vertical pointer can then be connected to a spiral groove on the cylinder, which will move to one end of the cylinder or the other, like the lines on a rotating barber's pole.

The turning of the speedometer shaft can also be used to answer the question *How many miles has the car run?* The gadget that an-

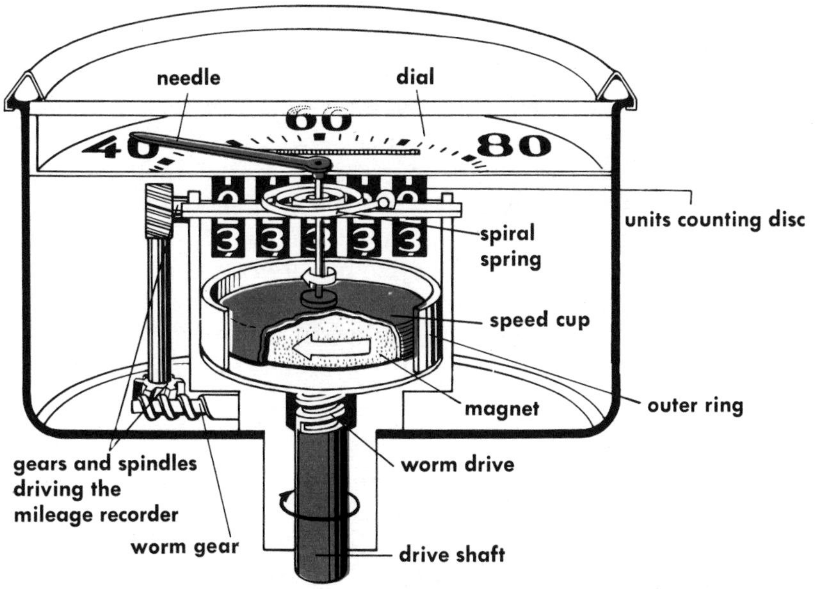

WORKING PARTS OF A SPEEDOMETER. THE GEARS AT LEFT, WHICH ARE DRIVEN BY THE SAME SHAFT AS THE SPEEDOMETER, ARE PART OF THE MILEAGE RECORDER

swers this question is called an **odometer.** It works through gears that greatly reduce the number of turns made by the speedometer shaft, transmitting the reduced number of turns to a cylindrical gear called a *worm gear.* The turns of the worm gear are then transmitted through one or two further gears to a little drum painted with ten digits, 0 through 9. This drum is at the far right of the mileage counter. When it has turned full circle, a slotted catch on its side makes the next drum turn by one-tenth of a circle, moving it from 0 to 1; the total mileage then reads 00010, and so on.

DIESEL ENGINES

Most trucks and buses don't use regular gasoline engines. They use Diesel engines. The reason is simple: Diesel engines are cheap to run.

Like gasoline engines, Diesel engines are INTERNAL-COMBUSTION ENGINES—they burn fuel inside their cylinders. But their fuel is Diesel oil, a heavy part of PETROLEUM that has a low boiling point and can be obtained cheaply, with little processing at the oil refinery.

Since 1900, we have been using up many of the easily reached deposits of petroleum. Remaining reserves are still good for many years but are more expensive to reach. If gasoline becomes more expensive, more and more people will want Diesel engines for their private cars. In Europe, this change-over has already begun.

The reason a Diesel engine can use a heavy fuel that doesn't vaporize easily is that it operates at a much higher level of temperatures and pressures than does a gasoline engine.. The cycle of strokes is very much like the four-stroke cycle pictured on page 89 or the two-stroke cycle on page 92. But there's an important difference in the compression stroke. Instead of compressing a fuel mixture down to about one-sixth of the volume of the cylinder, in a Diesel the piston

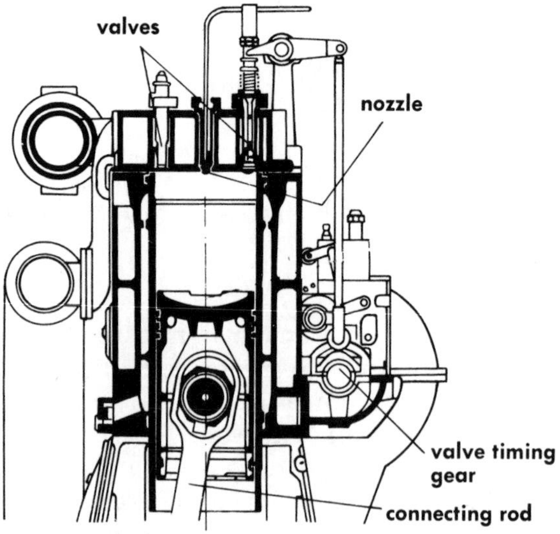

Fig. 1 DIESEL ENGINE IN WHICH FUEL IS INJECTED DIRECTLY INTO NOZZLES

compresses the air—just plain air—to a space only about one-third of that.

Now, as anyone knows who has worked a bicycle pump, putting air under pressure makes it hotter. In a Diesel engine, the pressure of the air is so high that the temperature rises to anything between 900° and 1500° Fahrenheit, depending on the engine. As the air reaches its top pressure and temperature, fuel oil is released into it from a *nozzle* (Fig. 1). Because of the high temperature, the fuel catches

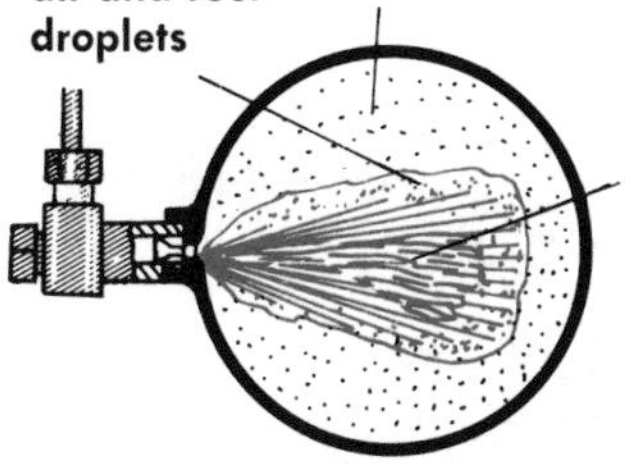

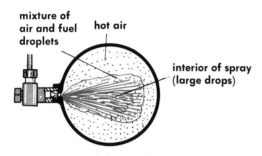

Fig. 2a HOW JET OF DIESEL FUEL MIXES WITH AIR IN CYLINDER

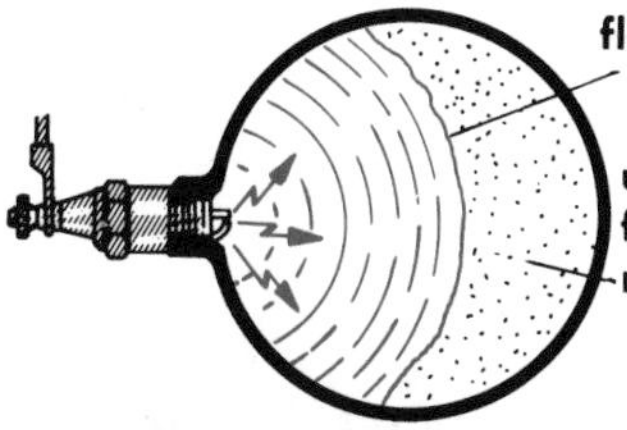

Fig. 2b HOW FLAME FRONT MOVES OUTWARD IN STANDARD GASOLINE ENGINE

fire without the need of a spark plug or ignition system. The nozzle is designed carefully, so that its spray fills as much of the air as possible (Fig. 2a), avoiding the sharp divison between burned and unburned portions that occurs in a gasoline engine (Fig. 2b).

No matter how carefully the fuel nozzle is designed, some of the fuel sometimes escapes burning when it should and catches fire later, causing the engine to "knock." Special ways have been found to pre-

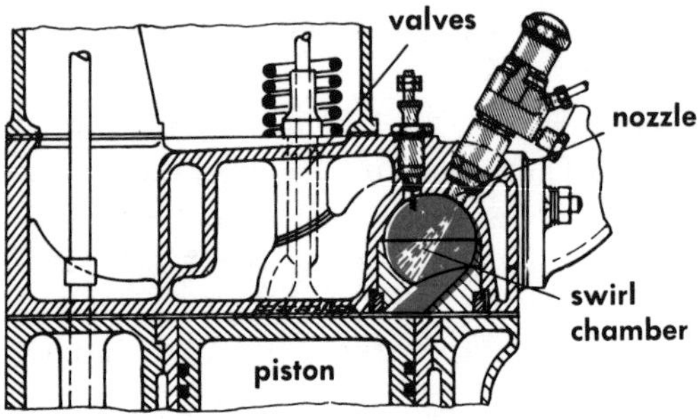

Fig. 3 HOW SWIRL CHAMBER HELPS AIR MIX WITH FUEL FROM NOZZLE

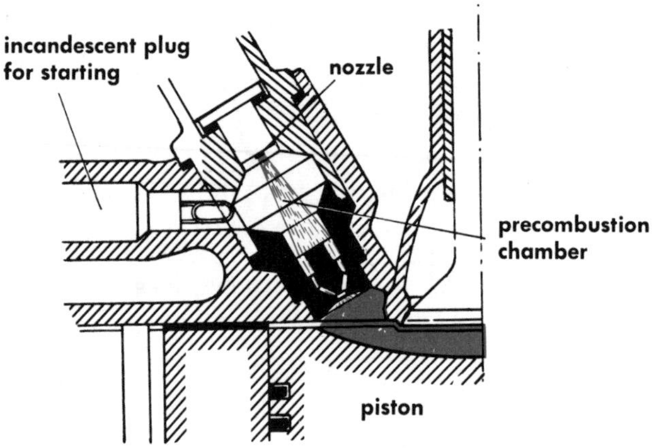

Fig. 4 PRECOMBUSTION CHAMBER

vent this from happening. In one design (Fig. 3), the *piston* pushes the air into a **swirl chamber,** in which swirling air mixes thoroughly with the incoming fuel. In another design (Fig. 4), an *incandescent plug* (like the glowing wire in a light bulb) starts the fuel burning in a **precombustion chamber;** the resulting gases expand into the cylinder, where the burning is completed.

FARM TRACTORS

In 1910, 35% of the population of the United States lived on farms; today the figure is 9%, and yet food is plentiful. The big difference between farming then and farming now is *power*. And the key source of power on the farm is the tractor.

A tractor (Fig. 1) is much like an automobile, but an automobile is designed for speed and comfort, whereas a tractor is designed for pulling power. It has many of the basic mechanical features of an automobile, except that its engine is often a DIESEL ENGINE, and instead of the three- or four-speed GEAR TRANSMISSION of the old-style passenger automobile, it has an eight- or ten-speed gearbox. This it needs because its pulling power depends on the *torque*, or twisting push, developed by the engine, and the simplest way to get more of it is to let the crankshaft turn at its natural speed but have the gears make a smaller number of turns (page 108).

But no matter how powerful the engine, a tractor won't pull if its huge rear wheels are slipping. All sorts of ways have been found to weigh down the rear axle of a tractor and make the wheels "grip" the ground: extra weights have been piled on at the rear, attachments have been designed to bear down on it, and on some tractors the rear tires have even been filled with water.

No farmer is likely to let a huge power source like a tractor work only at plowing time and stay idle the rest of the year. Two features make it convenient for him to put the tractor to work on other jobs: the power take-off shafts and the hydraulic control system.

The **power take-off shafts** allow a tractor's Diesel engine to be used for any job around the farm that requires power. Two of them are at the tractor's rear end; one rotates at 540 revolutions per minute, the other at 1,000 rpm. A third one, mounted in front and also turning at 1,000 rpm, is specially adapted to driving a grass- or wheat-cutting machine.

The cutting part of a **grass cutter** consists of a row of knife blades (colored red in Fig. 2a) that moves back and forth over a set of fingers —the stems of the plants are caught between the two and are nipped off. Since a tractor's take-off shaft produces only round-and-round motion, it is fitted with a *crank disk* (Fig. 2b) that works a *connecting rod*—much as on the STEAM ENGINE shown on page 60. The result is just the back-and-forth motion that the cutter blades need.

The **hydraulic control system** is a circuit of pipes that includes a

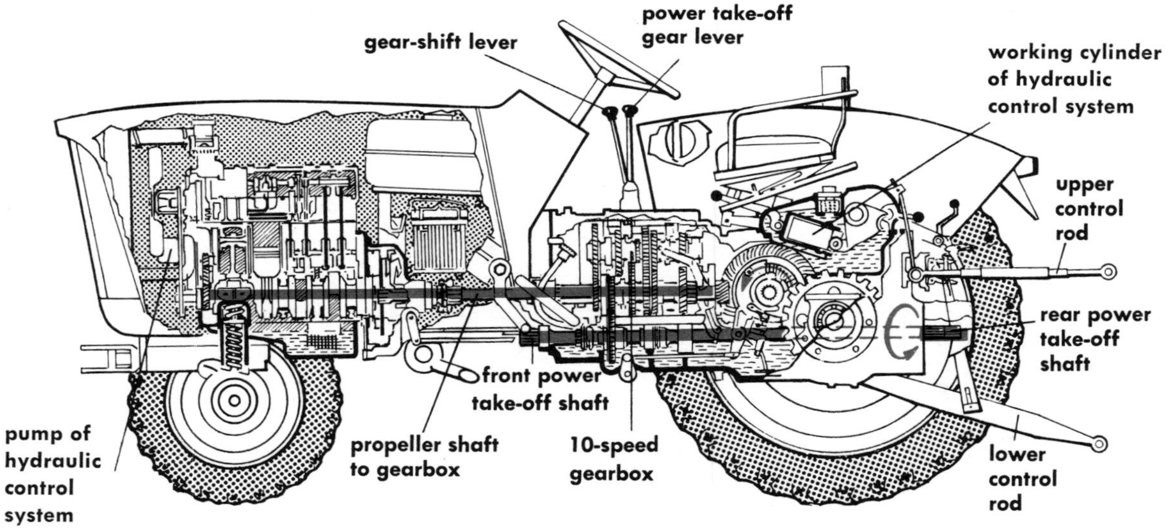

Fig. 1 FARM TRACTOR. ORIGINALLY INTENDED FOR PULLING, IT IS ALSO EQUIPPED TO ALLOW THE OPERATOR TO DRIVE AND CONTROL OTHER MACHINERY

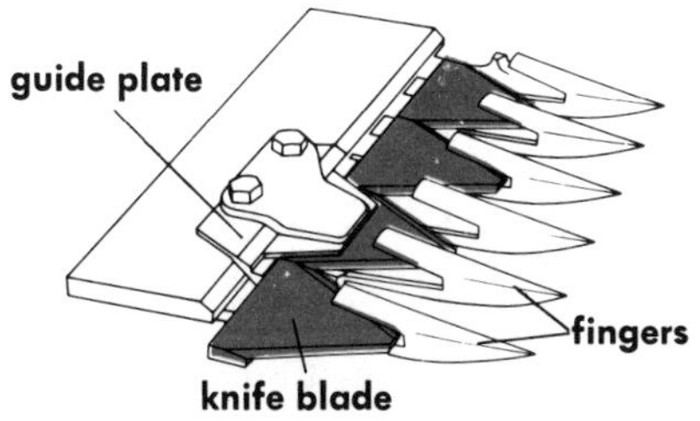

Fig. 2a BLADES OF GRASS-CUTTING ATTACHMENT SLIDE SIDEWAYS, BACK AND FORTH

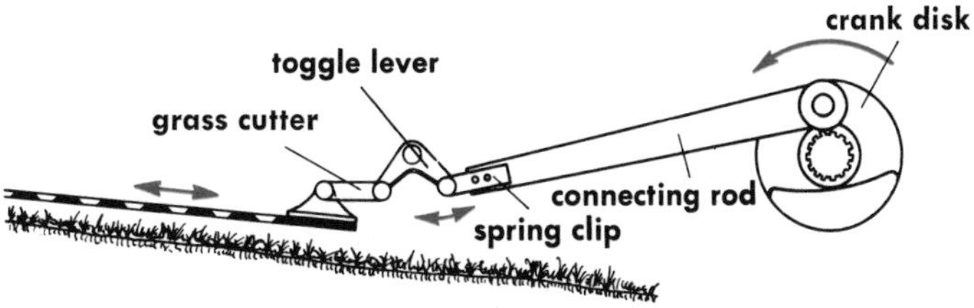

Fig. 2b CRANK DISK AND CONNECTING ROD CONVERT ROTARY MOTION OF TRACTOR SHAFT TO BACK-AND-FORTH MOTION OF GRASS CUTTER

pump and a *working cylinder.* The pipes connect to a supply tank filled with oil. The circuit also includes a control valve that allows the operator to fill the working cylinder so that its piston exerts great forces, very slowly. These forces can raise the two *lower control rods* that allow a tractor to tow heavy machinery. When the operator wants to disconnect the machinery, he sets the control valve so that the machinery's own weight, bearing down on the control rods, forces the oil to flow back to the supply tank.

COMBINE HARVESTER

The whole point of growing a crop of wheat is to harvest the grain, which may be in the form of 50 or so little kernels, each in a bearded husk, packed in the head at the top of a stem 4 feet high. But before the grain can be used to make bread, macaroni, and pie crusts, it has to be harvested. This used to be an enormous job, in which everybody within sight lent a hand. Today it is an even bigger job (the population of the United States has been doubling every 50 years), but it is done by vast machines called **combine harvesters,** or "combines" for short.

What the combine does is to cut the stalks, thresh the grain (even cleaning it), and leave long trails of straw behind called "windrows." If it has a baling attachment, it even ties the straw neatly in bales. A DIESEL ENGINE provides the power for the threshing and for the forward travel of the entire machine.

This is how a combine tackles its job:

As it moves forward, *spring prongs* on a *revolving reel* way out at the front set the wheat stalks upright; a *cutter bar* (like the one on page 133) cuts them and the *auger* (pronounced AW-gur) sweeps them up into the machine. The actual threshing is done in the *threshing cylinder,* where a roller called the *concave* bashes the heads against the knobby inside surface of the cylinder, shaking the grains out (along with some of the husks, or "chaff"). The grain falls into a space called the *cleaning shoe,* where it is separated from the chaff (and from stray wisps of straw) and is cleaned by *sieves* and a blast of air from a *fan.* Meanwhile the straw has been sent traveling to the rear of the machine, from which it shoots out in a continuous stream.

There are drawbacks to this system. Some grains will fail to separate out in the threshing cylinder—they will hitch a ride with the straw and be thrown out. Others will come out nicely in the threshing cylinder but will then be blasted to the rear with the chaff, skipping the sieves altogether.

So a few corrective mechanisms are added. For the grains left in the straw, *check flaps* do the trick. They catch the grains, which are then shaken out of the straw on screens on the straw rack and are emptied forward, where they join the incoming grain.

As for the grains that miss the sieves and are blasted away with the chaff, they too can still be retrieved: they are heavier than the chaff and fall within the machine. A return auger (the *tailings auger*) catches them and whips them onto a moving belt (the *tailing elevator*) that carries them upward and forward, dropping them into the threshing cylinder, where they get their second chance to go through the mill.

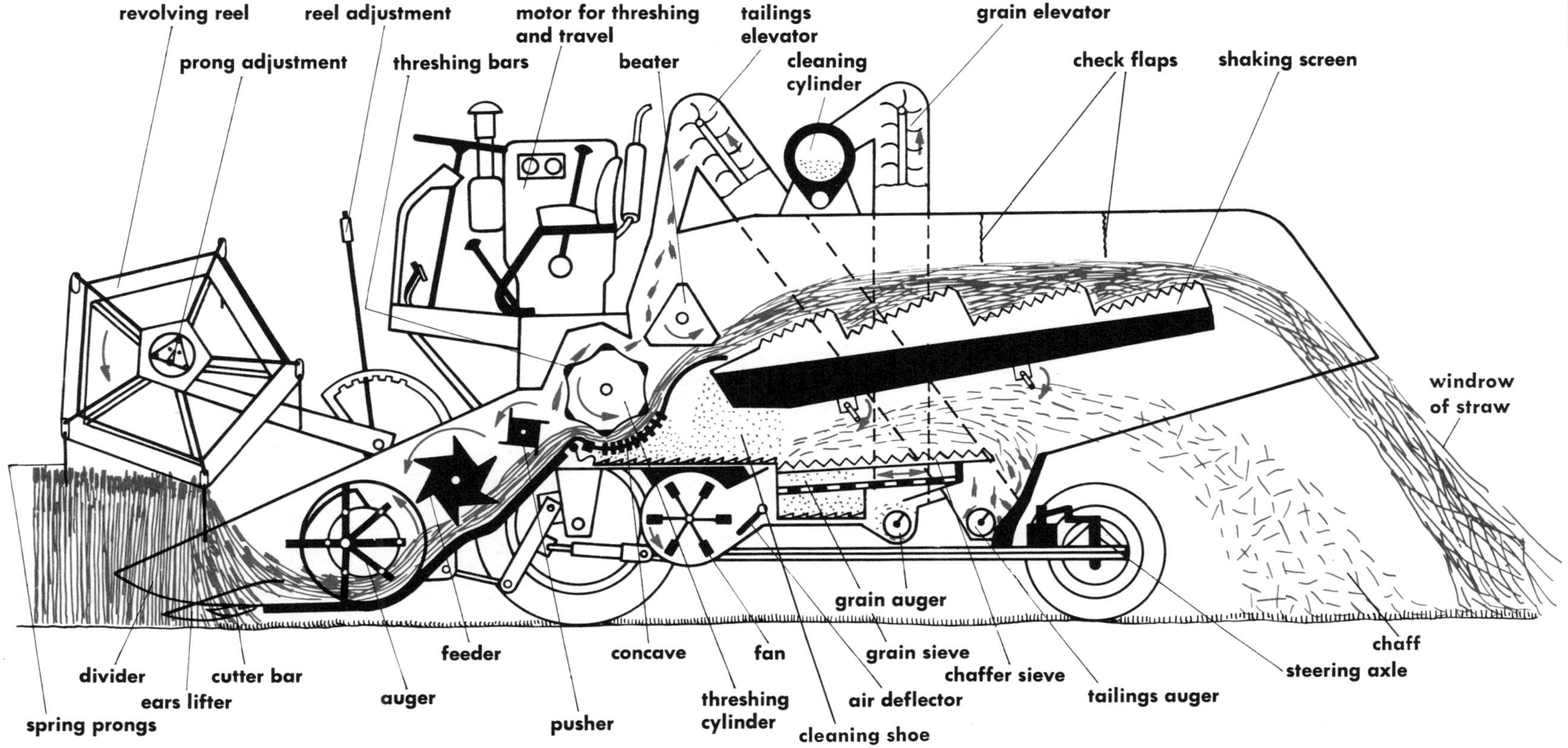
revolving reel
reel adjustment
motor for threshing and travel
tailings elevator
grain elevator
prong adjustment
threshing bars
beater
cleaning cylinder
check flaps
shaking screen
windrow of straw
divider
cutter bar
ears lifter
spring prongs
auger
feeder
pusher
concave
fan
threshing cylinder
grain auger
grain sieve
air deflector
cleaning shoe
chaffer sieve
tailings auger
steering axle
chaff

HELICOPTER

Airplanes have to move fast—keeping the air moving over their wings is the only way they have of obtaining the lift forces that keep them up in the air (page 52). And yet some jobs—like picking an astronaut out of the ocean—*require* that an aircraft stand still, or "hover," in the air for a while; and others—like patrolling a beach, a forest or a pipeline—require flight at low speeds.

What is needed for these jobs is an aircraft whose wings will produce "lift" even while it is moving slowly or even hovering over a fixed spot. The solution is the **helicopter**—a beast that at first sight

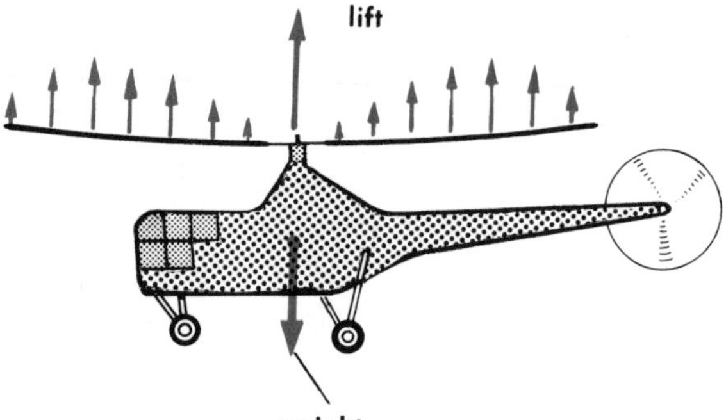

Fig. 1 WHIRLING ROTOR BLADES DEVELOP LIFT THAT COUNTERACTS HELICOPTER'S WEIGHT

does not seem to have wings at all. But all that has happened is that, in the helicopter, the wings have been taken off the main body, or *fuselage*, and placed above it, fitted onto a spinning hub. As they turn round and round, the wings—which have now become *rotor blades* —can have air flowing past them at high speed, producing "lift," even while the rest of the craft is not moving (Fig. 1).

So there is no problem about getting the craft airborne and keeping it airborne. Unfortunately, with a single rotor spinning away, forces will be set up that will start twisting the rest of the craft. The three standard ways of correcting this twist suggest the types of helicopter most often seen at airports and on television. These are: **dual rotors** placed at opposite ends of the fuselage (Fig. 2a); a **single main lifting rotor** with a small *antitorque* (that is, antitwist) *rotor* spinning vertically at the tail of the craft (Fig. 2b); and **two contrarotating rotors** mounted "coaxially"—that is, turning in opposite directions, with the shaft of the upper rotor running right through the middle of the shaft of the lower rotor (Fig. 2c).

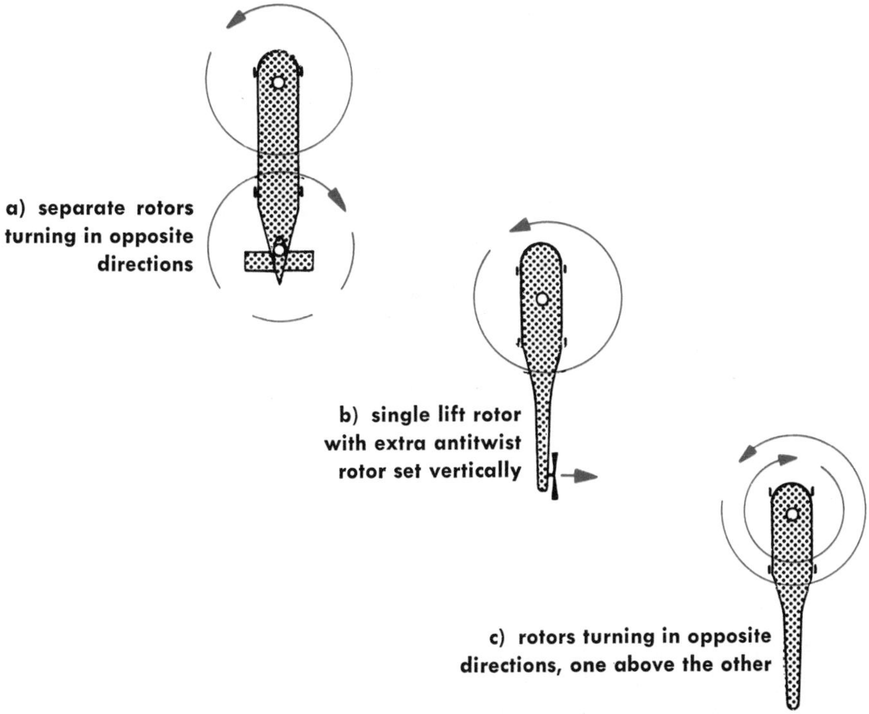

Fig. 2 TO PREVENT HELICOPTER FROM ROTATING DURING FLIGHT, SOME DESIGNS CALL FOR A SECOND HORIZONTAL ROTOR, OTHERS FOR A SMALL EXTRA ROTOR MOUNTED VERTICALLY

Now, a rotor directed straight up will clearly counteract the weight of the helicopter—but how will the craft move forward? The rotor could be tipped slightly forward—it would then still produce vertical forces to counteract the weight, but also a forward thrust. Unfortunately, this would also mean tipping the whole craft. What modern helicopters do instead is to tip the individual rotor blades as they turn.

Figure 3 suggests how this is done. Each rotor blade is free to swivel in such a way that the slant at which it pushes the air changes continuously as it sweeps through its 360°. This swiveling motion of the blades is controlled through a slim vertical *link* riding a *swash plate* that wobbles around the shaft. To head the craft on a given course, the pilot tilts the blades downward in the direction he has chosen. To do this, he changes the tilt of the swash plate, which in turn determines the tilt of the rotor blades. (The blades can also be

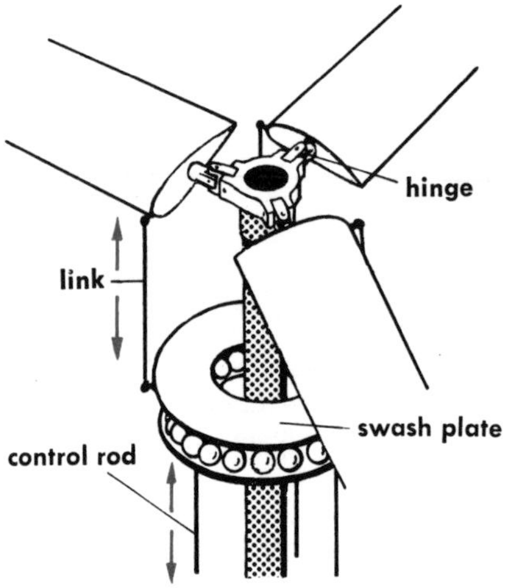

Fig. 3 PITCH OF ROTOR BLADES IS GOVERNED BY LINK, WHICH TRANSMITS WOBBLING MOTION OF SWASH PLATE. HINGES ALLOW BLADES TO FLAP, RELIEVING STRESS THAT WOULD OTHERWISE CAUSE REACTIONS IN REMAINDER OF HELICOPTER

attached with hinges that take the stress off their connection with the fuselage, allowing them to flap slightly during each cycle.)

During flight, the pilot manages the craft mainly through two controls. To change the direction of flight, he moves the *cyclic pitch stick* —called "cyclic" because it changes the pitch of the rotor blades at only one point in their cycle. To take the craft up or down, he uses the *collective pitch stick,* which changes the pitch of the rotor blades throughout their whole 360° cycle, carrying the craft as a whole higher or letting it descend. If the pilot, while traveling eastward, discovers that the craft's fuselage is facing in a slightly different direction, he works pedals that vary the pitch of the tail rotor until the craft "faces" its direction of travel again.

GAS TURBINES

In their source of power—they burn fuel in air and use the push of the resulting gases—gas turbines are INTERNAL-COMBUSTION ENGINES, just as much as the ones described on page 88. Except that in gas turbines, the hot expanding gases are not used to push pistons—they are used, instead, to turn the blade wheels of a turbine and produce rotary motion directly.

The best-known (and noisiest) varieties of gas turbine are the JET ENGINES of airplanes, described separately on page 140. But jet engines convert only as little of their power as possible to rotary motion—whereas other gas turbines devote all the power they produce to turning a main axle, or *shaft*. They are used to power the world-record-setting racing cars and high-speed ships like the Navy's PT boats—and, sometimes, simply as stationary power plants.

The gas turbine shown in the diagram is of the sort one might find used as a "stand-by" in electric-power plants to run an ELECTRIC GENERATOR. It has a single shaft that runs straight through it like a skewer from left to right. At its left end is a small *starter motor*, which is used at the very beginning to start the shaft rotating but not afterward.

The engine's three main parts are the air compressor, the combustion chamber, and the turbine. The **compressor** is itself much like a turbine, only operated backward: the blade wheels have the power and *they* push the air. Sandwiched between the moving, or rotating, blade wheels are stationary blade wheels. The moving blade wheels catch the incoming air and pack it between their own blades and the stationary blades, building up the air's pressure as it is tossed from one pair of wheels to the next. The air leaves the compressor under great pressure and rushes into the **combustion chamber,** where it meets the fuel, which is sprayed into the chamber all the time, without stopping. The fuel burns and the hot gases that result then expand against the blades of the **turbine,** making it turn. The power produced by the turbine is transmitted to the shaft, which passes on part of it to the compressor; only what is left is available for outside work, such as running an electric generator.

In Fig. 1, the exhaust gases are shown leaving at upper left after passing through a *heat exchanger*. Of course, after giving up most of their energy to the turbine, they could simply have been released immediately to the outside air. But they are still hot, and their heat can be put to good use by allowing them to warm up the fresh incoming air that is on its way to the compressor. This is done in the heat exchanger, in which pipes carrying air to the combustion chamber cross the exhaust channel; the gases themselves don't mix—only heat is exchanged.

Turbines are efficient, but they are expensive. Part of the reason is that the liquid fuels they use are more expensive than coal; another

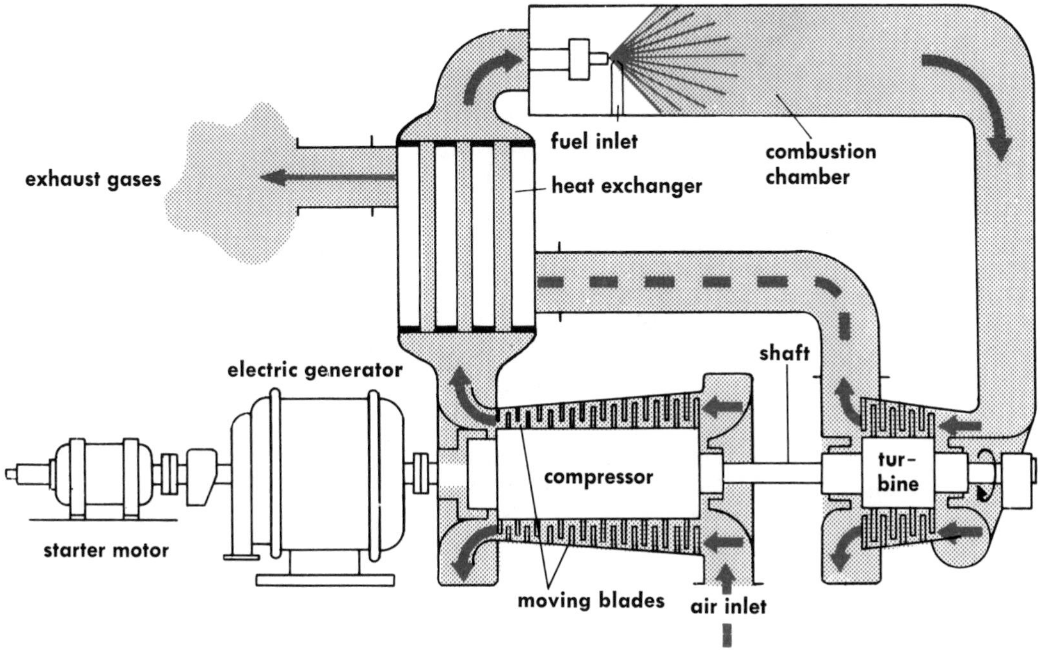

PATH OF GASES THROUGH GAS TURBINE

is that they keep hurling gases at temperatures around 1200° Fahrenheit at the turbine. Even the best steels can't take this forever—after a few thousand hours, the turbine blades are hopelessly eaten away and have to be replaced. As a result, gas turbines are seldom used in electric-power stations as main round-the-clock sources of power—but they are valuable as extra engines that can be started up quickly in times of sudden need.

JET ENGINES

Like ROCKETS, jet engines push themselves forward by building up pressure on gases in a combustion chamber, then releasing them from a nozzle at high speed. All the pressures across any diameter of the container are in balance except along one axis, in which pressure builds up at one end but is relieved by release of gases at the other. And so, as it expels exhaust gases from the rear, the engine is pushed forward (Fig. 1).

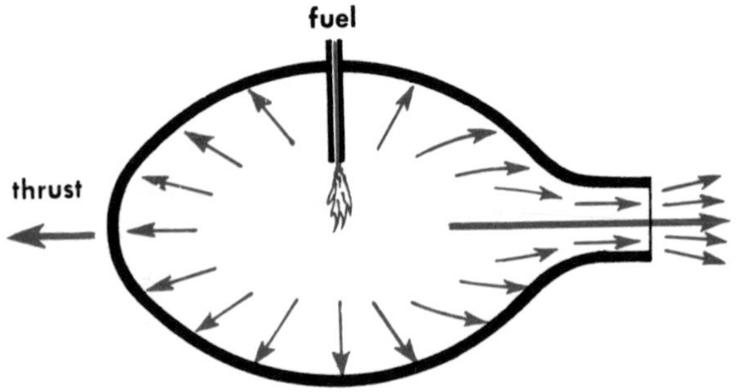

Fig. 1 EXPANDING GASES PUSHING AGAINST OPPOSITE SIDES BALANCE EACH OTHER, BUT ESCAPE OF GASES FROM REAR CREATES FORWARD THRUST

Unlike rockets, however, jets burn their fuel in ordinary air from the earth's atmosphere, building up the air's pressure in *compressors*. Their engines are much like the ones described under GAS TURBINES, except that in these other turbine engines, of the stationary kind, as much power as possible is turned into rotary motion—whereas in a propellerless airplane as much of it as possible is converted into building up the speed of the exhaust jet.

The key jet engine of today is the **turbojet,** which is the one used in high-speed, high-altitude long-distance flights (Fig. 2). Air is swallowed in at the front, where a *compressor*, made of rows of whirling fans sandwiched between fixed blades (as on page 139), compresses it. (This automatically raises its temperature.) The air rushes out from the last stage of the compressor and hurls itself into the *combustion chamber*, where a kerosene-like fuel is sprayed into it. (There is no cycle of different steps taking place in turn and then repeating, as in an automobile engine—the air and fuel keep coming continuously.)

Up to this point, the engine has not been producing power. But when the fuel starts burning in the compressed air, combustion gases expand with tremendous force. As they push their way to the exhaust, they give some of their energy to the turbine, making it turn at high

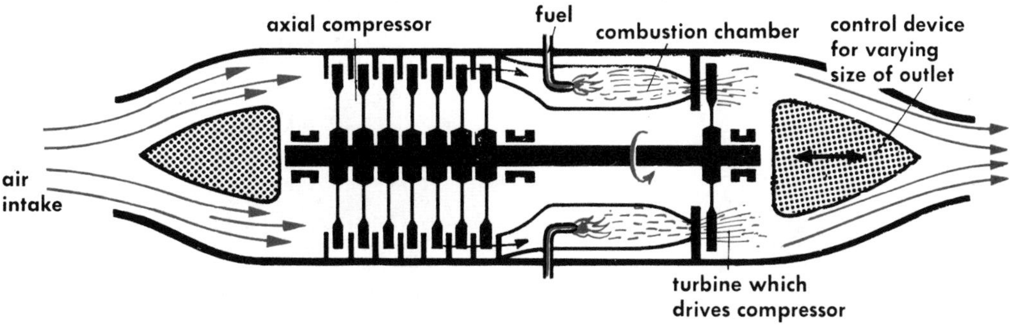

Fig. 2 IN TURBOJET ENGINE, A SMALL FRACTION OF ENERGY OF EXPANDING GASES TURNS TURBINE—REMAINDER SIMPLY GIVES SPEED TO EXHAUST JET

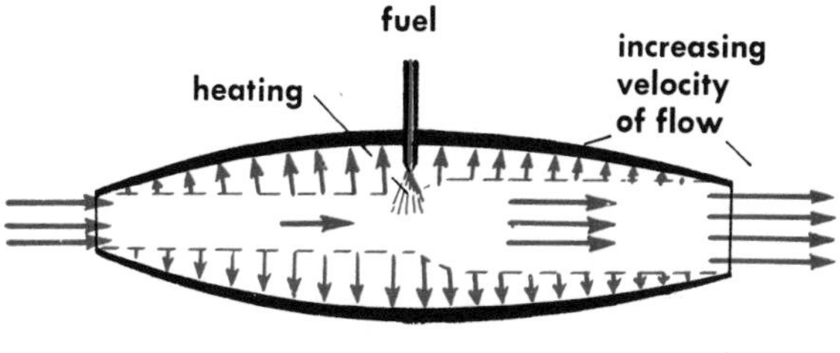

Fig. 3 IN RAMJET, FORWARD SPEED OF ENGINE MAKES COMPRESSOR UNNECESSARY

speed, but most of the energy shows itself directly in the speed of the exhaust jet—typically from 1,200 to 1,700 feet per second.

Why are the turbines needed? To drive the compressor. But when the engine reaches speeds around 300 and 400 miles an hour, the outside air "ramming" into the engine builds up so much pressure that the compressors are less and less needed—and neither, in that

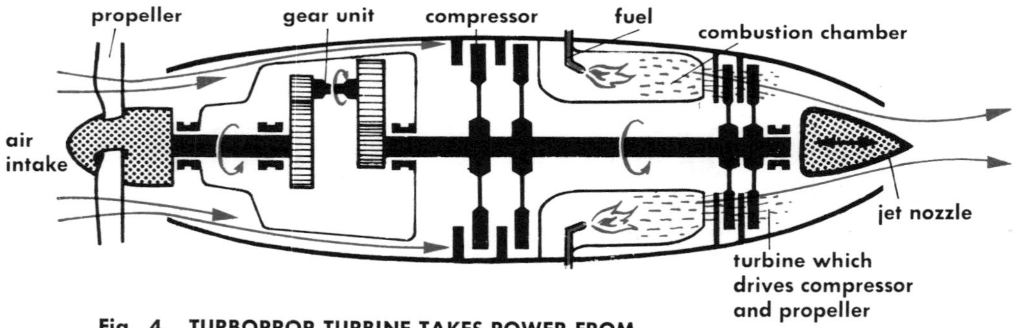

Fig. 4 TURBOPROP TURBINE TAKES POWER FROM EXPANDING GASES TO DRIVE PROPELLER

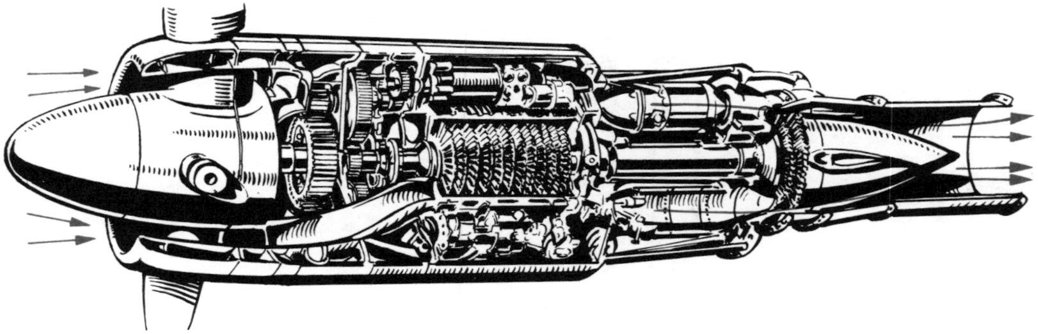

Fig. 5 TURBOPROP'S FANS (CENTER) ARE ITS COMPRESSOR; TURBINE WHEELS ARE AT RIGHT BETWEEN COMBUSTION CHAMBERS AND EXHAUST NOZZLE

case, are the turbines. An engine constructed on this principle from the start is called **ramjet.** It's beautifully simple (Fig. 3), but it always needs *something* to launch it and get its speed up at the beginning.

Among jet engines, the opposite of a ramjet (in which *no* power is taken from the jet to turn a shaft) is the **turboprop,** in which about 90% of the jet's power is drawn off by the turbine. The turbine turns a shaft, which drives not only a compressor but a *propeller* (Fig. 4). It may seem a shame to do this, after going to the trouble of building a jet. But for short low-altitude hops between cities, during which high speeds are never reached, the turboprop works out nicely. It still makes more sense than the old piston engines, with their wasteful back-and-forthing and their heavy cylinders. The turboprop engine (Fig. 5) works just like the GAS TURBINES described on page 138, except that the shaft now drives a propeller instead of an ELECTRIC GENERATOR.

SUPERSONIC SPEED

Supersonic speed refers to travel at a speed greater than the speed of sound. Since (at sea level) sound travels at 761 miles per hour, for a long time the only people who did practical work with such speeds were the people interested in bullets and the powders that propel them. Sound travels through the air as pressure waves, and the peculiar thing that happened when a bullet reached the speed of sound was that it caught up with its own pressure waves. These waves folded back over the bullet in the shape of a cone starting at the leading end (Fig. 1), forming also another cone at its rear end within which trails of eddies gathered in a low-pressure area.

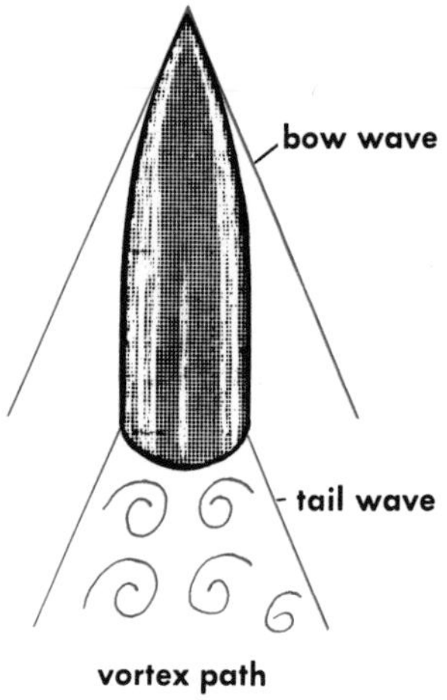

Fig. 1 SHOCK WAVES AROUND BULLET MOVING AT SUPERSONIC SPEED

The situation changed in 1947. On October 14 of that year, the American test pilot Charles E. Yeager took an airplane, the Bell X-1, right "through the sound barrier," reaching a speed 1.06 times the speed of sound. The Bell X-1 was rocket-propelled—but since then standard turbojet planes (see JET ENGINES) have crossed over into the supersonic region thousands of times.

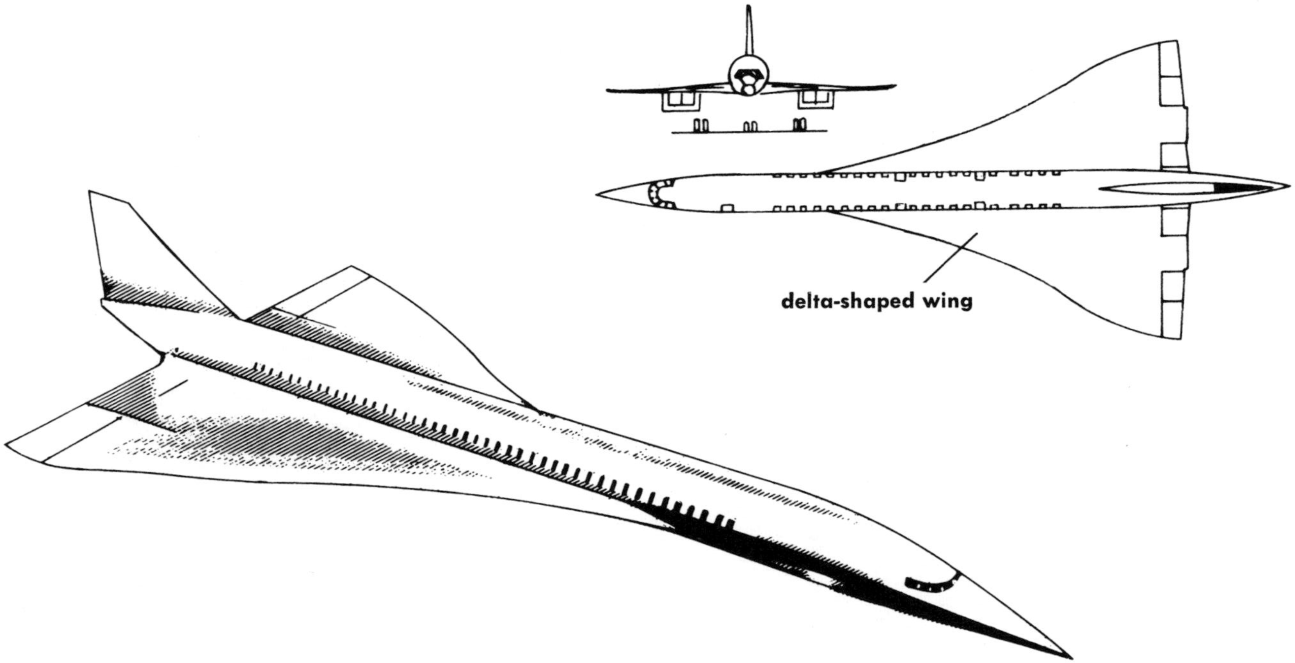

Fig. 2 SUPERSONIC PASSENGER AIRCRAFT (*CONCORDE*) DESIGNED TO FLY AT 2.2 TIMES THE SPEED OF SOUND

The usefulness of supersonic speeds is this:

When an aircraft approaches the speed of the pressure waves it has been pushing out ahead of it, these begin to pile up around it, creating sharp *shock waves* of extremely high temperature and pressure that make the craft difficult to manage and put dangerously high stresses on its materials. These conditions last throughout the range from about 0.8 to 1.05 the speed of sound. But between 1.05 and 2 times the speed of sound is a nice range of speeds that make good sense for high-altitude long-distance flight and that offer few problems once the craft has reached them.

Unfortunately, one cannot design a plane only for its cruising speed. One has to design it also for the low speeds its requires at take-off and landing. With planes flying at only a few hundred miles an hour, this is no great problem, and adjustable flaps on the wings' trailing edges give the plane whatever extra lift it needs at low speeds. But the difference between conditions above and below the speed of sound is enormous, and designs for supersonic planes include arrangements that allow the craft to transform itself in flight almost from one kind of plane into another.

The three large transport planes designed for supersonic flight in the early 1970's are the French-English *Concorde* (Fig. 2), the Soviet TU-144, and the Boeing SST (since postponed). For low speeds and for take-off and landing the American SST would carry its wings

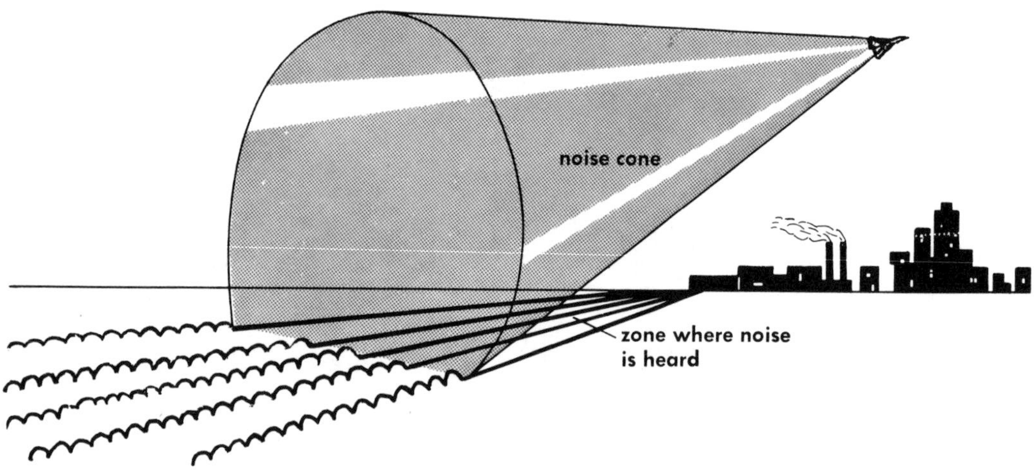

Fig. 3 NOISE PRODUCED BY BOW WAVE OF SUPERSONIC AIRCRAFT

forward; these would then sweep aft when the plane reached its cruising speed, which is 1,800 mph. (At 64,000 feet, the planned cruising altitude, this is 2.7 times the speed of sound.) It would be powered by four turbojet engines, each of them 6 feet in diameter and 25 feet long, and for take-off it would require a field 6,800 feet long—or about 1¼ miles.

As it flies through the air, a plane flying at supersonic speed sweeps a huge shock wave along with it, in the shape of the wall of a cone that stretches around and behind it (Fig. 3). As the edge of the cone passes by him, a person on the ground will hear the "sonic boom"—a powerful low-pitched sound (just like an explosion) that is heard for miles around.

IV Electricity At Work

ELECTRIC CHARGE

The lightning that follows the swift rushing of raindrops in a thundercloud, the shock one gets on touching a metal doorknob after one's shoes have been brushing against the pile of a rug—both represent the discharge, or unloading, of electric charge.

A good way of experimenting with these charges of electricity is to set up a post with an overhanging top (like a modern street light) and hang two balls of pith from it by silk threads—pith being the light, spongy core of marshland rushes and some trees.

If the two pith balls have been charged by being touched with a dry *glass rod* that has been rubbed with *silk* (Fig. 1) and are then allowed to swing free, they will shy away from each other—they *repel* each other (Fig. 3a). The conclusion is that "like charges repel." If they have both been charged by contact with a *hard-rubber comb or rod* that has been rubbed with *flannel* (Fig. 2), the same thing happens (Fig. 3b). But if one has been charged by glass and the other by hard rubber, they rush toward each other (Fig. 3c). The conclusion is that "unlike charges attract." Once they have touched each other, however, they lose their charge and are said to have been *neutralized* (Fig. 3d).

Further experimenting, with other materials, confirms that there are two different kinds of charge, but only two. By agreement among all people interested in the question since Benjamin Franklin, the plus signs ("positive") are saved for the charges from glass, the minus signs ("negative") for those from hard rubber.

One cannot give a positive charge to the glass rod without leaving the silk negative. This is easily checked by bringing the silk near a negatively charged ball: it immediately pushes it away. And if the rod and the silk it was rubbed with are brought back together, snugly, their charges disappear. These experiments suggest that the positive and negative charges are in balance. No surplus of either kind was created. The charges can be merged (the materials carrying them

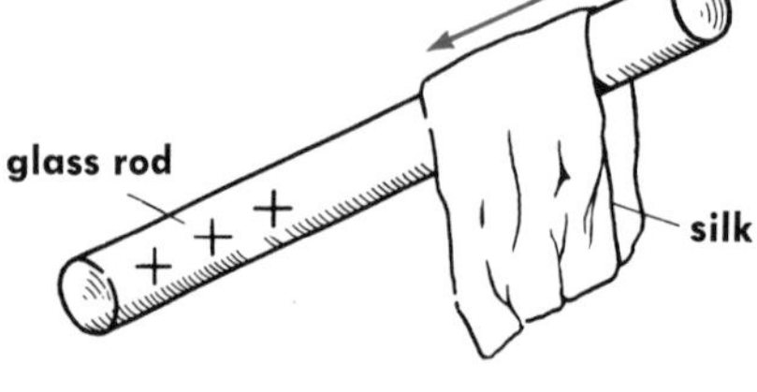

Fig. 1 GLASS ROD RUBBED WITH SILK DEVELOPS POSITIVE CHARGE

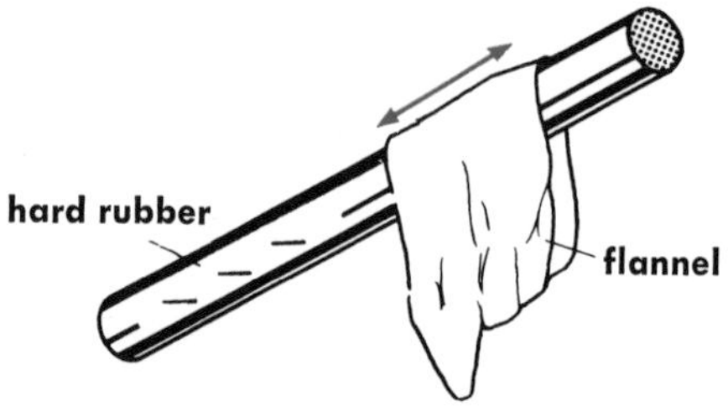

Fig. 2 HARD RUBBER RUBBED WITH FLANNEL DEVELOPS NEGATIVE CHARGE

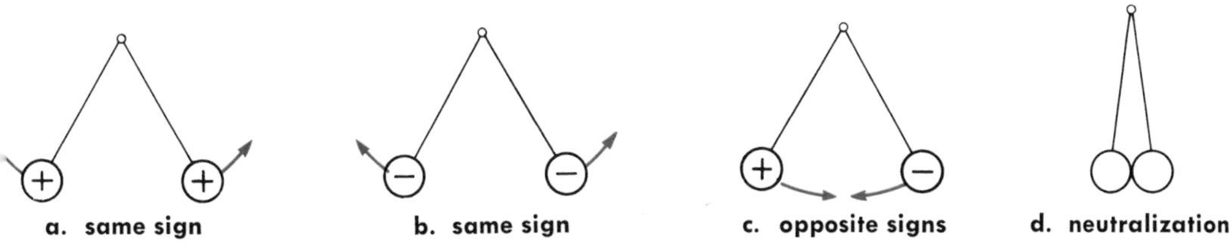

Fig. 3 HOW PITH BALLS ATTRACT AND REPEL EACH OTHER, DEPENDING ON THEIR CHARGE

then being neutralized) or they can be reseparated and brought out into the open, but they cannot be created or destroyed.

These observations acquired new meaning when, in the early years of this century, atoms came to be thought of as made up of small, heavy, positively charged cores surrounded by shells of light, negative electrons. Negative charge could then be understood as a local surplus of electrons, positive charge as a shortage.

The mention of metal doorknobs and silk threads suggests something else: some materials (silver, copper) *conduct* electric charges, passing them right on to the next object or to the ground. Others (silk, glass, rubber) act as insulators, stopping charges in their path. **Capacitors,** in which charge can be stored, take advantage of this difference. They consist of plates that conduct electricity separated

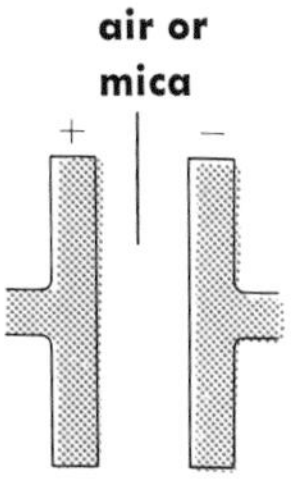

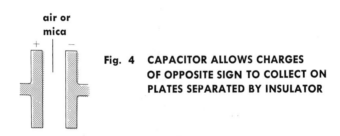

Fig. 4 CAPACITOR ALLOWS CHARGES OF OPPOSITE SIGN TO COLLECT ON PLATES SEPARATED BY INSULATOR

by thin spaces that don't (Fig. 4). (The space can be air—or mica or wax paper.) By bridging the two end plates of a capacitor with a conductor, all the electrons that have been collected on one side can be discharged.

Every radio contains capacitors—traditionally, little cylinders in which layers of metal foil alternating with wax-paper insulation are rolled up and sealed from moisture. The radio's tuning control governs a **variable capacitor.** It has two sets of parallel aluminum plates; when the listener turns the knob, the two sets mesh into each other or separate, as one's fingers do when one is clasping or unclasping one's hands.

INCANDESCENT LAMP

(LIGHT BULB)

A good many metals won't glow when heated—they melt first. But *tungsten* will not melt till heated to some point beyond 6100° Fahrenheit, and for this reason tungsten is at the heart of every incandescent lamp, or light bulb. When a lamp glows, it is because a very thin, tightly coiled wire of tungsten is being heated to more than

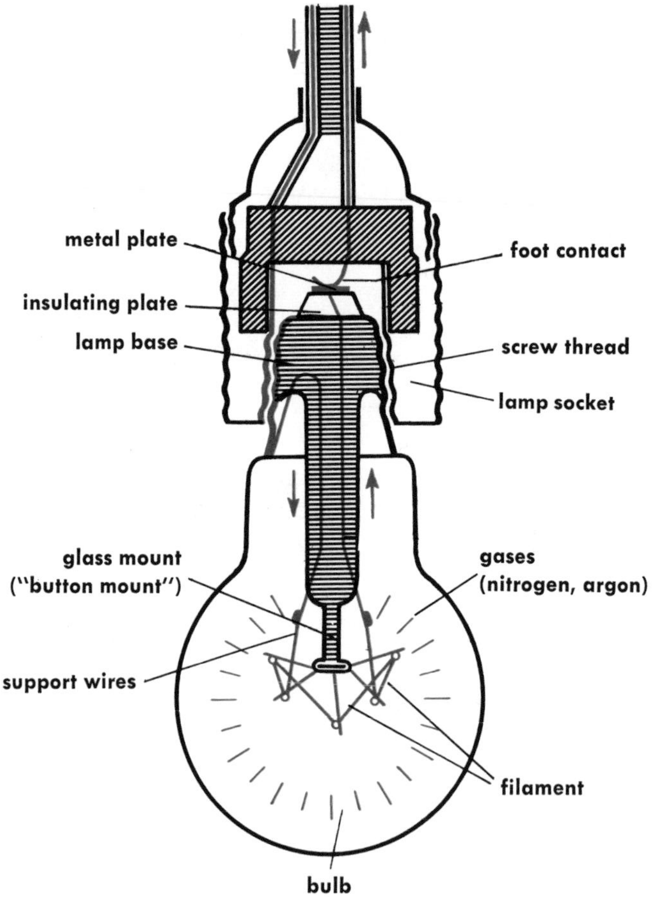

Fig. 1 PATH OF CURRENT (RED) IN INCANDESCENT LAMP. IN ALTERNATING-CURRENT SYSTEMS, CURRENT SWITCHES DIRECTION 120 TIMES PER SECOND

5000° Fahrenheit by the resistance it offers to ELECTRIC CURRENT. The heat one feels near the bulb is wasted, but it is the only way the lamp will also produce light. In fact, much of the *light* it produces is wasted because its vibrations are too slow (infrared) or too fast (ultraviolet) for the human eye to respond to them.

When the light switch is turned on, the little wire, called a *filament,* is cold. It offers little resistance to the current, which rushes through at a great rate, so that for the first fraction of a second a 60-watt bulb is in fact consuming a little over 600 watts of electric power. But the tungsten's resistance to electric current increases as it heats up—the bulb's power-gobbling quickly levels off to 60 watts and the filament takes on the familiar yellow-white glow.

If the air in the room were now allowed near it, the tungsten would simply burn up. So it is sealed in a glass bulb, and the bulb is filled with a mixture of *gases,* like nitrogen and argon, that don't readily react with metals. The engineers who design bulbs know that the higher the temperature, the more light the filament will offer for each watt of power. But they have also discovered that very high temperatures excite the tungsten atoms to leave the filament—they then settle on the inside of the glass bulb in the form of a black dust. The filament is less than a thousandth of an inch thick, and the more its material flies off, the sooner it breaks. So the engineers settle on a compromise between brilliant light and a bulb that will last.

In the usual screw-base design, the electric current reaches the bulb and leaves it through the brass collar surrounding the base and through the spot of lead at the tip of the base. Ordinary household current is alternating current—it switches direction 120 times per second—so that each terminal is used in turn as an entrance and as an exit. Flashlight bulbs work from BATTERIES, which yield current that flows in only one direction. Since a filament glows whenever it offers resistance to a current, it doesn't matter which way the current is flowing.

Three-way light bulbs have two filaments that can be used separately or together to produce 100, 200, or 300 watts—just as a nickel and dime can, between them, produce 5, 10, or 15 cents.

ELECTRIC CURRENT

Current is a process, an activity—not a "thing." So we cannot draw a picture of electric current and say, "This is what it looks like." But we can connect a flashlight bulb to a battery and watch it light up; and afterward, when we touch the bulb, it feels warm.

We can also obtain a current by joining the two sides of a *capacitor* that has been charged (page 151), but this will produce only a single surge of current. After this current has spent itself, whatever difference in ELECTRIC CHARGE there was between the two sides of the capacitor has disappeared and there is no reason for electrons to flow along the wire. To obtain a current that will *keep* flowing, we connect the bulb to a source that *maintains* a difference between its terminals, like a battery.

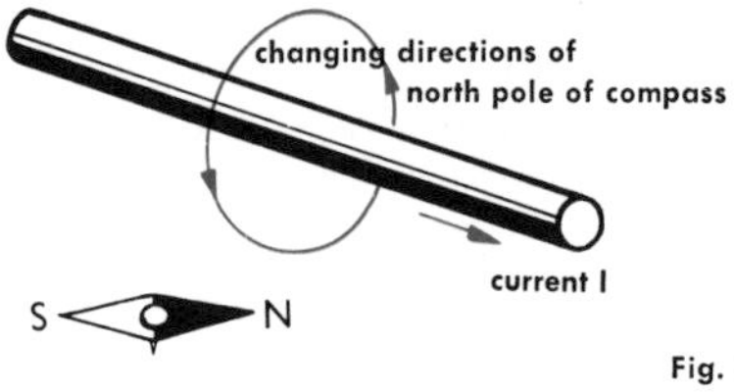

Fig. 1 WHEN WIRE IS CARRYING CURRENT AS SHOWN, NORTH POLE OF MAGNETIC COMPASS WILL FACE INWARD INTO PAPER IF HELD UNDER WIRE, OUTWARD FROM PAPER IF HELD ABOVE

Apart from their heating effect, used in an INCANDESCENT LAMP (light bulb), electric currents have ways of arising in chemical reactions (as in BATTERIES and FUEL CELLS) and, in other situations, of building fields of magnetic influence around them. When an electric charge moves along a wire, it acts as if it were a magnet. In Fig. 1, the north (dark) tip of the magnetic needle moves downward if it's held on this side of the page; if carried under the wire, it would point into the page. If carried behind the page, it would point upward; and if held above the wire, it would point toward us, out of the page. (In the diagram, this circling magnetic field is indicated by the red loop with arrowheads.)

One can make use of this effect in the following way:

Considering the wire as if it were seen from above, the magnetic force pulling the north needle upward is on the left. If one now bends the wire to the left, and continues to bend it (keeping it level) till one has looped it full circle, the space with the circle will be filled with magnetic forces that will all tend to tilt the north end of the compass needle upward. If one continues coiling the wire (using insulated wire), one ends up with a modestly effective magnetic coil.

An iron core (Fig. 2) will make the magnet stronger. (The best iron for this is "soft iron," which contains almost no carbon.) But the magnet is not "permanent"—as soon as the current is switched off, the magnetic force disappears. It is called an **electromagnet,** and can, for instance, be used at the end of a crane cable to catch hold of scrap metal in junk yards. Or two coils (wound in opposite directions) can be yoked together (Fig. 3), horseshoe style. An immense number of electrical devices (among them FUSES, RELAYS, buzzers and LOUDSPEAKERS) are built around electromagnets.

The motion of electric charges and their magnetic effect are knotted together in fundamental ways that make them quite inseparable. Imagine, for instance, a copper wire, not connected to a battery, held vertically between the two poles of a horizontal magnet (Fig. 4). Now, if this wire (kept vertical) is moved from left to right, the outer electrons of its atoms of copper will be charges in motion in a magnetic field. They will be propelled at right angles to the field (which is horizontal) and at right angles to their own motion—the result

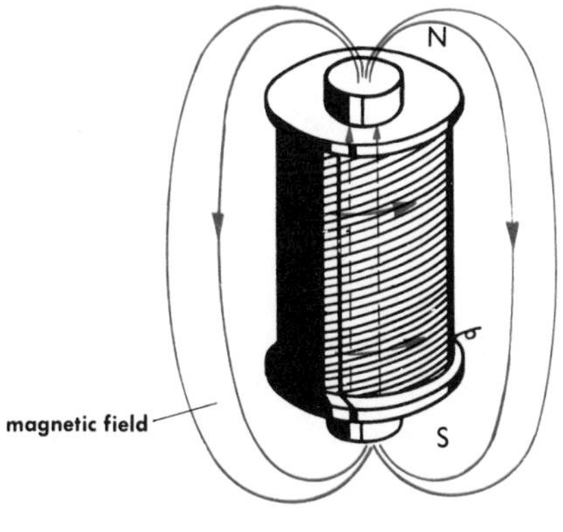

Fig. 2 COILED WIRE ALLOWS AN EFFECTIVE MAGNETIC FIELD TO BUILD UP ALONG AXIS OF COIL, MAKING ELECTROMAGNET. IRON CORE INCREASES STRENGTH OF FIELD

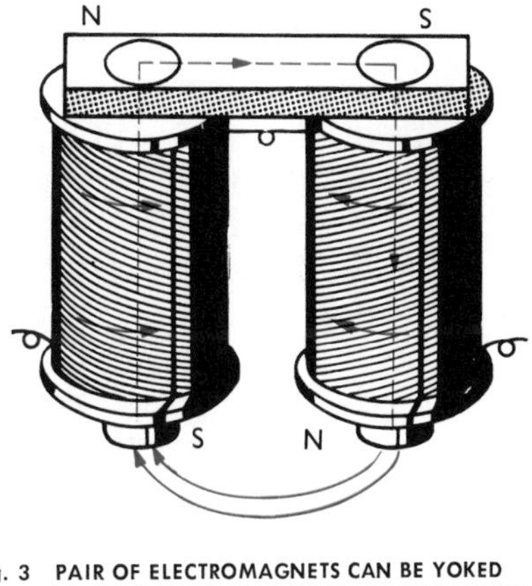

Fig. 3 PAIR OF ELECTROMAGNETS CAN BE YOKED TO FORM HORSESHOE WITH OPPOSITE POLES SIDE BY SIDE (THE TWO COILS ARE WOUND IN OPPOSITE DIRECTIONS)

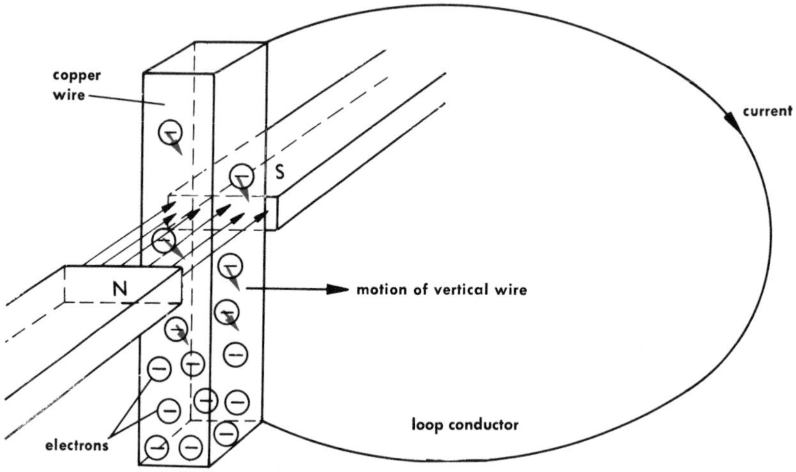

Fig. 4 MOVING WIRE ACROSS MAGNETIC FIELD STARTS A FLOW OF CURRENT

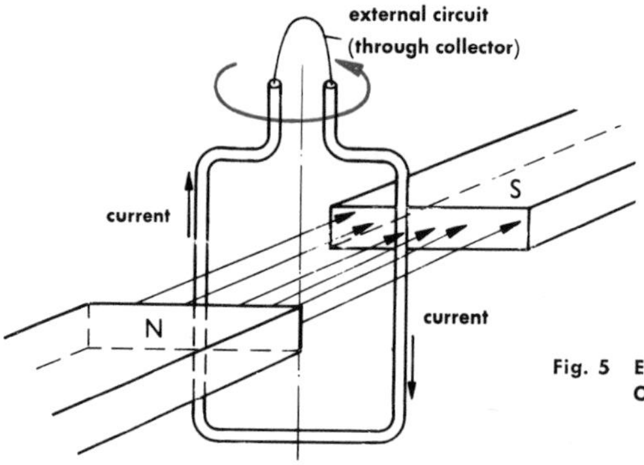

Fig. 5 ELECTRIC GENERATOR IS MADE BY TWIRLING LOOP OF WIRE IN MAGNETIC FIELD

being that they will be flowing as a current in the wire. This current is called an *induced* current and the effect is known as *induction.*

This is the effect used at power stations to produce electricity for cities. A version of the setup using a turning loop appears in Fig. 5. In full-scale installations, thousands of turns of fine wire are mounted on a frame called an *armature* that is turned by a motor within a circle of magnetic fields placed around the turning frame. As the frame turns, current is "induced" in its copper windings and is sent to the city's underground power cables.

SWITCH

Electricity differs from other forms of power in the ease with which it is switched on or off. By operating a switch, an electric circuit that has been open can be closed (as in buzzers, telephone dialing systems, automobile ignitions); a circuit that has been closed can be opened (burglar alarms); or ELECTRIC CURRENT can be switched from one circuit to another (traffic lights, channel selectors on television sets).

In an electrical wire, all one needs is a single break to stop current from flowing. Switches offer firm (YES or NO), safe ways of interrupting the current and of letting it run again. Apart from special low-current situations, such as radio circuits, in which transistors or radio tubes conduct electric current and interrupt it, a switch is usually a link of metal that bridges two terminals. The simplest switch is the **knife switch** (Fig. 1), in which a copper knife, or rod, pivoted on one contact is swung onto or off the other.

There is no problem in closing a circuit, but breaking it tends to cause a small arc—very much like lightning—to leap up between the

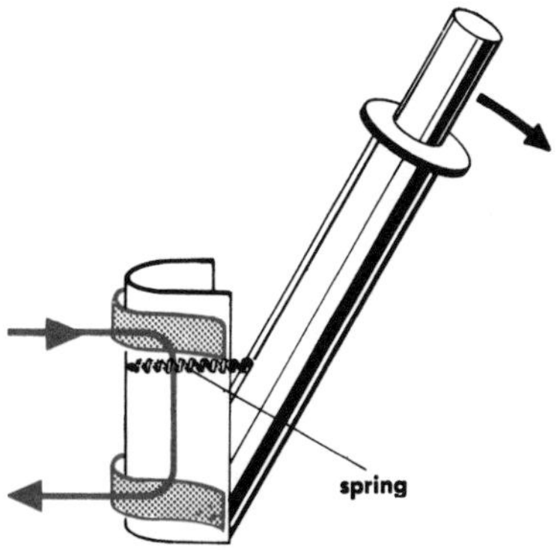

Fig. 1 KNIFE SWITCH—PATH OF CURRENT SHOWN IN RED

terminals. The flash can easily pit or melt the metal in the switch and destroy it (quite apart from the danger to the person throwing the switch). To guard against this, household switches are made with a "snap" feature. In the **turn switch** (Fig. 2), **tumbler switch** (Fig. 3), and **push-button switch** (Fig. 4), one's thumb or knuckle first meets resistance from a spring—one pushes but nothing happens. Then,

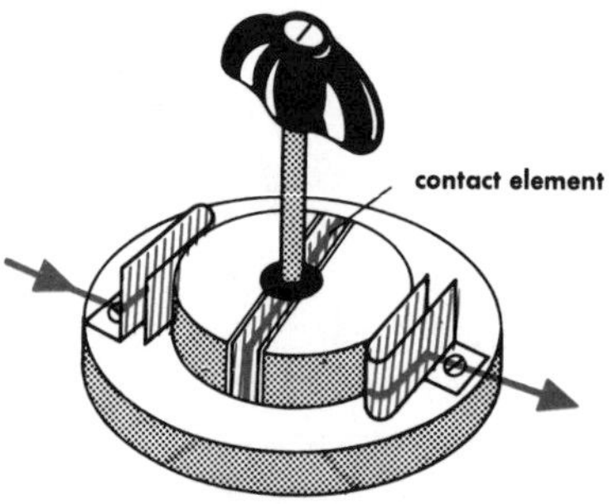

Fig. 2 TURN SWITCH—GAP PROVIDES RESTING POINTS

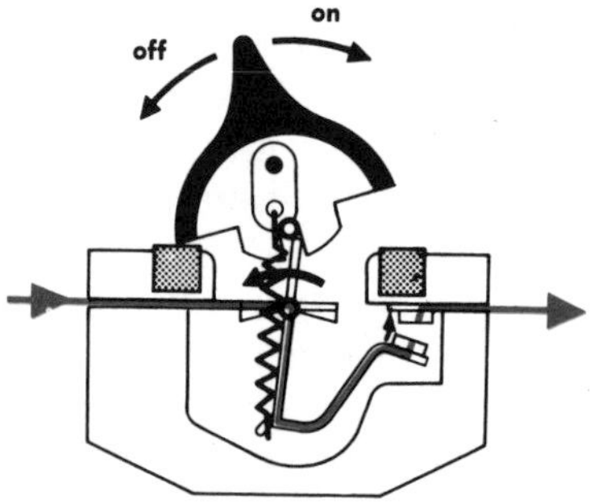

Fig. 3 TUMBLER SWITCH

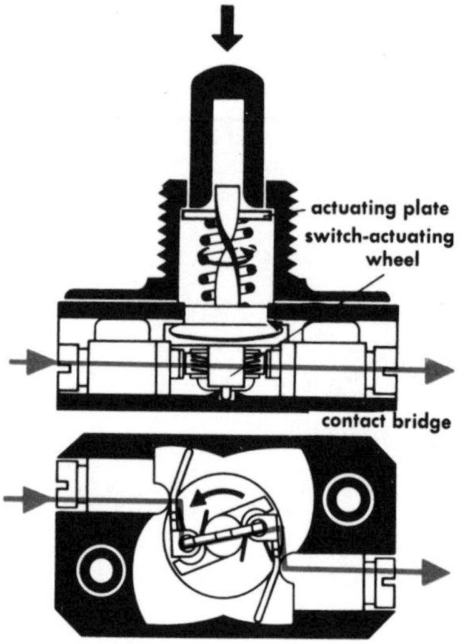

Fig. 4 PUSH-BUTTON SWITCH SEEN FROM THE SIDE (TOP VIEW) AND FROM ABOVE THE BUTTON (BELOW)

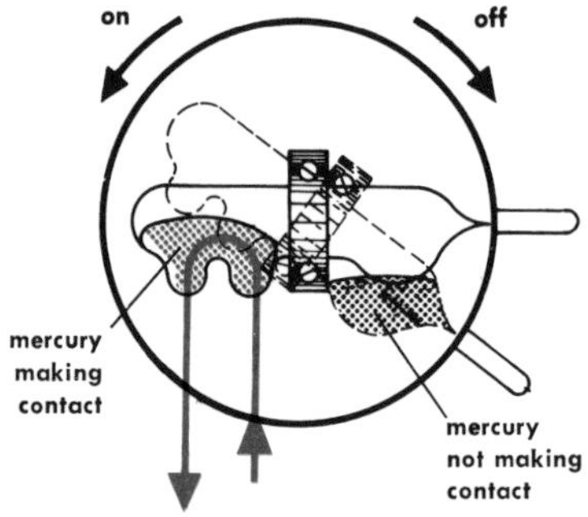

Fig. 5 MERCURY SWITCH. TILTING BULB ALLOWS MERCURY TO MAKE CONTACT

suddenly, the energy stored in the spring is released and the switch opens or closes smartly.

The **mercury switch** (Fig. 5) also closes the circuit with a metal link—but the metal, being mercury, is liquid. Flipping the switch tilts the bulb and lets the mercury flow, making or breaking the contact. In the bulb, the space above the mercury is filled with a protective atmosphere of nitrogen; since nitrogen is inactive chemically, the contact area stays clean.

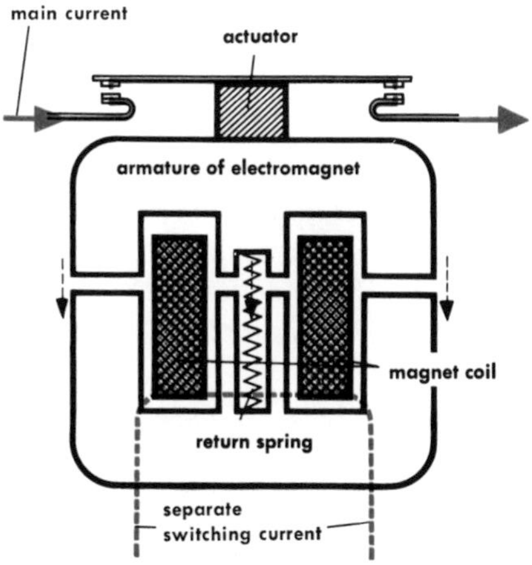

Fig. 6 ELECTROMAGNETIC SWITCH. DOWNWARD THRUST OF ARMATURE COMPRESSES SPRING; RELEASE OF SPRING BREAKS CONTACTS IN MAIN CURRENT AT TOP

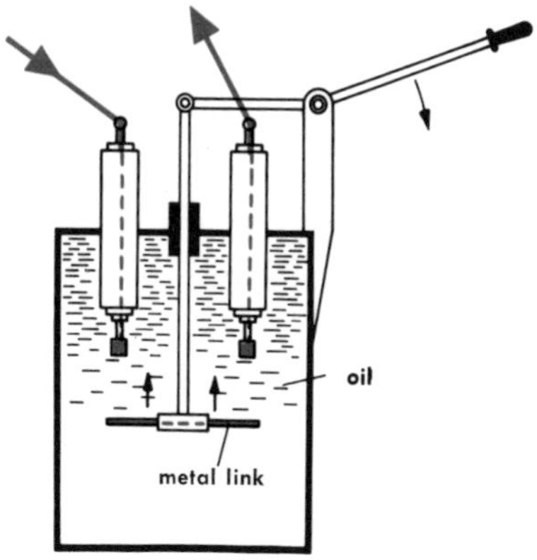

Fig. 7 OIL-BREAK SWITCH

One design, useful where a great quantity of current has to be stopped, is the **electromagnetic switch** (Fig. 6), in which a spring is compressed by an electromagnet (page 155). When the spring is released, it forces the circuit's elements apart and breaks the current. In the **oil-break switch,** which can be operated by hand (Fig. 7) or through an electromagnet, the contacts are separated under oil. As soon as the arc begins to form, the oil releases bubbles of hydrogen that break it up.

FUSE

A fuse is a part of a circuit that is made weak on purpose—it melts before anything else does (Fig. 1). In almost every situation in which electricity is used, a fuse is included at some point. It is placed between the circuit it protects and the wires or house mains that bring in the power. In this way, all the electricity has to pass through a small metal link in this fuse. This link is usually made of tin, a metal that melts even more easily than lead.

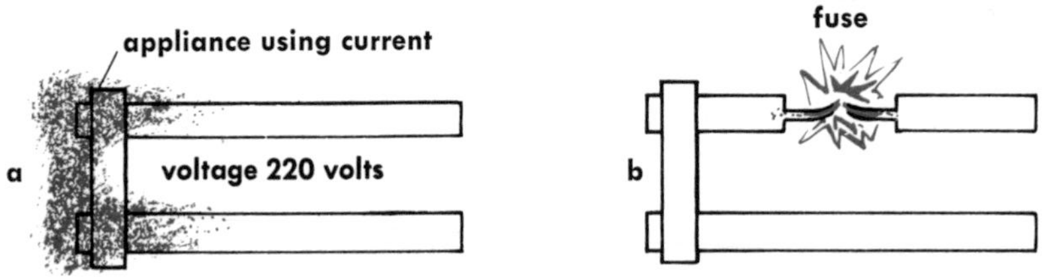

Fig. 1 ELECTRIC CURRENT GENERATES HEAT WHEREVER IT IS USED (a). BY INSERTING FUSE IN CIRCUIT (b), ONE ENSURES THAT EXCESS CURRENT PRODUCES EXCESS HEAT AT FUSE—AUTOMATICALLY STOPPING FLOW OF CURRENT

A flashlight has no fuse. That's because a flashlight is cheap and the electricity flowing in it is of no danger to anyone. But air conditioners are protected by fuses because if some of their parts gave out and suddenly allowed tremendous currents to flow straight through the machine, other parts would burn out and be expensive to replace. Every house or apartment has a whole boxful of fuses because if for any reason an electric wire or SWITCH started carrying more current than its insulation was designed for, enough heat might develop to set nearby parts of the house on fire.

The main differences among fuses are in the amount of current for which they are "rated"—that is, the amount of current they will let through without melting and breaking the circuit. Fuses also have difference shapes, but these differences simply reflect differences in the amount of current they are meant to carry.

Electrical appliances like radios sometimes have small fuses that are no bigger than the little capsules that enclose antibiotic drugs. Heavy-duty fuses used in factories are cylinders, or "cartridges," about the size of a finger, with metal tips. These carry currents of 30 amperes or more without burning out, or "blowing."

House fuses, in basements or in apartment hallways, are usually plug fuses (Fig. 2). Their "shells" carry a brass screw thread (like the bases of light bulbs). The part one sees when one looks at a fuse in a fuse box is the transparent flat face. When the metal has melted, a colored spot appears—the circuit is open and no electricity can flow through.

Most fuse boxes hold fuses rated to carry a current no stronger than 15 amperes, or "amps," for short. Most house wiring is also rated to carry currents of 15 amperes. (This refers to steady currents, or to currents lasting more than a few seconds. Occasional quick surges lasting only a fraction of a second don't raise neighboring temperatures enough to be fire hazards.) If a 15-amp fuse blows, it is not a good idea to replace it with a 20-amp fuse "so that it won't blow"—because if one did, the house wiring would then be the "weakest link" in the circuit and the house itself would be endangered.

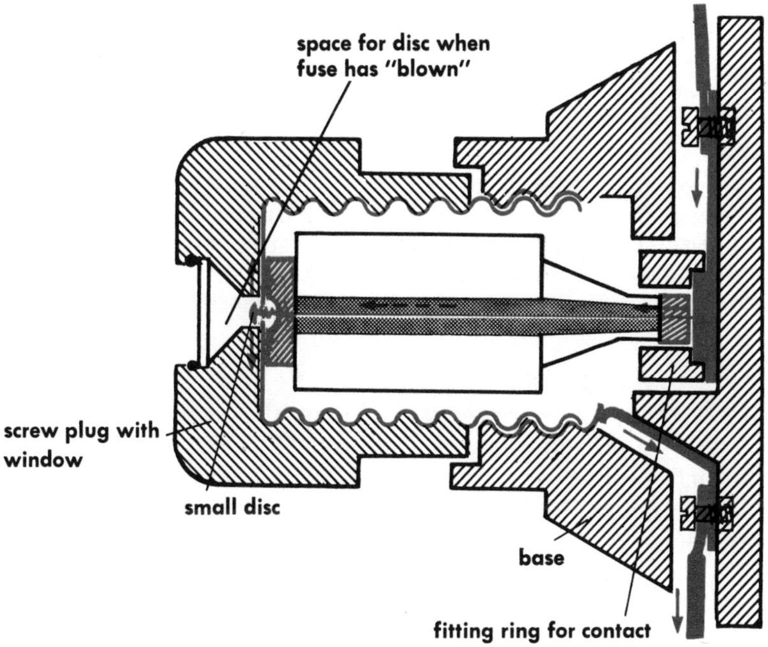

Fig. 2 SIDE VIEW OF PLUG FUSE SCREWED INTO SOCKET (PATH OF CURRENT IS SHOWN IN RED)

RELAY

Once one has discovered how strong the magnetic field of a coil is when it has an iron core (as on page 155), one can watch a vertical coil "grab" the core when one turns it off. If one holds the core steady, and flicks the switch on and off, it will grab and release any piece of iron brought near it. But suppose one used this motion to open and close a switch? The switch could then control *another* ELECTRIC CURRENT: the coil and switch would then be working as an **electromagnetic relay.**

The word "relay" is the same as that used in "relay races"; electromagnetic relays were originally used to help stretch the range of TELE-

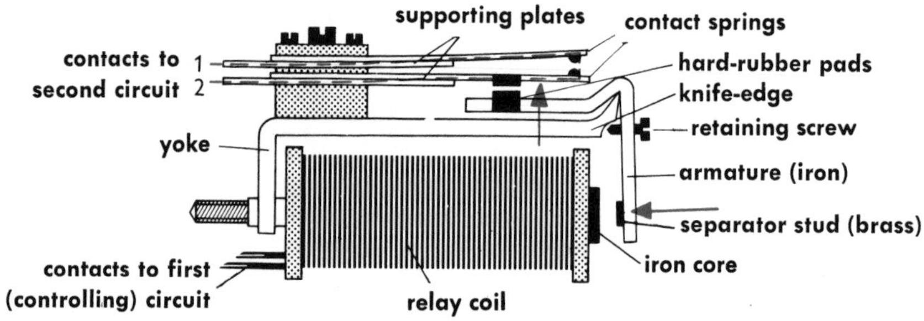

ELECTROMAGNETIC RELAY ALLOWS CURRENT IN ONE CIRCUIT (CONNECTED AT LOWER LEFT) TO CONTROL OPERATION OF ANOTHER CIRCUIT (CONNECTED AT UPPER LEFT). ARMATURE IS FREE TO TEETER ON KNIFE-EDGE. WHEN COIL ATTRACTS LOWER ARM OF ARMATURE, UPPER ARM MOVES UPWARD, PRESSING CONTACTS TOGETHER. THIS ALLOWS CURRENT TO FLOW IN SECOND CIRCUIT

GRAPH signals—by triggering a relay, the original signal could start a fresh signal going in a new circuit. This second circuit could again, through another relay, trigger a third one even farther away.

Although the various stretches of relay-linked circuits reached farther and farther out, each was similar to the preceding one. But electromagnetic relays can also be used to join different *kinds* of circuits. For instance, a visitor standing on the twelfth floor of a building can "push the button" to call an elevator. This button will not have to be connected to heavy-current lines that control the motor of the elevator—it can simply lead to a relay. The relay will then close a second circuit that will start current flowing in the electric motor that controls the elevator—and this second circuit, meanwhile, can contain another relay that allows current to flow only when the elevator is not already running. Standing near the elevator shaft at the top floor of a building, one can sometimes hear the relays clicking away as call signals come from the floors below.

In its actual design, an electromagnetic relay has three main parts: a part that starts it, or "actuates" it; a part that moves (the *armature*, or "clapper"); and a set of electrical *contacts* (which are part of the second circuit).

The relay in the diagram is set into action by current reaching from bottom left in the diagram and passing through its coil. As the coil develops its magnetic field, its core becomes strongly magnetic and pulls the lower part of the armature toward it. The armature as a whole teeters on the *knife-edge*, sending a *hard-rubber pad* (the lower one) upward. This pad then kicks the upper one, which is mounted on a flexible plate. This plate is bent upward, causing the two metal *contacts* to join. The result of this whole train of events is that the *second* electrical circuit, reached through the contacts in the upper left corner, has now been switched from open to closed.

Apart from being useful (it is found by the *millions* in telephone exchanges), a relay is an interesting sort of animal. It begins as a purely electrical connection; then goes on to develop magnetism; then transfers energy purely mechanically (teetering, pushing); and finally becomes a purely electrical contact again. (It is to make electrical contact quite impossible in the middle part that the pads are made of hard rubber.)

Nothing has been said of the brass *stud* on the armature. It is there because the armature, made of iron, after being exposed over and over to the magnetic field of the coil, tends to pick up a lingering bit of permanent magnetism—it tends, after a while, to want to hug the iron core and stay there. A brass separator, put between the two parts, ensures that the armature bounces away neatly after the current of the coil is shut off.

ELECTRIC GENERATOR

Generators are machines that are used to produce large amounts of electrical energy. They operate on the principle of electrical induction, in which electricity is produced in a circular conductor by the periodic changing of the direction of magnetism passing through the conductor. To accomplish this, the circular conductor, called a loop, is rotated in a constant magnetic field, or the loop can be keep stationary and the magnetic field rotated. In the first instance the loop is formed by the *armature winding* on the *stator* (Fig. 2) which revolves around the fixed magnetic poles of the *rotor*. Alternatively, the armature is

Fig. 1 ALTERNATING-CURRENT GENERATOR
(*internal pole machine, schematic*)

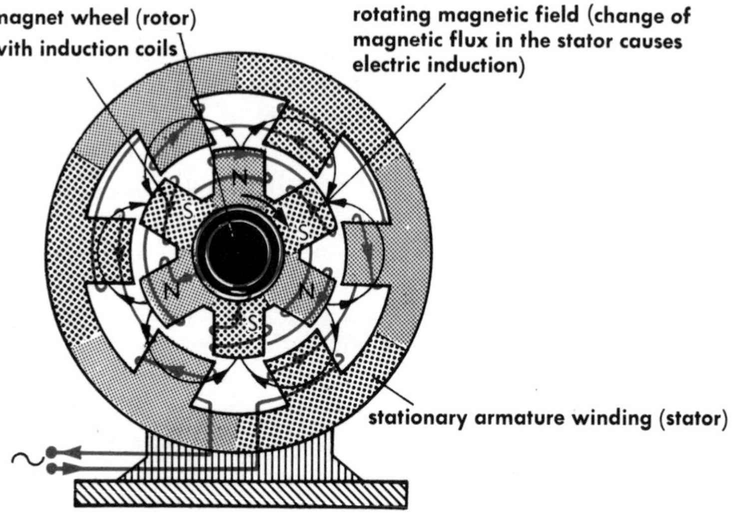

stationary and the magnetic poles on the stator revolve instead (Fig. 1).

The stator consists of an iron ring with induction coils mounted on the inside; the magnetic poles on the rotor move past the ends of these induction coils, at a very short distance from them (Fig. 1). In this method, the current produced by the generator is taken directly from

Fig. 2 DETAILS OF A GENERATOR FOR HIGH VOLTAGES
(internal pole machine)

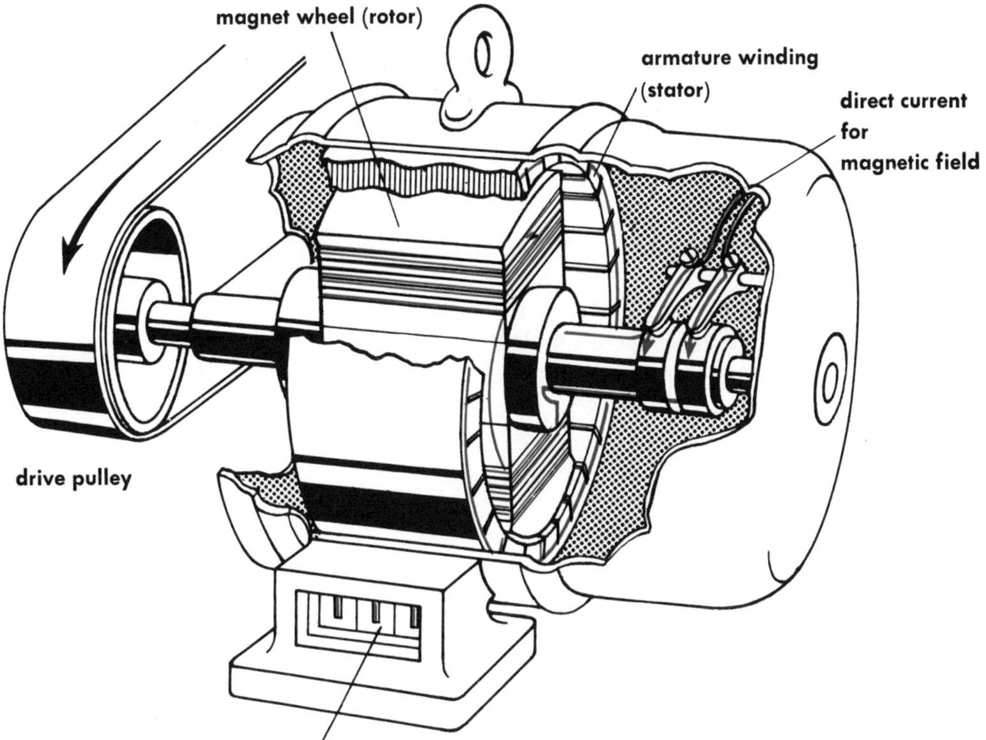

the stator, without the aid of special current collectors known as brushes. This form of generator construction is particularly suitable for the creation of high-voltage alternating current because the sparking that occurs at high voltages (around 20,000 volts) in large generators would destroy the brushes. The relatively low output of *direct current* needed for producing the stationary magnetic field is fed to the rotor by means of slip rings and carbon or copper-mesh brushes. The successive coils in Fig. 1 are wound in alternate directions, which ensures that the generated current always flows in the same direction. Heavy-duty generators are usually coupled directly—on the same shaft—to STEAM or WATER TURBINES.

TELEGRAPH AND TELETYPE

If a man in Denver wants to send some information to a man in San Francisco, he can write him a letter. But a letter is a clumsy sort of thing—it has to be carried by planes and postmen, and the planes and postmen have to carry their own weight in addition to the weight of the letter.

This is a waste of energy. Let's assume that all the man in Denver wanted to say was "Unable to ship twenty units till January 15." This is simply information—it has no weight at all. With a telegraph, the message is converted from spelled-out words into bursts, or pulses, of ELECTRIC CURRENT along a telegraph line. In this form, it *still* has no weight and can be sent quickly and efficiently to San Francisco, where it is printed out automatically.

What makes this possible is the magnetic effect of electric current, which shows up whenever current is switched on or off near a magnetized compass *needle* (Fig. 1). In the Morse telegraph and its descendants, an *electromagnet* is put in place of the compass needle (Fig. 2).

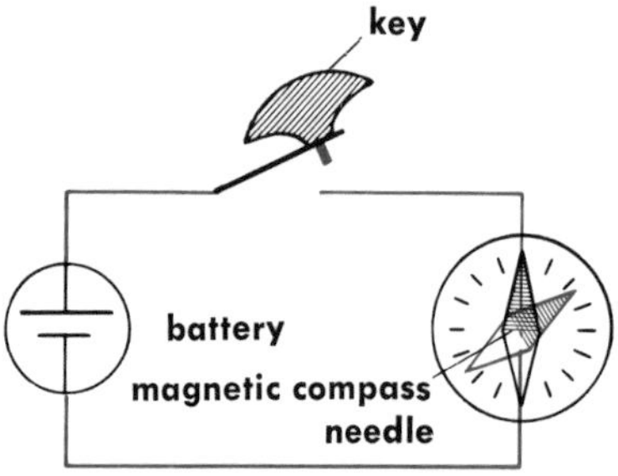

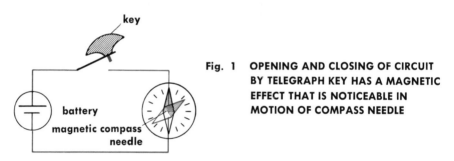

Fig. 1 OPENING AND CLOSING OF CIRCUIT BY TELEGRAPH KEY HAS A MAGNETIC EFFECT THAT IS NOTICEABLE IN MOTION OF COMPASS NEEDLE

In Fig. 2, when the sending *key* is pressed, current flows in the electric circuit (colored red); the *coil* at the left then works like a magnet, pulling the left arm of the gray seesaw down toward it. This pushes the right arm of the seesaw upward; its *stylus* (a sharp writing point) then marks a dot or dash on a moving strip of paper. (For a dash, a sending key is held down about three times as long as for a dot.)

The circuit can be wired so that current flows all the time *except* when the sending key is pressed (as in America) or *only* when the key is pressed (as in Europe). This second, or "open circuit," system is shown in Fig. 3. Its two telegraph stations are connected by a circuit that is completed at the top by a telegraph wire (in red) and at the bottom through the ground. (The ground doesn't conduct electricity as well as a copper wire, but it's much cheaper.)

When *key* 1 of *transmitter* 1 is pressed, it closes the circuit to its BATTERY and breaks the connection to *electromagnet* 1 at left. Current (*dashed arrows*) now flows through battery 1, the right arm of key 1, the telegraph wire, the left arm of *key* 2, *electromagnet* 2, through ground, back to battery 1, and back to key 1. The current flowing through electromagnet 2 draws down *armature* 2, which is pivoted; its left arm now kicks upward, pressing one side of the moving strip of paper, which is inked on its other side by a small roller. Dots and dashes can be read on the inked side of the paper.

When *transmitter* 2 is used as a sender, its connection with its printing-out strip is broken by the rise of the left arm of key 2 and

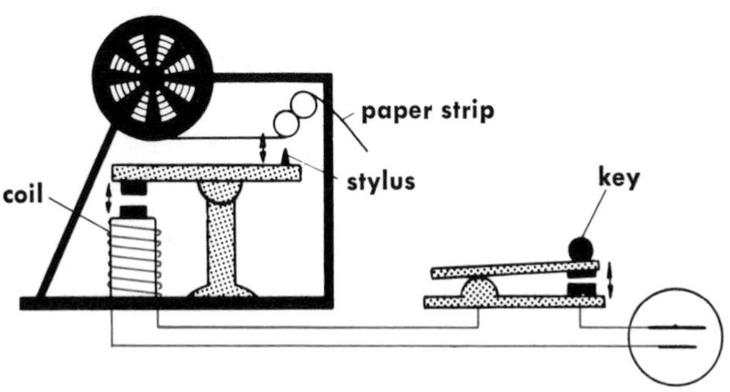

Fig. 2 IN EARLY FORM OF MORSE TELEGRAPH, STRONG MAGNETIC EFFECT ACHIEVED BY COILING WIRE IS USED TO DRAW DOWN ONE END OF PIVOTED LEVER. OTHER END, WITH STYLUS, KICKS UPWARD AND MARKS PAPER.

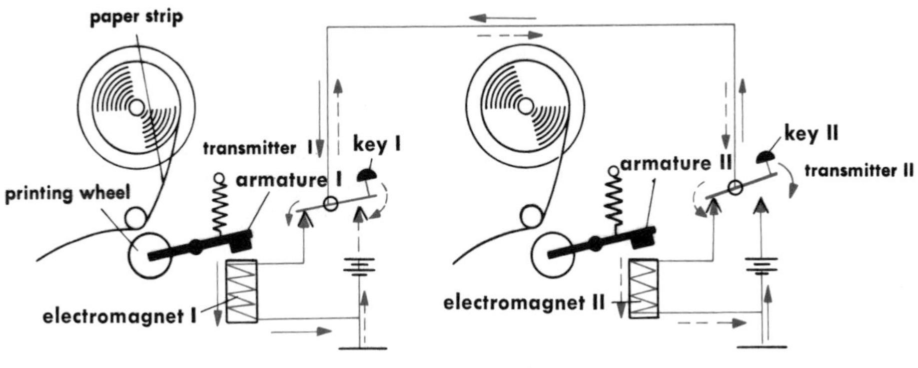

Fig. 3 WHEN KEY I IS PRESSED DOWN, BATTERY I OPERATES ELECTROMAGNET I AND ELECTROMAGNET II RECEIVES THE SIGNAL. WHEN KEY I IS NOT PRESSED DOWN, ELECTROMAGNET I CAN ACT AS RECEIVER FOR SIGNALS FOR TRANSMITTER II

a	•—	n	—•	1	•————
b	—•••	o	———	2	••———
c	—•—•	p	•——•	3	•••——
d	—••	q	——•—	4	••••—
e	•	r	•—•	5	•••••
f	••—•	s	•••	6	—••••
g	——•	t	—	7	——•••
h	••••	u	••—	8	———••
i	••	v	•••—	9	————•
j	•———	w	•——	0	—————
k	—•—	x	—••—		
l	•—••	y	—•——	period	•—•—•—
m	——	z	——••	distress signal	•••———•••

Fig. 4 TELEGRAPH CODE USED IN INTERNATIONAL COMMUNICATION

the current (*full arrows*) triggers the receiving mechanism of the station on the left.

Obviously there has to be agreement between sender and receiver as to what each combination of dots and dashes will stand for. Not all symbols that have been agreed to internationally are useful in English; those that are appear in Fig. 4. For speed, letters like small *e* and small *t* that appear most commonly in any page of English text (including this one) have been given the shortest and simplest signal.

In the early days of telegraphy, every big-city newspaper paid a man who sat all day with earphones clamped over his head, the *telegraph operator*. His job was to listen to everything that came over the wires in code and to write it down in ordinary letters of the alphabet.

Today this work is done by a machine, the **teletype,** that allows a typewriter in one city to operate a typewriter in another. The typewriter at the sending end punches holes into a moving tape; the tape holes then work a telegraph switch. At the receiving end, the telegraph signals punch holes into a moving tape and the various hole combinations work the keys of the typewriter.

Most teletypes use groups of five pulses of current. (By being ON or OFF, a signal pulse could distinguish between two letters; two pulses could distinguish between four; three pulses could handle eight.) With its groups of five pulses a teletype can produce 32 different patterns of holes in the tape. These are enough to control a typewriter keyboard because two of these patterns are reserved to instruct the typewriter whether to shift to "figures" or back to "letters." (A new seven-pulse code was launched in 1963. Its 128 different signals allow for 64 message characters, plus 64 extra combinations that enable data-processing machines to handle the messages.)

LOUDSPEAKER

To hear a clarinet, we don't have to press the clarinet against one of our ears. We hear it simply because the air around us is vibrating. If a loudspeaker (or "speaker") can make the air vibrate *just* as a clarinet would, it should sound like a clarinet.

A loudspeaker gives out sound, but without receiving it. What it receives is ELECTRIC CURRENT that varies several thousand times per second. If these electrical changes match the vibrations of the air in a clarinet, the speaker may then sound like a clarinet—that is, if it is a good speaker.

To accomplish this result, the speaker is given an *electromagnet* in which changes of current in a coil set up magnetic forces that can pull an iron plate with a constantly changing amount of force (Fig. 1). In early loudspeakers, the vibrations of the metal were passed on to a cone, made of stiff paper, which then passed them on to the air of the room.

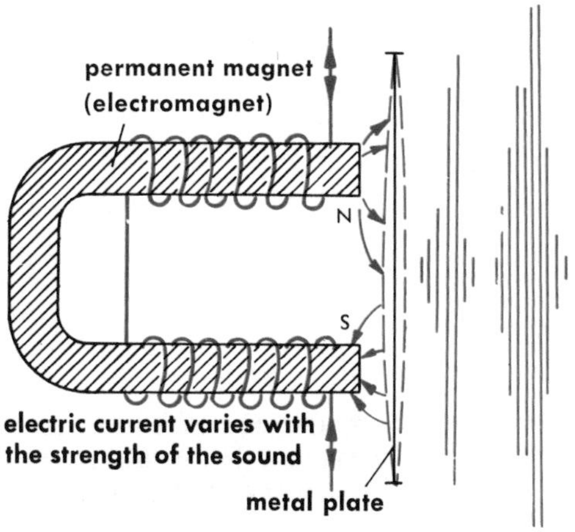

Fig. 1 IN THE SIMPLEST FORM, LOUDSPEAKER RECEIVES A VARYING ELECTRICAL CURRENT THAT SETS UP A MAGNETIC FIELD OF VARYING STRENGTH NEAR POLES OF ELECTROMAGNET. THESE VIBRATING PULLING FORCES ACT ON IRON PLATE, WHICH TRANSFERS ITS MOTION TO SURROUNDING AIR

In later designs, it was decided that making a piece of iron vibrate was not a good idea—the iron is heavy and is sluggish at following vibrations. So the *coil* was made movable (Fig. 2) and the narrow tip of the cone was attached to the coil. There are other ways of designing a loudspeaker, but the moving-coil design, or "dynamic loudspeaker," is the one usually used today in a reasonably good speaker. (The speaker is here seen from the side, as if sliced down the middle, so that the magnet looks like a capital E. Seen from in front or from behind, it would simply be circular.)

The purpose of the loudspeaker is to set up vibrations in the air of the room. In the speaker of Fig. 2, the coil is made to vibrate by magnetic forces; but once it is in vibration, the way it passes on its vibrations to the cone is purely mechanical. The cone's center is attached to the coil (firmly), and the cone's outer rim is attached to

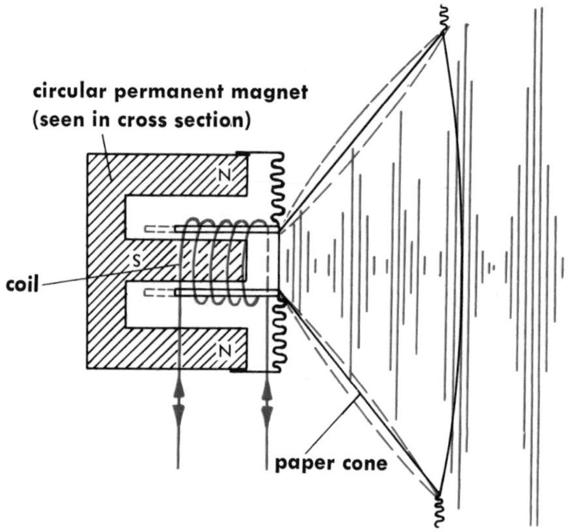

Fig. 2 IN "DYNAMIC" OR "MOVING-COIL" LOUDSPEAKER, HEAVY MAGNET HOLDS STILL WHILE LIGHT COIL VIBRATES, TRANSFERRING MOTION TO TIP OF PAPER CONE. AIR THEN PICKS UP VIBRATIONS OF CONE

the wooden cabinet (not so firmly). Whenever the coil vibrates backward and forward, the cone (usually made of stiff paper) bounces along with it. The low, "boomy" tones require a large vibrating area—the large cone acts somewhat like the head of a big bass drum.

Most loudspeakers today have little trouble reproducing a wide range of loudness, not only of a single tone as a whole but also any fluttering or pulsation within a tone; and some reproduce fairly high-pitched tones about as well as low ones—vibrating several thousand times per second or merely one or two hundred times per second. What is more difficult for a speaker is to sound sometimes like a flute, sometimes like a clarinet.

When a flute plays a single musical tone, such as the A above middle C on the keyboard of a piano, it makes the air vibrate 440 times per second; a very small proportion of its vibrational energy appears as vibrations that go 2, 3, 4, 5 times as fast (these are called *harmonics,* or *partials*). But when a clarinet plays an A at the same pitch, a good deal of its energy is channeled into its third harmonic, at $3 \times 440 = 1{,}320$ vibrations per second, and into its fifth harmonic, at $5 \times 440 = 2{,}200$ vibrations per second. This means that even when the tones being played are not especially high, the vibrations needed to give the right "color" to each instrument can be of several thousand cycles per second.

We are not normally aware of these high-pitched harmonics—all we notice is that if they're not there, all instruments sound pretty much the same. But even when the loudspeaker does not do quite as good a job as it should in the very low and very high frequencies, we usually supply what is missing automatically as we listen. We "hear" the low tones of a cello even when a small speaker doesn't quite manage to produce them, and offers us a set of harmonics instead. A good deal of the loudspeaker's work is actually done by the listener.

TELEPHONE

The telephone is a relatively simple but remarkable instrument consisting of a **transmitter** and a **receiver.** Its two functions are (1) to accept sound waves in the transmitter and convert them into electrical impulses and (2) to receive electrical impulses and change them back into sound waves.

When a person talks into a telephone, the sound waves from his voice are carried through the air. They enter the transmitter and

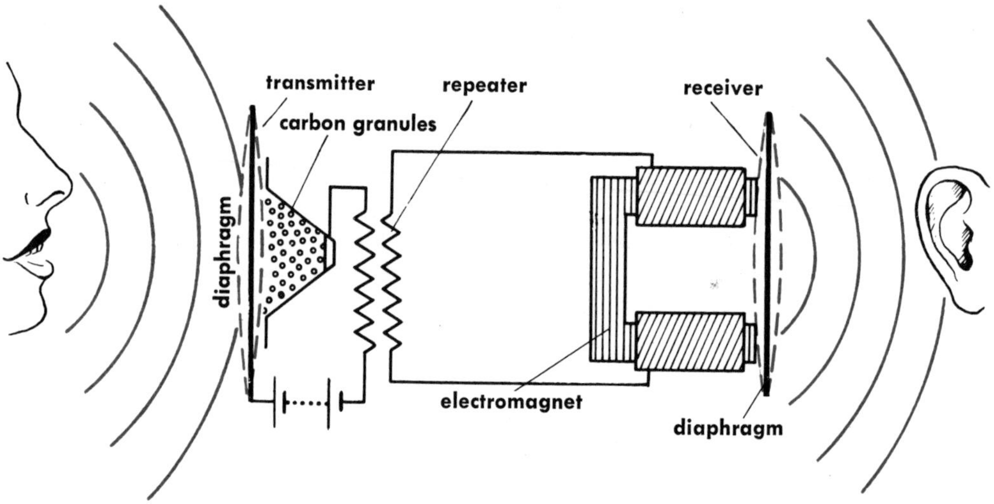

CARBON MICROPHONE AND TELEPHONE

cause a thin metal *diaphragm* to vibrate. Behind the diaphragm is a small metal box of *carbon granules* through which an ELECTRIC CURRENT flows. The vibrating diaphragm exerts a pressure on the granules, compressing and relaxing them in direct relation to the vibrations from the person's voice. When the granules are compressed, or close together, they conduct more current; when relaxed, or loosely spaced, they conduct less. And so we now have a pulsating electric current that imitates the sound waves from the person's voice.

The current, strengthened by amplifiers called *repeaters,* can be carried great or short distances to its destination—the receiver at the other end of the phone call.

Now the electrical impulses have to be changed into sound waves again. This is done with the aid of an *electromagnet,* one of science's more outstanding inventions. Basically, an electromagnet is a piece of iron wound with coils of insulated wire. When an electric current passes through the wire, it magnetizes the iron—the more current, the more magnetism; the less current, the less magnetism.

Inside the telephone receiver is another highly sensitive metal diaphragm backed by an electromagnet. As the incoming electric current fluctuates, the strength of the magnet fluctuates, thus attracting and relaxing the diaphragm in varying degrees. The diaphragm, then, is converting the current back into the same sound waves that were transmitted. The sound waves re-create the caller's voice and, once again, travel through the air to the receiver's ear. The whole procedure outlined here is instantaneous.

FLUORESCENT LIGHT

Before investigating fluorescent lighting, it might be helpful to redefine the principle of the incandescent light bulb, the common electric bulb used in most lamps. In this bulb, the ELECTRIC CURRENT is passed through a fine wire filament, heating it to an extremely high temperature. The white-hot glow of the filament produces the light. Usually incandescent light is softened, or diffused, by use of a frosted-glass bulb.

A fluorescent lamp does not depend solely upon heat for its light. The inside of the tube is coated with chemical salts that have the ability to glow when struck by ultraviolet rays produced in the tube. Different salts emit different-colored lights; the standard tubes used for home lighting are usually warm white (slightly yellow) or cool white (bluish).

Fig. 1 shows the chain of events that causes the coating in the tube to glow. When the current is switched on, it first lights a small *glow lamp.* The resulting heat causes the *bimetallic contact* to close and to create a short circuit. This sends the full voltage into the *cathodes,* making them incandescent. (If you have a fluorescent lamp, try pushing the starter switch and holding it down. You can see the incandescent light burning at both ends of the tube.) For just an instant, the *autotransformer* boosts the charge to the high voltage needed to activate the light. The hot cathodes send streams of *electrons* through the tube. The tube contains *mercury,* which is vaporized by the ELECTRIC CHARGE. As the electrons collide with the mercury atoms, the atoms emit invisible *ultraviolet rays.* (Even though you can't see ultraviolet radiation, you may sometimes be painfully aware of it when it causes sunburn.) The ultraviolet rays, in turn, strike the salts on the wall of the tube, exciting the atoms and causing them to radiate (see Fig. 2). This radiation, which *is* in the visible range of the spectrum, produces the soft glow of fluorescent light.

FLUORESCENT LAMP

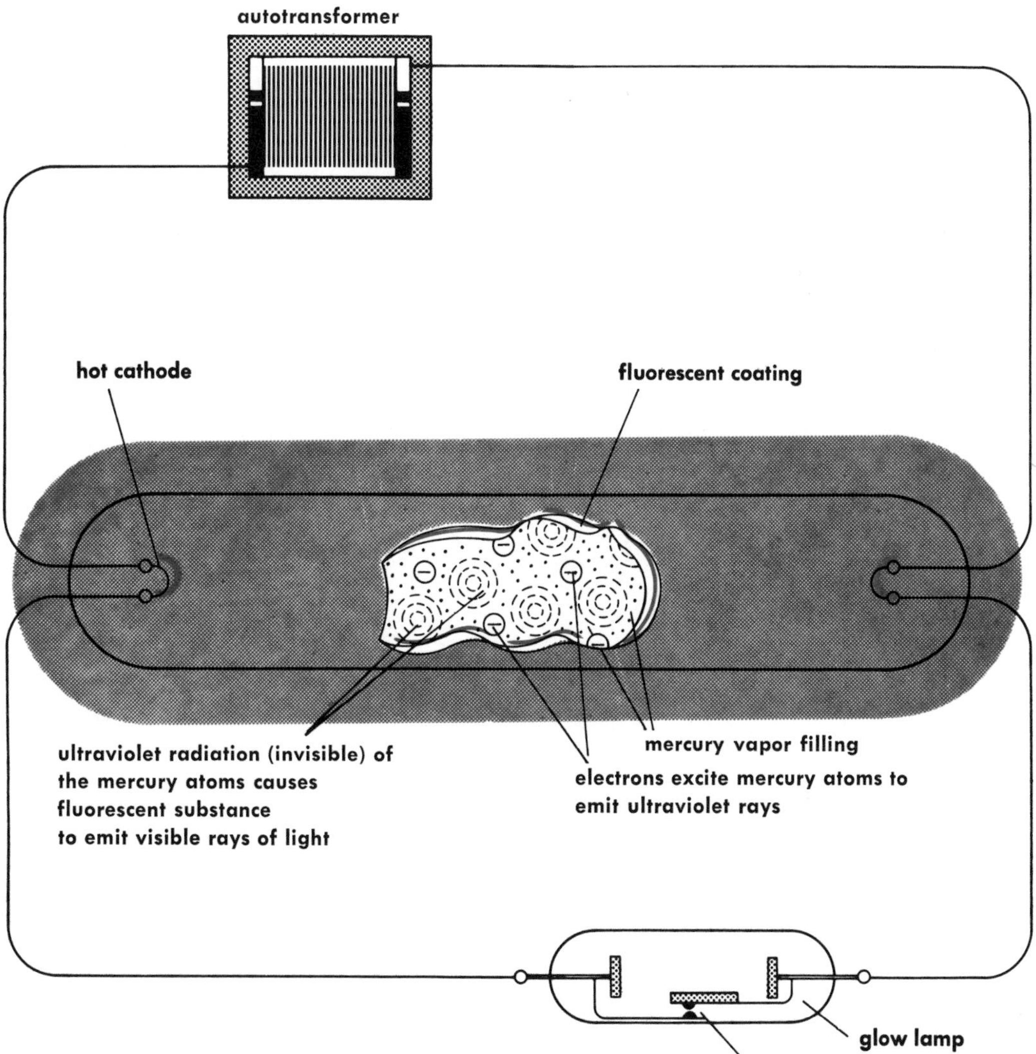
autotransformer
hot cathode
fluorescent coating
ultraviolet radiation (invisible) of
the mercury atoms causes
fluorescent substance
to emit visible rays of light
mercury vapor filling
electrons excite mercury atoms to
emit ultraviolet rays
glow lamp
bimetallic contact

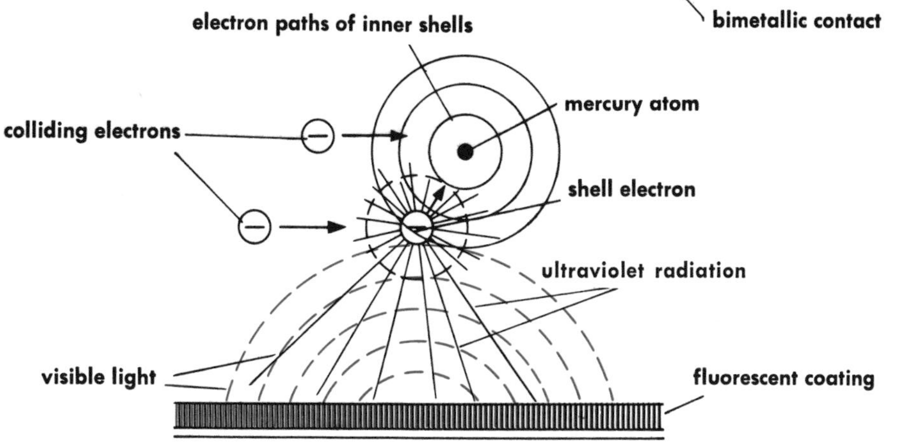
electron paths of inner shells
mercury atom
colliding electrons
shell electron
ultraviolet radiation
visible light
fluorescent coating

V Light, X Rays and Photography

MICROSCOPE

Telephone poles in a row, though you may *know* they are all the same size, *appear* to be smaller as their distance from you increases. This is because the *apparent size* of any object depends on the size of the image formed on the retina of the eye. The light rays from a distant pole enter the eye at a narrow angle and form a small image. The light from a nearby pole enters the eye at a wide angle and forms a

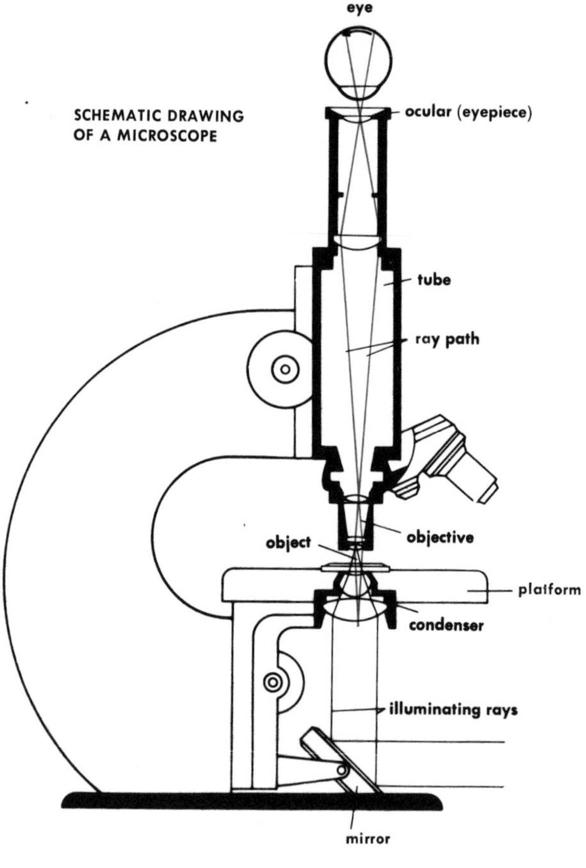

SCHEMATIC DRAWING OF A MICROSCOPE

large image. The *visual angle*, then, determines the apparent size of an object.

Distant objects can be magnified (the visual angle increased) by a TELESCOPE so that they can be seen more clearly. But in the case of very small objects, such as specks of dust, the visual angle remains too small even when they are viewed from the shortest possible distance. The limiting factor is the eye itself, which cannot focus on anything closer than about 5 inches. With the aid of a microscope, however, it is possible to bring an object right up next to the eye, thereby greatly increasing its visual angle, and yet view it as though it were comfortably within the eye's focus.

The magnifying power of a microscope is the ratio of the apparent size of the magnified object to the actual size as seen by the naked eye. For instance, a microscope with a magnifying power of 300 will show an object 300 times as large as it appears to the eye at a distance of about 10 inches.

The illustration shows the general workings of a microscope. Starting at the bottom, *illuminating rays* are picked up by an adjustable *mirror* and are reflected into the *condenser*. The original source of illumination is often a small, intense lamp that can be moved to throw the light where it is needed. The condenser concentrates the light through a hole in the *platform* and through the *object* (on a glass slide) to be examined. Magnification takes place in two stages: the *objective*, which usually consists of more than one lens, forms an enlarged image inside the *tube;* the image is further magnified as it passes through the *ocular*, or eyepiece. The result is that the image enters the eye at a wide visual angle, thus greatly increasing its apparent size.

CAMERAS

All cameras, whether simple or sophisticated, work in the same basic way, and they have the same fundamental parts: a *lightproof box* with a tightly sealed door; a *film holder,* which holds the film to be exposed in a flat position and also provides a means of advancing or changing the film; a *lens* to bend incoming light rays and focus the image on the film; a *shutter,* which opens and closes to let light reach the film for a precise amount of time; a *diaphragm* to control the size of the lens opening (some simple cameras have one fixed opening, while more advanced cameras have an adjustable diaphragm); and a *viewfinder* to let you see what your picture will look like.

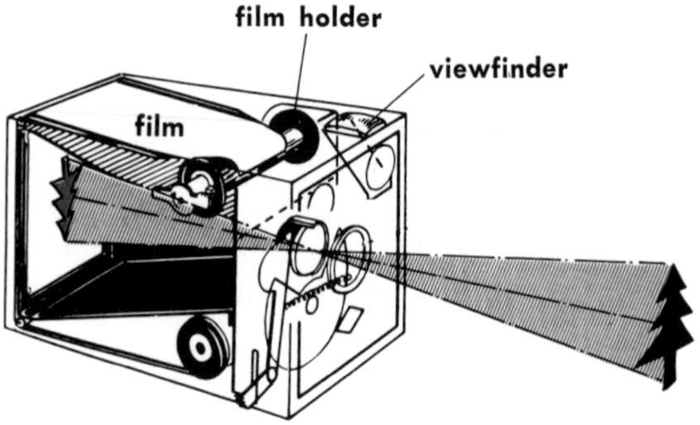

Fig. 1 BOX CAMERA

The easiest cameras to use are **box cameras** (Fig. 1) because they have so few manual controls. The lens opening, or aperture, and shutter speed are preset to take good pictures under average conditions. Some camera models accept a preloaded film cartridge that simply drops into the back of the camera. The lens in a box camera is usually composed of only one or two elements (see camera lenses, page 183). The simplicity of these lenses keeps the cost of the camera down, but also limits the quality and sharpness of the picture.

The more complicated cameras have adjustable controls that are set automatically or manually or by a combination of both ways. This feature allows the photographer to take pictures under conditions in which a preset box camera could not be used. Adjustable settings provide two basic controls: the lens opening and the shutter speed. The lens opening determines *how much light* will be allowed to reach the film in a given time. This is done by opening or closing down the diaphragm. The speed of the shutter controls the *length of time* the light will be allowed to expose the film.

Three extreme situations will illustrate how the settings can be balanced to provide just the right exposure. When taking pictures of clouds or water on a bright day, the problem is to avoid overexposing the film with *too much light.* In this case, the lens opening may be closed way down and the shutter speed may be fairly fast. Conversely, a picture taken on a cloudy, dark day would require a slow shutter speed and a wide lens opening to let in *enough* light. Action pictures, such as those taken of sports events, usually require very fast shutter speeds to avoid a blurred picture. In order to compensate for the speed and to expose the film correctly, the lens is usually opened wide.

Of the cameras with adjustable settings, the *35-millimeter cameras* (Fig. 2) are perhaps the most popular. They are compact and many

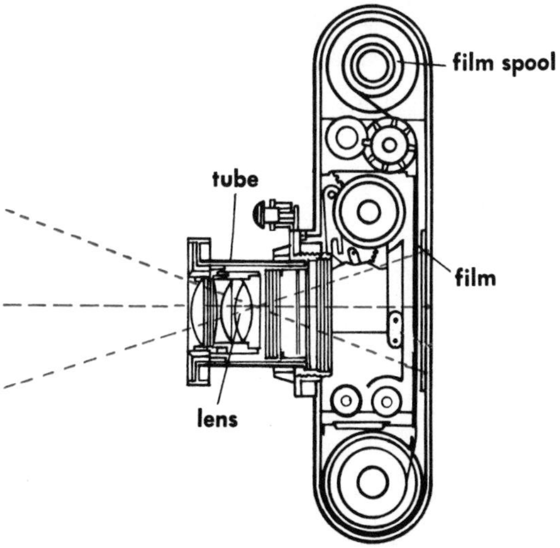

Fig. 2 35-MILLIMETER CAMERA

will accept a variety of accessories, such as close-up and telephoto lenses. The viewfinder on a camera is located above, and/or to the side of, the lens. Therefore they are not both aimed at *exactly* the same area. The difference between what you see in the viewfinder and what the lens "sees" is called *parallax.* (This is also true of your eyes. Try holding a pencil in front of you and making it jump back and forth by alternately closing one eye and then the other.)

The **single-lens reflex camera** (Fig. 3) is designed to eliminate the parallax problem, which is especially important in close-up work. The image that comes through the lens is reflected into the viewfinder by the *deviating mirror* and the *viewing prism*. When the shutter is released, the mirror flips out of the way, allowing the film to be exposed. In this way, you can see *exactly the same area* that the lens is aimed at.

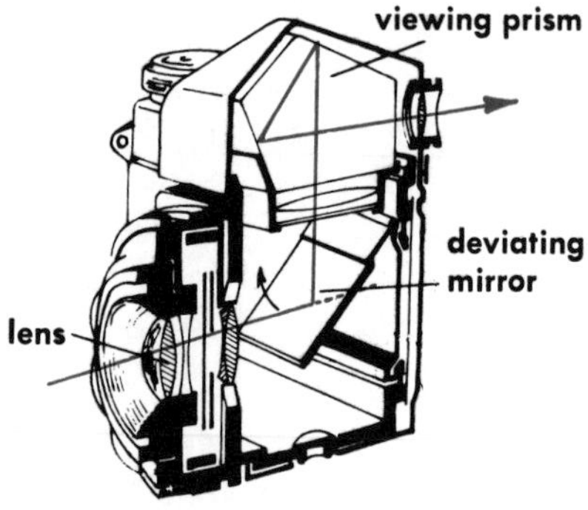

Fig. 3 SINGLE-LENS REFLEX CAMERA

CAMERA LENSES

The performance (and the cost) of a CAMERA is largely dependent on the quality of its lens. The camera lens does the same job as the lens of the human eye—it bends incoming light rays so that they form a clear image on the film, whereas the eye focuses the image on the retina. This bending of light is called *refraction*.

If you have ever watched an eclipse through a "pinhole viewer" you know that it is possible to project an image with no lens at all, though the results are somewhat dim and fuzzy. Figure 1 shows what happens to *points* of light as their rays enter a **pinhole camera.** They are projected as *spots* of light that cannot be smaller than the pinhole itself. Also, because of the hole's small size, its light-transmitting power is extremely low.

Light rays travel in a straight path unless something interrupts the path and refracts the rays. Figure 2 shows the rays from the same two points of light entering the camera through a lens. The lens bends the spread-out rays, making them converge on the film as a sharp point once again. Note that only the rays passing through the center of the lens continue in a straight line. As the diagrams show, the image is formed upside down; light rays emanating from an object travel in a straight path. The rays from the top of the object "seen" go straight through the small opening of the camera lens or the eye to the bottom of the viewing surface—the eye's retina or the camera

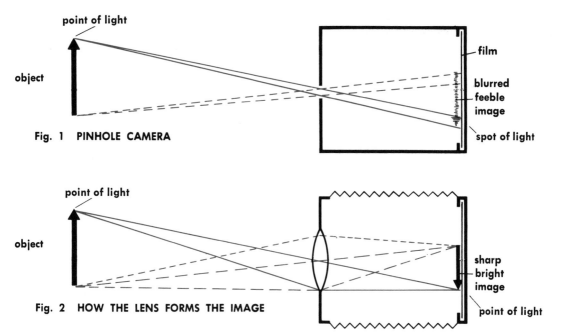

Fig. 1 PINHOLE CAMERA

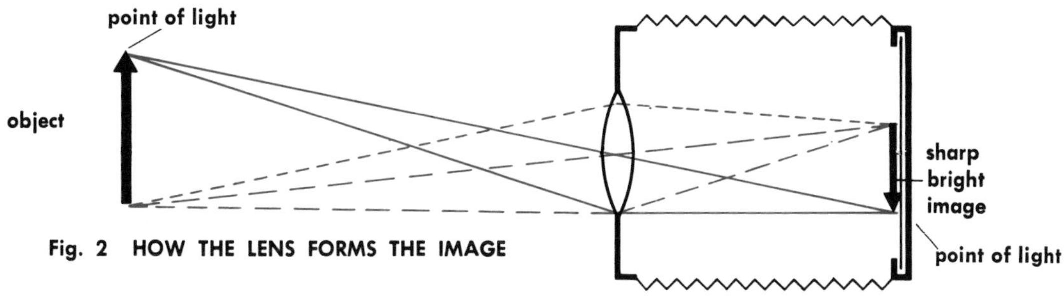

Fig. 2 HOW THE LENS FORMS THE IMAGE

film. Likewise, rays from the bottom of the object go to the top of the viewing surface. By the same principle, the images formed on the retina of the eye are inverted. The reason that we see them right-side up is that the visual centers in the brain correct our perception.

The imperfections, or distortions, in lens images are called *lens aberrations*, or errors. One common error is **spherical aberration** (Fig. 3) wherein the *marginal rays* entering the edge of the lens are not bent to the same focus as those entering nearer the center. In

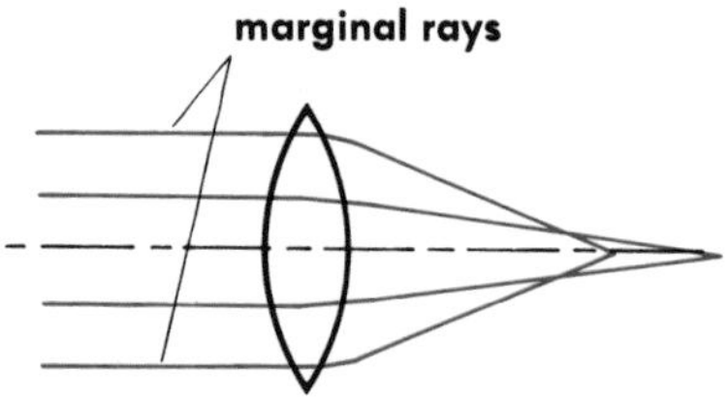

Fig. 3
SPHERICAL ABERRATION

correcting this and other imperfections, the art of lens making becomes highly complicated and often involves the use of several different pieces of glass (elements) to make up a single lens.

There are two main types of lenses: **converging lenses** (Fig. 4) reflect light rays in the direction of the thickest part of the lens (the center) and concentrate them at one point; **diverging lenses** (Fig. 5) are thicker at the edges than in the middle, causing light rays to spread outward in the direction of the edges. Camera lenses, more correctly called *objectives*, are usually composed of a combination of these elements. And the elements can be made of a great variety of glasses possessing different optical properties.

Fig. 4 CONVERGING LENSES

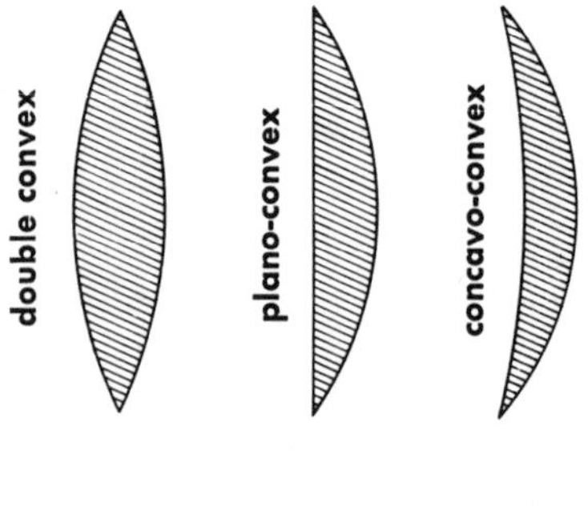

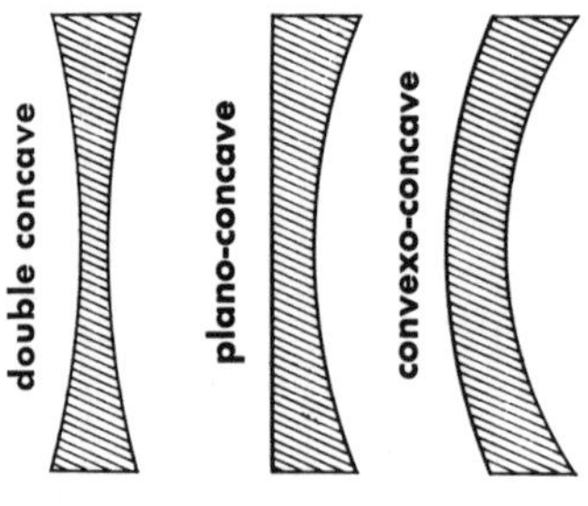

Fig. 5 DIVERGING LENSES

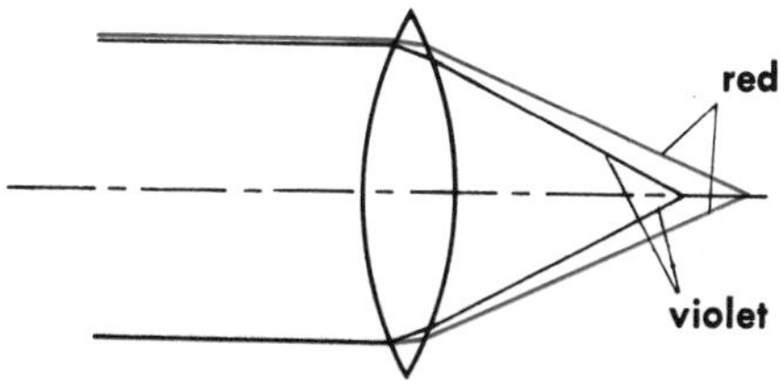

Fig. 6 CHROMATIC ABERRATION

Fig. 7
CORRECTION OF
CHROMATIC ABERRATION

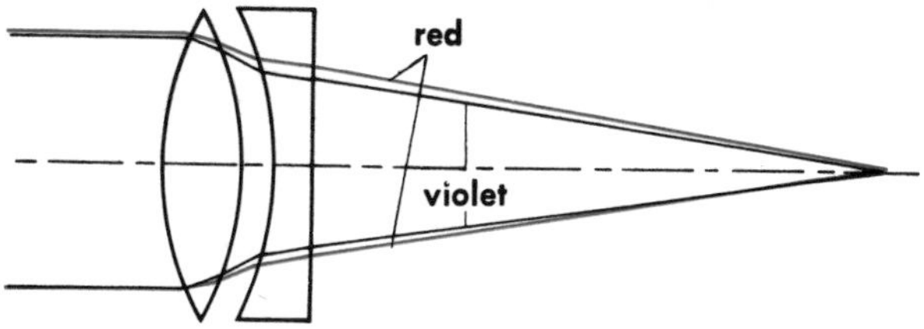

A simple example of a combination lens is the achromatic lens used to correct **chromatic aberration** (Fig. 6). This is caused by the inability of a single lens to focus all colors at one point due to their varying wavelengths. Violet light (shorter wavelength) is refracted at a sharper angle than red light (longer wavelength). The addition of a *plano-concave lens* (Fig. 7) solves the problem. This lens used alone would diverge the light rays, but the combination of the two makes the colors converge at the same point.

Fig. 8 shows a **six-element lens,** the kind often used in fast 35-millimeter cameras, though for additional corrections even more elements can be added. By varying the number and type of lenses, the type of glass, the curvature, the lens thickness, and the gaps (if any) between the elements, it is possible to achieve nearly optically perfect lenses for general or specialized work.

Fig. 8 SIX-ELEMENT LENS

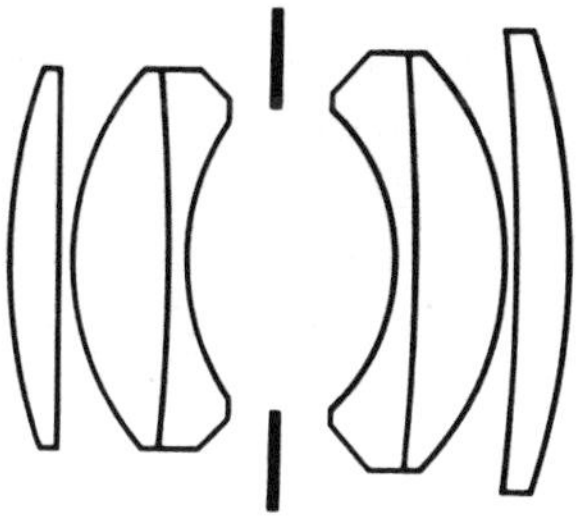

BLACK-AND-WHITE FILM

If we take a pencil and try to draw a picture of a model airplane, we notice that the outline doesn't take shape clearly unless there is a *contrast* between the plane and the background—as, for instance, when the plane, seen against a dark background, is just "catching" the light. This contrast becomes even more important when we try to *photograph* the plane—that is, to make the light draw the picture for us. And we will then need to let the light from the model plane hit a surface that will react differently to light and to darkness.

Photographic film has a surface that does just that. The supporting part of the film is not light-sensitive—it's merely a broad ribbon of cellulose acetate, five-thousandths of an inch thick. But over it is a layer of gelatin, made from the skin of cattle and containing traces of sulfur; and within the gelatin, which is only one-tenth as thick as the supporting film, are thousands of crystals of silver bromide. Under a microscope, some of these look like hexagons, some like triangles with their corners clipped.

In the dark, nothing happens to these crystals. But when light reaches them, some of their molecules break down, apparently in spots where silver has gotten entangled with sulfur from the gelatin. What the light then does is to release small, invisible specks of silver, right at the spots where the light has been strongest.

This silver is not visible. To get it to make a picture, the film is taken to a darkroom, where it is dunked in a tank of liquid called a *developer*. After that, the film is washed in a solution of a special form of sodium sulfate called "hypo" to clear away all remaining traces of the original silver bromide—otherwise the film would go on darkening whenever it was brought out of the darkroom.

These grains of silver, or silver sulfide, are now large and dark. The brighter the light source (as when the sunlight bounced off a metal part of the plane), or the longer the film is allowed to soak up the light, the more silver will break loose from the silver bromide. These spots that have received the most light are the darkest; those that have received the least light remain light. The picture that results is called a **negative.** To get a **positive** (in which light objects would look light, dark objects dark), we need to take a photograph of the negative. The best way to do this is to shine light not *on* it but *through* it. To make this possible, all negatives are printed on transparent film.

The positive can be made by laying the negative flat down on photographic paper, then turning on a bright light for a few seconds. The spots receiving the most light will be those under the lightest areas

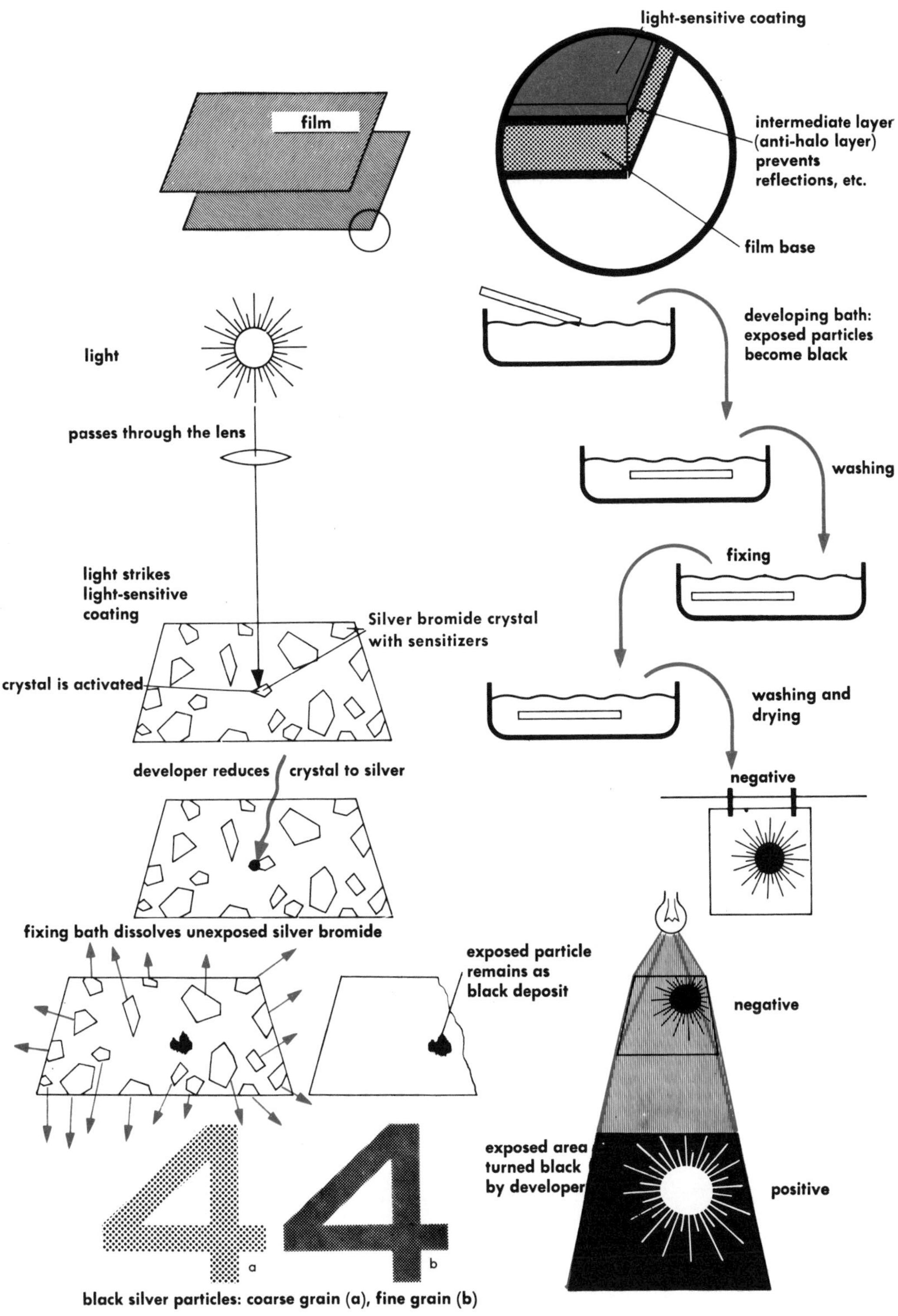
light-sensitive coating
film
intermediate layer
(anti-halo layer)
prevents
reflections, etc.
film base
light
passes through the lens
developing bath:
exposed particles
become black
washing
fixing
light strikes
light-sensitive
coating
Silver bromide crystal
with sensitizers
crystal is activated
washing and
drying
developer reduces crystal to silver
negative
fixing bath dissolves unexposed silver bromide
exposed particle
remains as
black deposit
negative
exposed area
turned black
by developer
positive
a
b
black silver particles: coarse grain (a), fine grain (b)

of the negative. A developing solution will make these areas appear dark in the print—light and dark have again been switched, and what we now have is a positive. The print is then washed in a bath of *fixative,* which will stop, or "fix," the printing process at the point it reached when we turned off the light. (Otherwise, the print would still be sensitive to light and we could never take it out of the darkroom.)

The kind of print we will have made is called a *contact print,* because the negative was in contact with the paper we were "printing" the positive picture on. If our negative was small, the contact print will be small.

To make an enlargement, we slip the negative into the holder of an enlarger, where it is held horizontally over a table. On the table we set out a large sheet of light-sensitive printing paper. (All this takes place in a darkroom.) To bring out a positive picture on the printing paper, we shine a light through the negative and through a *lens,* which will project an enlarged image onto the paper. After that, we put the print through the same steps as for a contact print.

X RAYS

Although the only radiations that can be *seen* are in the form of visible light, there are many with longer or shorter wavelengths that cannot be seen. One such radiation is the X ray, which, because of its short wavelength, has the power to penetrate the lighter elements, of which materials such as wood, cloth, or human flesh are composed. And, though the X ray's light is invisible to the eye, it can pass through opaque substances and expose a photographic plate or show an image on a fluorescent screen.

The structure of the atom plays a large part in the workings of an X-ray tube. The *nucleus* is the central mass of the atom and is charged with positive electrical units. Around the nucleus, somewhat like planets in orbit, whiz *electrons*, which are negative charges. They

Fig. 1

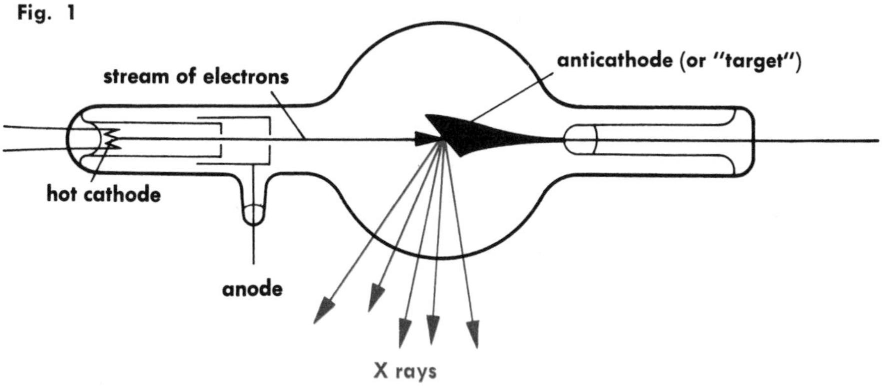

revolve in their orbits, or shells, at the rate of several billion times a second. While the nucleus is hard to break up, the electrons can be easily displaced or driven off.

In an X-ray tube (Fig. 1), a *stream of electrons* is shot out of a *hot cathode* (electric terminal) under extremely high voltage. They are focused on a metal target, or *anticathode*, which is usually made of tungsten. As the electrons bombard the metal atoms of the target, they upset the atomic structure, causing them to emit energy in the form of X rays.

Figure 2 shows what happens to a single atom in the target. A high-energy electron from the cathode knocks an electron out of the inner shell of the metal atom. An electron from another shell leaps into the vacant place, thus emitting X rays. Many targets are water-cooled or rotated by motors to prevent them from melting under the impact of the bombardment.

X rays are used extensively in research and industry. Many products are routinely inspected by X ray for internal cracks, flaws, and other imperfections. But the major significance of the X ray is in the medical field of *radiology*, where it is used for both diagnosis and treatment of certain diseases.

Fig. 2

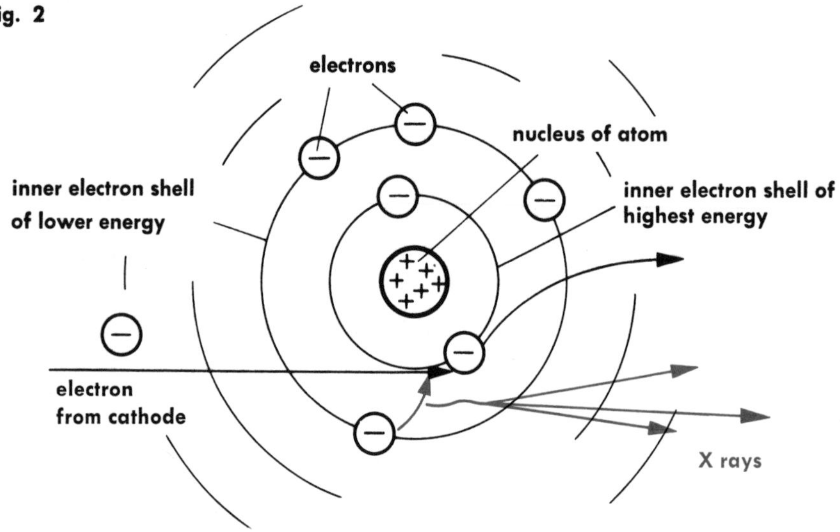

When X rays are used to take pictures of bones or teeth, they pass through the lighter tissues (flesh) but do not penetrate the bone area as easily because bones are made of heavier atoms. In other words, the amount of light reaching the film varies with the density of the material it must pass through. The result is a clear shadow picture that can show up fractures, growths, cavities, etc. Extremely heavy elements, such as lead or gold, cannot be penetrated by X rays. This is the reason for using lead casing around X-ray equipment and lead-lined clothing for workers who are exposed to possible harmful amounts of radiation.

Some internal organs, such as the stomach, may be too transparent to show up on an X-ray photograph with sufficient contrast. In this case, the patient is given a drink containing chemicals, often barium sulfate, which will absorb the X rays and register distinctly on the film.

While overexposure to radiation can result in harmful burns, controlled exposure can be used to advantage for therapeutic purposes. Certain abnormal cells, such as those found in tumors or cancer, can be destroyed by X rays while leaving the healthy cells relatively unaffected. This is an exacting procedure and is often done with ultrahard X rays. (*Hard* X rays are radiated at very high voltages and have shorter wavelengths. *Soft* X rays have longer wavelengths and are not as penetrating.) Often the X-ray tube is moved about so that the radiation remains focused on the tumor but does not constantly penetrate the same healthy tissue.

COLOR PRINTING

A color photograph or painting is usually reproduced by the *four-color printing process.* The standard inks used (process colors) are blue, yellow, red, and black. When superimposed on each other, they appear as compound colors. Standard inks will achieve a fairly accurate replica of the original colors, though sometimes different inks are used to obtain special effects.

Basically, this is how the process works:

First, the original picture is photographed four times to separate the colors. This is done by using colored filters on the camera. The filters cut out certain colors and allow others to reach the film. For instance, the red filter allows only blue colors to pass through it. The result is a black-and-white negative on which only the blues are recorded. This step is repeated three times, using a blue-violet filter for the yellow plate and a green filter for the red plate. A partial exposure through each of the three filters is made to obtain black tones so that black will print where it is needed for outline, depth and detail.

The negatives are next developed, then photographed through a screen that breaks up the solid areas into small dots. The four separate dot images are printed on copper plates that are coated with a photosensitive solution. In order to make a raised printing surface, the plates are chemically etched so that the dots remain raised while the white areas are "eaten away."

The plates are then inked and printed, one over the other. Figures 1 through 7 show prints of the separate color plates along with the step-by-step build-up of the picture as each color is superimposed. In order to achieve a sharp clean print, great care is taken to keep all of the plates in exact register.

The dots are so fine that they appear to be a solid wash of color. But Fig. 8, an enlargement of the boxed area on the grapes, show how the dots blend to create this effect.

Fig. 1

+

Fig. 2

=

Fig. 5

+

Fig. 3

=

Fig. 6

+

Fig. 4

=

Fig. 7

Fig. 8

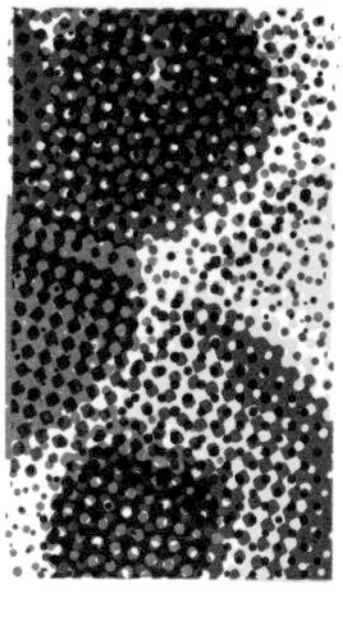

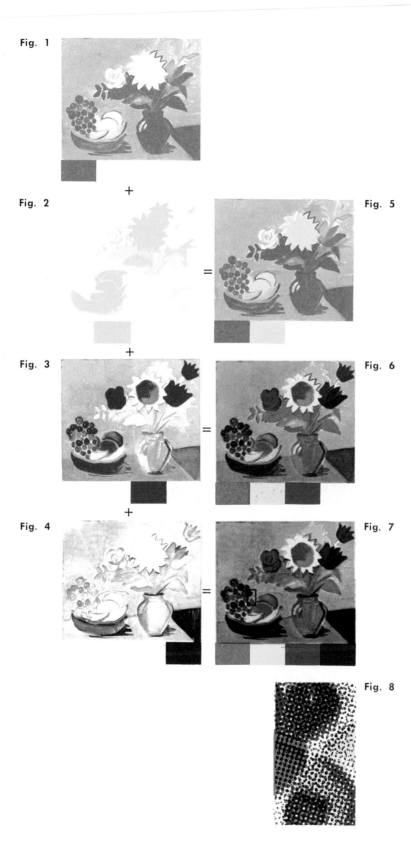

COLOR PHOTOGRAPHY

Color photographs come in two different forms. One is the *color transparency*, or "slide," in which light is passed *through* the photograph. The other is the *photographic print*, which shows colors just the way most other objects do—that is, by taking advantage of the fact that daylight already has so many different wavelengths of light vibrations in it that it can produce all the colors of the rainbow. Like any other object lying about, a color print sends forth only some of the colors, absorbing the others.

Both kinds of color photographs start from film that is not only light-sensitive (like BLACK-AND-WHITE FILM) but, in its various layers, sensitive to certain colors. Once the films have been processed, they again make use of three carefully balanced colors to re-create the orginial scene. (The POLAROID color process, which works differently, is described on pages 198–201).

Transparencies look simple—their surface shows the right patches of color in the right places, and when light from the projector shines through them, the colored images appear on the screen, enlarged. But the process that *gets* the color onto the slide is quite devious.

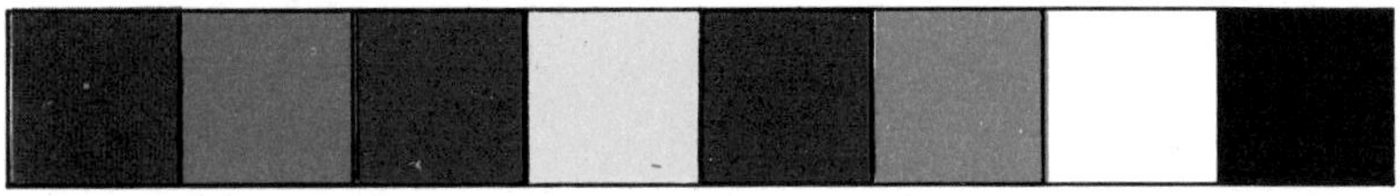

Fig. 1 FULL RANGE OF COLORS THAT WILL BE PHOTOGRAPHED IN TRANSPARENCY IS REPRESENTED BY SELECTED HUES OF TEST STRIP

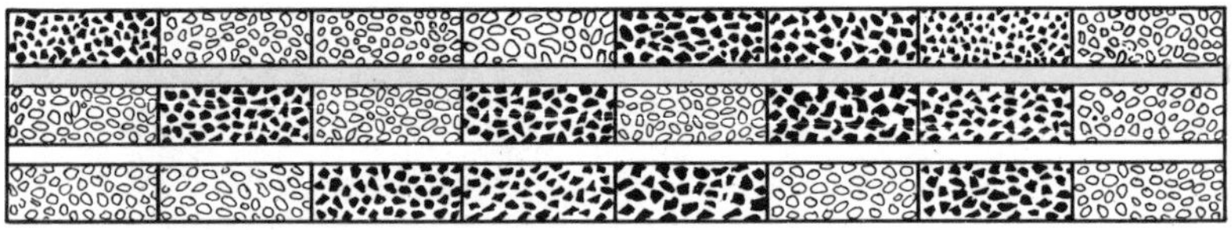

Fig. 2 FILM'S TOP LAYER IS SENSITIVE TO BLUE, MIDDLE LAYER TO GREEN, BOTTOM TO RED. AFTER FIRST (BLACK-AND-WHITE) DEVELOPMENT, BLACK GRAINS APPEAR WHEREVER A LAYER WAS RESPONDING TO A COLOR IN FIG. 1. BECAUSE SILVER BROMIDE IN FILM IS NATURALLY SENSITIVE TO BLUE, FILM INCLUDES YELLOW FILTER LAYER THAT PREVENTS BLUE LIGHT FROM REACHING LOWER LAYERS

Only one layer of the original film (the middle layer) responds to green (Fig. 2). It is sandwiched between a layer that responds to blue and a layer that responds to red. Now, you may have noticed that the colors in the original scene (Fig. 1) include yellow. On looking at the layers in Fig. 2, you may think, This is one combination that will never produce yellow! You're right. It won't. At this stage, it doesn't have to.

In the processing, after the film has been passed through a developing solution to bring out the little dark grains of silver that will form the picture (Fig. 2), the film is exposed to a red light, then is dunked in a tank that deposits a greenish-blue "cyan" dye on the red-sensitive layer. So far, the film has only one dye. But it is now passed on to another light and another tank where its blue-sensitive layer picks up yellow dye, and then to a third light and a third tank in which the middle layer picks up a purplish-red "magenta" dye.

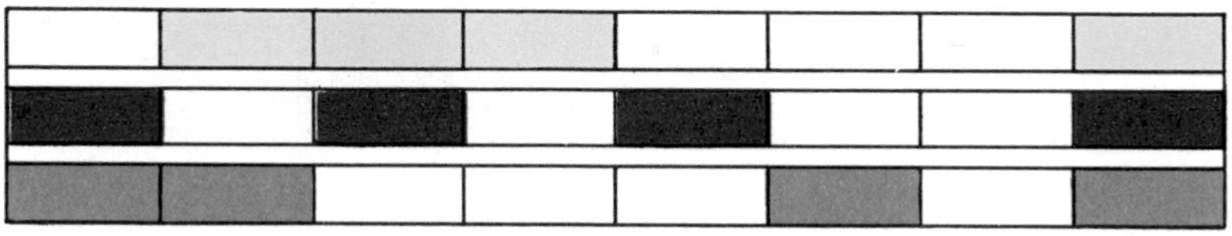

Fig. 3 AFTER PROCESSING, TRANSPARENCY'S THREE LAYERS HOLD YELLOW, MAGENTA, AND CYAN DYES IN PATTERN GOVERNED BY COLOR SENSITIVITY OF ORIGINAL LAYERS

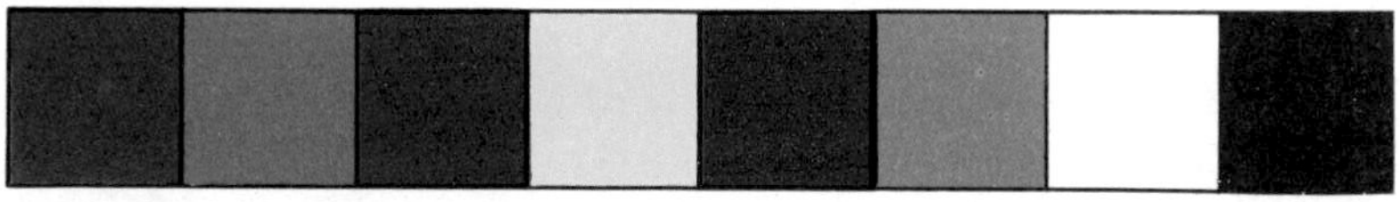

Fig. 4 COLORS OFFERED BY TRANSPARENCY AFTER PROCESSING COMBINE EFFECTS OF THE THREE LAYERS OF FIG. 3

From then on, it is up to these three dyes (Fig. 3) to recombine light into the original colors. But will these three dyes reproduce green? Yes, they will. The second blocks from the left in Fig. 3 show how the yellow and cyan layers will combine to produce the green of Fig. 4.

Some photographers prefer to use a film that will give them **negative prints** (as in black-and-white photography) that can later be used

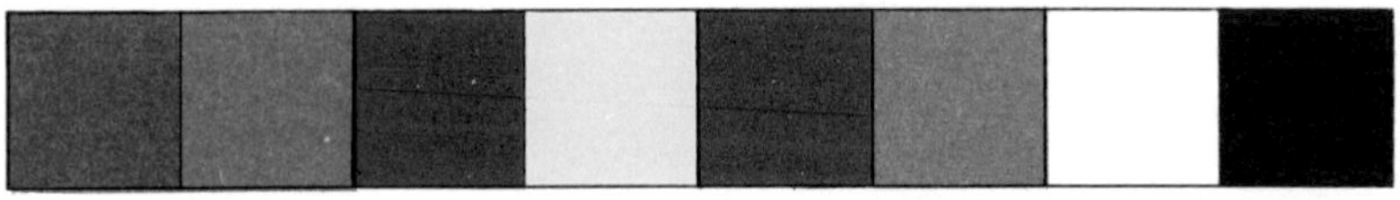

Fig. 5 FULL COLOR RANGE OF NATURAL SCENE THAT WILL APPEAR IN PHOTOGRAPHIC PRINTS IS REPRESENTED BY SELECTED HUES IN TEST STRIP

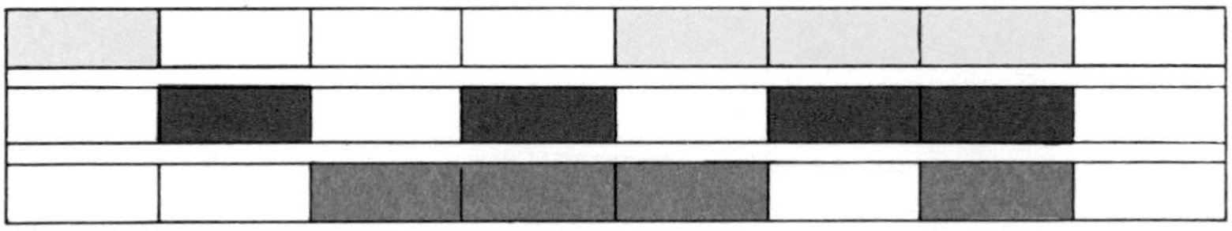

Fig. 6 IMAGES FORMED OF YELLOW, MAGENTA, AND CYAN DYES REMAIN IN SEPARATE LAYERS OF NEGATIVE PRINT AFTER DEVELOPMENT AND REMOVAL OF SILVER

Fig. 7 IN NEGATIVE PRINT, THE COLORS PRODUCED BY THE THREE LAYERS ARE, SQUARE BY SQUARE, COMPLEMENTARY TO CORRESPONDING COLORS OF ORIGINAL SCENE. MEANING OF "COMPLEMENTARY" WILL APPEAR IN FIG. 9

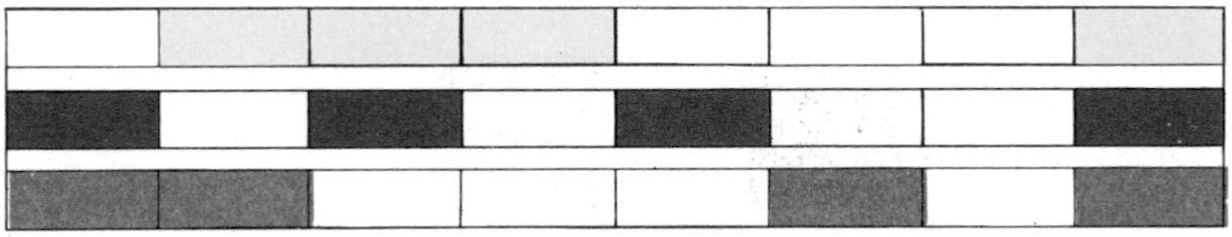

Fig. 8 IMAGES FORMED OF YELLOW, MAGENTA, AND CYAN HUES ARE NOW PRODUCED IN SEPARATE LAYERS IN A POSITIVE PRINT

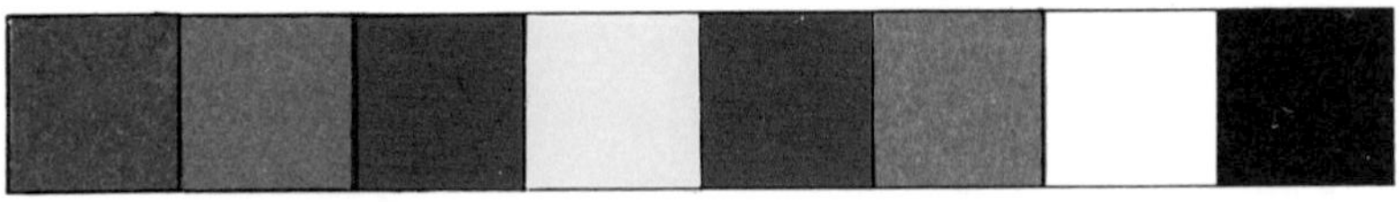

Fig. 9 IN POSITIVE PRINT, COLORS PRODUCED BY THE THREE LAYERS ARE COMPLEMENTARY TO CORRESPONDING SQUARES IN FIG. 7. THE COMPLEMENTARY (FIG. 9) OF A COMPLEMENTARY (FIG. 7) IS AGAIN THE ORIGINAL (FIG. 5)

to make **positive prints.** These require a different sort of film to begin with. After photographs have been taken, the film is processed in a developing solution that brings out separate silver-and-dye images in three layers (Fig. 6). The silver is then removed, leaving a color negative. (Color negatives are reversed not only in their brightness—light becoming dark, dark becoming light—but also in their hue, or "color": green for magenta-red and magenta-red for green.) This can be seen by comparing Figs. 7 and 9. Later, when positive prints are made, paper is used that reverses the images all over again (Fig. 8), so that the colors in the final positive print (Fig. 9) are those of the original scene (Fig. 5).

POLAROID COLOR FILM

Photography is a chemical process, and most people aren't chemists. So, once a picture has been taken, the negative film is usually taken to a laboratory where the negative is developed and a positive print is made from it. But with Polacolor film, the camera itself becomes the lab. As a matter of fact, the actual chemical work is done not in the camera as a whole but right in the film—in a layer only two-thousandths of an inch thick!

If you have ever watched a football game, you'll have no difficulty understanding what goes on in Polacolor film—in both cases, it's simply a matter of whether something is going *one way* down the field or the *other way*. In our illustrations, the "field" in Figs. 1 and 3 is set up vertically and shows a cross-section of the film. In Fig. 1, light moves downward; in Fig. 3, a substance with a technical name moves downward and bits of dye move upward.

The first thing that moves downward (Fig. 1) is the light, when the shutter is snapped. It can land in any one of three light-sensitive

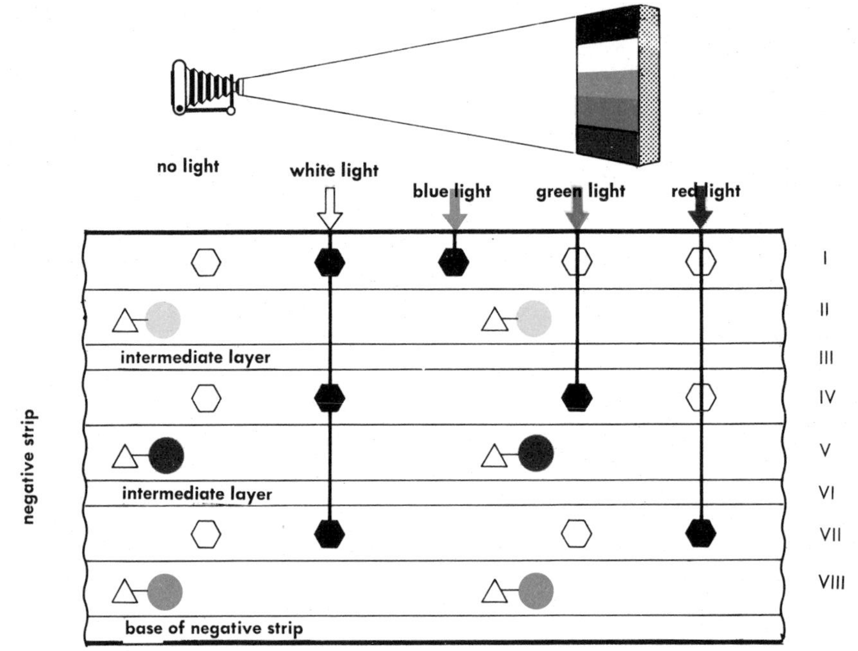

Fig. 1 EXPOSURE OF EIGHT-LAYER FILM

layers (numbers I, IV, and VII). Each layer is sensitive to light of only one color (blue, green, or red). Let's say we are photographing a red barn. The red light from the barn will go all the way down to layer VII, where it will hit a grain of silver bromide and "expose" it. (For just what this means, see BLACK-AND-WHITE FILM.) The red light will have no effect on layers I through VI as it passes through them. Blue light, the sky behind the barn, will expose grains of silver bromide in layer I, which is blue-sensitive; green light from the grass will affect layer IV.

The picture has now been taken. Now we take the film to the laboratory—that is, we convert the film itself into a lab. To do this, we pull the film tab at one end of the camera. Doing this squeezes the film between two rollers (Fig. 2) and breaks open a pod, or cap-

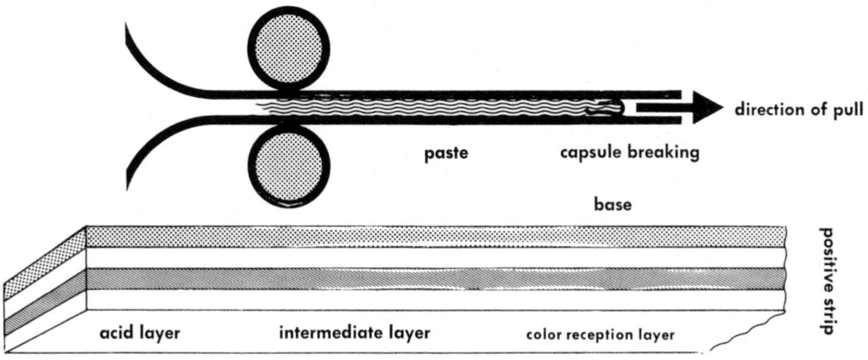

Fig. 2 THREE-LAYER POSITIVE STRIP IS PRESSED AGAINST NEGATIVE STRIP; DEVELOPER-ACTIVATING PASTE SERVES AS "GLUE"

sule, of paste that can be called alkaline activator. (This is a "substance" with a technical name mentioned earlier—informally, its inventors have usually called it "goo.") It is this goo, spreading through neighboring layers, that starts a chemical reaction that will bring out images in color—first negative, then positive.

The goo's first work (Fig. 3) is *downward*—seeping into layers II, V, and VIII, it releases compounds that work both as developers and as dyes. Each bit of developer-dye moves upward toward the silver bromide just above it.

At this point what is being developed is a *color negative*. It is not only dark where the original scene was light, but it's a purplish red, or magenta (see layer V), where the original grass was green. The following conversion now takes place:

Layers I, IV, and VII, which originally were sensitive to blue, green, and red, are now invaded by developers that are dyeing them yellow, magenta, and cyan (a blue with a slight suggestion of green). As the

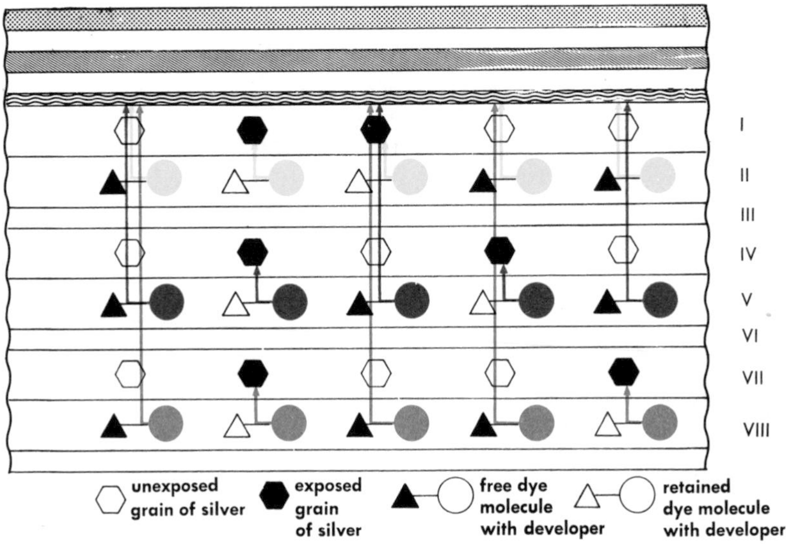

Fig. 3 DEVELOPMENT PROCESS

three images now develop in layers I, IV, and VII, each image is going to come out a color opposite, or "complementary," to the color the layer was sensitive to when we began. To accomplish this, cyan dye (layer VIII) moves into red-sensitive layer VII; magenta dye (layer V) moves into green-sensitive layer IV; and yellow dye (layer II) moves into blue-sensitive layer I. In each case, a negative is turned into a positive.

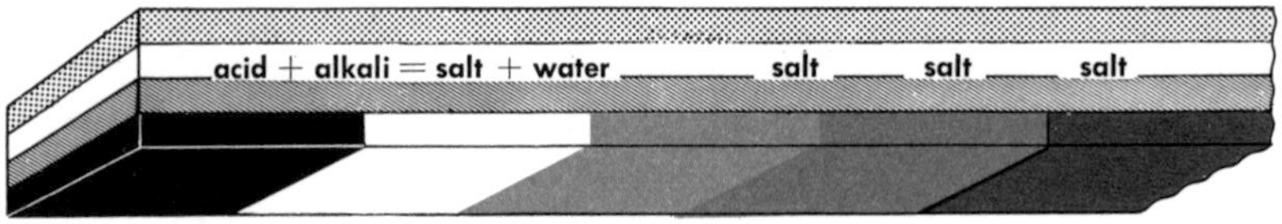

Fig. 4 FINALLY DEVELOPED POSITIVE

The dyes keep on moving upward until they reach the positive layer on the top. Blue is formed wherever cyan and magenta dyes reach the surface at the same spot, green wherever cyan and yellow emerge together, and red wherever there is a mixture of magenta and yellow.

Some of the goo, meanwhile, has also spread *upward* from its original layer. When the printing paper, which is acid, is invaded by this goo, which is alkaline, water is produced (Fig. 4). This water washes away whatever goo remains and all chemical activity stops. The result is a finished color print.

MOVIE PROJECTORS

A movie projector operates on the same principle as a movie camera, although more or less in reverse order. In the camera, the light rays reflected from the subject being photographed are focused on the unexposed film by the lens. In the projector, a light *behind* the processed film passes through the image. The image is then projected by the lens onto a viewing screen. In other cases, hundreds of pictures showing progressive movement are made, and each picture, or frame, must be exposed, or projected, rapidly enough to give the illusion of continuous motion to the human eye. This action may be slower than one would expect due to a built-in retaining quality in the eye called *persistence of vision.* The most fleeting image that registers in the eye does not fade away for one-sixteenth to one-twentieth of a second. Most home movie projectors show 16 separate frames of film per second—enough for the eye to blend the pictures into one smooth motion.

Figure 1 shows the construction of a typical projector. In order to throw an enlarged film image onto a screen some distance away, a powerful light must be beamed through the transparency. A concave collecting *mirror* is mounted behind the *lamp* to direct as much light as possible toward the *lens.* To ensure even lighting, the center of the mirror is directly behind the filament. The *condenser* concentrates the light on the *film* while the lens enlarges the image and focuses it on the screen.

Intense light creates the problem of intense heat, which can cause the film to buckle (or even to melt in a slide projector). The heat is

Fig. 1 SCHEMATIC DIAGRAM OF A MOVIE PROJECTOR

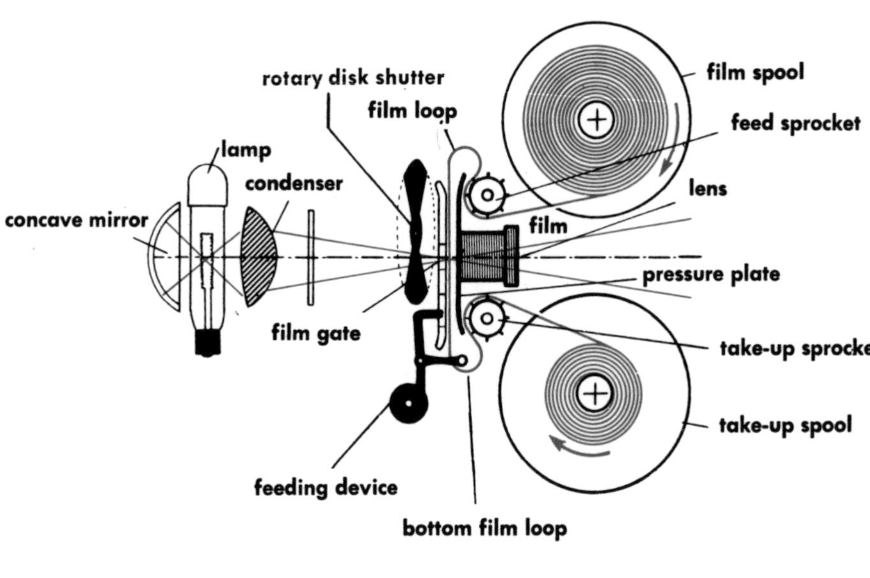

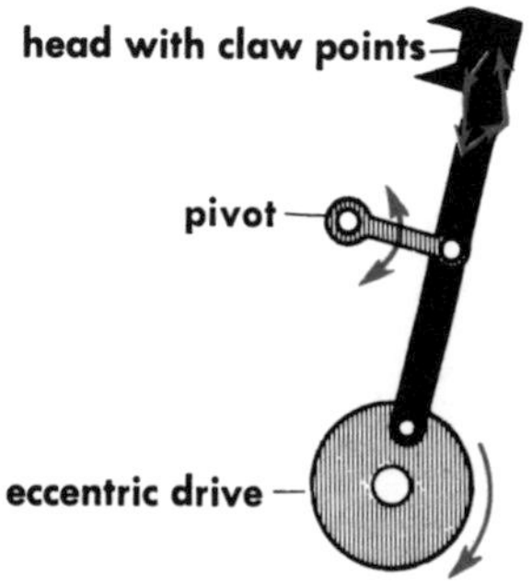

Fig. 2 CLAW-TYPE FEEDING MECHANISM

Fig. 3 OPERATION OF ROTARY DISK SHUTTER

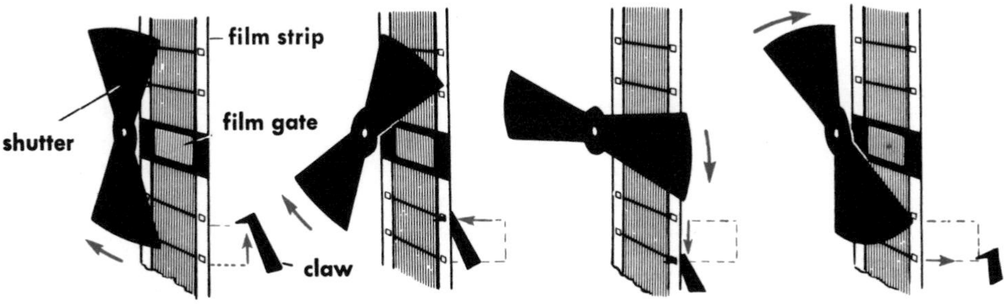

controlled on most projectors by a small motor-driven fan that pulls in cool room air and blows out hot air.

The same motor controls the *sprockets* and *feeding device.* The sprockets rotate at a constant speed, but the feeder advances the film in quick jumps, making it necessary to have loops of slack film above and below the *film gate.*

One type of feeding mechanism is shown in Fig. 2. The lower end of the claw is mounted eccentrically (off-center) on a rotating drive wheel. With each turn of the wheel, the rotating motion, along with the *pivot* action, moves the *claw points* in the path shown by the red arrows. The results can be seen in Fig. 3. The claw points engage with the perforations on the edge of the film, pull it down one full frame, release it momentarily, and move up to continue the cycle. While the film is being pulled down, the film gate must be covered to avoid a blurred image. The *rotary disk shutter* shown here is exactly synchronized with the feeding device to cover the film while it is in motion.

Projectors for showing slides (individual "still" transparencies) work optically on the same principle as movie projectors, though they are built to accommodate a larger-size film. And, except for the cooling fan, they don't require motor-driven parts.

VI Radio and Television

RADIO WAVES

An ELECTRIC CURRENT that periodically changes the direction in which it flows is called an *alternating current.* Alternating currents are characterized by their *frequency*—that is, the number of cycles, or complete changes of direction, in the flow of the current per second. Such cycles are also called *double waves.* High-frequency alternating currents are used in radio communication because an alternating current produces an electromagnetic field that varies with the frequency of the current and that is propagated through space with the speed of light—that is, 186,000 miles per second. With low-frequency alternating current, the energy that is transmitted into space has sufficient time to return to the electrical conductor each time the alternating current changes its direction of flow. With very high frequencies, however, the change of direction takes place before all of the energy has had time to return. A portion of the energy is, therefore, cut off and is transmitted into space as *electromagnetic radiation.* Because of the periodic character of this radiation, and because of its similarity to the propagation of a wave in water, it is also called an electromagnetic wave, or radio wave.

The generation of radio waves is always associated with the existence of a high-frequency alternating current whose energy is radiated into space. This radiation process, which depends on the frequency of the

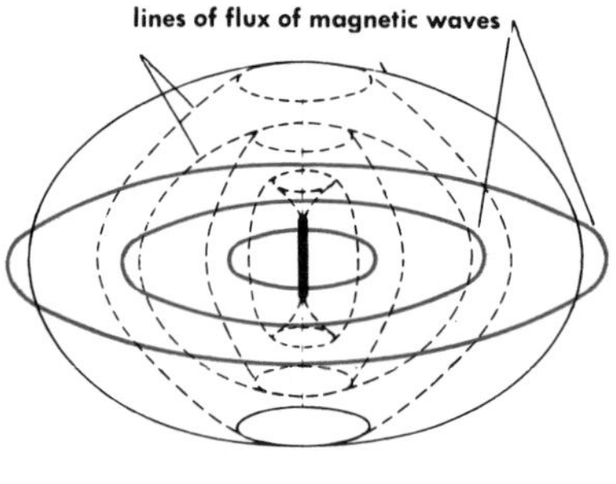

Fig. 1 SPHERICAL WAVE SYSTEM AROUND A HERTZ DIPOLE

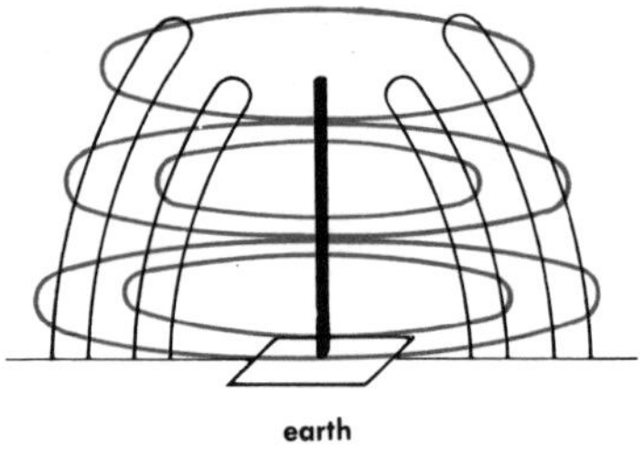

Fig. 2 DIPOLE GROUNDED ON ONE SIDE

alternating current that produces it, can best be demonstrated with reference to the so-called **Hertz dipole** (Fig. 1). This device consists of a conductor whose length is related to the wavelength of the electromagnetic wave produced. The wavelength equals the distance traveled per second divided by the frequency—the number of periods, or cycles, per second. If a high-frequency alternating current is passed through this conductor, a high-frequency alternating electromagnetic field will be formed around it, as shown in Fig. 1. If one end of a dipole is earthed, or grounded, we have the simplest form of an aerial, or antenna (Fig. 2). A circuit whose electrical and magnetic properties are tuned to the frequency of the alternating current—that is, is in resonance with it—is called an **oscillating circuit.** The latter is

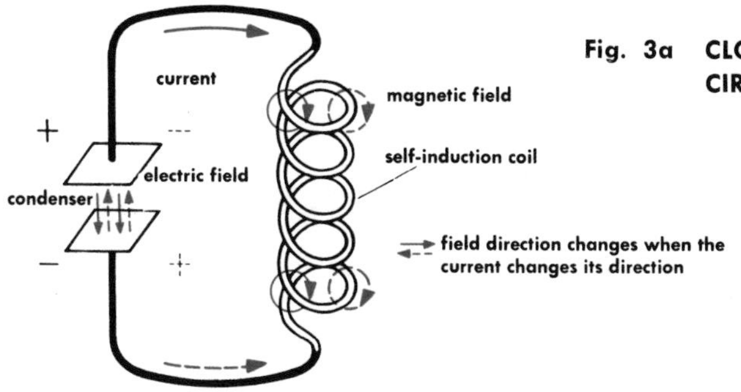

Fig. 3a CLOSED OSCILLATING CIRCUIT

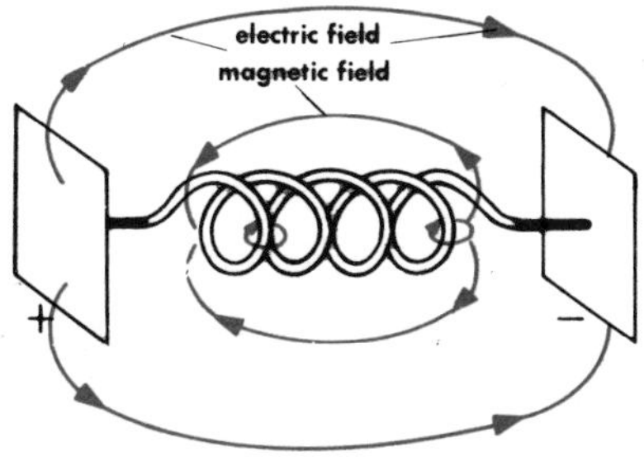

Fig. 3b OPEN OSCILLATING CIRCUIT

made of a *condenser* and a *self-induction coil.* Once it is charged, the condenser discharges itself through the coil, so that electrical energy that was stored up in the condenser is converted into magnetic energy (Figs. 3a and 3b). After the discharge of the condenser has taken place, the magnetic field breaks down and induces a current in the coil. This current gives the condenser a charge of opposite sign to its

Fig. 4 TUBE TRANSMITTER (amplitude modulation)

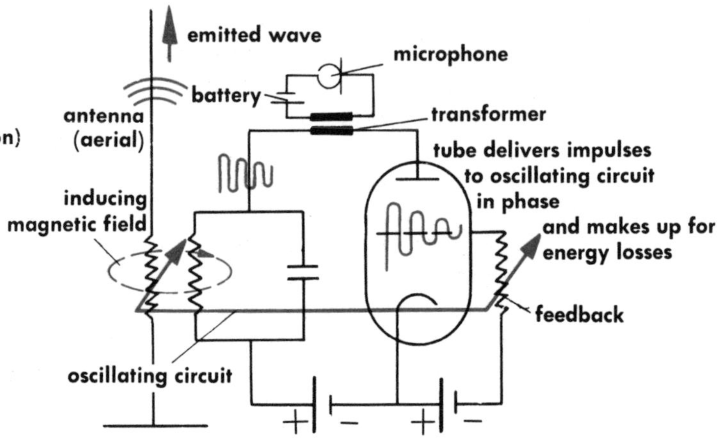

Fig. 5 TUBE TRANSMITTER (frequency modulation)

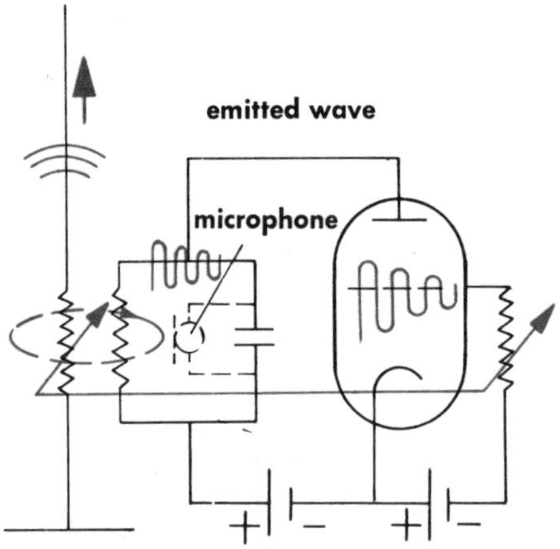

Fig. 6 TRANSISTOR TRANSMITTER

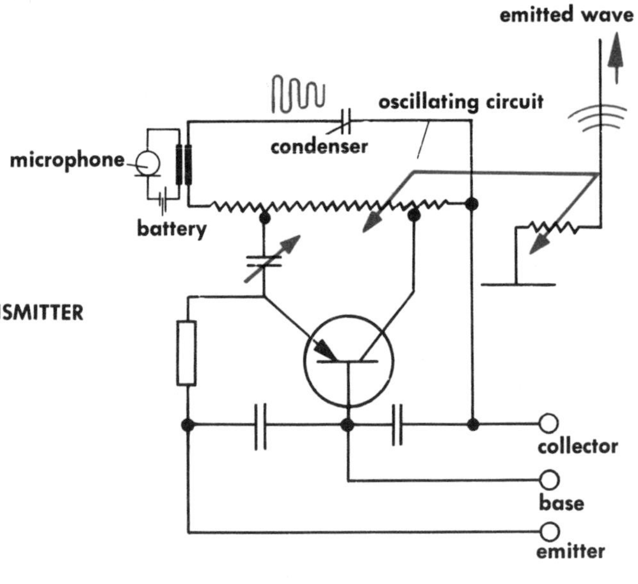

original charge. If no losses occurred, the charge would go on oscillating—changing its sign indefinitely.

Oscillating circuits are used, in the form of aerials, as transmitting and receiving devices for electromagnetic energy in radio transmitters and receivers. As the emission of electromagnetic waves constantly withdraws energy from the oscillating circuit of the transmitter and therefore damps it, it is necessary constantly to supply fresh energy to it. This is done by means of a triode or a transistor in a feedback circuit (Figs. 4, 5, and 6).

VACUUM TUBES AND TRANSISTORS

The vacuum tube is a sensitive electronic device that can detect radio signals and amplify them with great accuracy. In a metal, the "free," or loosely bonded, electrons can be shaken loose by the addition of energy. The easiest way to do this is to heat the metal. The emission of the electrons can then be seen as a kind of evaporation process (Fig. 1). When heat is applied, the atoms of the metal collide and high-energy electrons are released, which can break out from the surface of the metal and escape. This emission of electrons from an incandescent metal (usually an electrically heated filament) can most easily be made to take place in a vacuum, which prevents oxidation

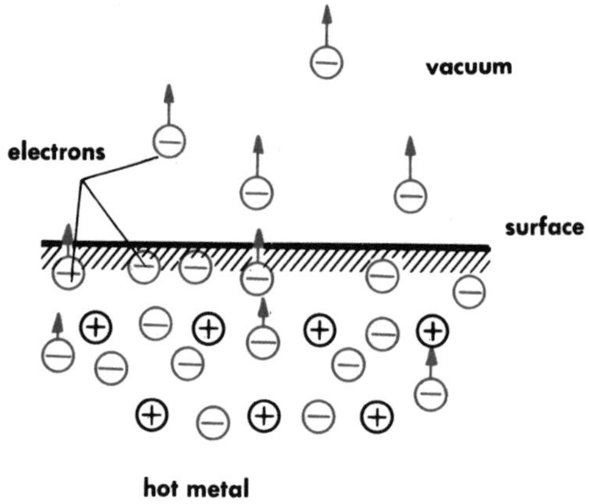

Fig. 1 EMISSION OF ELECTRONS FROM A HOT METAL

of the very hot surface of the metal and allows the electrons to emerge unobstructed—that is, without colliding with, or being neutralized by, gas molecules and ions of the air. The thermionic, or vacuum, tube does this. It contains at least two electrodes, the *cathode* and the *anode* (thus it is called a **diode**), and may have more (Fig. 2). The **triode** has a third electrode, the control *grid*. It allows the electrons to pass through it and controls them by appropriately modifying the space charge. The circuit connections for a triode are shown in Fig. 3. The vacuum tube has the property of unipolar conductivity—that is, the electrons can flow in one direction only, from the (hot) cathode to the (cold) anode.

In contrast to metals, certain elements known as semiconductors contain only a relatively small number of "free" electrons at room temperature. Silicon and germanium are two commonly used semiconductors. By adding atoms with a higher or lower number of "free"

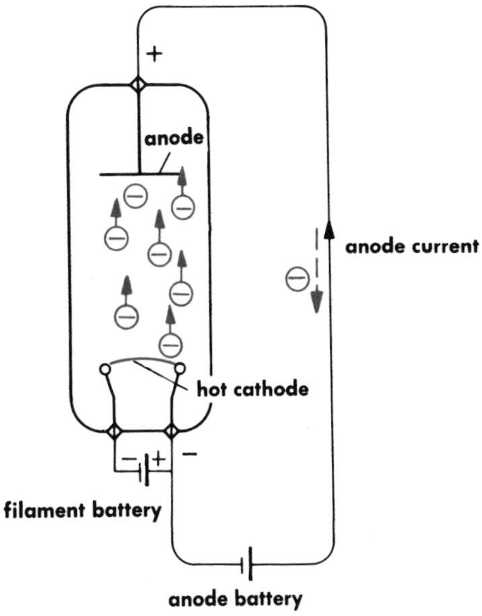

Fig. 2 DIODE

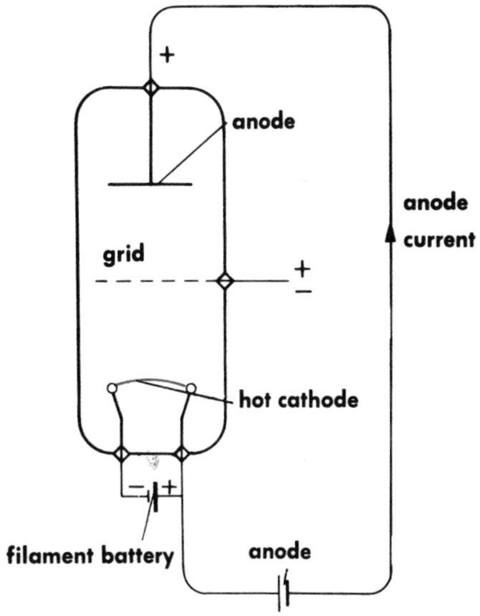

Fig. 3 TRIODE

electrons, the conductivity properties of semiconductors can be varied very widely. Thus, the flow of ELECTRIC CURRENT can be increased or decreased (or blocked) depending on the kind of material added to it. Semiconductor elements that comprise a transition from positive to negative conduction are called semiconductor diodes, while those that comprise two such transitions are called **transistors.** The transistor is a semiconductor triode. Its three electrodes are called the *emitter*, the *base*, and the *collector*. The significant feature is that the base should be narrow (50 microns) to enable the charge carriers from the emitter to pass through the boundary layer 1 and traverse the base so that they can thus affect the processes taking place at the boundary layer 2. Control of the passage of current between base and collector is thereby achieved. This enables the transistor to be used for the purpose of amplification and the generation of oscillations. It is progressively superseding the vacuum tube. Besides taking up far less space, transistors have the advantage of dispensing with the filament current.

Fig. 4 HOW A TRANSISTOR WORKS: CURRENT IN COLLECTOR CIRCUIT CONTROLLED BY CONDUCTION IN EMITTER CIRCUIT

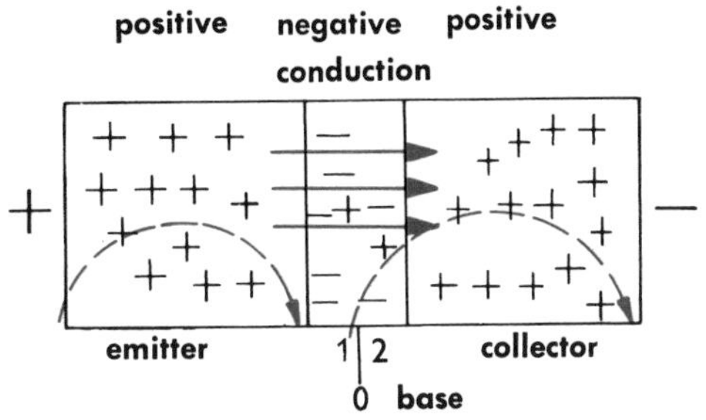

RADAR

The word "radar" comes from the initial letters of the phrase "radio detecting and ranging." It is a method of scanning an area by means of high-frequency RADIO WAVES that are sent out from a powerful transmitter and are reflected by any objects that they encounter. The reflected beam of radio waves is picked up by a receiver; the beam's strength and direction give information on the size, distance, altitude, etc., of the object it has encountered.

Fig. 1

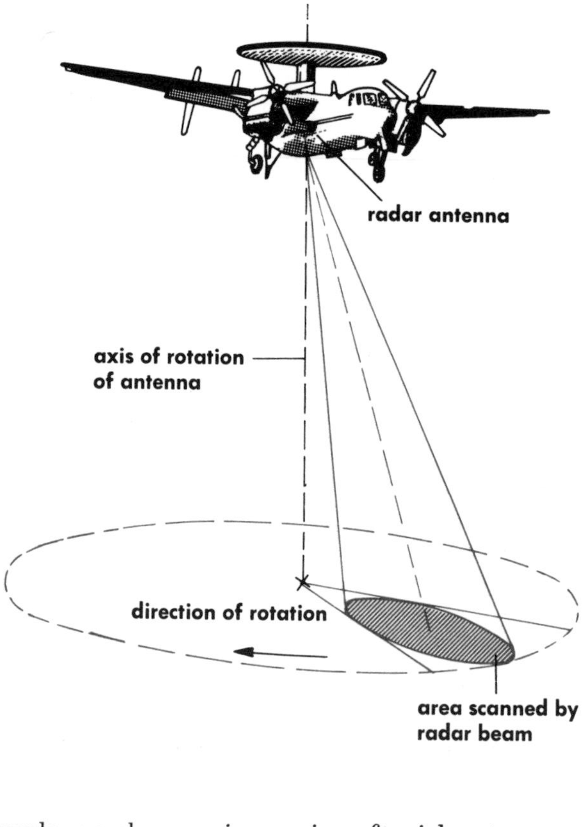

If, for example, an observer in an aircraft wishes to survey by radar the land over which he is flying (Fig. 1), a rotating radar beam is directed downward from the aircraft. The beam scans a circular area in the form of a sector that sweeps around and around. Depending on the nature of the reflecting objects (in this case, located on the surface of the earth), the intensity of the reflected beam will vary (Fig. 2). The transmission and reception of the high-frequency waves are done in the radar apparatus. The radar waves are generated in the transmitter, which is equipped with radio tubes of a special design. The transmitting *antenna* usually also functions as the receiving antenna by means of a periodic change-over. The transmitter sends out short intense bursts, or pulses, of energy with a relatively long interval between pulses. The receiver is active during this interval. When sufficient time has elapsed to permit the reception of echoes from the most distant objects of interest, the transmitter sends another short pulse and the cycle repeats.

Fig. 2

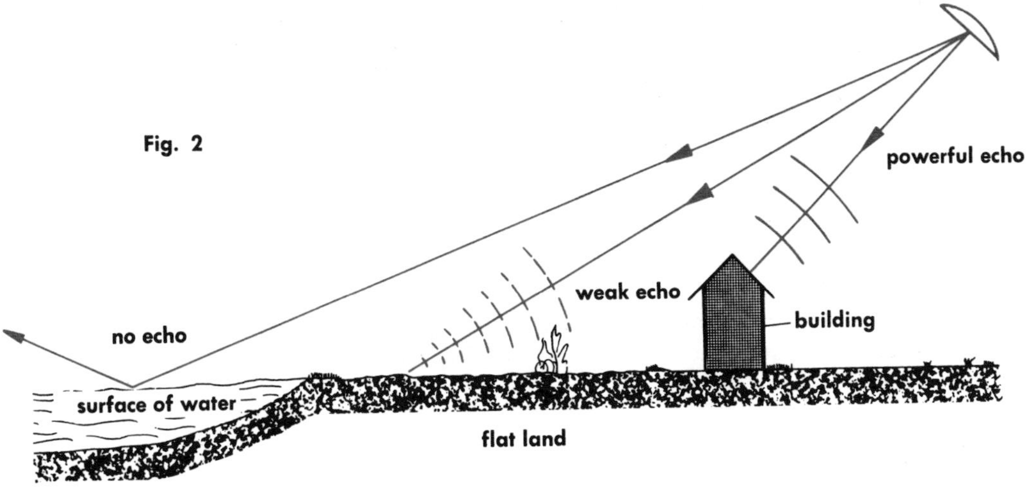

The reflected beam is picked up by the receiver and the corresponding ELECTRIC CURRENTS are used to deflect an electron beam in a cathode-ray tube.

The radar beam is so deflected that it scans the luminescent screen from the center to the edge while it rotates at the same speed as the antenna. An echo picked up by the receiver strengthens the flow of electrons in the tube, causing a point of light to appear on the screen and to remain visible by phosphorescent afterglow until fresh echoes are picked up on the next revolution of the scanning antenna. In this way the points of light build up a picture of the area, or space, scanned by the beam. The brightness of the display of the signal

Fig. 3 **HOW A HURRICANE APPEARS ON A RADAR SCREEN**

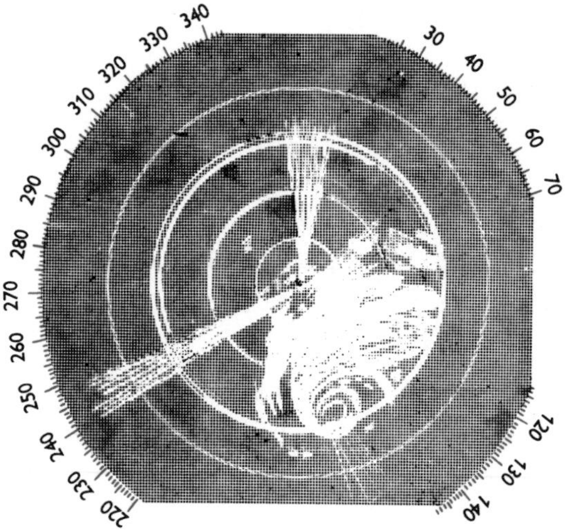

(the radar echo) on the luminescent screen of the cathode-ray tube depends on the reflecting power of the object with regard to the high-frequency radio waves sent out by the radar transmitter. For this reason a radar image generally looks quite different from an optical image, although as a rule they will have the same outlines (Fig. 3).

BLACK-AND-WHITE TELEVISION

Television uses the movie-projection principle in that it shows a series of pictures at a rate of at least 30 per second and thus produces the visual impression of continuous motion. The picture to be projected is divided into many lines and each line must contain several hundred individually identifiable shades of gray—called "halftone light values." This is known as "scanning." To obtain a reasonably good picture, the image must be thus analyzed into at least 100,000 (and preferably 200,000) **picture elements** (Fig. 1).

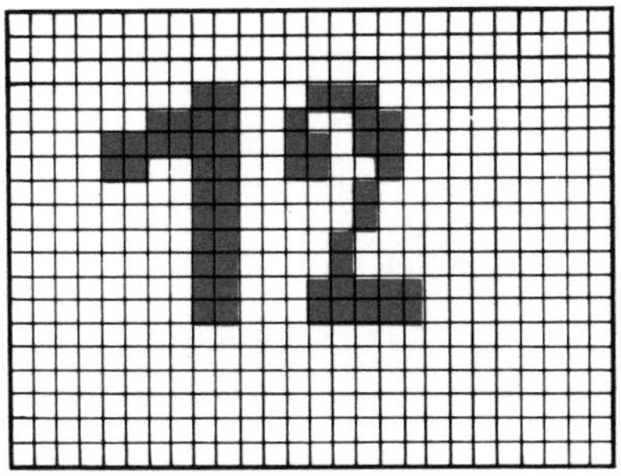

Fig. 1 PICTURE ELEMENTS

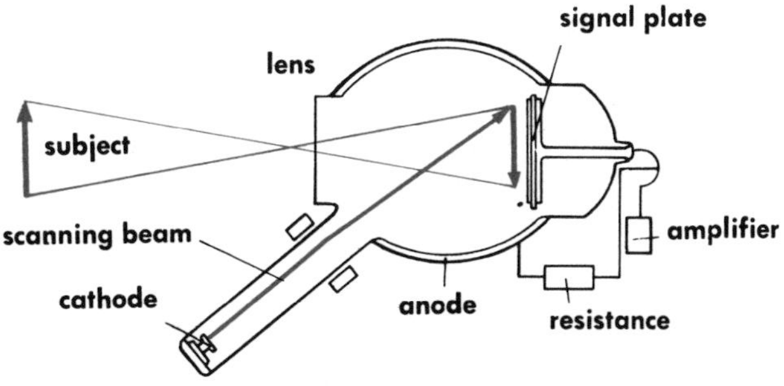

Fig. 2 TELEVISION CAMERA

In the **television camera** (Fig. 2) the image is focused on a plate called the *signal plate* whose surface is covered with a mosaic of photosensitive points. Each of these points, corresponding to one picture element, acquires a positive ELECTRIC CHARGE whose strength depends on the strength of the illumination falling on it. An *electron beam*, forming a scanning spot on the signal plate, zigzags its way, line by line, across the plate every one-thirtieth of a second and thus discharges each photosensitive point 30 times per second (Figs. 2 and 3). Each point thus gives an electric impulse whose strength corresponds to the strength of illumination at that point at that particular instant. These impulses (forming the picture signal) are amplified and transmitted. In the television receiver the incoming impulses, after amplification, are fed to the **control electrode** of the picture tube (Fig. 3) in which an electron beam is zig-zagged across a fluorescent screen synchronously with the beam in the camera tube, with an intensity varying with the strength of the electric impulses. In this way a pattern of luminous points of varying brightness, and formed in rapid succession, is produced on the screen, thus making the picture that the viewer sees.

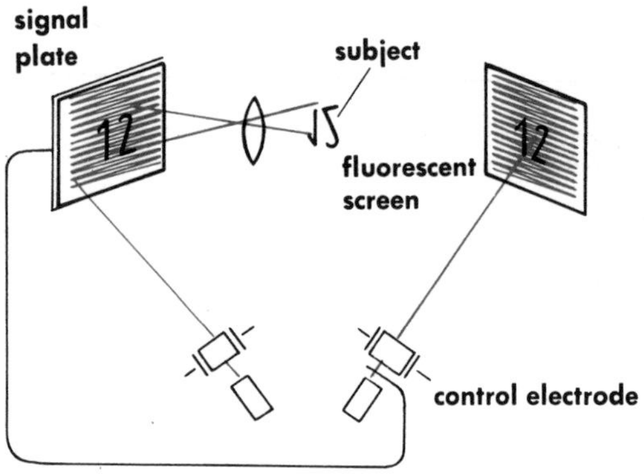

Fig. 3 ICONOSCOPE (transmission) AND CATHODE-RAY TUBE (reception)

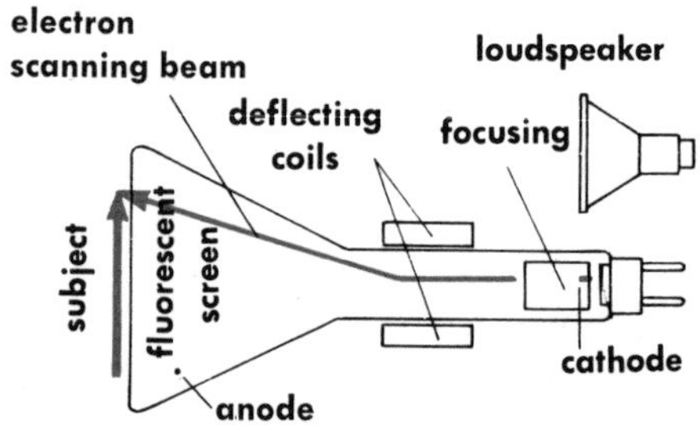

Fig. 4 SOUND AND PICTURE REPRODUCTION AT RECEIVER (loudspeaker and cathode-ray tube)

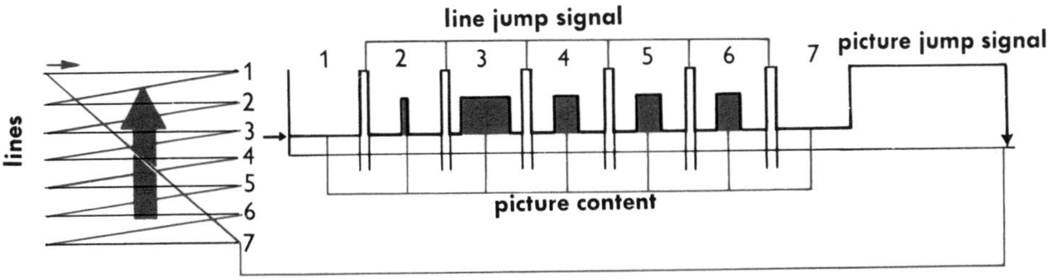

Fig. 5 SCANNING OF AN IMAGE AND CORRESPONDING ELECTRIC SIGNALS

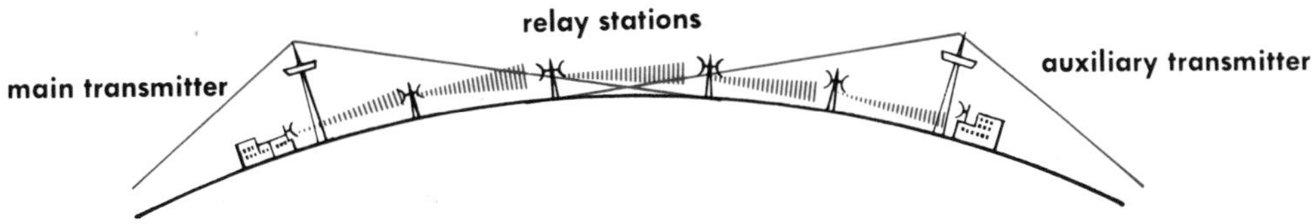

Fig. 6 TELEVISION TRANSMISSION WAVES TRAVEL IN STRAIGHT PATHS; RELAY STATIONS AND AUXILIARY TRANSMITTERS ARE THEREFORE REQUIRED

The picture *signals* (Fig. 5) can be conveyed to the receiver by cable, but they are usually transmitted by means of waves similar to those used in ordinary radio broadcasting, but of shorter wavelength. These high-frequency shortwaves are able to travel only in straight paths from the transmitter so that, because of the earth's curvature, the range is, broadly speaking, limited to the visual horizon. It is for this reason that television transmitters are installed on tall masts or towers, which have to be spaced about 50 miles apart in order to provide good television coverage throughout a region (Fig. 6).

COLOR TELEVISION

All colors of light can be created by mixing, in varying amounts, primary colors—red, green, and blue light. (While in painting, red, yellow, and blue are called the primary colors, in photography, green replaces yellow as one of the primary colors.) The color-television camera separates the objects to be viewed into the three primary colors, and these colors are then converted by a device called a color coder into a *luminance*—a brightness, or "brilliance"—signal and a *chrominance* signal. Chrominance refers to two characteristics, *hue* and *saturation*.

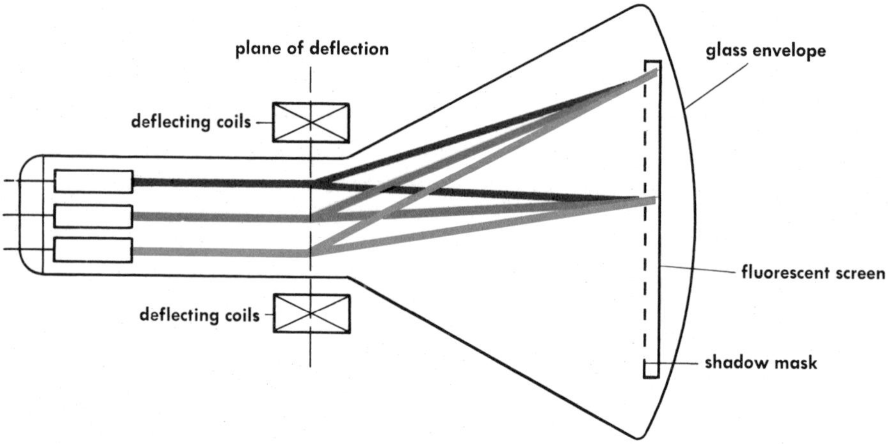

Fig. 1 COLOR TELEVISION TUBE

The primary-color signals, which have been recast into luminance and chrominance components at the transmitter, must be reconverted into primary-color signals at the receiver before they can be applied to the color picture tube. The system used in the United States employs a picture tube, known as a *shadow-mask tube*, that contains three electron guns that produce three separate electron beams. These beams move simultaneously in the scanning pattern over the viewing screen and produce a red, green, and blue image. The screen is composed of three separate sets of uniformly distributed phosphor dots. The dots of each set glow in a different color. Electrons discharged by the gun controlled by the red color signal hit only the red-glowing phosphor dots and are prevented from hitting the green- and blue-

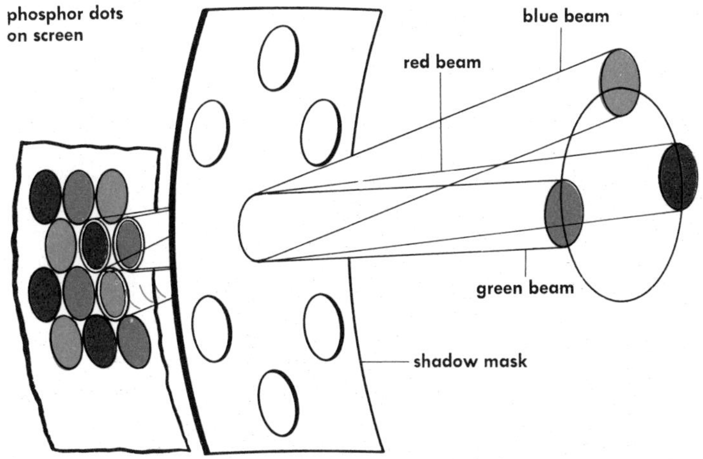

Fig. 2 SMALL PORTION OF SHADOW MASK SHOWN ENLARGED

glowing dots by a mask that contains about 200,000 tiny holes, each of which is accurately aligned with the different-colored phosphor dots on the screen. In the same way, the electrons from the other two guns fall only on the green and blue dots, respectively. In this way, three separate primary-color images are formed simultaneously. The dots producing the three different colors are so small and so close together that the eye doesn't see them as separate points of light.

VII Handling Messages and Data

TYPEWRITERS

About one hundred years ago, Philo Remington, a gunsmith and arms manufacturer, was responsible for making the first practical typewriter with most of the essential features of the modern machine. It had a moving carriage with a hard-rubber cylinder, or platen, on which the paper was wound and held in place by rubber pressure rolls. The type bars were arranged in a radial arc so that they struck the paper through an inked ribbon at a common center, leaving the imprint of the raised letter on the paper. The early Remington had one letter on each type bar and wrote only in capitals. There were other machines that supplied both upper- and lower-case characters by using a double keyboard, but they were bulky and complex to operate.

The problem was solved with the introduction of the *carriage shift*, which is now an important feature on all typewriters. The shift allows two letters to be carried on each type bar along with numbers, symbols, and punctuation marks. Normally the lower-case letter at the bottom of the bar strikes the inked ribbon. When the shift key is depressed, it works a lever that raises the carriage a short distance, causing the capital letter at the top of the bar to strike the ribbon. The shift can also be locked in this position when *all* capital letters are wanted. The compact keyboards of shift machines can be operated without having to look at the keys, a system called "touch typing."

Figure 1 shows the lever action of a single type *key*. On portables, the springs are often horizontal, but their function is the same: to pull the *type bar* back into position after it has struck the ribbon. The action between key and type bar can be traced quite clearly in a typewriter with a removable top section; use a flashlight and slowly depress a key that works one of the outside bars.

Fig. 1 MECHANISM OF A MECHANICAL TYPEWRITER

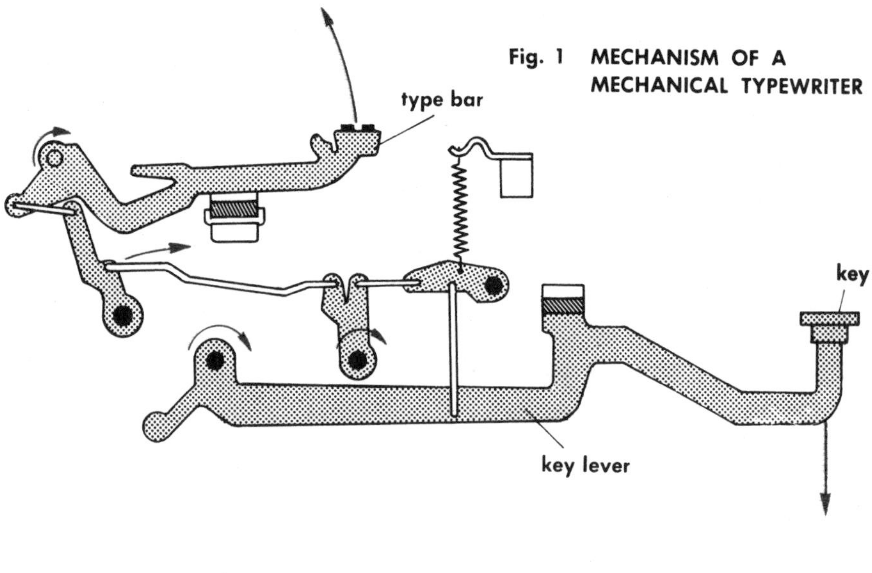

Fig. 2 SECTION THROUGH AN ELECTRIC TYPEWRITER

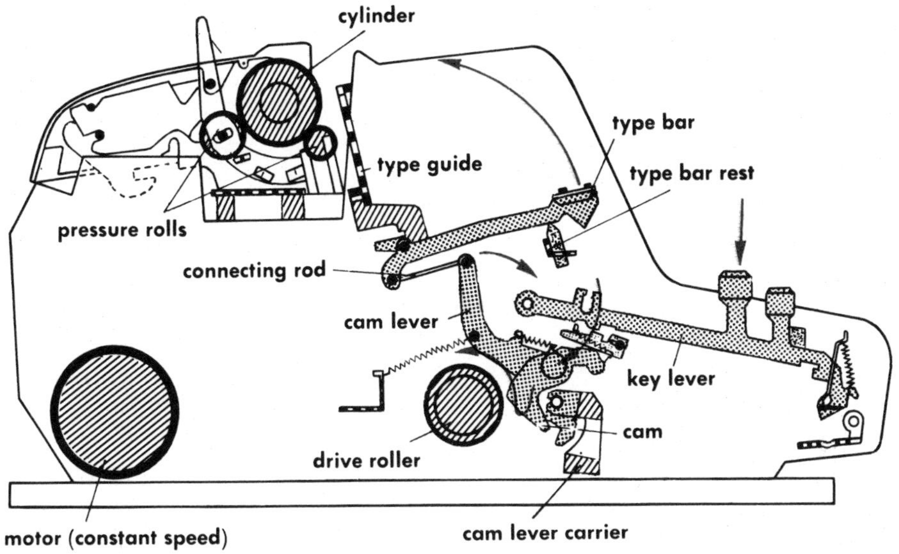

Each time a key is pressed and released, the carriage moves a fixed distance from right to left to make room for the next letter. This action is controlled by an escapement mechanism consisting of a pawl and ratchet wheel. The pawl acts as a brake to arrest the teeth of the wheel, release them momentarily, arrest them again, etc., allowing the carriage to move to the left in quick short jumps. The escapement can also be activated by the space bar when blank spaces, such as those between words, are wanted. The carriage is returned to the right by pushing a lever that also controls the line spacer. The latter, again, is done with a pawl and ratchet designed to rotate the cylinder (and the paper) a fixed distance. The ribbon is carried on two spools and is taken up automatically so that it unwinds and wears evenly.

An **electric typewriter** (Fig. 2) works basically on the same principle as the mechanical one. It has the advantage of being easier and faster to operate and produces more uniform typing. Instead of actually striking the keys, the typist needs only to touch them lightly —an electric motor does the rest of the work. The motor rotates the *drive roller* at a steady speed. When a key is touched, a *cam* is brought into contact with the roller, activating the lever system that raises the *type bar*. The carriage return and the line spacer are also controlled electrically, which adds to the saving in time and effort.

TYPESETTING: HAND AND MECHANICAL COMPOSITION

In the language of printing, the words "type" and "letter" include many characters that are *not* letters: for example, punctuation marks, numbers, symbols, borders, musical notes, etc. *Type faces* are made in a variety of designs and sizes and are made of metal composed of lead, antimony, tin, and sometimes copper. The size (height) of the type is designated in *points*, one point measuring one seventy-second of an inch. Ten-point type (about ⅛″) is a fairly standard readable size, though smaller sizes are often used for greater condensation. Twelve- and 14-point types are popular sizes for children's books.

The compositor's job is to set the separate pieces of type into lines. When setting type by hand, he works from a large case that is subdivided into about 130 compartments. The complete font of type is distributed in the boxes, each in a standard location. The capital letters are on top (upper case); the small letters are below (lower case). There is also an assortment of space pieces for separating words and lines, indenting, etc., and some "furniture" to fill the larger blank spaces.

The type is set, letter by letter, in a *composing stick* (Fig. 1), which can be adjusted to make lines of the desired length. Each piece of type has one or more *nicks* cut into one side (Fig. 2), the number depending on which type face is being used. The compositor can tell when the letters are right-side up by feeling the nicks. When the line is loosely filled, additional spaces are added between words to make the type fit snugly, a process called *justification*. Groups of justified lines from the composing stick are transferred to a tray called a

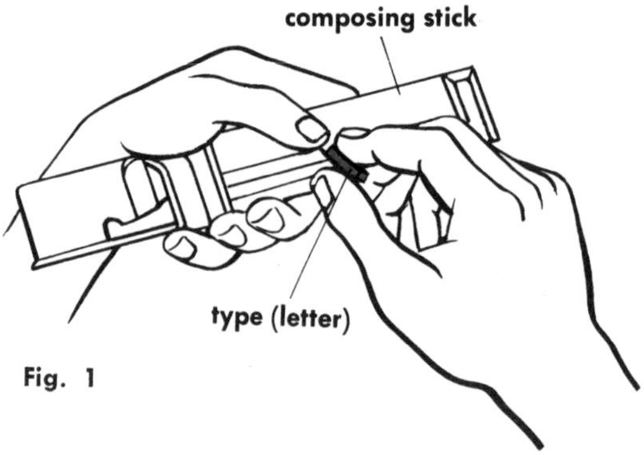

Fig. 1

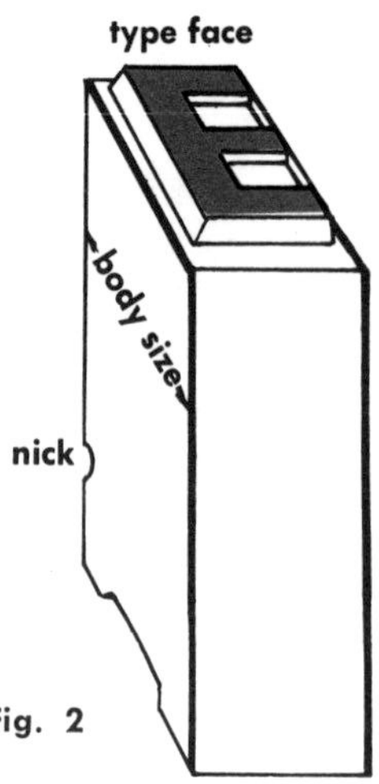

Fig. 2

galley. When a column has been assembled, it is inked, proved (a galley proof), and corrected before the final printing.

While hand composition is used for specialized jobs, such as letterheads, leaflets, etc., there are great advantages in mechanical typesetting. The speed and accuracy of the machines makes them invaluable for commercial volume work. Another advantage is that they use clear newly cast type that does not have to be sorted and used again; it is simply melted for recasting.

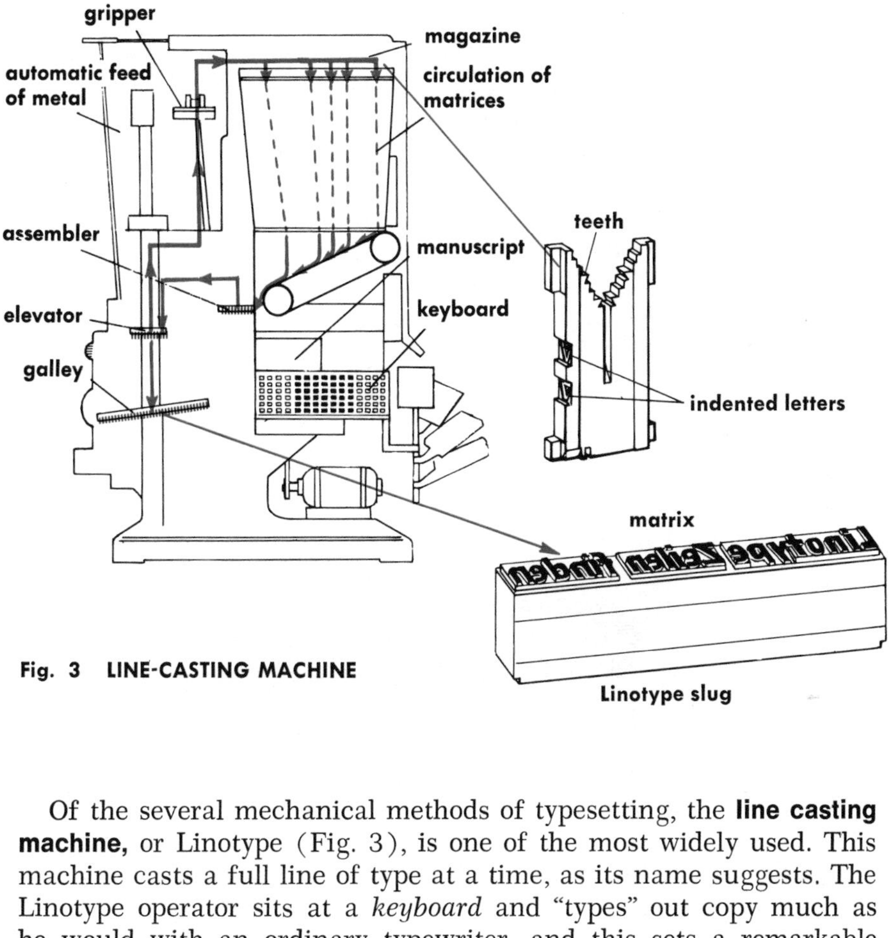

Fig. 3 LINE-CASTING MACHINE

Of the several mechanical methods of typesetting, the **line casting machine,** or Linotype (Fig. 3), is one of the most widely used. This machine casts a full line of type at a time, as its name suggests. The Linotype operator sits at a *keyboard* and "types" out copy much as he would with an ordinary typewriter, and this sets a remarkable chain of events in motion. As each key is touched, a *matrix* with the equivalent letter *indented in its edge* is released from a *magazine* where the matrices are stored in stacks. It slides down an incline onto a moving belt that carries it to the *assembler,* placing it next to the previous matrix. Wedge-shaped spaces called *spacebands* are dropped in between the words. They consist of double wedges with their wide edges at opposite ends. When a line has been completed, it can be justified automatically by pushing the sliding wedges against each other. This widens the spaces until the line fills out to its full length.

The operator next presses a lever that raises the completed line and transfers it to a molding wheel where it is held in position in front of a melting pot. In the pot, a pump forces molten metal up through a slot and into the hollow indentation of the matrices. The metal cools quickly and forms a *slug,* as the line casting is called. The wheel then rotates and the slug is automatically trimmed, ejected, and positioned on a long metal galley tray from which it is proved and corrected before it is made ready for the final printing.

There is a continuous cycle being carried out while the machine is operating: when the finished slug goes to the galley, a new one is all ready to be cast; the previous line of matrices has been picked up and redistributed in the magazine. The latter operation is controlled by the *teeth* at the top of the matrices, which act much like the notches in a door key. Each letter has its own combination of teeth allowing it to be released into the proper bin as it slides along a grooved rod at the top of the magazine.

Fig. 4 LINE OF MONOTYPE LETTERS

Another popular machine is called the **Monotype,** which casts single letters instead of full lines. The advantage is that a galley can be corrected more easily because individual letters can be replaced (Fig. 4), whereas with the Linotype a whole line has to be replaced if there is an error in it.

PHONOGRAPH RECORDS AND RECORD PLAYERS

Sound is audible noise, or tone, that is transmitted through the air in the form of pulsating waves, or vibrations. Until methods of reproducing sound electrically were perfected, man had to be content with sounds reaching his ears directly from the original sources. Then came the development of the TELEPHONE and radio, making it possible for sound to travel long distances. This is done by changing the sound waves into ELECTRIC CURRENTS and then changing them back into audible sound waves again. A phonograph record goes a step beyond that by capturing the vibrations and storing them in another form for future use.

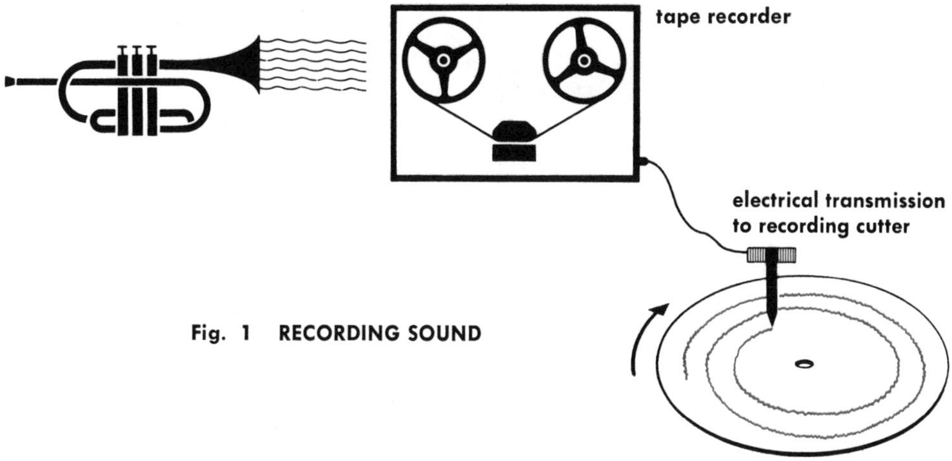

Fig. 1 RECORDING SOUND

The master recording for commercial records used to be made directly from a live performance. For better fidelity, the sound is now recorded on tape first (page 230). Then it is transferred from the tape to a rotating disc with a soft wax-like surface (Fig. 1). As electrical impulses from the tape are transmitted to a sharp cutting stylus, the vibrations cause the stylus to fluctuate as it scratches a spiral groove into the disc. The resulting groove has a zigzag pattern that duplicates the pattern of the sound waves.

Next, a metal casting is made from the original record. The casting serves as the master disc, or matrix, and is used, along with a second master, to press out plastic records in volume (Fig. 2). The plastic material used is pliable under heat and high pressure and it yields exact copies of the first wax impression. In examining a record through a magnifying lens, it seems astounding that its microscopic wavy grooves can store the sound of a full orchestra with such precision.

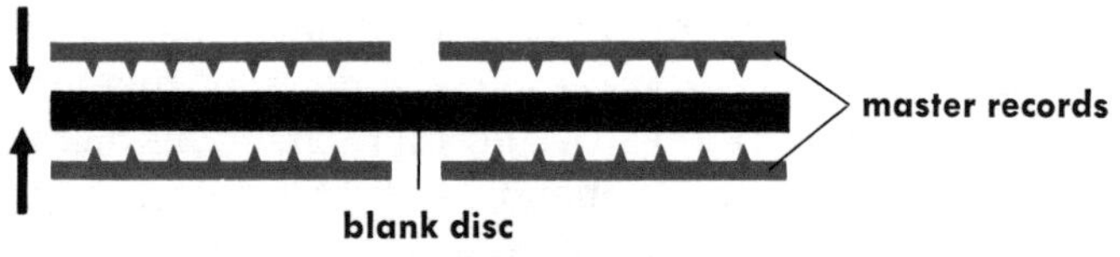

Fig. 2 PRESSING A RECORD

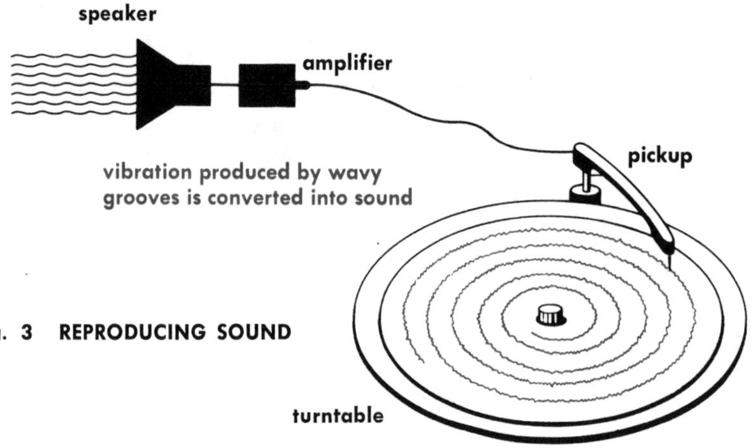

Fig. 3 REPRODUCING SOUND

The job of a record player is to translate these fine scratches back into sound waves—the reverse process of making the recording. A record player consists of three basic parts: a *turntable* with a *pickup* arm, an *amplifier*, and one or more *speakers* (Fig. 3). These parts can be combined in one cabinet but are frequently bought and used as separate units.

The motor-driven turntable is timed to rotate the record at the same speed at which the original recording was made. The stylus, or needle, in the pickup is placed in the groove where it fluctuates as it follows the pattern of the waves in the groove. The magnetic pickup, the kind used in most high-fidelity sets, converts this motion into electric pulsations. These signals are strengthened in the amplifier and sent to the speaker. Here, the electrical impulses cause a diaphragm to vibrate and send out sound waves almost identical to those that were originally recorded. The process is similar to the workings of a telephone receiver (page 172).

Stereophonic sound is designed to give more depth and realism to the recordings. This is done by picking up the original sound in two microphones placed some distance apart (for example, to the left and right of center stage). The resulting stereo record has a double groove, each producing a separate signal. These are picked up by a special stylus on the turntable, amplified, and sent into separate speakers located in two parts of the room. Given good acoustics in that room, the sound will be more nearly like the sound heard in a concert hall.

TAPE RECORDER

The magnetic tape recorder, though a fairly recent invention, is being manufactured in great quantities for home and office use. It is also widely used by radio stations to tape broadcasts for original and repeat use. Live performances are now initially recorded on tape before being transferred to PHONOGRAPH RECORDS.

TELEPHONES, RECORD PLAYERS, and radios deal with the conversion of sound waves into ELECTRIC CURRENTS and back to sound waves again. A phonograph record introduces the added feature of *storing* the sound for future use, which a tape recorder also does in quite a remarkable way.

In making a tape recording, the original *sound waves* enter a *microphone* where the vibrations are converted into a pulsating electric signal (Fig. 1). The signal is then strengthened by an *amplifier* and

Fig. 1 RECORDING

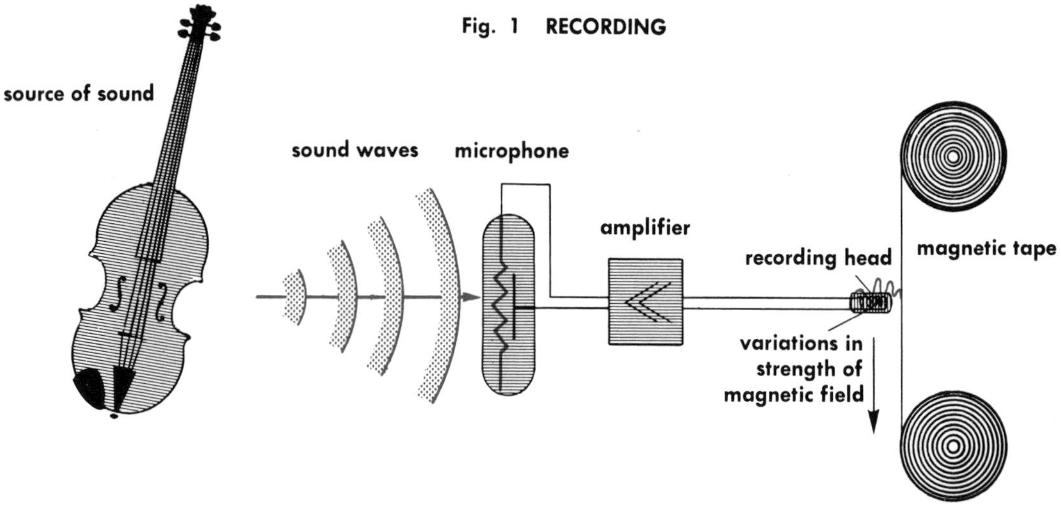

passed into a *recording head,* which is a small electromagnet (page 155) with a gap in it. Its magnetism fluctuates in direct relation to the varying current flowing through it, and a strong *magnetic field* is produced in the tiny gap.

The tape itself is made of thin tough plastic coated with a substance containing iron oxide. The particles of iron oxide are easily magnetized and will retain a given magnetic pattern until they are purposely demagnetized by an erasing device. The tape is on a reel that feeds it to the take-up reel at a preset speed. As the tape is drawn across the gap of the recording head, the oxide particles become magnetized in a pattern corresponding to the fluctuations in the magnet.

The original sound has now been transformed from *sound waves* to *electrical impulses* to *magnetic variations.* In playing the tape back, these forms have to be repeated in reverse order to reach our ears as sound. The tape is rewound and played back at the same speed used in the recording process. It is drawn across the *reproducing head,* (Fig. 2), which, on some small units, is the same electromagnet used for recording. The magnetized tape sends a weak pattern of signals into the electromagnet. The pulsations are amplified and sent into a LOUDSPEAKER. This causes the diaphragm in the speaker to vibrate and send sound waves through the air. Thus the electric signal is turned back into an almost exact reproduction of the original sound.

Along with the accuracy of the sound, there are other advantages in recording on tape. As there is no physical contact with the surface (as with a needle), there is no scratching noise and no wear and tear on the recording. Tapes can be erased and used over and over again without wearing out, and they can be edited, cut, and spliced like movie film to eliminate errors or unwanted parts.

Fig. 2 REPRODUCTION

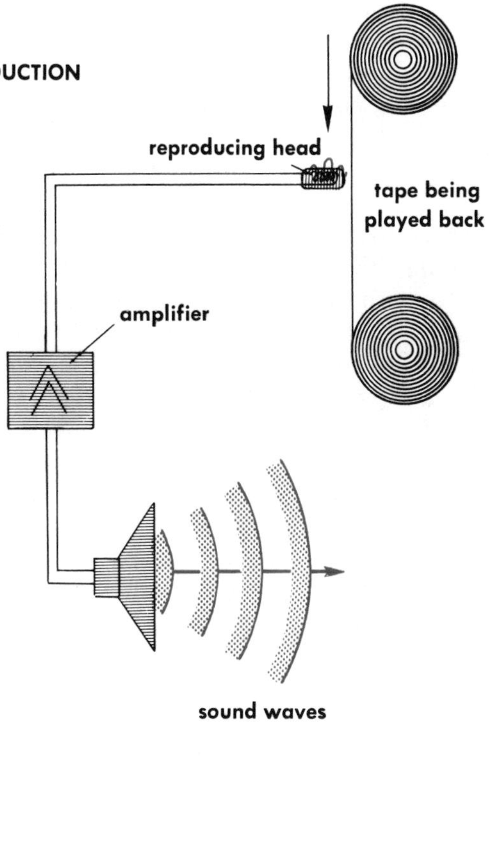

PUNCHED CARD SYSTEMS

Punched cards are stiff rectangular cards into which a machine has punched small, square holes. By their position on the card, the holes represent various numbers and the numbers stand for certain kinds of information that a company may want to record and have easy access to when needed.

The cards may be used for storing and withdrawing information (called the input and output of data) in mechanical information-processing. Such cards can be sorted at a rate of more than 100,000 cards per hour and may be arranged in various ways as well.

A punched card is divided into columns whose rows contain figures from zero to 9. For example, if the number 403 has to be recorded in the first three columns of a card, the fourth row in the first column, the zero row in the second column, and the third row in the third column must be punched. The usual punched cards have 80 columns. In addition, appropriate holes for conveying nonnumerical code information may be punched in rows in which the places are not numbered.

When the punched cards are passed through any of various machines, the punched holes cause electrical impulses to be transmitted. The usual machines involved are the *punching machine,* which punches data into the cards; the *sorting machine,* which sorts out cards according to various classifications; and the *tabulating machine,* which prepares printed reports from the sorted cards.

Figures 1 and 2 show how a sorting machine operates. The stack of cards to be sorted is placed in the *feed hopper* on the right, in which *feed blades* moving forward and backward seize the bottom card and push it under the *transport roller* (Fig. 2). The card passes between a *contact roller* and a *scanning spring.* The scanning spring scans the rows 9 to 0 in the selected columns. In the neutral position the *sorting springs* are close above the card transport track. Cards that contain no punched hole in the scanned column will pass unhindered under all the sorting springs and fall into the receiving box for unperforated cards. But if the column contains a hole, the card concerned will slide along under the sorting springs only until the hole reaches the scanning spring. When that happens, an electrical circuit is completed that energizes an electromagnet, causing an *armature* on which the sorting springs are resting to be pulled down. The sorting springs whose front edges have then not yet been reached by the card will now drop below the level of the card, so that the

Fig. 1

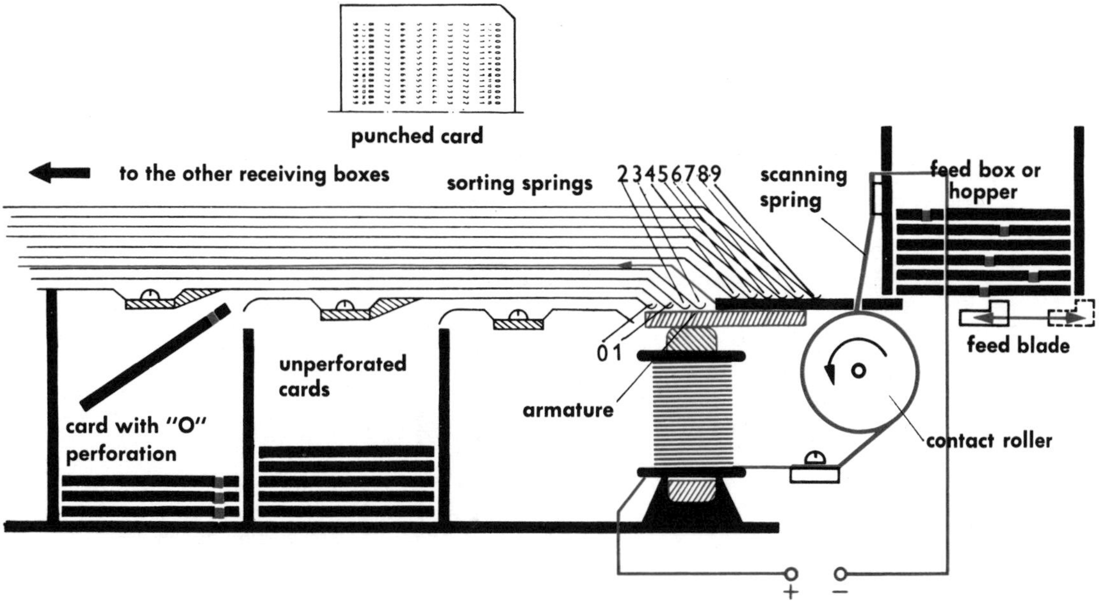
punched card
to the other receiving boxes
sorting springs
23456789
scanning spring
feed box or hopper
feed blade
0 1
unperforated cards
armature
contact roller
card with "O" perforation
+
−

Fig. 2

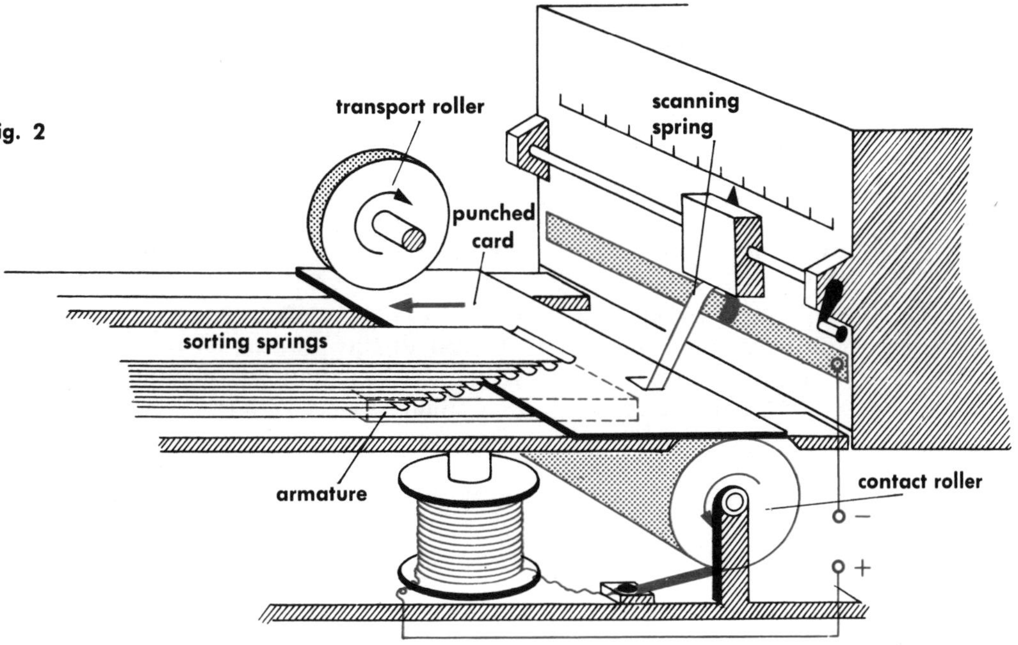
transport roller
scanning spring
punched card
sorting springs
armature
contact roller
−
+

card slides between two of these springs and is thus delivered into the appropriate receiving box.

A stack of cards can also be sorted according to the value of a multi-digit number. This involves several successive sorting operations (Fig. 3). First the cards are sorted according to the figure in the units column. Then the cards must be restacked in the feed box in

Fig. 3 SORTING WITH REGARD TO MULTI-DIGIT NUMBERS

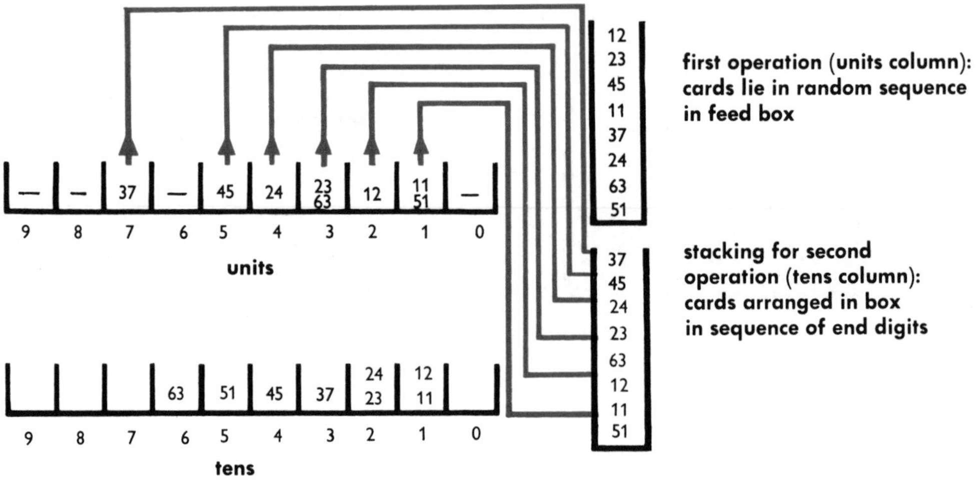

the sequence of their end digit (first the end digit 0, then 1, and so on up to 9). When the cards are now sorted according to the "tens" digit, the cards with the lowest end digits should be lowest down in the "tens" box; the other cards are stacked on top of these in the sequence of their respective end digits. In the next sorting operation the cards are sorted with regard to the "hundreds" and then to the "thousands" and so on. Thus, with only four sorting operations, 10,000 cards are arranged in their correct order.

VIII Around the House

DOOR LOCKS

A mechanical door lock consists essentially of a sliding bolt to hold the door closed and a mechanism for engaging and releasing the bolt, usually activated by a key. The movable obstruction in a lock is called a *tumbler*. Figure 1 shows a very simple lock with one tumbler held in place by a *spring*. When the key is turned, it pushes the tumbler up and moves the *bolt* forward into the slot in the doorframe. At the same time, the *catch* slips into the next notch, holding the bolt in locked position.

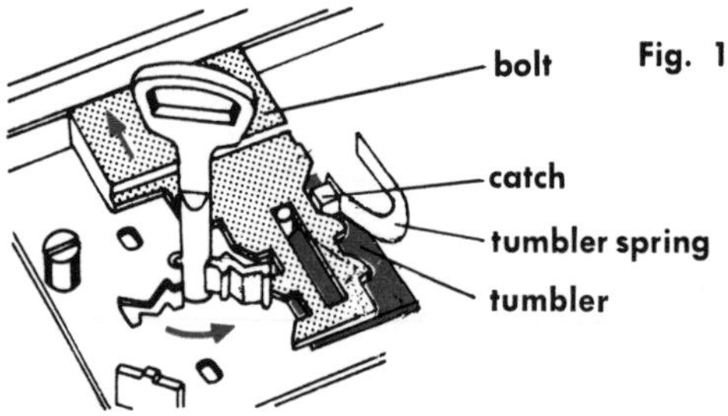

Fig. 1 LOCK WITH ONE TUMBLER

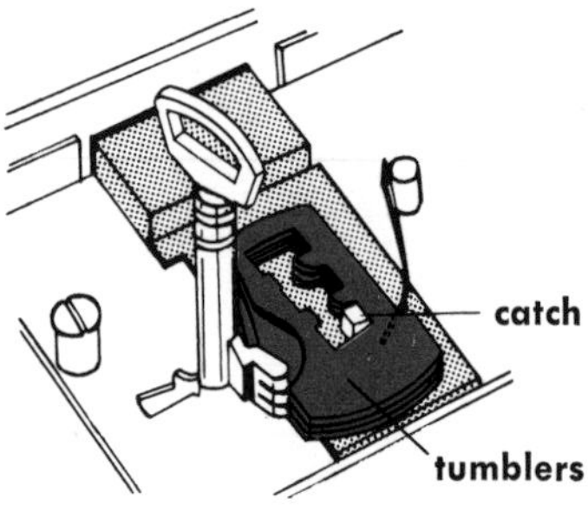

Fig. 2 LOCK WITH SEVERAL TUMBLERS

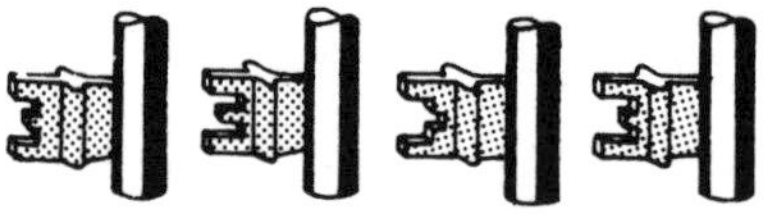

Fig. 3 KEYS FOR LOCKS WITH SEVERAL TUMBLERS

Locks with several tumblers (Fig. 2) provide greater protection, though it is still fairly easy to open them with "skeleton" keys. The bolt has a catch that engages with the notches inside the tumblers. The key (Fig. 3) is provided with cuts and projections designed to raise each tumbler the exact distance needed for the catch to clear the notches and allow the bolt to be pushed forward.

The lock most commonly used for outside doors is the **cylinder lock.** The bolt is connected to a metal shaft with a strong spring to hold it in place when locked. From outside, the mechanism that pulls the bolt back can be activated only by turning the cylinder with a key specially made to fit that lock. (A knob controls it from the inside.) Figure 4 shows a cross section of the *barrel* and the *cylinder* in locked position. Five holes are drilled in the barrel and in the top part of the cylinder. These holes contain *pin tumblers*, each having three parts: a pin with a rounded or triangular end (striped), a pin with flat ends (white), and a spring to keep tension on them. Note that the *pins* are of different lengths.

The key for a cylinder lock has ridges running the length of its flat sides. These must fit into corresponding ridges in the keyhole. The key also has a series of notches along its top. When inserted, it lifts the pins and settles them into the notches, which have been cut to raise the pins an exact distance (Fig. 5). Now the lower pins are lined up flush with the top of the cylinder, allowing it to be turned by the key. Attached to the end of the rotating cylinder is a metal projection, the *pawl,* which pushes a lever, or cam, which, in turn, pulls back on the bolt and unlocks the door.

Figure 6 shows a situation where the wrong key is inserted in the keyhole. Even though it happened to have the right set of ridges to allow it to enter, the notches are not raising the pin tumblers to the right alignment for turning the cylinder. As you can see, the possible combinations of pin arrangements and key notches are practically endless.

There are many variations on locks, their efficiency usually geared to their purpose. For instance, a bookcase or a bicycle probably doesn't require the protection needed for the door to a house. Many safes have **combination locks** in which the tumblers are aligned in the right positions by turning a knob to a certain set of numbers. Other safes have two or more different locks. The **time lock** is probably the most efficient of all. It is connected to a clock timer that allows *no one* to open it except at a certain preset time.

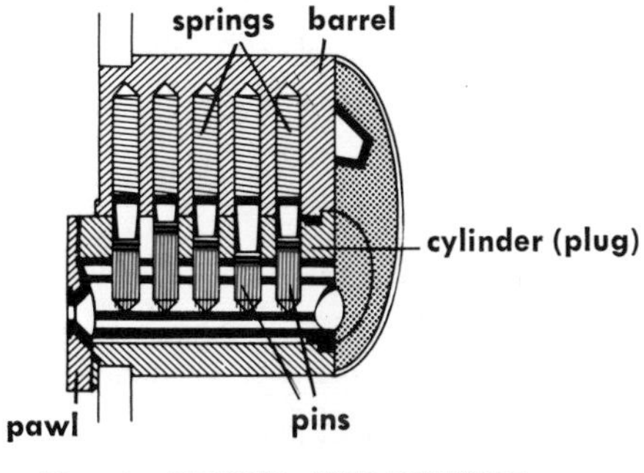

Fig. 4 LOCKED: PINS PREVENT CYLINDER FROM ROTATING

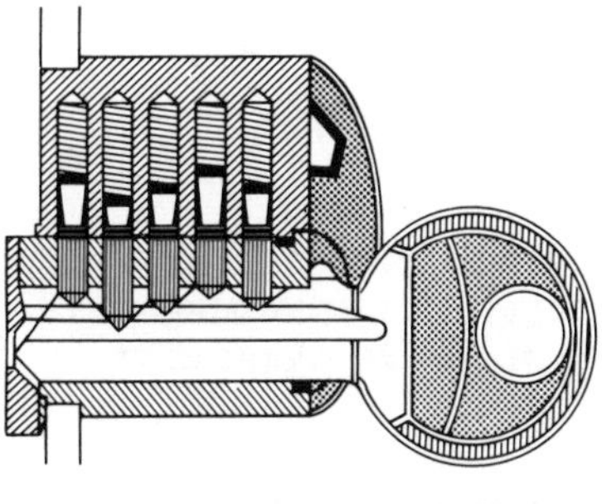

Fig. 5 UNLOCKED: KEY PUSHES UP THE PINS SO THAT CYLINDER CAN BE ROTATED

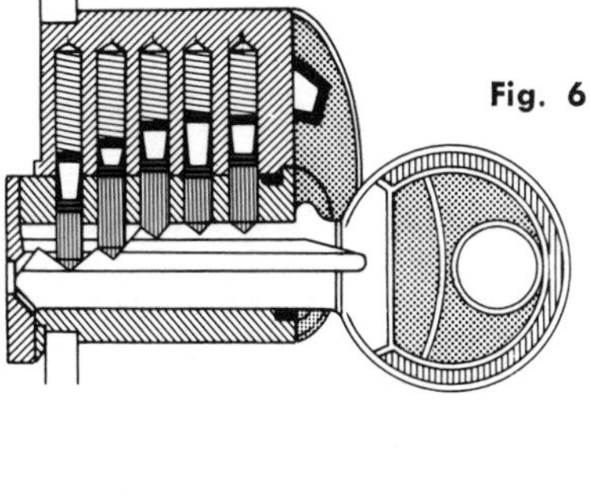

Fig. 6 WRONG KEY INSERTED: NOT ALL THE PINS ARE LIFTED A SUFFICIENT DISTANCE; CYLINDER CANNOT BE ROTATED

ZIPPER

The word "Zipper" was launched in 1924 by the B. F. Goodrich Company as a trade name for galoshes that closed with slide fasteners. As of today, the future of galoshes looks uncertain but the zip fastener is well established in clothing and luggage.

Zippers are quite different from the buttons previously used in clothing—or from the toggles used by Eskimos. Toggles and buttons are now made by machine, but for centuries they were carved by hand. There's no reason why they shouldn't be—they don't have to be exactly alike. If a button is too large or too small, the buttonhole can be adjusted—and with a toggle there is no problem at all. But in a zipper, each tooth in one row fits into the gap between the two facing teeth in the row opposite (Fig. 1a), and the two sides of the zipper won't mesh unless the teeth line up exactly. This is easy to accomplish, since they are all made on a machine.

The zipper embodies two different ideas. One is the idea of a ladder of little platforms, each with a *bump* (Fig. 1b) that fits into the hollow of the platform opposite—or *almost* opposite (they are staggered). The other is the idea of the *slide* (Fig. 2), which allows one to mesh a hundred teeth in one pull. The slide's channels are in the shape of a Y. The angle of the two arms is important—the rows won't mesh unless the angle is right.

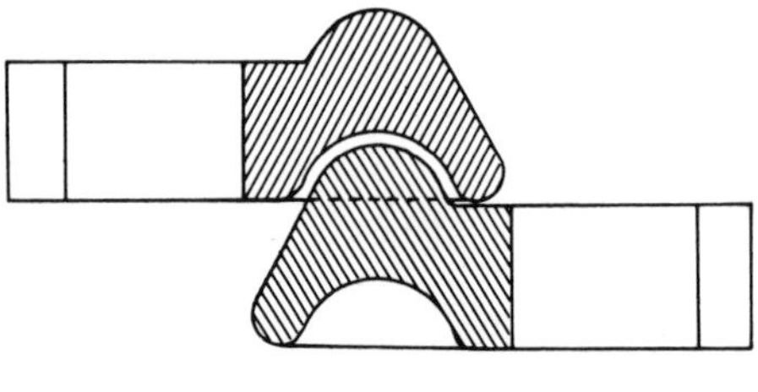

Fig. 1a INTERLOCKING OF STAGGERED TEETH IS PRODUCED BY LETTING BUMP OF ONE TOOTH NEST IN HOLLOW OF THE NEXT

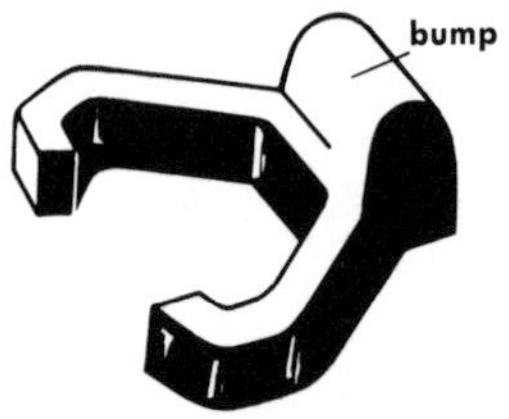

Fig. 1b TO WORK SMOOTHLY, ZIPPER MUST BE MADE OF ELEMENTS THAT ARE IDENTICAL

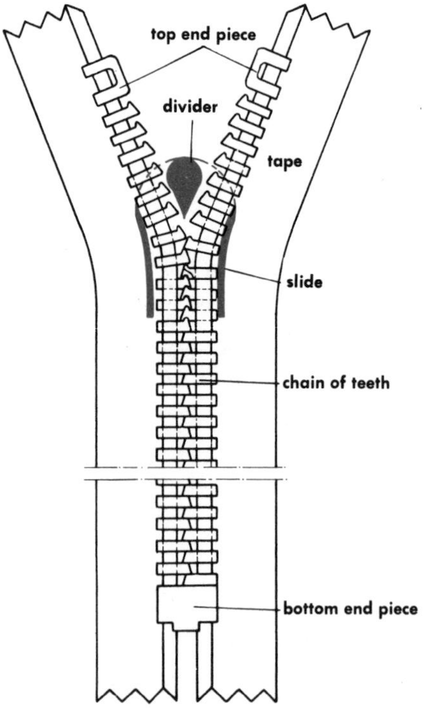

Fig. 2 ZIPPER WOULD NOT WORK WITHOUT THE SLIDE, WHICH BRINGS THE TWO COLUMNS TOGETHER AT AN ANGLE THAT ALLOWS THEM TO MESH

CLOCKS AND WATCHES

A driving mechanism providing a steady source of power is one of the basic requirements for mechanical clocks and watches. The power is used to turn a series, or train, of interconnected gears that rotate the hands of the clock. One driving device used on early clocks was a weight on a string or chain that was wound around the axle of a wheel. The falling weight turned the wheel that drove the clock. But until the invention of the pendulum, these clocks were more ornamental than accurate because there was no good method of controlling the rate of fall.

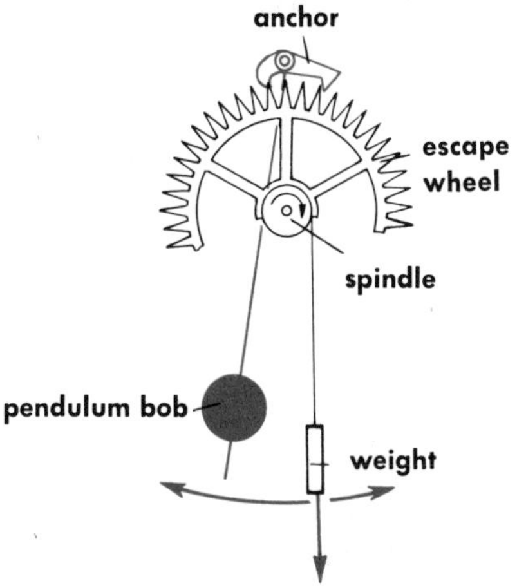

Fig. 1 PENDULUM DRIVE

The **pendulum drive,** most often seen on grandfather clocks, is reliable and can be regulated to keep accurate time. Figure 1 shows how the four parts of this mechanism are interrelated. The *weight* causes the *escape wheel* to rotate while the *anchor,* which is linked to the pendulum, acts as a brake to control both the wheel and the falling weight. (The combination of wheel and anchor is called the *escapement.*) When set in motion, the pendulum swings back and forth and rocks, or "walks," the anchor on the escape wheel. The anchor projections, called *pallets,* release one tooth at a time (which accounts for the "tick tock" sound). This causes the wheel to rotate a corresponding distance and the weight to drop imperceptibly.

There is a reciprocal action between the escapement and the *pendulum.* Each time the pendulum rocks the anchor into a new tooth, the anchor transmits an impulse (a light tap) to the pendulum, which keeps it swinging with a steady motion. The clock can be regulated by moving the *pendulum bob* down or up to slow or speed up the swinging.

The word "clock" comes from the French word *"cloche,"* which means "bell." Many of the early clocks had no dials or faces, but simply announced the time by striking the hour or quarter hour. Pocket timepieces were named for the fact that most had no bells—and they had to be *watched.* Watches, as well as other kinds of clocks, work on the same principle as the pendulum clock, though the design and power sources may vary. Figure 2 shows the workings of a widely

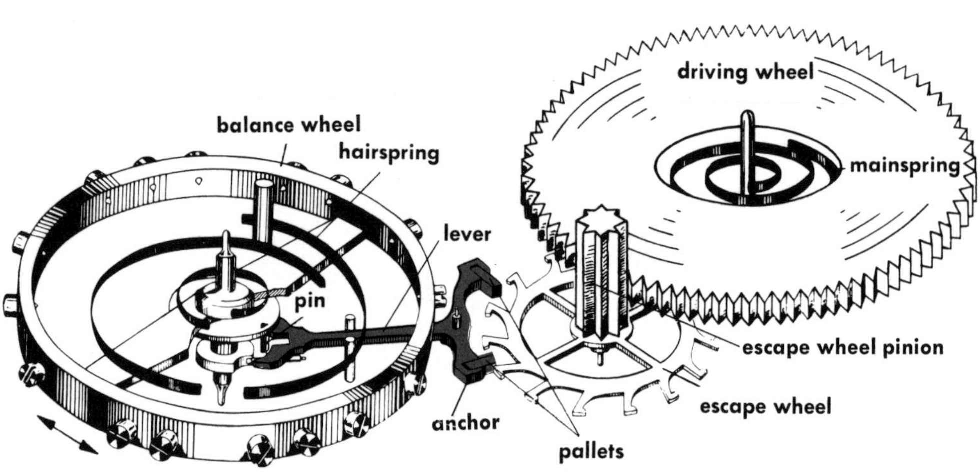

Fig. 2 DRIVE MECHANISM OF A WATCH

used design called a *lever escapement.* In place of the weight, the tension on the *escape wheel* is provided by a wound-up spring, the *mainspring.* The equivalent of the pendulum is the *balance wheel,* which is connected to a *hairspring.* The balance wheel swings steadily back and forth, or oscillates, under the tension of the spring. This causes the attached *lever* and *anchor* to rock and release one tooth at a time on the escape wheel. Again, there is a reciprocal action between the escapement and the balance: each time the anchor releases a tooth, an impulse is sent back to the balance to keep it oscillating steadily. The escape wheel connects with the train of gear wheels that control the hands of the clock. Figure 3 shows the gearing calculated to allow the minute wheel and hand to make one revolution in an hour and the hour wheel and hand to make one revolution in twelve hours.

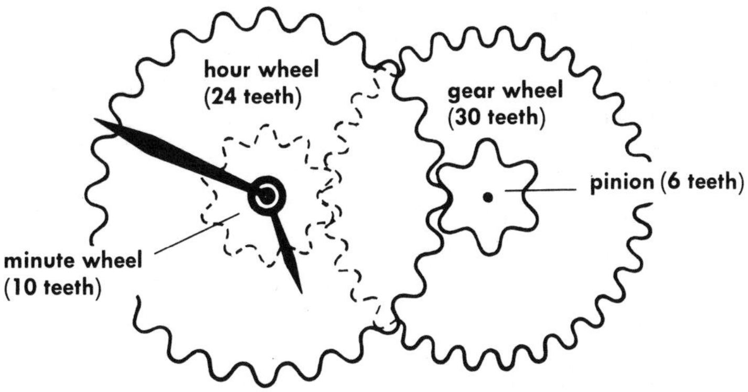

Fig. 3 TRANSMISSION OF MOTION FROM THE MINUTE AND HOUR WHEELS TO THE HANDS

SEWING MACHINES

Modern electric sewing machines for home use are compact and versatile. Many have adjustments and accessories that make it possible to baste, darn, make buttonholes and a variety of decorative stitches. But probably the most intriguing aspect of the machine is how it makes stitches that don't pull out.

Most modern machines use two separate threads to form a lock stitch. The upper thread is led through the eye of a vertical needle, while the under thread is carried on a bobbin. Many popular machines use a **rotary bobbin** with a hook on its outside rim. Figures 1–6 show how the needle and the bobbin interact to form a lock stitch.

1—The threaded needle is lowered and goes through the fabric, while the bobbin hook advances to meet it.

2—The hook catches on to the thread and makes a loop.

3—The needle withdraws and the inner rim of the bobbin holds the front end of the loop in a stationary position.

4—The outside rim of the bobbin pulls the other side of the loop around with it and the thread slides over the bobbin case.

5—The bobbin thread is now captured inside the loop.

6—As the hook comes back to its top position, the loop slides off. The thread take-up level at the top of the machine pulls up the slack thread and locks the stitch tightly. The presser foot holds the fabric flat while a toothed feeding device moves it forward for the next stitch.

Other machines use what is called a **vibrating,** or **reciprocating, shuttle,** which is a somewhat simpler mechanism. Figures 7–10 show the steps.

DRIVING MECHANISM OF A SEWING MACHINE

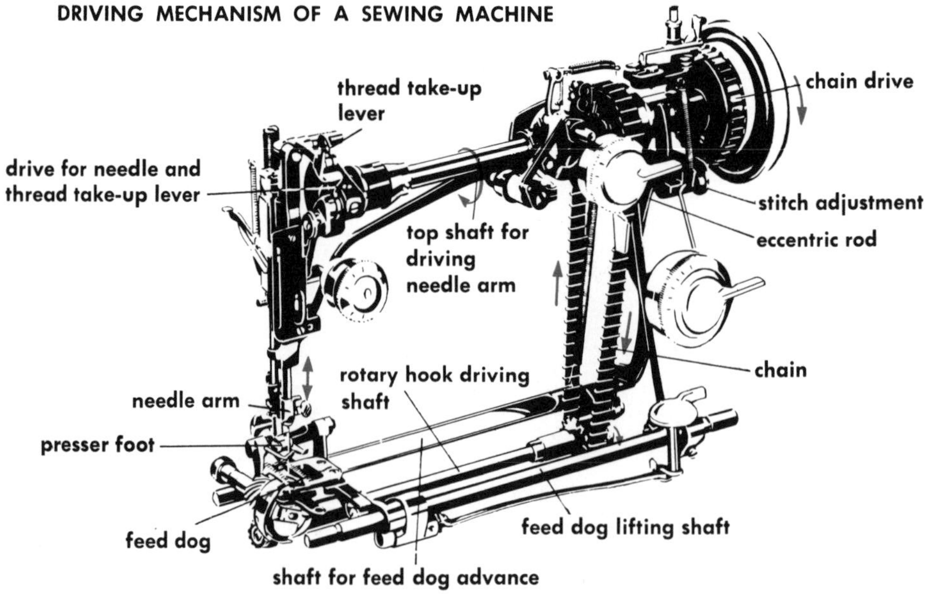

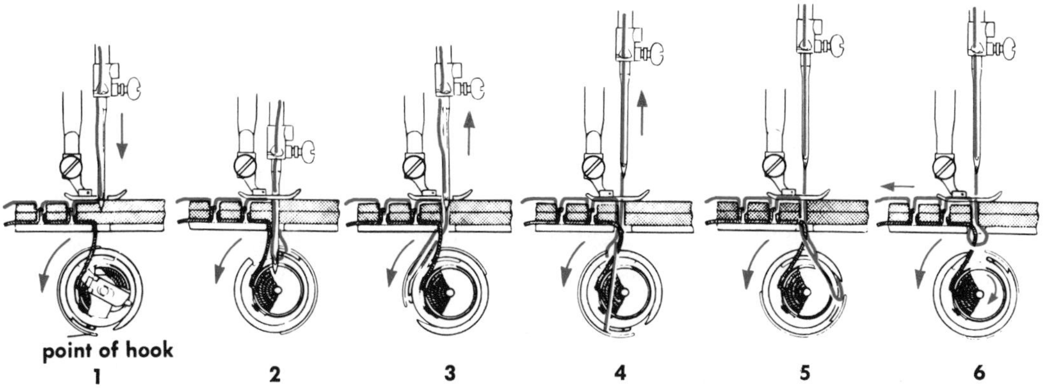

ROTARY BOBBIN

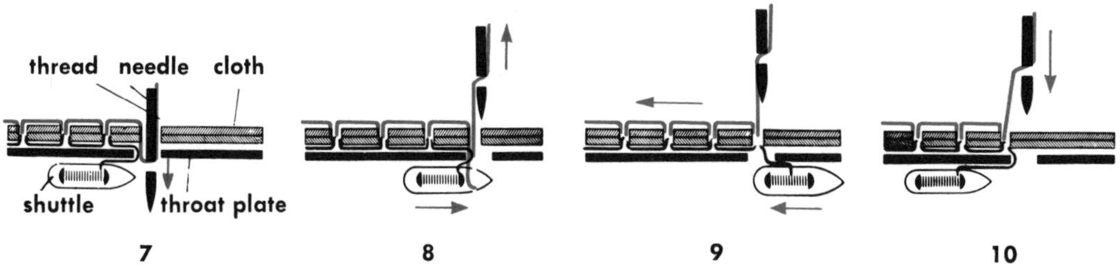

VIBRATING SHUTTLE

7—The needle and thread are lowered through the fabric.

8—The needle rises, leaving a loose loop, and the bullet-shaped shuttle starts to move forward.

9—The shuttle containing the bobbin of thread moves all the way through the loop.

10—The fabric is then fed forward for the next stitch while the shuttle, having caught the loop, returns to its original position. These two actions take up the slack in both threads and lock the stitch.

The first workable sewing machine, patented in 1790, was designed for sewing leather. It used a single thread that formed a chain stitch in the fabric. This was accomplished by pushing a loop of thread through the material. The loop was caught underneath by a hook and was pulled forward. The next loop penetrating the fabric fell inside the preceding one and was again pulled forward by the hook, thereby forming a chain. The only real disadvantage of the chain stitch was that if the thread should break in any one place the whole seam would unravel as it does in straight knitting. But the same principle, because it involves fewer delicate parts, is used in some machines today—usually those designed for sewing leather, canvas, and other bulky materials.

FLUSH TOILETS

If, for simplicity, one thinks of the human species as having existed for 2,000,000 years and the water-sealed toilet as having existed (at least as a patent) for 200 years, it is apparent that toilets of the kind we are used to have existed for only one ten-thousandth of the life of mankind. By great good luck, this fraction of time is the period we are living in now.

The mechanism of a flush toilet is extremely simple. A valve, operated by hand, releases a few gallons of water from a tank into the toilet bowl. This causes an overflow back of the bowl and all the wastes and extra water spill over into a pipe that leads to the city

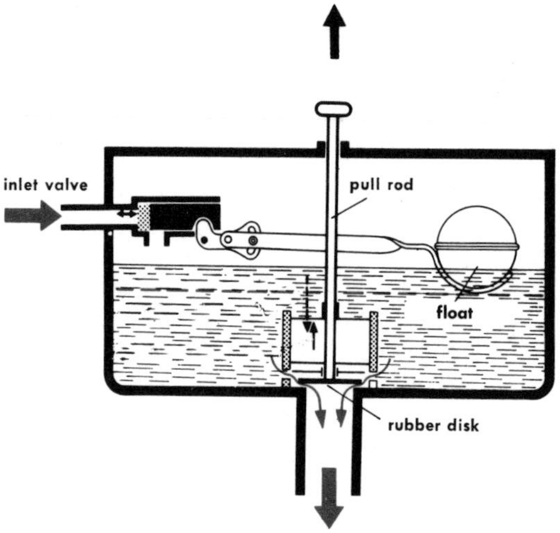

RAISING THE PULL ROD LETS WATER OUT FROM BOTTOM OF TANK.
AS WATER LEVEL IS LOWERED, FLOAT IS LOWERED WITH IT, OPENING INLET VALVE.
AS WATER FILLS TANK, FLOAT RISES WITH IT, TILL ANGLE OF ITS STEM SHUTS OFF INCOMING WATER.
(IN OTHER MODELS, PULL ROD IS RAISED BY USING LEVER ON FRONT OF TANK)

sewer. After the water has stopped flowing, two things happen: a *seal* of water—just as effective as a metal lid on a jar—forms in the bottom of the bowl. This water seal is important—it is the only thing that stands between us and the city sewer. The other thing that happens concerns the *float* that rests on the water within the tank. As the water sank, the float moved down with it, so that the stem holding it opened the *inlet valve,* letting new water in. Now, as the water in the tank rises, the float rises—until its stem reaches the angle that makes it close the valve. The tank is now full and can be used again.

Now you may think: Well, if that's all there is to a flush toilet, it could have been in use *centuries* ago. People could have had this kind of toilet in Shakespeare's time—even Julius Caesar could have had a flush toilet. But the answer is No. And the reason people of former centuries never had this kind of toilet is that *they weren't scared enough.*

Although the two important patents (covering the valves and the water seal) date from around 1780, very few such toilets were built. They were a nice idea, it was thought, but they weren't necessary. When the typhoid bacillus was discovered in 1882, people's ideas changed. It was now a frightening thought to them to have sources of infection reaching into their own homes. They now decided it was not only *pleasant* to have a water-sealed toilet in the home—it was *necessary.* It kept typhoid epidemics from spreading, and it also held other diseases in check—such as cholera and (as was discovered only much later) polio.

However, by 1882 we had also reached the age of large cities. Flush toilets were not self-contained gadgets that could be installed all by themselves. They required a city water supply and they required sewers. The water supply was not too difficult a problem (the population of the United States was only a quarter of what it is today), but sewers were expensive. They were usually built under the city streets, and the millions of gallons of sewage they carried had to be taken to treatment plants that would clean them up chemically. This was an enormous job, and the condition of our rivers and beaches shows that the problem is still far from solved.

TEMPERATURE MEASUREMENT

Many activities, from baking to controlling a nuclear reactor, depend on someone's knowing how hot something is, and on his ability to tell about it so that another person knows exactly what he means. The thermometers and other devices that make this possible are based on something's changing in a dependable way as it is warmed or cooled, and on its scale being marked off in a way that has been agreed on. Some of these devices are sensitive to small changes; others are less sensitive but good over a wide range of temperatures. Some work in extreme heat, others in extreme cold. Among the instruments that have been invented to do these specialized jobs are the following:

Thermometers use a liquid that expands when heated. In a mercury thermometer, the liquid mercury is held in a pocket, or *bulb* (Fig. 1). To make even a small expansion noticeable to the eye, the mercury is allowed to expand only in a very narrow column. In America, most thermometers are marked off in such a way that the height at which water freezes (at sea level) is marked 32 and the point at which it boils is marked 212. The length between the two marks is divided evenly into 180 degrees. This is the Fahrenheit scale. (In laboratories these two points are marked 0 and 100; that is called the Centigrade scale.)

Since mercury freezes at –26° Fahrenheit, weather thermometers use alcohol instead. (A red dye is added to the alcohol to make it easy to read.)

The **bimetallic thermometer** (Fig. 2a) also is based on the fact that most substances expand when their temperature rises—but it uses *two* metals that have been joined (Fig. 2b). As the temperature in a room rises, each metal expands at its own rate. The one that expands less tends to pull back on the other one and makes the combination

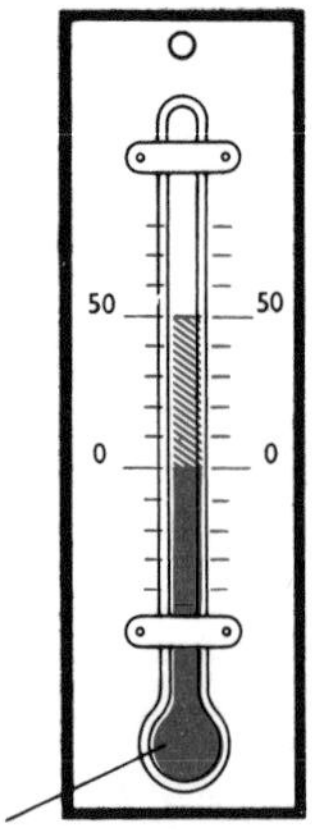

liquid expands on heating

Fig. 1 THERMOMETER

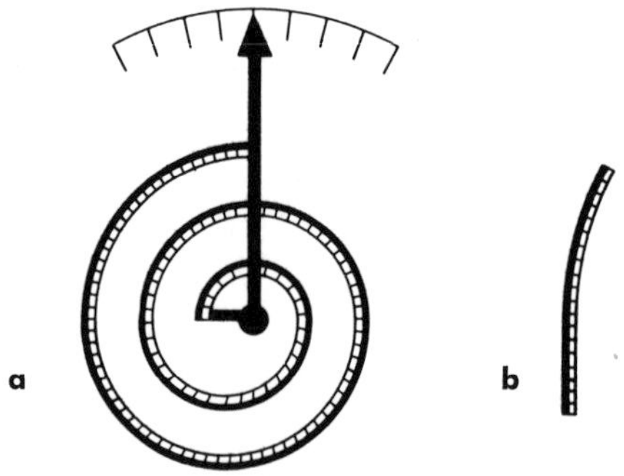

Fig. 2a THERMOMETER BUILT FROM BIMETALLIC STRIP

Fig. 2b CURVATURE OF BIMETALLIC STRIP WITH INCREASE IN TEMPERATURE

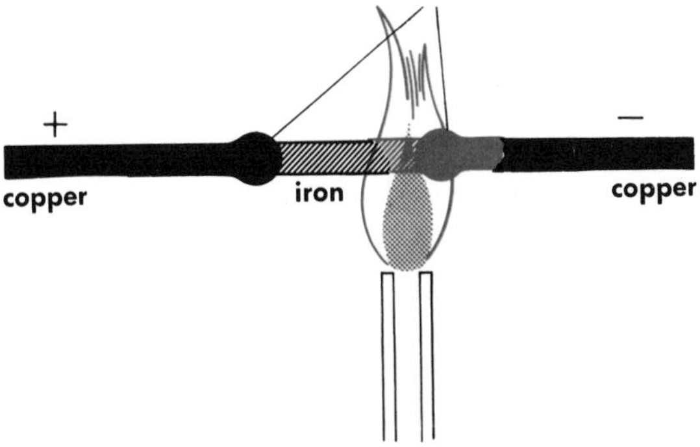

Fig. 3 THERMOCOUPLE

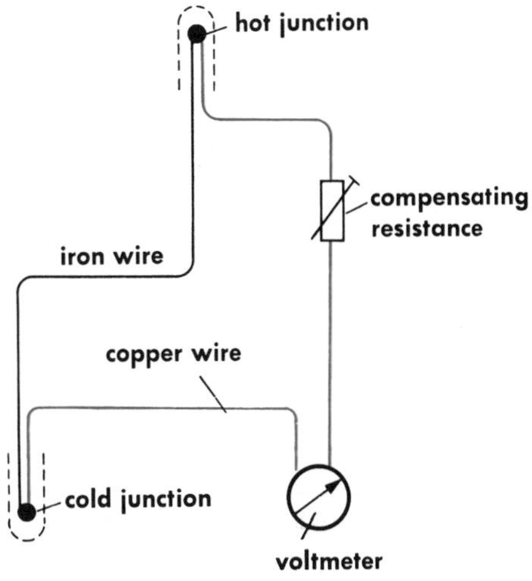

Fig. 4 ELECTRICAL CIRCUIT FOR TEMPERATURE MEASUREMENT WITH THERMOCOUPLES

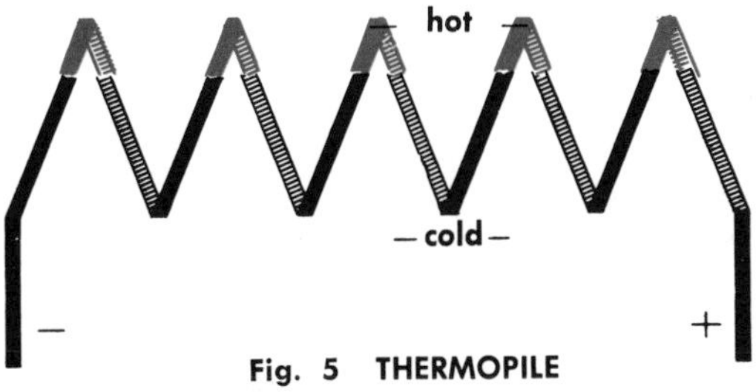

Fig. 5 THERMOPILE

curve toward it. By designing the combination as a spiral, one can let the increase in curvature move a pointer. The pointer is seen against a dial marked off in degrees of temperature.

The **thermocouple** indicates temperature by using an odd property of metals: if rods of two different metals, say copper and iron, are joined together end to end to make two joins (Fig. 3) and one of the joins is heated, the two outer ends develop opposite ELECTRIC CHARGES. If one now completes the circuit (Fig. 4) with some *wire* and a *voltmeter*, an ELECTRIC CURRENT will flow. One can then follow the difference in temperature between the two joins by watching the needle on the meter. The dial of the meter can be marked off in degrees of temperature. Since thermometers are unusable above the boiling points and below the freezing points of their liquids, thermocouples have become important in measuring extreme temperatures.

By hooking up a large number of thermocouples together, one can make a **thermopile** (Fig. 5). This device is so sensitive that astronomers use it to measure the radiation from individual stars.

THERMOSTATS

A thermostat is designed to keep the temperature of a room constant. It does not do quite that, but what it *does* do is almost as useful. Suppose, one January night, you should decide, "I'll turn off the radiator whenever the living room gets as warm as 70° Fahrenheit. When it cools down to 65°, I'll get up and turn it on again." You could be getting up to fix it all evening long. After a while, you might just prefer to install a **direct-acting thermostat.**

This thermostat would have tubes filled with a liquid that expands when heated (Fig. 1). By having a large enough supply of liquid, or by channeling its expansion into a narrow tube (as in a THERMOMETER), the increase in volume can be made to show up as a noticeable change in length. If the liquid is warm enough, it expands just far enough to close a *valve* in the heating system (Fig. 2). Once the heat has been cut off, the room starts to cool. Slowly, the liquid in the thermostat shrinks back, causing a *spring* in the valve to stretch out; the valve opens and the heat comes on again.

This system does not keep the temperature of the room really *constant,* but it keeps it going up and down within a fairly narrow range.

Fig. 1 HOW EXPANSION OF LIQUID IS CHANNELED TO PRODUCE MOTION IN A STRAIGHT LINE

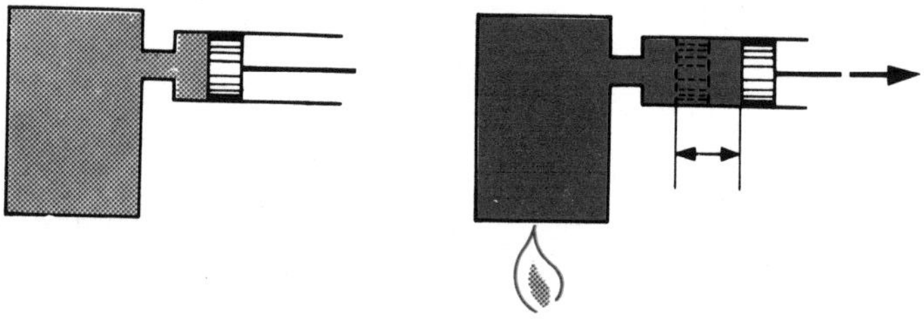

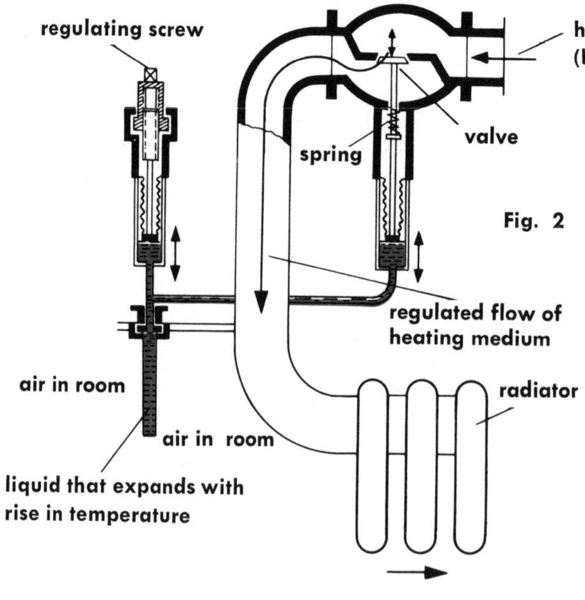

Fig. 2 DIRECT-ACTING THERMOSTAT

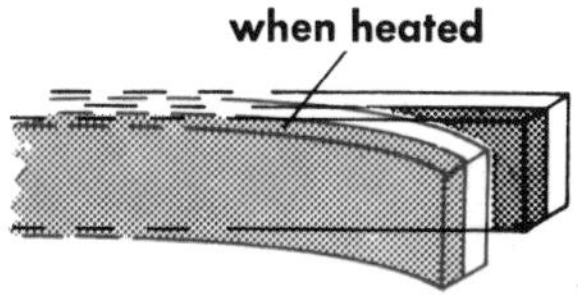

Fig. 3a HOW BIMETALLIC STRIP CURVES WHEN TEMPERATURE RISES

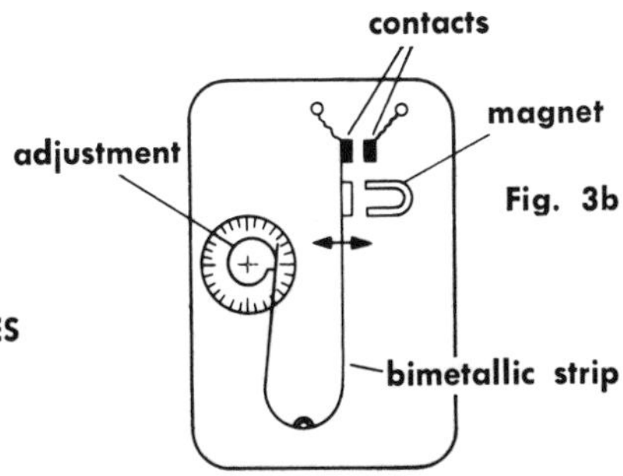

Fig. 3b HOW MAGNET AND BIMETALLIC STRIP CONTROL ELECTRIC CURRENT

In the thermostat shown in Fig. 2, the opening or closing of the valve depends on a pushing contest between the expanding liquid (shown in red) and a spring. The spring is set at the factory, but the volume available to the liquid can be changed by turning the *regulating screw* right in one's living room. With the screw turned down, the expanding liquid (red) rises high under the valve, keeping it shut except when the temperature is very low; with the screw turned upward, the liquid under the valve tends to remain low, allowing the spring to keep the valve open except when the temperature is very high.

In the **indirect-acting thermostat,** the liquid or metal that expands when it is heated does not itself turn the furnace off. It relies on an outside agent—usually electricity—which it triggers. Through the electricity, it transmits its *Cut!* signal to an electromagnetic RELAY that then pushes the valve spring that turns the heater off. The advantage of this indirect action is that it does not require the sensitive element (the liquid) to do the mechanical work (pushing the valve).

In the indirect-action thermostat, the first job—the job of reacting to the temperature—is sometimes assigned to something other than a liquid. For instance, it can be done by a *bimetallic strip* (Fig. 3a), which curls when the temperature rises (page 246). As the end of the strip curls up, it makes or breaks an electric *contact* (Fig. 3b), which in turn governs the heater valve. In other designs, the same job is done by a *bellows*—a container that can expand or shrink. When the gas in the bellows is warm, it expands; the outward shift of its loose end is then used (through levers) to control the heater valve by making or breaking an electric contact (Fig. 4), which in turn governs the heater valve as before.

Fig. 4 HOW BELLOWS AND SPRING CONTROL ELECTRIC CURRENT

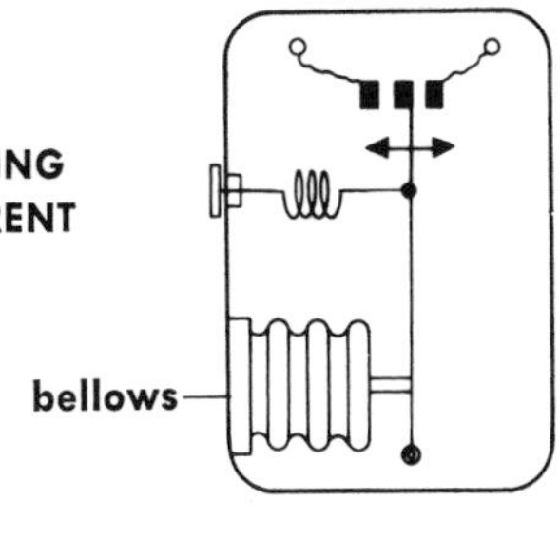

REFRIGERATOR

Heat can be created by simply burning fuel and releasing its energy. But creating cold takes more ingenuity—the only way to make anything cold is to *remove the heat.*

A refrigerator system removes heat by applying two basic laws of physics: (1) *The boiling point of a liquid* (the temperature at which it turns to vapor) *can be raised or lowered by its surrounding pressure* —the less pressure, the lower the boiling point (conversely, the boiling point can be raised by increasing the pressure). (2) *Liquid absorbs heat in the process of changing to vapor; when vapor condenses, it gives off heat.* There is an evaporation-condensation cycle, based on these laws, that makes a mechanical refrigerator work.

OPERATING PRINCIPLE OF COMPRESSION REFRIGERATOR

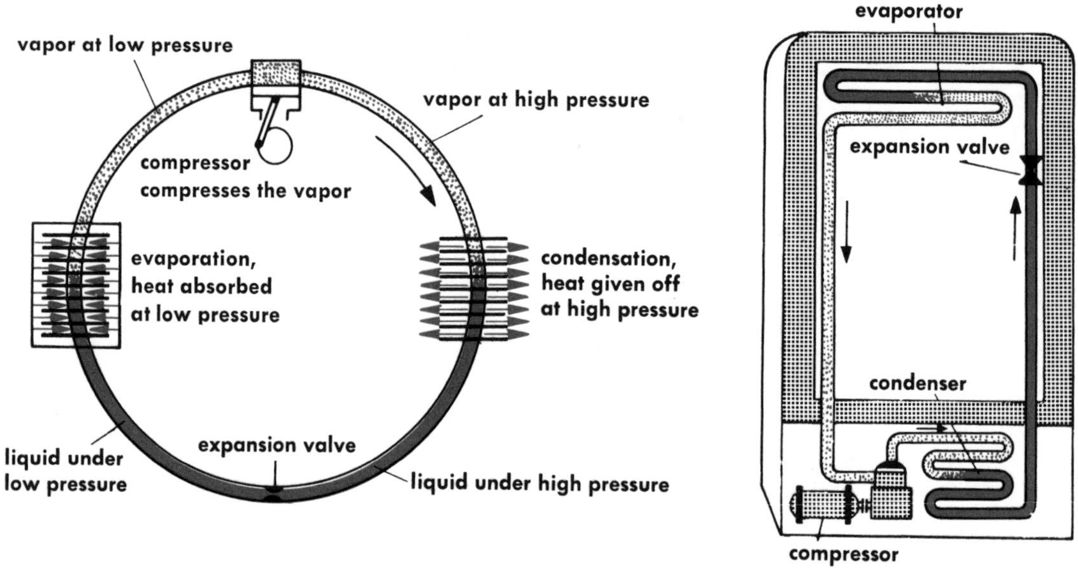

Most modern refrigerators operate on a compression system that involves four mechanical units: an *evaporator, compressor, condenser,* and *expansion valve.* A sealed-in refrigerant with a very low boiling point is circulated through these units. A chemical compound called Freon is widely used for this purpose because, in case of leakage, it is both nonflammable and nontoxic.

The liquid refrigerant runs through the evaporator, which is installed in the freezing compartment. Because of the low pressure and reduced boiling point, it vaporizes and absorbs heat from its surroundings (air, ice-cube trays, etc.). The warmed vapor is then pumped through a compressor, which squeezes the molecules into a smaller space. Now the pressure is raised, thus raising the boiling point. This causes the vapor to become a liquid again as it goes through the condenser. At this point it gives off heat which, in most home refrigerators, dissipates into the room much as it would from a small radiator. This is the same heat that was absorbed earlier—it is just being transported from the inside of the refrigerator to the outside. Next, the liquid passes through an expansion valve, which decompresses it (or lowers its pressure) before returning it to the evaporator.

If this cycle ran continuously, the temperature would drop progressively lower. A thermostat is used to turn the compressor on and off at intervals in order to maintain the desired degree of cold.

DETERGENTS

Dirt has always been with us, but household detergents, bought at the supermarket, have been with us only since 1946. The reason detergents are useful has something to do with the nature of dirt, something with the nature of water, and something with the nature of detergents.

Laundries have come to expect 2 to 4 pounds of dirt with every 100 pounds of washing they take in. In cities, much of this will be waxes, petroleumlike substances, proteins (dandruff, wisps of hair), greasy sweat, and odd bits of sand and dust. On a shirt, for instance, some of the dirt will be held by ELECTRIC CHARGE, some (like juice from cherries or blueberries) by chemical bonding, some by simply being "jammed in" between the fibers of the cotton.

Since the soot and the grease are mixed, washing the shirt in plain water accomplishes nothing—the water is repelled by the grease.

Fig. 1 SOAP IS ADDED TO WATER TO HELP REACH DIRT THAT IS CARRIED IN GREASY FILMS

Fig. 2 SHAPE OF ONE MOLECULE OF SOAP

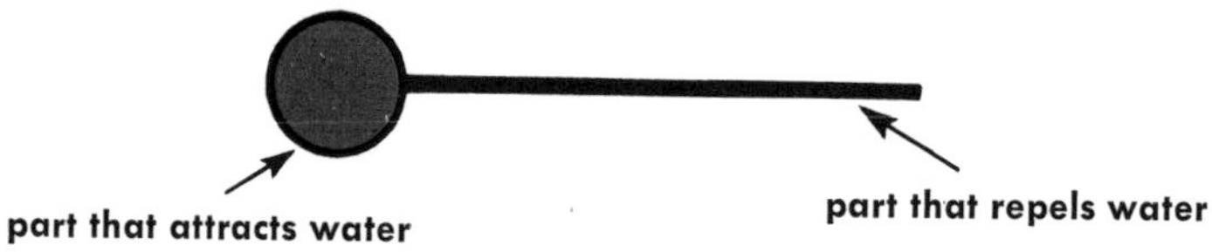

Adding soap helps because of a peculiarity of its molecules (Fig. 1). Each soap molecule has a head and a tail (Fig. 2). The head is attracted to the water, but the tail—made up of a long string of carbon atoms, each flanked by two hydrogen atoms—always tries to face *away* from it. If a shirt collar, with its film of dirt, is in soapy water,

Fig. 3 TAILS OF SOAP MOLECULES MOVE TOWARD GREASE ON FIBER

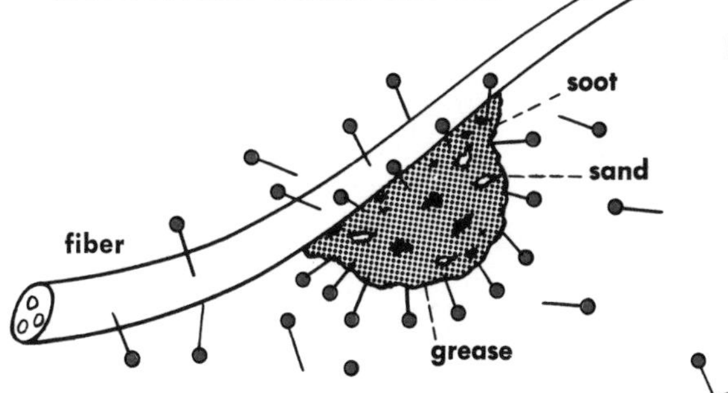

Fig. 4 DIRT PARTICLES ARE DISLODGED

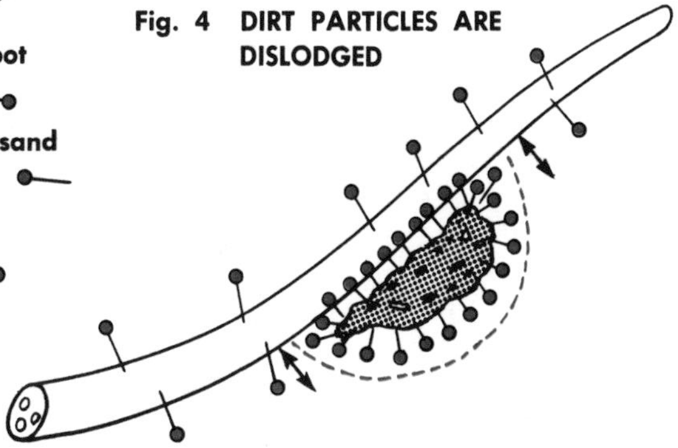

Fig. 5 PARTICLES OF GREASY DIRT ARE SURROUNDED BY MOLECULES OF DETERGENT AND ARE CARRIED AWAY BY RUNNING WATER

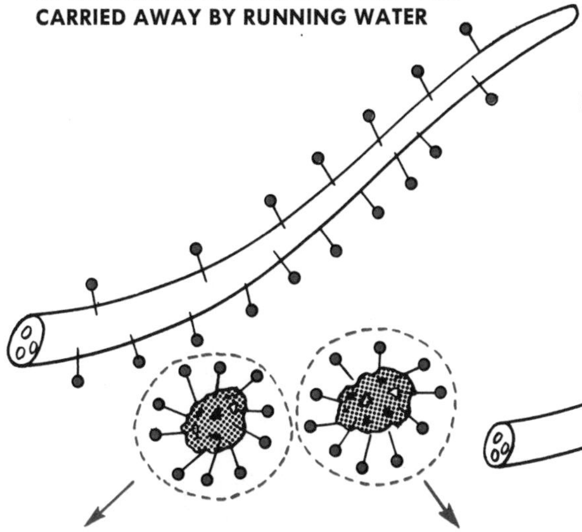

Fig. 6 REMAINING FIBER IS RINSED

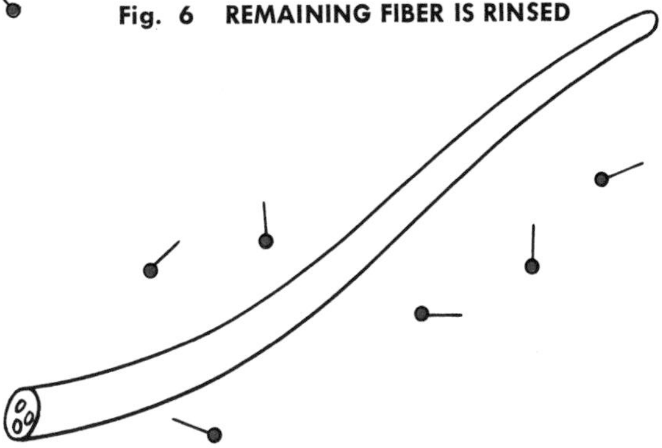

the tails of the soap molecules (known to chemists as "paraffin chains") face away from the water and into the dirt particles (Fig. 3), surrounding them and enabling them to be carried away by rinsing (Fig. 4).

But there is one difficulty with soap: in some kinds of water ("hard water"), it forms a scum. The trouble lies in the head of the soap molecule, which is unable to keep itself from reacting with some of the things it finds in hard water. Hard water contains calcium, sometimes magnesium. The calcium and magnesium like to get into the act, forming "soaps" of their own, which do not dissolve in water.

This is how "scum" is born. Meanwhile the original soap has been blocked from doing its job.

There are two solutions. One is to add a *water softener,* which tackles the calcium or magnesium in the water, keeping it from reacting with the soap. The other is to use a compound whose molecules are just like those of soap but whose "heads" are less vulnerable to attack. These are the *synthetic detergents,* or, simply, *detergents.*

The detergent boxes available at supermarkets do not reveal exactly what they contain. Half the contents may simply be "filler" added to make the package look bigger. The ingredients will also usually include a foaming agent. A little bit of this is fine, but the amount usually included simply causes the used water to bubble up into the neighbor's plumbing. It invades the sewers, keeps on bubbling, and risks carrying the filth from the sewers up into whatever sinks and toilet bowls happen to be nearby.

Most detergent powders also include phosphates. These do a good job of tackling the dirt and then keeping it suspended in the water until the water's own movement carries it away. But they also happen to be fertilizers—that is, they help plants grow. If the town sewers empty into a river or a lake, the phosphates start a population explosion among the plants (including algae and pondweeds) that live in the water. Some of the plants grow so thick that they clog the waterways; after they die, they decay, using up the oxygen in the water. The fish and other little animals swimming in the water then lack oxygen and *they* die. The water, at that stage, is not only unsafe to drink but is even unsafe for swimming.

The amount of phosphates released into the sewers by dishwashers is not considered dangerous, but the much larger quantities used in laundering have polluted the water in many parts of the United States and Canada.

Other ingredients often included are the *sulfonates,* which reduce the water's tendency to form a stretched surface, allowing it to reach the clothing fibers and give them a good soaking. Unfortunately, sulfonate molecules do not break up naturally in the ground after use, and in many small towns they have made the water in neighborhood wells undrinkable.

IX A Man-made World

PAPER

When the Babylonians—some 4,000 years ago—wanted to record information, they punched their words and numbers into *clay tablets,* which could later be baked. The Egyptians wrote on *papyrus,* made from the pressed stems of marsh plants that grew along the Nile. Medieval writers favored *parchment*—the scraped skin of some hapless donkey or calf, a material we now use only for drums and banjos. In more recent centuries, especially since the invention of printing, we have turned to paper. It can be made cheaply from the fibers surrounding the seeds of cotton plants and even more cheaply from the wood of Scandinavian and North American forests.

When paper is used in this way, it helps us to fulfill the role that most easily distinguishes us from other animals: when we learn something, we can transmit it to other people and to other generations. (Whether a lobster or a kangaroo ever thought of doing this we don't know. In any case, it can't.)

As used today, paper is given a great many jobs—as bathroom tissue, newsprint, typewriter paper, or kraft paper for grocery bags. The substance of the paper (*cellulose*—see WOOD) can even make it possible to use it in making clothes and in building houses.

Huge tracts of forest are devoted today to growing trees for *newsprint,* the somewhat coarse paper—made mostly from wood—that newspapers are printed on. The illustration on the facing page shows how newsprint is made. It is a "flow chart" with two inputs: one of them is the log of wood (upper left); the other is the container of rags—and waste paper—just under it. Products of the two are mixed with water in a great vat (center of page), where their fibers are converted to pulp. (Pulp can be 100 or 200 parts water to 1 part fiber.) This pulp is the basic "makings" from which any particular variety of paper will be made. The effect of all the grinding, dissolving, and beating is to break down the original structure of the wood (or rags) and serve up the cellulose molecules in smaller chains that can be reassembled into paper.

All this sopping pulp is not yet paper. It is first bleached; then glue is added, along with various compounds that allow the glue "sizing" to stick to the fibers rather than get lost in the water between them; and the pulp is drawn onto screens—sometimes an endless screen stretched over rollers. At this point the pulp acquires enough "body" to be passed through the air from one roller to the next in huge machines several hundred feet long. The water is dried out of it; it is passed over a succession of highly polished rollers that give its two surfaces a smooth "calendered" finish; and finally it is reeled (at a rate of a thousand feet per minute) into large rolls carried by trucks to the printing plants.

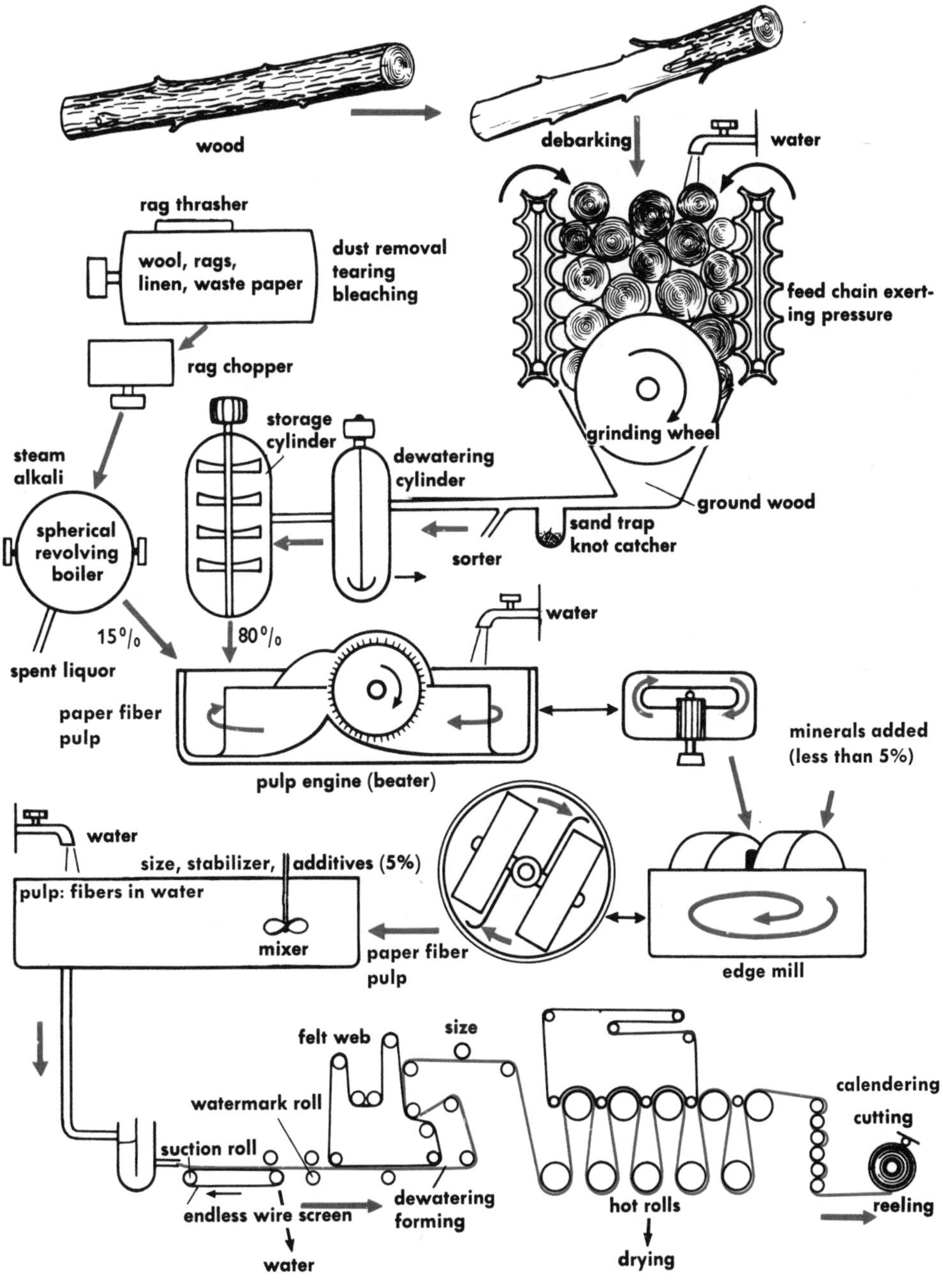

WOOD

Wood, over the centuries, has been our most faithful material. We've had stone and bone for exactly as long, but we've outgrown bone and the uses of stone have been getting fewer. Wood, on the other hand, has "grown" along with mankind, revealing new qualities as our skills have developed.

A violin, a cedar pencil, a longbow of yew—each shows up wood's special qualities of workability, lightness, or ability to spring back; and wood's sturdiness on a larger scale is what led to the log cabin and to the *Niña*, the *Pinta*, and the *Santa Maria*. In these uses the original wood has been *seasoned*—that is, the moisture in the lumber has been allowed to evaporate—but in its substance the wood has hardly changed: it is wood's structure that is being used.

Anyone who looks at finely ground wood under a microscope can confirm that wood is made up of fibers—each about a thousandth of an inch thick. But chemists who have analyzed wood report that the bulk of it is *cellulose*. Now, how is the cellulose made up into fibers? The beginning of a cellulose molecule—two molecules of glucose laid end to end—appears toward the top of Fig. 1. In each glucose unit, five carbon atoms and one oxygen atom form a hexagon, with various packets of H or OH hanging on to the C's. The condensed formula for cellulose, $C_6H_{10}O_5$, is enclosed in parentheses followed by a number *in the thousands*—meaning that it takes a chain of several thousand of these units to make up the cellulose molecule as it actually occurs in a tree. About a thousand of these chains then go to form a filament, a few dozen filaments form a microfibril, and a few dozen microfibrils form a fibril. The fibrils, which lie alongside one another but entwined in a multiple helix, are shown in the lower part of Fig. 1 as they take their place in a *day ring*. Between all these cellulose fibrils is a substance called *lignin*. (Chemists have identified the various compounds that occur in lignin, but have so far been unable to put them together into a picture that makes sense as a whole.)

The two extremes in the use of wood are (1) to use it just as it comes from the lumberyard (as in construction) and (2) to use it as fuel, destroying it completely. If these were the only things we could do with it, wood would be on the way out.

More interesting things happen when wood is transformed into something with brand-new properties. *Plywood* hardly counts in this regard—wood slices an eighth of an inch thick have simply been glued together, each sheet turned with its grain at right angles to the next. But PAPER, in which the wood's fibers are broken up by converting wood into a watery pulp and then drying it, lends itself to printing the Des Moines *Register* or *The Way Things Work* in ways that a block of wood couldn't really match.

But it's through *chemical change* that the greatest transformations of wood come about (Fig. 2). The wood can be heated in a closed container (a process known as *destructive distillation*) in which the cellulose molecules are broken down into smaller units that chemists then use to build something else. When the wood reaches temperatures in the neighborhood of 600° Fahrenheit, it yields a liquid that contains wood alcohol (methanol) and from which turpentine and a variety of oils and solvents can be drawn. (In its own right, methanol is poisonous stuff unfit for man or beast. By putting it through processes that enable it to pick up extra oxygen, chemists convert it to *formaldehyde;* a solution of 40% formaldehyde in water, called

Fig. 1 THE GLUCOSE MANUFACTURED IN GREEN PLANTS IS TRANSFORMED INTO LONG MOLECULES OF CELLULOSE THAT GIVE WOOD ITS STURDINESS. THESE MOLECULES FORM MICROFIBRILS, WHICH FORM FIBRILS, WHICH IN TURN FORM THE FIBERS IN A PIECE OF LUMBER

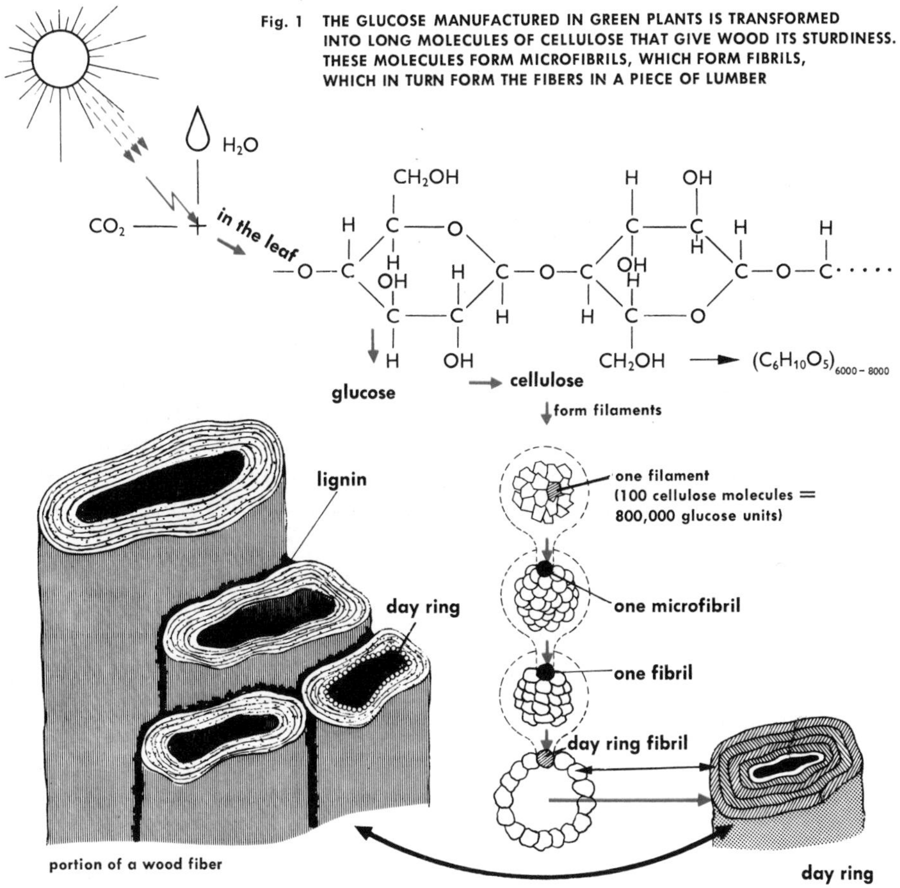

Fig. 2 THE FUTURE OF WOOD LIES NOT IN BURNING IT BUT IN TRANSFORMING ITS CELLULOSE AND LIGNIN BY SUCCESSIVE CHEMICAL REACTIONS

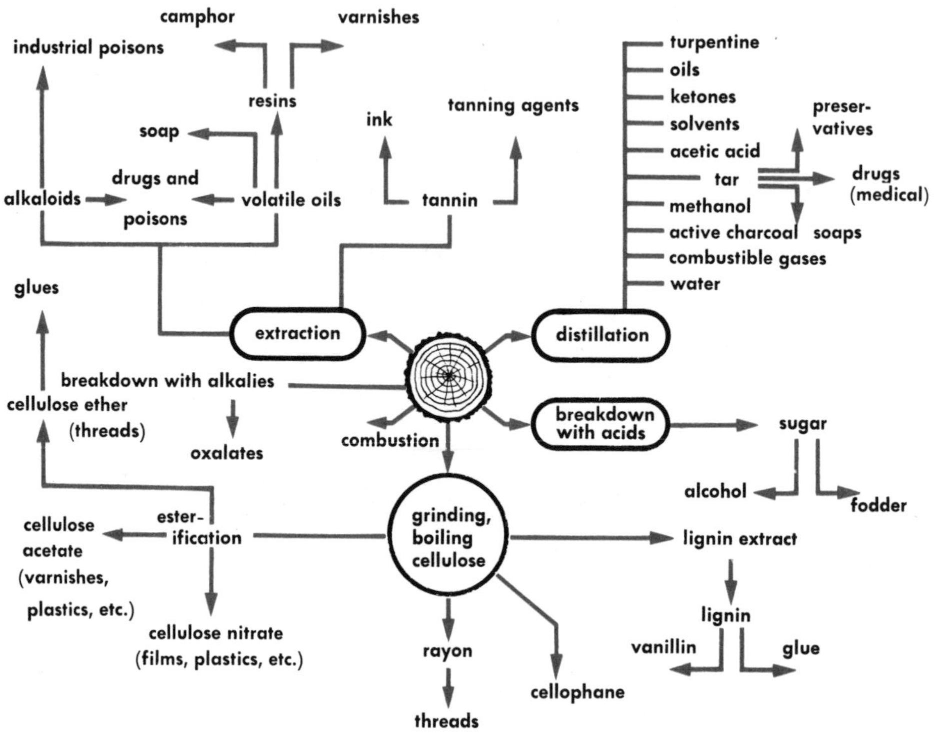

formalin, is good for preserving frogs, moles, and snakes.) Figure 2 also diagrams the transformation that wood undergoes on being treated with certain acids or by having its cellulose made available by grinding and boiling. Wood contains—notably in its lignin—small amounts of compounds that can be extracted to serve in the making of leather-tanning preparation and drugs.

One often hears woods divided into "softwoods" and "hardwoods." As generally used today, these terms no longer describe the wood but the tree it comes from. *Softwood,* in the lumber trade, simply refers to wood from trees that keep their leaves or needles throughout the year—pine, redwood and spruce, cedar and fir; *hardwoods* come from trees that shed their leaves in the fall—elm and maple, walnut and oak. Though not always harder than the softwood, hardwoods split less readily.

WEAVING

For most of the history of mankind, the only clothing people had was what they could put together from animal skins. (This tradition survives in our shoes, which are usually still made of leather.) The discovery of ways of assembling small bits of animal hair (sheep's wool) or plant fiber (flax, for linen) was a tremendous step forward.

This step took two forms: felting and weaving. In **felting,** bits of hair from an animal's hide are soaked or steamed, then matted together under pressure. (Little bits of roughness on each hair enable the fibers to hook on to one another and stay matted; plant fibers, being smooth, don't allow felting.) Today men's hats are often made of felt, but so are many insulating materials used in buildings. A felt pad does a beautiful job of absorbing vibration—for instance, under a clattering typewriter.

Weaving depends on a more indirect approach. Instead of taking little bits of hair or plant fibers as they are, the weaver has someone else (in former times known as a *spinster*) spin the fibers into thread by rubbing and twirling them together (stretching them out lengthwise at the same time) so that they form a long, twisted strand. The next step is to stretch the lengths of yarn side by side on a loom to form the *warp*. The warp has no yarn running across and through it to hold it together and is useless as cloth.

Yarn is now stretched across the warp, crosswise. If one takes a piece of yarn between thumb and fingers and runs it over and under the threads of the warp, one is not weaving—one is *twining*. For true weaving a system has to be worked out that allows the crosswise thread to go *straight through*, without a twisting over-and-under motion. How can this be done? By using a *heddle*, which lifts all odd-numbered threads of the warp at one stroke. The shuttle carrying the crosswise thread is then passed through the space (or "shed") between the odd-numbered warp threads and the even-numbered ones. The heddle is then let down and a shred rod is then turned up, raising every even-numbered thread of the warp, making a space for the shuttle to carry the crosswise thread back. The result of these two steps is that the crosswise thread has gone under and over the warp threads in one direction and over and under them on the return trip. The result is much the same as with twining, but since no twisting was involved, the process is much faster. The crosswise threads, which form the *weft*, are pushed up to keep the weave tight, and the weaving continues until a whole stretch of cloth has been made.

A modern working out of this system appears in the large hand loom in Fig 1, in which the yarn is shown in red. The odd and even

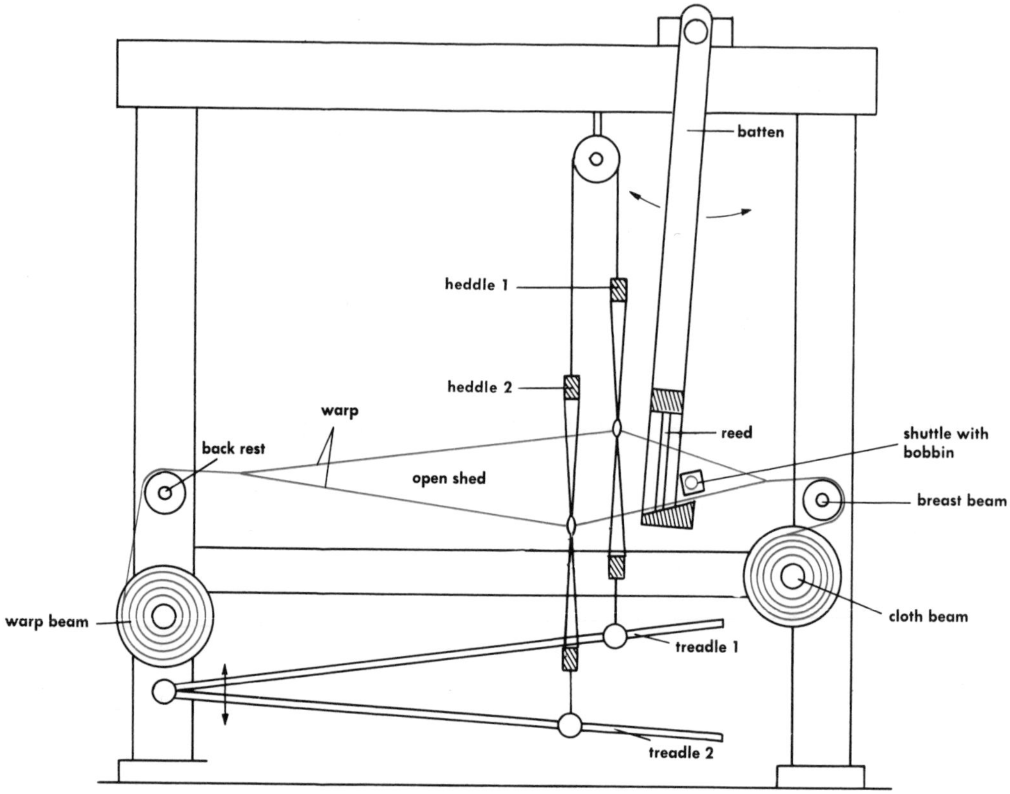

Fig. 1 IN THIS HAND LOOM THE WARP THREADS ARE HELD HORIZONTALLY BETWEEN BACK REST AND BREAST BEAM; FINISHED CLOTH IS GATHERED ON THE RIGHT. TREADLES ALLOW WEAVER TO RAISE HEDDLES THAT DETERMINE WHICH THREADS OF THE WARP WILL BE RAISED AS SHUTTLE PASSES THROUGH

warp threads have been pulled apart by liftable heddles (seen end on) suspended from an overhead pulley and controlled by *treadles*. In the position shown, treadle 2 has been pressed down, lowering heddle 2; this raises heddle 1 and warp threads 1, 3, 5, 7 . . . For the return trip of the shuttle, the weaver's foot will lower treadle 1; warp threads 1, 3, 5, 7 . . . will be low; warp threads 2, 4, 6, 8 . . . will be high. A swinging *batten*, as it swings to the right, packs the newly added weft threads tightly against the already completed fabric.

If the weaving proceeds in the simplest way, with the weft thread going once over and once under and so on as it makes its way across the warp, the result is a *linen weave*, or *plain weave* (Fig. 2; warp thread is shown in black, weft thread in red). The wiggly drawing at the foot of Fig. 2 shows how the weft thread (red) passes over and under the warp thread (black). In the shorthand checkerboard diagram to the right of Fig. 2, a filled-in square means warp over weft, a black square means weft over warp. If *two* weft threads are lifted over the same number of warp threads (Fig. 4), the result is a *double weave,* sometimes known as "basket cloth."

The double weave is still basically a plain weave, because in each pair the second thread stays "in step" with the first—simply doubling it. But now suppose that one weft thread crossed under two warp threads, then over one warp thread, and so on (Fig. 5), and imagine also that on the return trip the same 2:1 under/over ratio were kept, *but out of step by one square.* The result would be a cloth with "climbing" diagonals (Fig. 5) called *right twill.* Diagonals seeming to head "downward" make a *left twill* (Fig. 6). A close-up of a simple 1:2 twill appears in Fig. 3.

A close look at Figs. 5 and 6 will also reveal a different rhythm in the weaving—Fig. 5 is known as a 2:1 twill, Fig. 6 as a 3:1 twill. (The angle is 45° in both, because the ratios are used horizontally *and* vertically.) Since the warp in both diagrams is "above" the weft more often than not (that is, filled-in squares outnumber blank ones), the twills of Figs. 5 and 6 are called "warp-faced." (In the checkerboard diagrams, the groups of squares at lower left printed in black indicates the smallest "cell" from which a weaver can make up the pattern.)

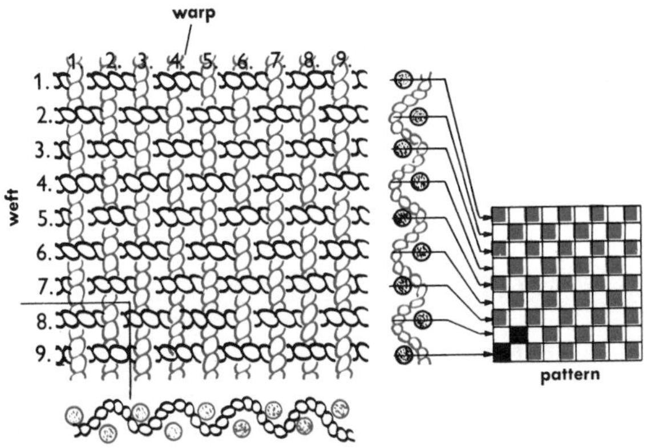

Fig. 2 IN PLAIN WEAVE, THE INTERLACING LINES UP HORIZONTALLY AND VERTICALLY, CREATING AN EVEN EFFECT

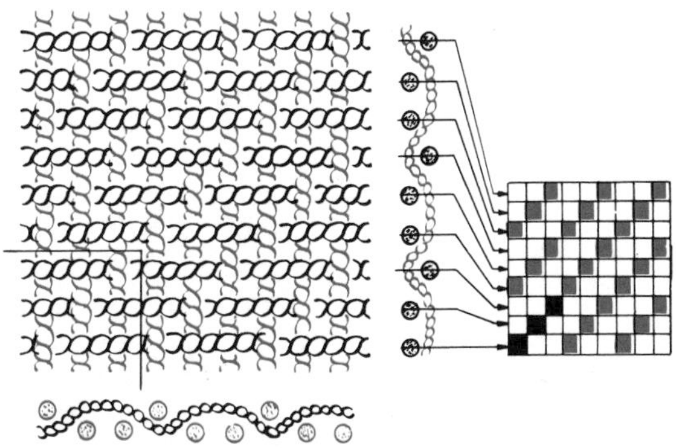

Fig. 3 IN TWILL, EACH NEW LINE BEGINS OUT OF STEP WITH PREVIOUS ONE, FORMING DIAGONAL "RIBS" IN CLOTH

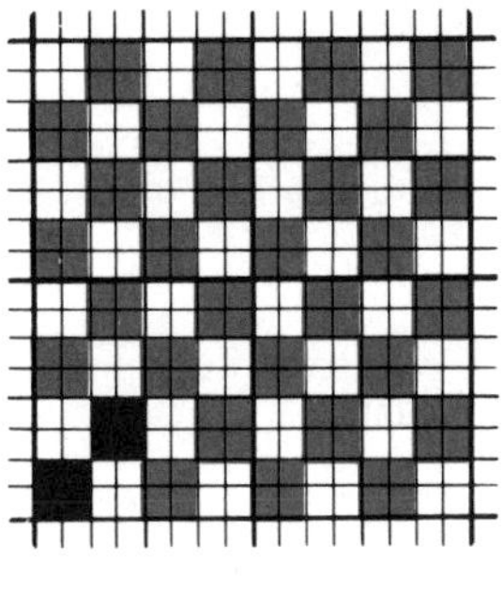

Fig. 4 "DOUBLE WEAVE" LINES UP LIKE PLAIN WEAVE, SIMPLY CREATING COARSER "GRAIN"

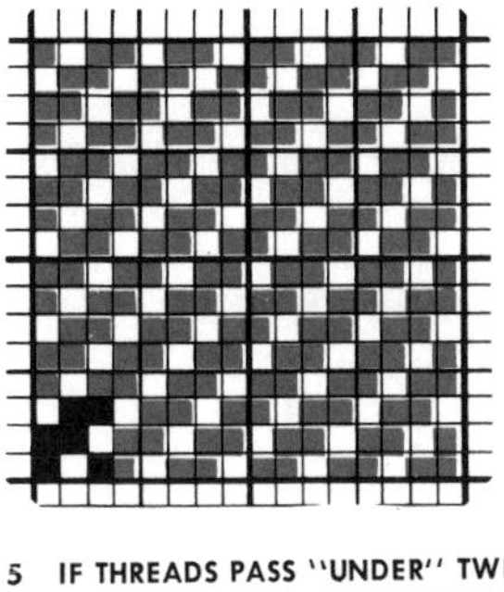

Fig. 5 IF THREADS PASS "UNDER" TWICE AS MUCH AS THEY PASS "OVER," RESULT IS A "WARP-FACED TWILL"

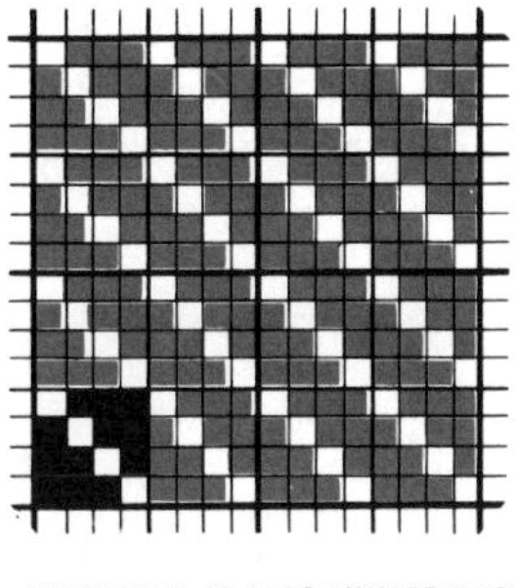

Fig. 6 THIS TWILL IS ALSO "WARP-FACED," BUT 3:1 INSTEAD OF THE 2:1 OF FIG. 5

RUBBER

Rubber is a highly useful and versatile product because of its varied properties. To name a few, it has flexibility (useful for hoses), water repellence (rainwear and diving gear), electrical resistance (wire insulation), resistance to abrasion (automobile tires), and elasticity (rubber bands). One of its earliest uses in Europe was as an eraser for rubbing out lead-pencil marks, which explains the name "rubber."

Natural rubber is made from *latex*, a milky fluid that comes mostly from the *Hevea brasiliensis* tree, though there are other latex-producing plants. The Hevea is grown on plantations in tropical climates. Latex is extracted by tapping the tree—cutting gashes in the bark and collecting the dripping sap in a cup. South American Indians aptly named the Hevea the "weeping tree."

The latex is coagulated, or solidified, by the addition of acid. Before shipping, the *crude rubber* is usually pressed into sheets and dried by smoke or rolled into thin crepe sheets and air-dried. In this form, rubber is not very useful because it becomes hard and brittle at low temperatures and soft and sticky at warm temperatures. A process called *vulcanization* is used to cure the rubber and give it the desired characteristics.

Pure crude rubber (rubber without additives) is a compound of carbon and hydrogen, the atoms of which are chemically joined together forming rubber *molecules*. It is the long chainlike structure of these molecules that gives rubber its elastic properties.

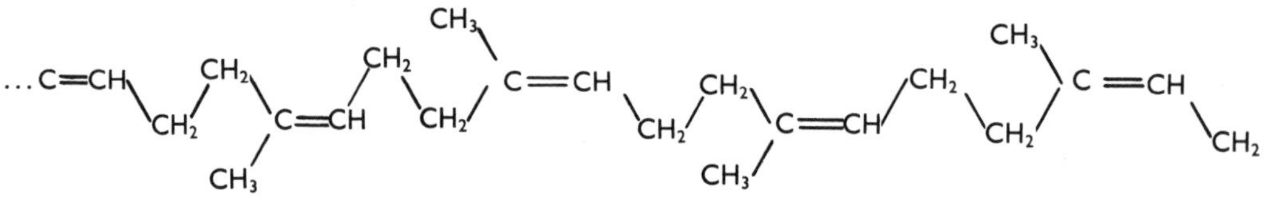

RUBBER MOLECULE

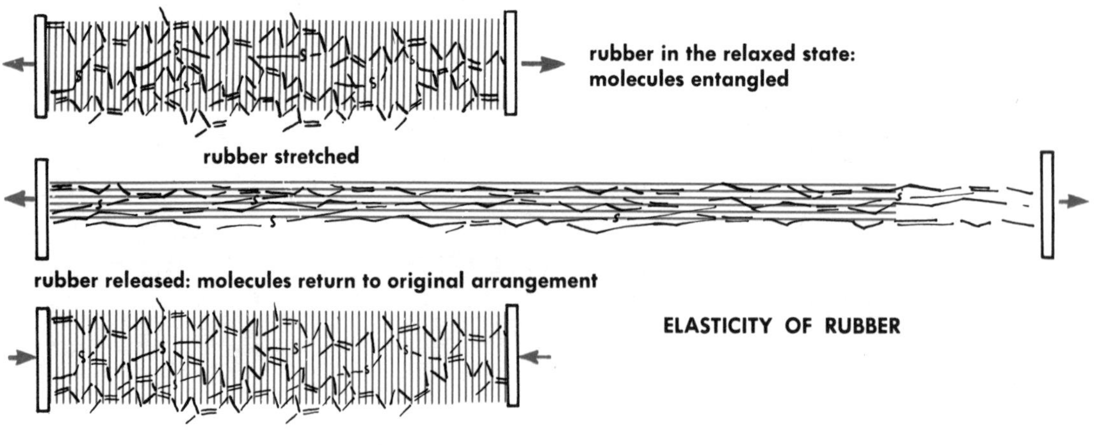

ELASTICITY OF RUBBER

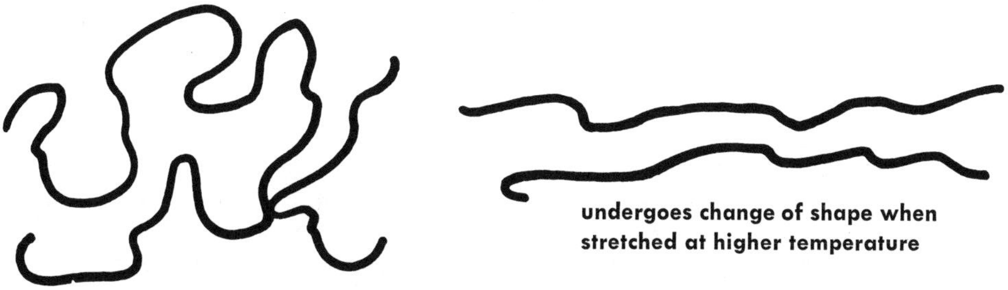

CRUDE RUBBER (NOT VULCANIZED)

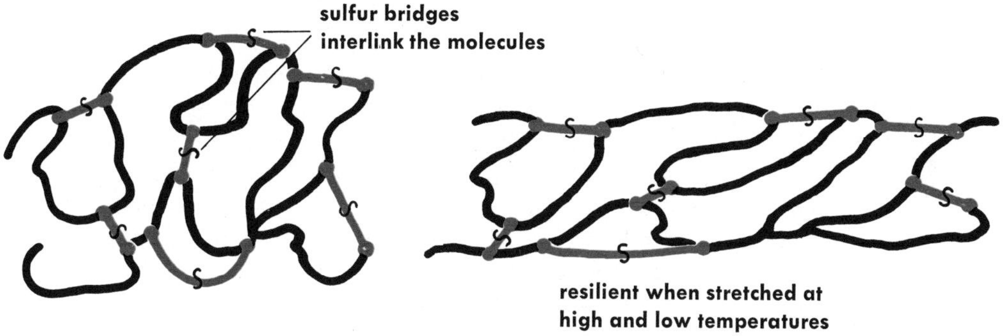

VULCANIZED RUBBER

In vulcanizing the raw rubber, it is reduced to its sticky plastic form and mixed with other ingredients—these depending on the product for which it will be used. Sulfur is the additive most widely used. It interlinks the long molecules and gives them greater strength and resiliency at relative high and low temperatures. Most rubber products are molded under high heat and pressure, which completes the vulcanization.

Foam rubber, used extensively in mattresses and seat cushions, is usually made by whipping the soft rubber in a frothing machine before molding and vulcanizing.

The chemical composition of natural rubber can be copied almost identically in the laboratory. The long filamentary molecules are produced by a chemical reaction called *polymerization*. This process involves the combining of two or more compounds to form a new compound. For instance, one of the leading synthetic rubbers, often used in automobile tires, is Buna S. It is a polymer of two liquids, butadiene and styrene. Buna S, like many other synthetics, can be mixed with natural rubber and can be vulcanized.

GLASS

The glass of a window, of a thermometer, of a CAMERA LENS, is obviously a very special substance. But quite apart from the properties that are easily noticed—the fact that it won't conduct electricity, that it is transparent—there is one thing about it that is even odder: although it looks like a solid, it is really a peculiar variety of liquid. Its atoms (mostly silicon and oxygen) aren't at all arranged in the orderly rows commonly found in solids. The silicon atoms are randomly distributed, each within reach of several oxygen atoms, and a few sodium atoms are strewn here and there among them, like raisins in a cake.

This, in fact, is the arrangement one expects to find in a liquid. But if glass is a liquid, why doesn't it slosh about and take on different shapes? The answer seems to be that it's a very slow-moving liquid—like molasses, only some 1,000,000,000,000,000,000 times as stiff. It's a *supercooled* liquid. Its main ingredient, silicon dioxide, normally melts at around 3100° Fahrenheit. When allowed to cool below this, it should "freeze" and form crystals. But glass doesn't! It goes right on cooling, simply becoming a stiffer and stiffer liquid. (At the factory, it is usually shaped at around 1200° Fahrenheit.)

If glass (like the mineral quartz) were *only* silicon and oxygen, it would melt at only a very high temperature and would be so sluggish even when melted that bubbles from air trapped in the sand wouldn't be able to escape. So the traditional way of making glass is to mix other substances with the sand; the oxygen they contribute breaks up the ready-made bonds between silicon and oxygen in the sand, loosens up the melt and lets the bubbles out.

One starts with a heap of clean, finely ground *quartz sand,* a heap of *soda ash* (sodium carbonate), and a heap of *limestone,* as in Fig. 1. Other ingredients sometimes include *dolomite* (a double carbonate of sodium and magnesium), which also contributes oxygen. After thorough mixing, the sandy mixture is heated in a *regenerative tank furnace* to a temperature above 2300° Fahrenheit; air bubbles and carbon dioxide are released, and a clear melt (consisting of calcium and sodium silicates dissolved in each other) can then be poured out. It can be passed between rollers (Fig. 2) to form window glass, or dropped into a mold (Fig. 3) to start the forming sequence that will result in a ginger-ale bottle.

If the sand contains traces of iron oxides, the glass will be green. In some uses (such as bottles) this does not matter; without resorting to purer and more expensive quartz sand, one can still make the glass

Fig. 1 FINELY GROUND QUARTZ SAND, SODA ASH (SODIUM CARBONATE), AND LIMESTONE ARE THE MAIN INGREDIENTS OF ORDINARY GLASS. IN REGENERATIVE FURNACE, FUEL AND EXHAUST ARE MADE TO SWITCH CHANNELS EVERY SO OFTEN TO ALLOW AIR AND FUEL GAS TO BE HEATED BY WARMTH OF EXHAUST PIPES

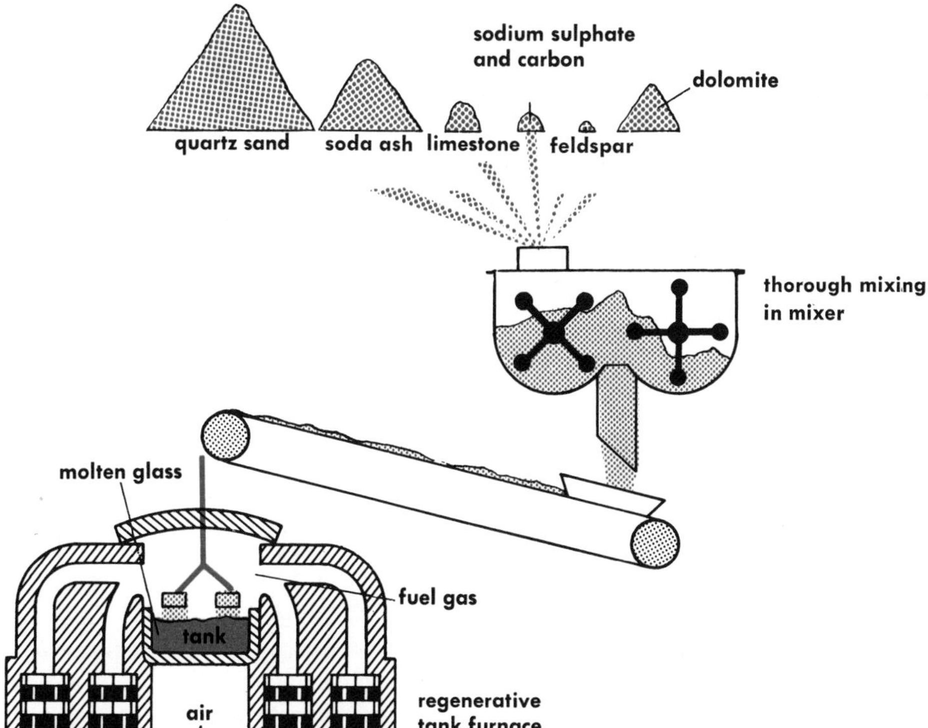

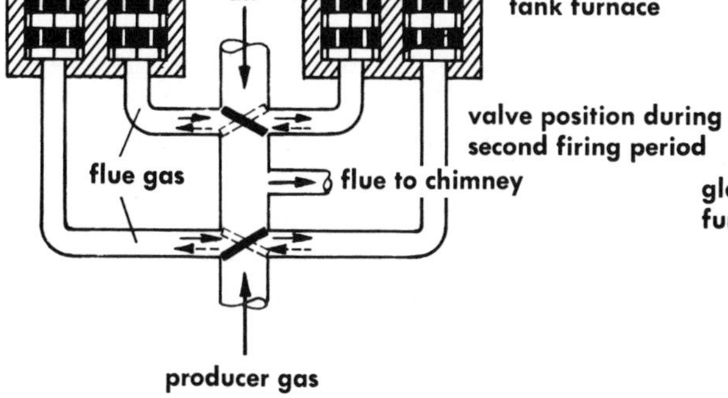

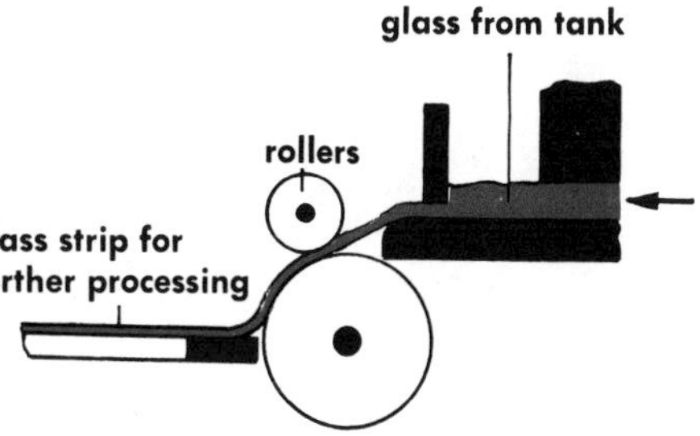

Fig. 2 TO MAKE WINDOW GLASS, BARELY COOLED MOLTEN GLASS IS PASSED BETWEEN ROLLERS

colorless by adding manganese dioxide into the mix. Optical glass, however—for instance, the glass in camera lenses—is made only from extremely pure ingredients, and the melt is stirred to ensure that the mixing is very thorough and even throughout, so that all parts of a lens will bend light rays by the same amount.

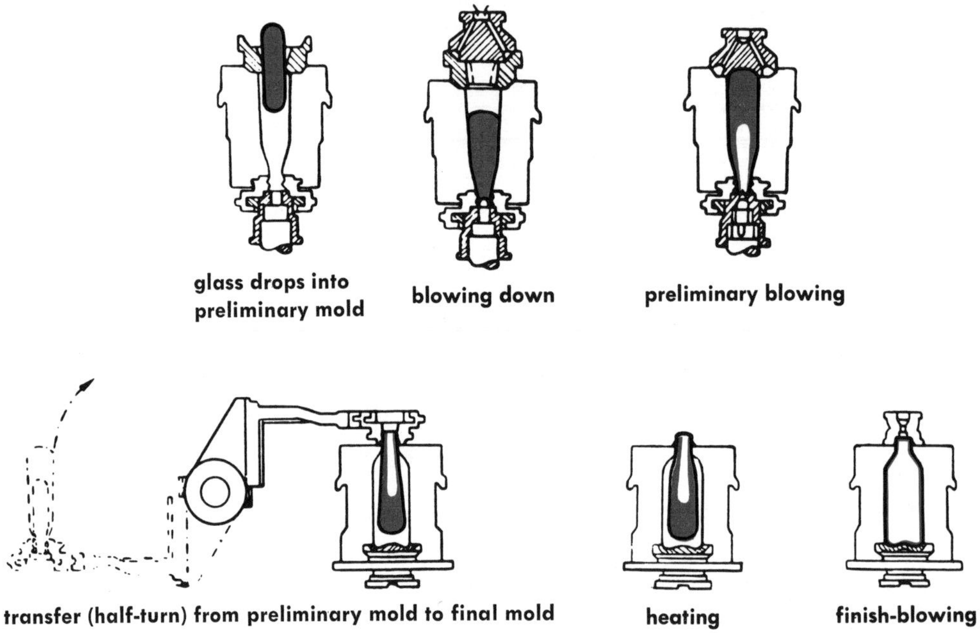

Fig. 3 IN SIX-STEP OPERATION, A CLUMP OF MOLTEN GLASS IS FORMED THROUGH COMBINED ACTION OF MOLDS AND AIR JETS

Adding boron oxide to the silicon oxide allows glassmakers to produce glasses that don't expand when heated and that don't shrink when cooled. Glasses of this kind—of which Pyrex is the best-known—are now used in baking dishes and saucepans, though their most spectacular use is in astronomy: California's 200-inch TELESCOPE mirror at Palomar, which weighs 500 tons, was cast as a single piece of Pyrex.

One surprising development in glassmaking is that glass can also be drawn into fibers and spun over a rotating drum. These fibers can be as fine as two ten-thousandths of an inch; they can be woven (for curtains) or matted (for insulating materials).

STEEL

Steel—the material from which we make such diverse items as pen-knives, ships' hulls, automobiles and skyscrapers—is taken for granted today. Yet it was only a bit over 100 years ago that this use became possible. Why? The iron ore was always present in nature and small pieces of steel had been made as early as the Middle Ages (as in armour), but man had not yet solved the problem of building furnaces large enough and providing heat high enough so as to convert large quantities of iron into steel.

Today to transform iron ore into steel, we heat the ore (and some added materials) to a temperature so high that it drives off much of the carbon and other impurities in the ore. We usually accomplish this in two stages, beginning by converting iron ore into pig iron.

In this first stage, the ore (along with limestone and a high-carbon coal product called *coke*) is poured in at the top of a 100-foot-high *blast furnace* and is kept "cooking" by a blast of air coming in from below at a temperature of about 1,300° Fahrenheit. The molten iron sinks to the bottom, and a layer of *slag* floats on top of it. The slag, which contains unwanted byproducts of the chemical reaction caused by the "cooking," is drawn off every so often, leaving molten pig iron at the bottom of the furnace. However, some of the impurities of the iron ore still remain in the pig iron, so it must be "recooked."

Fig. 1 IN OPEN-HEARTH FURNACE, PIG IRON UNDERGOES CHEMICAL CLEANUP THROUGH ACTION OF BURNING FUEL-AND-AIR MIXTURE. DIRECTION OF GAS FLOW IS SWITCHED EVERY 15 MINUTES

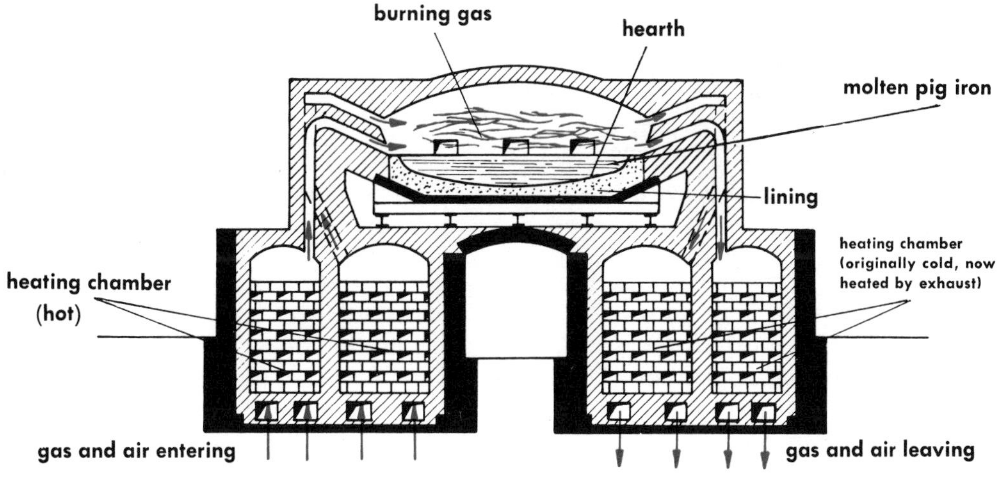

The second stage—the "recooking"—converts the pig iron into steel. Over the last 100 years, much of the world's steel has been made in an **open hearth** (Fig. 1). Molten pig iron is poured into a shallow tub, usually along with scrap steel, iron ore, and some limestone. A gas flame heats the mixture from above to a temperature of 3,240° Fahrenheit. As the metal mixture gets hot, a slag forms and is skimmed off. The steel is removed from the bottom of the hearth through taps.

A peculiarity of the open-hearth process is that the gas and air for the overhead flames are switched from left to right or from right to left every 15 minutes. If the gas and air first come from the left (as in Fig. 1), the pipes on the right are used for exhaust; when the direction is switched, forcing the new supply of gas and air to come from the right, these pass upward through pipes that have now been heated by the exhaust. By switching back and forth, the temperature is driven higher and higher (this is called a "regenerative" system). After about ten hours, the hearth will have produced 200 tons of steel.

Another device for converting pig iron into steel is the **Bessemer converter,** which burns the carbon out of the pig iron by blasting air

Fig. 2 BESSEMER CONVERTER, HELD UPRIGHT DURING "BLOWING" OF AIR THROUGH MOLTEN IRON, IS TILTED TO SKIM OFF SLAG

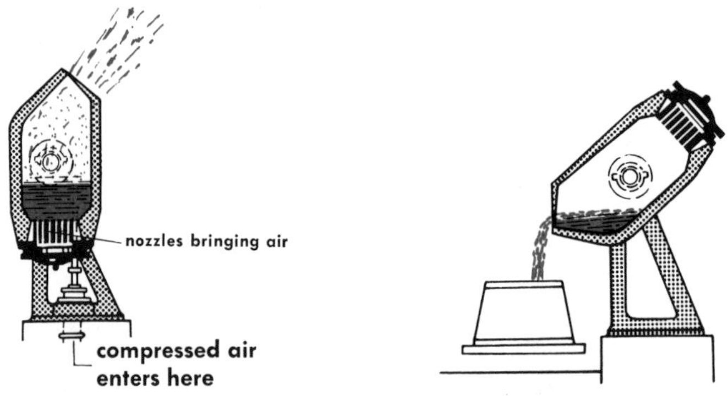

a position during blowing

b pouring off the slag

through it. The air is ordinary unheated air—no fuel is needed. It blasts upward through *nozzles* at the bottom of a huge container holding some 40 tons of pig iron (Fig. 2, upper part). As it bubbles upward, it oxidizes unwanted silicon and manganese, forming a slag that floats on the surface. (The converter can be tipped to pour the slag off—Fig. 2b.) As the converter heats up (simply from the heat released in chemical reactions with the incoming air), the carbon in the pig iron starts to burn off at the mouth of the converter. Controlled amounts of carbon and alloy metals are then added, the converter is tipped over all the way, and the steel is poured out.

Fig. 3 IN ELECTRIC ARC FURNACE MOLTEN IRON IS HEATED BY ELECTRIC CURRENT ENTERING AND LEAVING THROUGH ELECTRODES. BEARINGS ALLOW TILTING TO POUR OFF SLAG OR STEEL

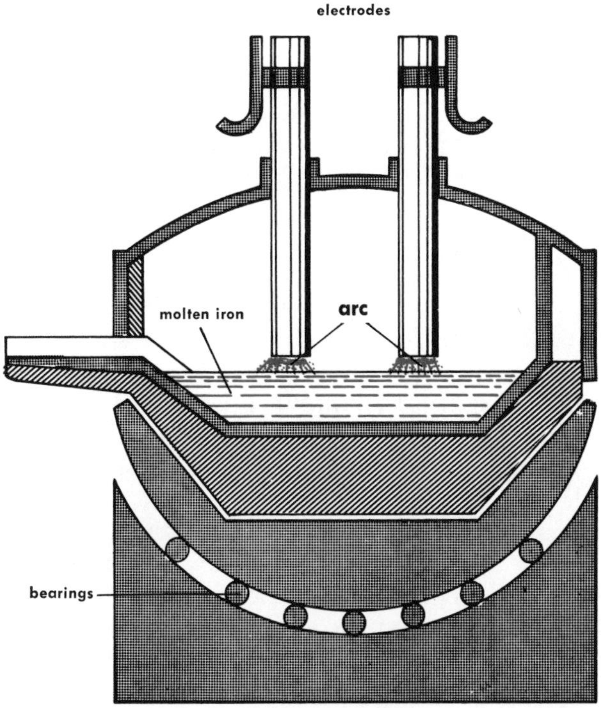

For tools and alloy steels, the pig iron can be processed in an **electric arc furnace,** in which temperatures and ingredients can be controlled with great accuracy. In the one shown in Fig. 3, ELECTRIC CURRENT coming down from one electrode passes *through* the molten steel before returning to the other electrode. As it passes through, it raises the temperature of the mixture. Since the metal can be sampled from time to time, and new alloy metals added at will, steel made in this way can have practically any purity or alloy proportion desired.

PLASTICS

In its broadest sense, the term "plastics" could be applied to any substances that can be molded to retain a given shape. This definition would include such materials as clay, *glass, steel,* and *rubber*. But in modern terminology, plastics are taken to mean solid substances made up of organic compounds (carbon compounds) derived either from the raw materials of nature or from synthetic chemicals. Plastics are sometimes described as being manufactured from coal, air, and water. This is true in that they contain the chemical elements present in that combination. The same elements, however, can be produced from a variety of other materials, such as plants, proteins, petroleum, natural gas, and wood pulp.

Synthetic plastics fall into two categories: **thermoplastics** and **thermosetting plastics.** Thermoplastics, such as Lucite and Plexiglas, can be softened by heat, shaped, and then rehardened by cooling. Thermosetting plastics, such as Bakelite, are "set," or hardened, by heat and cannot be softened again.

Plastics are made of very large molecules. Some are formed by *polymerization,* wherein two or more compounds made up of small molecules are combined to produce large molecules. When some chemicals are united they set free, or split out, water. This is what happens in the thermosetting plastics. For instance, when phenol and formaldehyde are heated together, they produce Bakelite resin and water.

The nature and formation of the molecules in the plastic determine its qualities. If the molecules are clustered in a spherical shape, they produce hard, rigid plastics. If they are long and filamentary in structure, they will produce pliable rubberlike plastics.

Celluloid is one of the oldest plastics. It was first produced in 1869 as a substitute for ivory and was basically made from cotton, acids, and camphor. It is still used for a variety of products, such as toys, but its high flammability presents a drawback.

Since the advent of Celluloid, plastics have been in a nonstop state of development. Their varieties and uses are now practically countless. Plastic materials can be formed in a number of ways. The liquid plastic can be molded, pressed, rolled, stamped, drawn into threads or ribbons, etc. Many can be *laminated* (built up in layers with other materials) to form rugged sheets, such as the Formica often used on table tops and wall panels. The wide range of plastic products includes toys, packaging, cases for radios, unbreakable dishes and bottles, flooring, wire insulation, fabrics, boat hulls, machine parts, lenses, and thousands of other items—ranging from powder puffs to gun barrels.

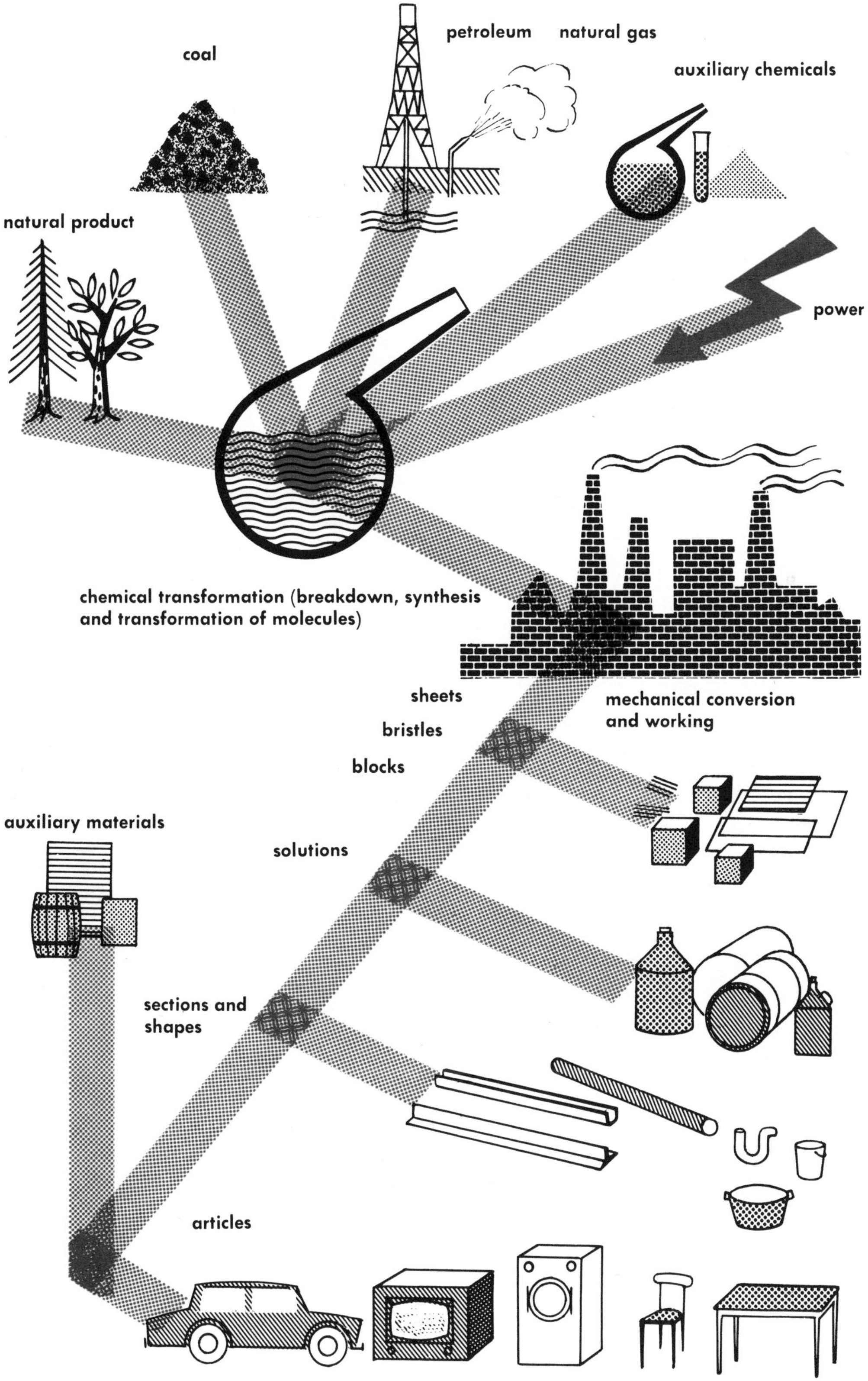
coal
petroleum
natural gas
auxiliary chemicals
natural product
power
chemical transformation (breakdown, synthesis and transformation of molecules)
sheets
bristles
blocks
mechanical conversion and working
auxiliary materials
solutions
sections and shapes
articles

X Navigation and Space

TELESCOPES (OPTICAL)

An optical telescope is an instrument that makes faraway objects appear to be closer, and therefore clearer, to the viewer. This is accomplished by gathering the light from the object by means of a lens or mirror, bringing it to a focus, and enlarging the image in an eyepiece. Though telescope designs vary somewhat, they all fall into two major categories—*refractors* and *reflectors*.

The **refracting telescope** (Fig. 1) has what is called an *objective lens* mounted near the end of the tube. The lens is *convex*—that is, curved like the *outside* surface of a sphere. It bends, or refracts, the incoming light and focuses a small image inside the tube. Then the *eyepiece lens* magnifies this image for the viewer to examine.

The **reflecting telescope** (Fig. 2) has a *main mirror* at the bottom of the tube. The mirror is *concave*—that is, curved like the *inside* sur-

Fig. 1 REFRACTING TELESCOPE

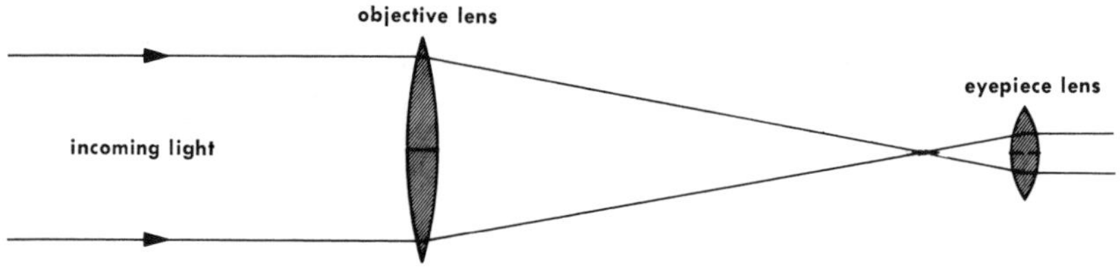

Fig. 2 REFLECTING TELESCOPE

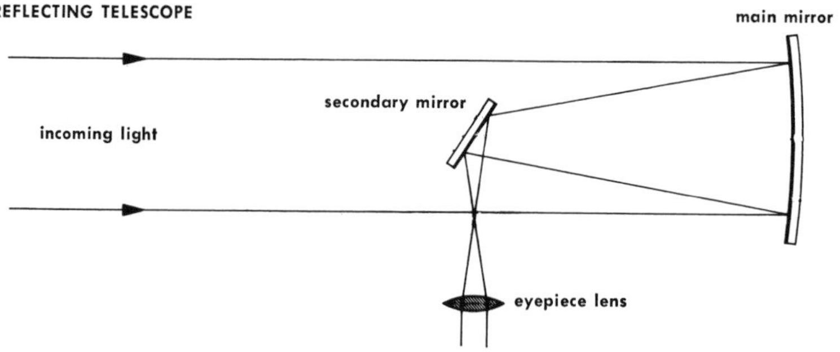

face of a sphere. It receives the incoming light rays and reflects them onto a second diagonal mirror. The image is brought to a focus and is reflected into the magnifying eyepiece.

While refractors may have fewer components, it is not practical to build them in very large sizes. The bulky objective lenses can be supported only around the rim—a delicate mounting problem. The largest observatory refractor now in use has a 40-inch-diameter lens.

The main advantage in the reflector is that light does not have to pass *through* the mirror, as it does with an objective lens. And so the mirror can have a solid support across its back to hold it in position. Also, only the top surface needs to be ground and polished to perfection, after which it is coated with silver or aluminum to give it a reflecting surface. The largest reflector now in use has a 200-inch-diameter mirror, though even larger ones can conceivably be built.

Fig. 3 TERRESTRIAL TELESCOPE

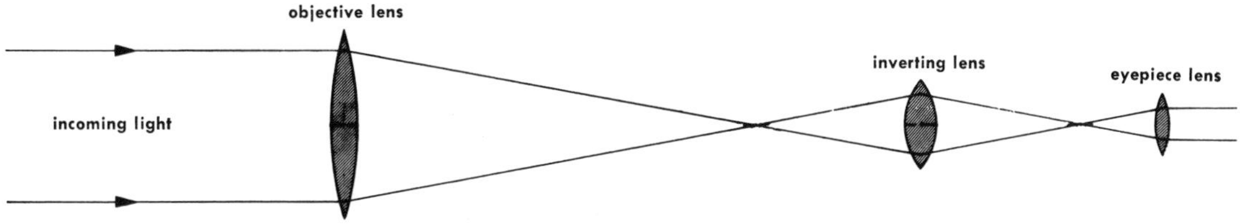

Astronomical telescopes show the observer an inverted image, which makes little difference when viewing celestial objects—there is no "right-side up" in space, anyway. But **terrestrial telescopes** (Fig. 3) often provide a third lens to turn the image upright again. Though this adds to the length of the instrument, it provides an added convenience.

ROCKETS

Rocket propulsion is based on Sir Isaac Newton's law of "action and reaction," which states that *for every force there is an equal and opposite force.* For instance, if you jump from a boat to a dock, you are exerting a force, or an *action.* But you are also pushing the boat away from you with an equal force—a *reaction.*

Newton's law, as it applies to rockets, can be simply demonstrated with a balloon (Fig. 1). When the balloon is inflated and tied, the compressed air inside is pushing on all parts of the wall with an equal force. The balloon remains stationary. But if it is untied and let go, the compressed air escapes and the balloon takes off in the direction *opposite* the opening. What happens is that the escaping air (action)

Fig. 1 BALLOON WITH COMPRESSED AIR

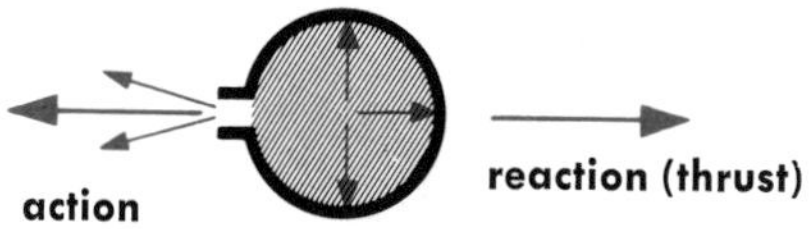

Fig. 2 ROCKET WITH HOT EXPANDED GASES

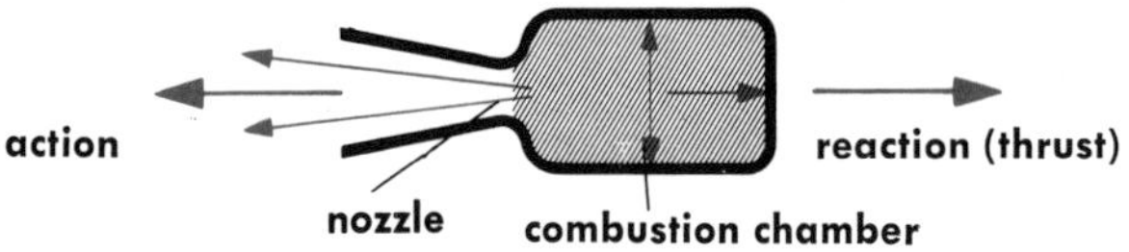

creates an unbalanced force inside the balloon causing the reaction force to push it forward. A rocket is thrust forward in the same way when hot expanded gases shoot out from the nozzle (Fig. 2). It might seem that this forward thrust is caused by the escaping gases pushing against the air. Actually, the force is completely internal and in no way dependent on the outside environment—it works the same way in a vacuum as it does in the atmosphere, which makes the reaction engine ideal for spacecraft propulsion.

Fuel is another important factor in propelling a missile outside the earth's atmosphere. Most fuels need the oxygen in the air for combustion. For instance, if you light a candle, the wax (fuel) combines with oxygen in the air (oxidizer) to make it burn. If you put an inverted glass over the candle, the flame will go out when the oxygen is used up. Aircraft JET ENGINES are also dependent on the atmosphere for combustion.

Rocketry differs from other means of propulsion in that a rocket *is not dependent upon air* to burn the fuel. It carries its own oxidizer along with the fuel. A rocket, then, need not be a prisoner of the earth's atmosphere if it can carry enough fuel to reach outer space.

In sending a rocket into space there are three major deterrents: the pull of the earth's gravity, the resistance of the atmosphere, and the rocket's own ponderous weight. It takes a tremendous amount of fuel to give the needed thrust to overcome these obstacles. As the rocket rises, the three problems diminish—gravity decreases, the air thins out, and weight lightens as fuel burns off, giving the rocket more and more speed as it climbs. To cut down on weight even more, most rockets have several stages (often three). When the first stage, the *booster*, is burned out, it drops off and the second stage fires. When that stage is dropped the third one fires. The last stage contains the *payload* that carries out the planned mission.

Rockets can be fueled with solid or liquid propellants, and sometimes a combination of solid fuel with a liquid oxidizer is used. A solid-propellant rocket contains dry chemical fuel mixed with the oxidizer in the form of grains. It is pressed against the wall of the combustion chamber. When ignited, it releases a high-pressure gas through a center core in the chamber. The gas escapes through the open-ended nozzle, thus producing the thrust. A liquid-propellant rocket (Fig. 3) carries both fuel and oxidizer in a liquid state. They are usually contained in separate tanks and are fed into the *combustion chamber* by a mechanical *propellant supply system*. When ignited they produce hot expanded gases that, again, escape through the *nozzle* and provide thrust.

While chemical propellants are being used at present, other means of propulsion are under consideration. Nuclear rocket engines are now in the experimental stage. Among other barriers, they present a problem of excessive weight, as do most other proposed systems.

Fig. 3 LIQUID-PROPELLANT ROCKET

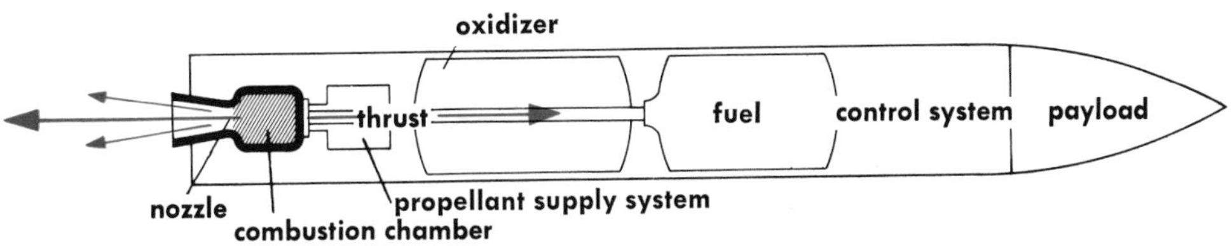

FUEL CELLS

Astronauts use a great deal of power for heat, for their instruments, and for communication with the earth. But although they take some BATTERIES with them (for use in re-entry), they get most of their electric power from fuel cells kept in the service module. These weigh only 15 times as much as batteries for every watt of electric power they produce.

Like many other power sources, fuel cells make use of chemical reactions. But the difference between a fuel cell and, for instance, the engine used in an automobile shows up in the *way* the two systems take advantage of the same kind of chemical reaction.

When carbon (in a fuel) combines with oxygen, producing carbon dioxide, two things happen: heat is produced and carbon atoms capture electrons from the outer shells of oxygen atoms. In combustion engines, the *heat* of the reaction is used—even when the final goal is to produce electricity. In fuel cells, the *electrons* are used—they are routed into an electric circuit, directly.

One of the earliest fuel cells was the **Ehrenberg cell** (Fig. 1), which works only at high temperatures. Carbon (left) is the electron taker and oxygen (pumped in from the right) is the electron supplier. Since carbon does not develop electrically charged atoms, the setup requires a metal (molten silver) on which electrons from the oxygen settle; and it requires a pool of molten sodium carbonate that acts as a middleman in the chemical reaction and as a conveyor belt for

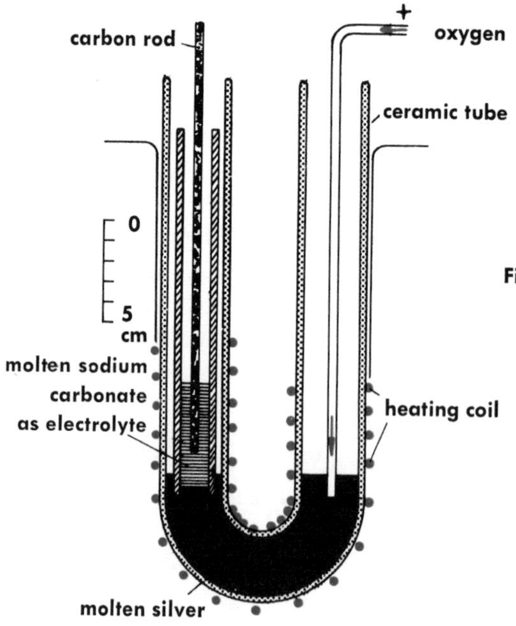

Fig. 1 EHRENBERG CELL

electrons. The Ehrenberg cell works—electrons liberated at the carbon end make a fine source of ELECTRIC CURRENT. But the temperatures it requires are so high (a little over 1000° Centigrade, or close to 2000° Fahrenheit) that the materials are eaten up in short order and keep having to be replaced.

To get away from the need for high temperatures, an Englishman named Francis T. Bacon designed his fuel cell with hydrogen as the fuel. The hydrogen and oxygen could produce an explosion if brought together directly—something has to be placed between them; but since they are both gases, high pressures—around 1,000 pounds per square inch—can be used to keep their molecules hopping. No high temperatures are needed.

The **Bacon cell's** electron giver is oxygen, which arrives from the left in Fig. 2. The two electric *terminals* are two plates shown in black; they are made of nickel, prepared in a form that leaves it with

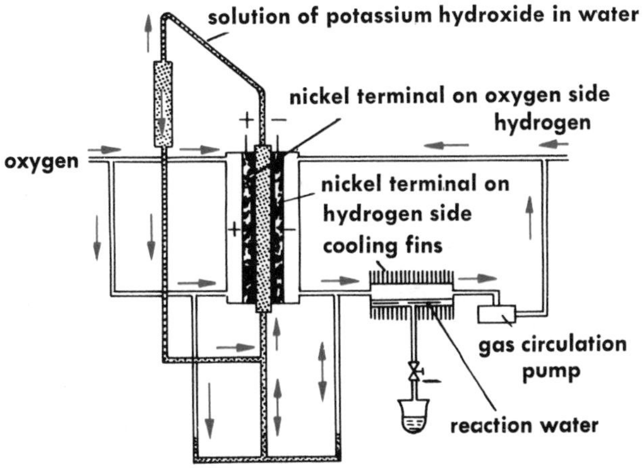

Fig. 2 BACON CELL

thousands of tiny little holes. Between these two nickel plates is a tank filled with *potassium hydroxide* dissolved in water. This solution (which keeps the hydrogen and oxygen from reacting directly with each other) conducts electricity and breaks up into electrically charged combinations of atoms. These react readily—some with the oxygen (which comes from the left), some with the hydrogen (from the right). The efficiency of the reactions depends very much on the size of the little channels in the nickel terminals (Fig. 3). The electrons

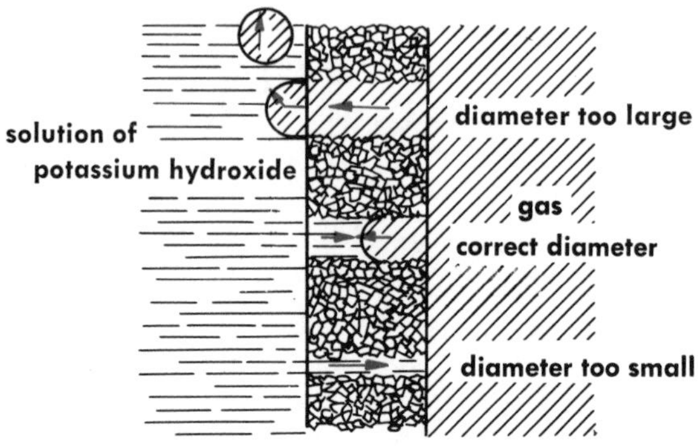

Fig. 3 WIDTH OF SMALL PASSAGES IN NICKEL TERMINALS

released appear on the terminal at the hydrogen side, circulate in the outside electric circuit, and return to the terminal on the oxygen side.

Fuel cells make our usual ways of getting electrical power look clumsy. When we plug a radio into a wall outlet, we are able to tap electrical energy only because, a few miles away, a power plant is burning fuel to produce heat, then using heat to convert water into steam. The steam is put to work in a STEAM ENGINE, which drives an ELECTRIC GENERATOR—which finally gives us the electricity.

In all these "conversions," from one kind of energy to another, energy is lost. Less than 40% of the energy offered by the original fuel reaches us as electricity. If ever a fuel cell is designed that works with common materials at low temperatures, it will become as common as the INTERNAL-COMBUSTION ENGINE is today.

INDEX

S

T